Carbon Markets or Climate Finance?

After the failure of the Copenhagen conference, climate finance has become the buzzword of international climate negotiations. A 'fast-track' sum of $30 billion has been promised by industrialized countries for emissions mitigation and adaptation activities in developing countries. A frantic race for access to these funds has begun with little consideration of how an effective allocation could be achieved. This could lead to a backlash against climate finance once the first headlines about misuse of funds appear.

This book builds on a decade-long experience with mechanisms provided by the Kyoto Protocol and the UN Framework Convention on Climate Change. It discusses the challenges of climate finance in the context of the post-Copenhagen negotiations and provides a long-term outlook of how climate finance in developing countries could develop. Written by climate finance experts from academia, carbon finance businesses and international organizations, the book provides background, firsthand insights, case studies and analysis into the complex subject area of climate finance.

Looking into the past decade of climate policy, we see that market mechanisms can be a surprisingly attractive and transparent way to promote emissions mitigation in the South. In contrast, the performance of development assistance spent as climate finance to date is mixed. Surprisingly, several advanced developing countries have been able to mobilize domestic finance for large-scale mitigation activities that are more successful than similar activities in industrialized countries. Learning from these lessons, we discuss how the Copenhagen fast-track finance should be governed to achieve a satisfactory outcome. New market mechanisms could build on the foundations set by the Clean Development Mechanism and innovative incentives could mobilize mitigation policies in the developing world. In a multi-decadal perspective, new financial instruments such as bonds linked to mitigation policies could be developed to harness the huge potential of the financial markets. We assess how a carbon-free backstop technology could be harnessed for climate finance.

Axel Michaelowa is researcher at the Center for International and Comparative Studies at the University of Zurich, Switzerland and Senior Founding Partner of the consultancy Perspectives.

Routledge explorations in environmental economics
Edited by Nick Hanley
University of Stirling, UK

1 **Greenhouse Economics**
Value and ethics
Clive L. Spash

2 **Oil Wealth and the Fate of Tropical Rainforests**
Sven Wunder

3 **The Economics of Climate Change**
Edited by Anthony D. Owen and Nick Hanley

4 **Alternatives for Environmental Valuation**
Edited by Michael Getzner, Clive Spash and Sigrid Stagl

5 **Environmental Sustainability**
A consumption approach
Raghbendra Jha and K.V. Bhanu Murthy

6 **Cost-Effective Control of Urban Smog**
The significance of the Chicago cap-and-trade approach
Richard F. Kosobud, Houston H. Stokes, Carol D. Tallarico and Brian L. Scott

7 **Ecological Economics and Industrial Ecology**
Jakub Kronenberg

8 **Environmental Economics, Experimental Methods**
Edited by Todd L. Cherry, Stephan Kroll and Jason F. Shogren

9 **Game Theory and Policy Making in Natural Resources and the Environment**
Edited by Ariel Dinar, José Albiac and Joaquín Sánchez-Soriano

10 **Arctic Oil and Gas**
Sustainability at risk?
Edited by Aslaug Mikkelsen and Oluf Langhelle

11 **Agrobiodiversity, Conservation and Economic Development**
Edited by Andreas Kontoleon, Unai Pascual and Melinda Smale

12 **Renewable Energy from Forest Resources in the United States**
Edited by Barry D. Solomon and Valeria A. Luzadis

13 **Modeling Environment-Improving Technological Innovations under Uncertainty**
Alexander A. Golub and Anil Markandya

14 Economic Analysis of Land Use in Global Climate Change Policy
Thomas Hertel, Steven Rose and Richard Tol

15 Waste and Environmental Policy
Massimiliano Mazzanti and Anna Montini

16 Avoided Deforestation
Prospects for mitigating climate change
Edited by Stefanie Engel and Charles Palmer

17 The Use of Economic Valuation in Environmental Policy
Phoebe Koundouri

18 Benefits of Environmental Policy
Klaus Dieter John and Dirk T.G. Rübbelke

19 Biotechnology and Agricultural Development
Robert Tripp

20 Economic Growth and Environmental Regulation
Tim Swanson and Tun Lin

21 Environmental Amenities and Regional Economic Development
Todd Cherry and Dan Rickman

22 New Perspectives on Agri-Environmental Policies
Stephen J. Goetz and Floor Brouwer

23 The Cooperation Challenge of Economics and the Protection of Water Supplies
A case study of the New York City watershed collaboration
Joan Hoffman

24 The Taxation of Petroleum and Minerals: Principles, Problems and Practice
Philip Daniel, Michael Keen and Charles McPherson

25 Environmental Efficiency, Innovation and Economic Performance
Massimiliano Mazzanti and Anna Montini

26 Participation in Environmental Organizations
Benno Torgler, Maria A. Garcia-Valiñas and Alison Macintyre

27 Valuation of Regulating Services of Ecosystems
Methodology and applications
Pushpam Kumar and Michael D. Wood

28 Environmental Policies for Air Pollution and Climate Change in New Europe
Caterina De Lucia

29 Optimal Control of Age-Structured Populations in Economy, Demography and the Environment
Raouf Boucekkine, Natali Hritonenko and Yuri Yatsenko

30 Sustainable Energy
Edited by Klaus D. John and Dirk Rubbelke

31 Preference Data for Environmental Valuation
Combining revealed and stated approaches
John Whitehead, Tim Haab and Ju-Chin Huang

32 **Ecosystem Services and Global Trade of Natural Resources**
Ecology, economics and policies
Edited by Thomas Koellner

33 **Permit Trading in Different Applications**
Edited by Bernd Hansjürgens, Ralf Antes and Marianne Strunz

34 **Carbon Markets or Climate Finance?**
Low carbon and adaptation investment choices for the developing world
Edited by Axel Michaelowa

Carbon Markets or Climate Finance?

Low carbon and adaptation investment choices for the developing world

Edited by Axel Michaelowa

LONDON AND NEW YORK

First published 2012
by Routledge
2 Park Square, Milton Park, Abingdon, Oxon OX14 4RN

Simultaneously published in the USA and Canada
by Routledge
711 Third Avenue, New York, NY 10017

Routledge is an imprint of the Taylor & Francis Group, an informa business

British Library Cataloguing in Publication Data
A catalogue record for this book is available from the British Library

Library of Congress Cataloging in Publication Data
Carbon markets or climate finance : low carbon and adaptation investment choices for the developing world / edited by Axel Michaelowa.
p. cm.
Includes bibliographical references.
1. Emissions trading–Developing countries. 2. Environmental impact charges–Developing countries. 3. Carbon dioxide mitigation–Developing countries. 4. Greenhouse effect, Atmospheric–International cooperation. I. Michaelowa, Axel.
HC79.P55C347 2012
363.738'746091724–dc23 2011033246

ISBN: 978-1-84971-474-7 (hbk)
ISBN: 978-0-203-12887-9 (ebk)

Typeset in Times New Roman
by Wearset Ltd, Boldon, Tyne and Wear

Contents

Boxes

Figures

Tables

Contributors

Jessica Brown is a researcher at the Overseas Development Institute (ODI) and at the US State Department. Jessica has a background in climate change policy and international development, and focuses on international climate finance. She previously worked as a consultant with California Environmental Associates based in San Francisco.

Jorund Buen is a senior partner at carbon advisors Perspectives, and invests in small-scale emission reduction technologies and project development. He has followed Chinese climate policy since the mid-1990s as a political science researcher and in his market-analysis work for Point Carbon, which he co-founded.

Sonja Butzengeiger holds degrees in Environmental Sciences and Protection and has worked on international climate policy since 1999. She was Research Fellow at the Hamburg Institute for International Economics and worked for the German Environment Ministry. In 2003, she co-founded the think-tank Perspectives, where she acts as Managing Director and Head of Climate Policy Advice.

Martin Cames joined Öko-Institut's Energy and Climate division in 1994 as Research Fellow and has headed the Berlin branch of the division since 2008. He studied Economics and Political Science at the Free University of Berlin and holds a PhD from the Technical University Berlin in Economics. Currently he is working on national and international climate policies with a specific focus on emissions trading and financial instruments.

Paula Castro is a researcher at the Department for Political Science of the University of Zurich, where she works on international climate policy. Her research focuses on international market mechanisms and domestic policies in developing countries, their interactions and role in the climate regime.

Björn Dransfeld studied Political Science and Economics at the University of Hamburg and has been involved in climate policy since 2005. Since 2007, he has worked for Perspectives, focusing on climate policy advice, CDM project development and capacity building.

Daisuke Hayashi is a PhD candidate at the University of Zurich, researching international technology transfer and carbon market mechanisms for climate change mitigation in developing countries. His prior professional experience includes working as a Research Fellow at the Hamburg Institute of International Economics and a Senior Consultant at Perspectives.

Sean Healy joined Öko-Institut's Energy and Climate division in 2009 as a Researcher. He studied Geography at the undergraduate level at Oxford University and also holds an MSc from Imperial College London in Environmental Technology. He is currently working on national and international climate policies with specific focus on emissions trading and flexible mechanisms.

Lena Hörnlein holds a Bachelor's degree in Philosophy and Economics from the University of Bayreuth. Before beginning her Master's studies in Environmental Economics and Climate Change at the London School of Economics, she worked as a Research Assistant at the University of Zurich and at Perspectives, with a focus on international climate negotiations.

Michel Köhler's studies at Flensburg University focused on energy and environmental management. He then joined the wind power developer SoWiTec. Since 2010 he has worked for Perspectives, focusing on climate policy advice, most notably studies for promoting mitigation and adaptation activities.

Axel Michaelowa is head of the research group on international climate policy at the University of Zurich. He is a senior founding partner of Perspectives and lead author in the fourth and fifth IPCC assessment report. He is a member of the CDM Executive Board's Registration and Issuance Team and has contributed to the development of six CDM baseline methodologies.

Katharina Michaelowa is Professor at the Department of Political Science, University of Zurich, and Director of the Center for Comparative and International Studies (CIS). Her research focuses on education/human capital development in Africa, the political economy of aid and the linkages between economic development and international climate policy.

Izabela Ratajczak-Juszko is a Research Fellow at the Climate Change Adaptation Programme, RMIT University in Melbourne. Her primary research focuses on international climate change policy, governance and finance for climate change adaptation in developing countries, multi-level governance and broad stakeholder engagement.

Martin Stadelmann is a PhD candidate at the Department for Political Science, University of Zurich, and analyses international climate finance. Prior to his PhD he was carbon offset manager at the Myclimate foundation. In 2009 he worked as short term consultant at the Global Environment Facility. He holds a Master's in Geography, University of Bern, with minors in Economics and Political Science.

Katie Sullivan is the Canadian Director at the International Emissions Trading Association. Prior to joining IETA, Katie worked as a Climate Change Consultant for ICF International. Katie holds a Master's in Environment, Development and Policy from the University of Sussex, and an Honours Bachelor's degree in Public Affairs and Policy Management from Carleton University.

Stefan Wehner holds a Diploma degree in Industrial Engineering from the University of Flensburg, Germany, with a major in Energy and Environmental Management. Currently, he is working for Perspectives, focusing on CDM project development, risk assessment and NAMAs, especially in the areas of energy efficiency and renewable energy.

Preface

Climate finance at the crossroads between market mechanisms and public funding vehicles

What is climate finance? Climate finance is the term given to the financial resources mobilized to mitigate climate change and allow developing countries to adapt to climate change impacts (Schalatek and Bird 2010). The Copenhagen conference in 2009 tried to conceal its failure to agree on a new climate policy regime by promises of large flows of funds from industrialized to developing countries. By 2012, US$30 billion were to be mobilized as 'fast track finance' for mitigation and adaptation activities in the South. So far, it is unclear what criteria are used for allocation of these funds, and what the efficiency of their use is. Finance has become a goal in itself, instead of the real goals of mitigation or adaptation. Allocation decisions are opaque and there is no transparency regarding funding volumes available and their use. This makes it likely that scandals taint climate finance as funds could be diverted from their planned use.

In the longer term, given the massive financial volumes required for mitigation to achieve the target of limiting global warming to 2°C, compared to pre-industrial levels, as well as adapting to the inevitable climate change impacts (UN 2010), innovative mechanisms for scaling up climate finance need to be developed and assessed. In this context a crucial question is whether market mechanisms or public subsidies are the better way to finance greenhouse gas reductions and adaptation to climate change in developing countries. Negotiators, consultants and the public interested in development and climate policy are eager to get an integrated perspective on how climate finance could be effective, and how it can avoid repeating the mistakes of development finance.

There is now 15 years of experience with market mechanisms and public funds under the Kyoto Protocol and UN Framework Convention on Climate Change (UNFCCC). Thus it is time to take stock, discuss the challenges of climate finance in the context of the post-2012 negotiations and assess how climate finance for developing countries could develop in the long term.

Despite the crucial role of climate finance in the development of the post-2012 climate policy regime, there is no other book bringing together researchers' and practitioners' perspectives on climate finance in developing countries. The only formal publication by Kingsbury *et al.* (2009) is a series of 36 short essays on climate finance. Parker *et al.* (2009) describe the finance proposals in the post-2012 negotiations without an in-depth analysis of their merits. Beyond these two publications, there is only a vast array of grey literature.

This book brings together a number of experts from research and business, who have worked on international climate policy for many years. It benefits from the close contacts of the international climate policy consultancy, Perspectives, with the international research world, particularly the University of Zurich. This guarantees a 'hands on' approach while safeguarding academic quality. Three sections address lessons learned, immediate challenges and long-term concepts.

The section on lessons learned provides case studies on four climate finance vehicles: market mechanisms, development assistance, unilateral financing by developing country governments and public funds.

The Clean Development Mechanism (CDM), the largest market mechanism under the Kyoto Protocol, is the topic of Chapter 1, by Axel Michaelowa and Jorund Buen. Against all expectations, the CDM, which allows emissions mitigation projects in developing countries to generate emissions credits, has been a resounding numerical success. Within five years, over 5,000 projects have been mobilized in almost 80 countries. Michaelowa and Buen discuss the reasons for this gold rush, and which technologies and countries benefited the most. The CDM gold rush was, inter alia, due to the fact that emissions credits are granted by an international institution without interference of the host-country government (Michaelowa *et al.* 2008). Companies in developing countries, especially the advanced ones, discovered that Certified Emission Reductions (CERs) are a valuable export commodity, leading to a race to unilaterally develop CDM projects. This had not been foreseen by anyone and is the key of CDM success. While the CDM project cycle is cumbersome, it has led to full fungibility of credits and their general acceptance as compliance tools. Nevertheless, in some fields the CDM underperformed and needs reform to enable upscaling.

In Chapter 2, Katharina and Axel Michaelowa assess whether aid flows for adaptation have been influenced by the development of international climate policy. In contrast to mitigation flows, where no relevant link between key milestones of the climate policy regime and mitigation aid flows could be found, adaptation aid has been increasing significantly over time in line with the development of international climate policy. Political-economic variables of donor countries that play a significant role in the context of mitigation are scarcely relevant in the adaptation context.

Chapter 3, by Jorund Buen and Paula Castro, discusses two important cases of unilateral financing of renewable-energy programmes by developing countries – the Brazilian ethanol programme and the Chinese wind energy expansion. Both programmes required multi-billion dollar subsidies and had a strategic component to build-up local industry. Buen and Castro stress that both supply and demand had to be supported over a long period, and a multi-layered approach involving R&D, strategic niche market introduction and diffusion into a domestic and international mass market was required. Both programmes had lengthy periods of near failure that could only be overcome through government persistence. Also, protectionism of the nascent industry was crucial in the initial phases. Buen and Castro found it surprisingly difficult to quantify the exact financial subsidy volume of each programme, which indicates that the rules for monitoring and verification for Nationally Appropriate Mitigation Action (NAMA) finance need to be very clear.

Izabela Ratajczak-Juszko's Chapter 4 assesses the role of the Adaptation Fund as a model for future, upscaled adaptation funding in the post-2012 UNFCCC era. The Fund, which is financed through a levy on CDM transactions, is actually an 'intergovernmental grant system' to finance concrete adaptation projects and programmes in developing countries. It has introduced a number of new concepts for international finance, such as a 'direct access modality' empowering governments of developing countries to implement proposals identified by them as national priorities. However, this direct access option is only utilized to a limited extent as countries fear to lose out in the race for project approval.

The section on immediate challenges addresses fast-track financing, new market mechanisms proposed for mitigation under the post-2012 regime and how developing countries can combine different sources of finance for national mitigation policies.

Martin Stadelmann, Jessica Brown and Lena Hörnlein assess experiences made with fast-start finance in Chapter 5. They assess whether the collective US$30 billion pledge for the period 2010–2012 is really being met and whether there is a balance between funds for mitigation and adaptation. Moreover, they analyse which funding goes through which international channels – bilateral and multilateral. While the total sum pledged seems to reach the promised level, the situation gets much more unclear when one moves down the chain to actual disbursements. On average, adaptation receives a lower share than mitigation. Data are often not comparable and lags of spending are considerable. Transparency of flows has improved over the last 18 months, but could be further increased, while effectiveness of spending remains virtually unknown.

Chapter 6 discusses the proposals for new market mechanisms for mitigation going beyond the project level, focusing on the incentives that are provided to those who actually can engage in mitigation. Sonja Butzengeiger, Björn Dransfeld, Martin Cames, Axel Michaelowa and Sean Healy scrutinize whether the shift in responsibility from emitters or investors to host-country government would limit or even eliminate emitters' incentives to seek cost-effective mitigation options and, if so, by which means such an outcome could be avoided or limited. Given the challenges that may be caused by the different responsibility structure under a new mechanism based on a 'no-lose target', strong governance skills of the host-country government in implementing climate policy are required. However, a number of potential policy instruments exists that could reduce free riding and would provide the necessary mitigation incentives with different degrees of direct or indirect linking with the global carbon market. Emissions above the target level could be penalized by a mandatory regulation or an emissions tax, or subsidies such as feed-in tariffs could be used. Pilot schemes would help to establish confidence in the new mechanisms and encourage their broader application.

Chapter 7 by Daisuke Hayashi and Stefan Wehner describes the concept of NAMAs in developing countries and proposes different ways of financing them. NAMAs receiving emissions credits would concentrate on mitigation with moderate costs and direct, short-term greenhouse gas (GHG) impacts. NAMAs supported by subsidies from industrialized countries could either cover activities with low or very high costs and relatively direct GHG impacts. Unilateral NAMAs financed solely by the host country work best for negative- to very low-cost mitigation actions and do not have to address the causality and timeframe of the reductions. A concept of combination of these NAMA types is applied to a programme of green mortgages in the Mexican housing sector, where the continuation of the current penetration level would serve as a baseline for a unilateral NAMA. Increased penetration and expansion of the energy-efficiency and renewable-energy technologies covered could be a supported NAMA, building on a revolving fund structure. A strengthening beyond that level could generate credits. CDM rules would have to be changed from the current exclusion of mitigation policies in the baseline to prevent disadvantages for the NAMA compared to CDM projects.

The third section covers climate finance issues that are just emerging – a market mechanism for adaptation, innovative loans for NAMAs and a levy on a backstop technology replacing fossil fuels in the electricity sector. Chapter 8, by Axel Michaelowa, Michel Köhler and Sonja Butzengeiger, discusses whether market mechanisms could become an instrument for adaptation financing. Compared to the current first-come, first-serve distribution of adaptation funding, market mechanisms could increase efficiency. There is a wide range of adaptation technologies with hugely differing costs. A credible adaptation market mechanism, however, requires specification of universally accepted trading units. Such units could relate to 'saved wealth' and 'saved health'. Demand for such adaptation units should be created by adaptation targets on the (industrialized) country level that then could be allocated to entities, that could then either finance adaptation projects themselves or buy credits from adaptation service companies. Alternatively, tender rounds for adaptation funding could be implemented. A pilot phase for adaptation market mechanisms should test the different concepts.

A new financial instrument to harness private finance for large-scale mitigation investment linked to NAMAs is outlined by Katie Sullivan in Chapter 9. The concept of 'Green NAMA bonds' would allow developing countries to issue loans for financing of NAMAs. These loans would have a low interest rate but would be entitled to carbon credits from the NAMA. If the NAMA does not reach its target and thus does not generate credits, an addition to the interest would be paid to the loan providers. General default on loans would be covered by guarantees from international financial institutions. To prevent countries getting into a debt spiral, they could only borrow up to a level depending on the country's emission performance.

Chapter 10, by Sonja Butzengeiger and Axel Michaelowa, discusses the potential to levy finance from a super transformational technology (STT) that could produce electricity at much lower cost than fossil fuel power plants. As the introduction of such a technology could have severe impacts on industrial competitiveness, a power transformation levy could skim off the cost differential between the incumbent power technology and the STT. The revenues from that levy should be used to set-up power plants in developing countries with suppressed electricity demand. Moreover, a large-scale Desert Greening Programme could be used for diversification of economies that have so far benefited from fossil fuel exports.

Chapter 11, by Axel Michaelowa, provides an overview of the question of whether public funds or market mechanisms are a better way towards large-scale climate finance. The multi-decadal experience with development finance has shown that it is challenging to reach ambitious targets for public funding, especially if performance of the activities funded is lacklustre. Public funds also usually require a long time for project implementation. Market mechanisms will lead to higher performance and transparency, but are dependent on the political willingness to set ambitious mitigation and adaptation targets. If this is not forthcoming, prices and thus incentives for emission reduction or adaptation will be low. This chapter also discusses whether the current 'valley of tears' of international climate policy could eventually lead to a crash programme of solar radiation management. To avoid this risky gamble, Michaelowa proposes a strong role for market mechanisms while public finance supports non-quantifiable 'soft' activities and capacity building. A levy on the market mechanisms could provide this public funding. But this path requires a willingness to seriously engage in climate policy through ambitious targets, which is currently lacking.

I hope that having read this book, the reader will have a clear view of the different options for climate finance in developing countries and understand the challenges in incentivizing high performance for mitigation and adaptation investments in the global South. Hopefully, we have contributed to an increase of transparency in this very opaque policy field.

References

Kingsbury, B., Rudyk, B. and Stewart, R. (2009) *Climate Finance: Regulatory and Funding Strategies for Climate Change and Global Development*, New York: New York University Press.

Michaelowa, A., Hayashi, D., Jung, M., Müller, N., Bode, S., Castro, P., Dransfeld, B. and Höhne, N. (2008) 'A review of the current state and options for reform of the CDM', London: UK Department for Environment, Food and Rural Affairs.

Parker, C., Brown, J., Pickering, J., Roynestad, E., Mardas, N. and Mitchell, A. (2009) *The Little Climate Finance Book*, Oxford: Global Canopy Programme.

Schalatek, L. and Bird, N. (2010) 'A normative framework for climate finance', *Climate Finance Fundamentals*, vol. 1, Washington, DC and London: Heinrich Böll Foundation North America, Overseas Development Institute.

UN (2010) 'Report of the Secretary-General's High-level Advisory Group on Climate Change Financing', New York: United Nations. Online. Available: www.un.org/wcm/webdav/site/climatechange/shared/Documents/AGF_reports/AGF_Final_Report.pdf (accessed 20 April 2011).

Acknowledgements

I would like to thank Lena Hörnlein for meticulous support in coordinating the contributions of the different authors of this volume. Moreover, I thank the following clients of Perspectives for giving assignments that allowed us to reflect upon innovative ways of climate finance: Point Carbon (Chapter 1), the German Federal Environmental Agency (Chapter 6), the German Federal Ministry for the Environment, Nature Conservation and Nuclear Safety (Chapter 7) and the Swiss Development Cooperation (Chapter 8).

Acronyms and abbreviations

ACM	approved consolidated methodology
AEAEE	Asociación de Empresas para el Ahorro de Energía en la Edificación, México
AFB	Adaptation Fund Board
AHM	Asociación Hipotecaria Mexicana
AHPPER	Asociación Hondureña de Pequeños Productores de Energía Renovable
ANII	Agencia Naçional de Investigaçión e Innovaçión
AOSIS	Alliance of Small Island States
BAU	business-as-usual
BIDD	Bond Issuance Design Document
CCS	carbon capture and storage
CDM EB	CDM Executive Board
CDM	Clean Development Mechanism
CER	Certified Emission Reduction
CFL	compact fluorescent lamp
CIF	climate investment fund
CO_2-e	CO_2 equivalent
CO_2	carbon dioxide
CONAVI	Comisión Nacional De Vivienda, México (Mexican National Housing Commission)
COP	Conference of the Parties (to the UNFCCC)
CPA	CDM Programme Activity
CSE	Centre de Suivi Ecologique
CSP	concentrated solar power
DAC	Development Assistance Committee of the OECD
DALY	disability-adjusted life years saved
DFID	Department for International Development (UK)
DGP	Desert Greening Programme
DNA	Designated National Authority
DOE	Designated Operational Entity
DSM	demand-side management
EC	European Commission

EDP	Energy Development Programme
EFC	Ethics and Finance Committee
EGAT	Thai national electric power utility
EIT	economies in transition
ERPA	emission reduction purchase agreements
ERU	Emission Reduction Unit
ETF	Efficiency Target Factor
EU	European Union
EU ETS	EU emissions trading scheme
FSF	fast-start finance
GCCU	Guaranteed Carbon Collateral Unit
GCF	Green Climate Fund
GDP	gross domestic product
GEF	Global Environment Facility
GHG	greenhouse gas
GIZ	Gesellschaft für Internationale Zusammenarbeit
GNB	Green NAMA Bond
GNI	gross national income
GW	gigawatt
HCFC-22	hydrochlorofluorocarbon 22/chlorodifluoromethane
HFC	hydrofluorocarbon
HFC-23	fluoroform
ICA	international consultations and analysis
IEA	International Energy Agency
IET	International Emissions Trading
IETA	International Emissions Trading Association
IFI	international finance institution
IMF	International Monetary Fund
INFONAVIT	Instituto del Fondo Nacional de la Vivienda para los Trabajadores, México (National Workers' Housing Fund)
IPCC AR4	Fourth Assessment Report of the IPCC
IPCC	Intergovernmental Panel on Climate Change
IPRs	intellectual property rights
ISB	International Supervisory Body
ITER	International Thermonuclear Experimental Reactor
JI	Joint Implementation
kW	kilowatt
LDC	least developed country
LDCF	Least Developed Countries Fund
LEC	levelized electricity costs
LoA	Letter of Approval
M&V	measurement and verification
MAC	marginal abatement cost
MDB	multilateral development bank
MEA	multilateral environmental agreement

METI	Japanese Ministry of Economy, Trade and Industry
MIE	multilateral implementing entity
MRV	monitoring, reporting and verification
MSG	Melanesian Spearhead Group
Mtce	million tonnes coal equivalent
Mtoe	million tonnes oil equivalent
MW	megawatt
N_2O	nitrous oxide
NAMA	nationally appropriate mitigation action
NEDO	New Energy and Industrial Technology Development Organization
NGO	non-governmental organization
NIE	national implementing entity
NPV	net present value
NSS	National CDM/JI Strategy Program
ODA	official development assistance
OECD	Organization for Economic Co-operation and Development
OOF	other official flows
PCF	Prototype Carbon Fund
PDD	Project Design Document
PECC	Programa Especial de Cambio Climático, México
PIJ	Planning Institute of Jamaica
PIN	Project Identification Note/Project Idea Note
PoA	Programme of Activity
PPA	Power Purchase Agreement
PPCR	Pilot Programme for Climate Resilience
PPRC	Project and Programme Review Committee
PTL	power transformation levy
PV	photovoltaics
R&D	research and development
REDD	Reduced Emissions from Deforestation and Forest Degradation
SCCF	Special Climate Change Fund
SDC	Swiss Agency for Development and Cooperation
SDM	Sustainable Development Mechanism
SEMARNAT	Secretaria de Medio Ambiente y Recursos Naturales, México (Mexican Environment Ministry)
SH	saved health
SHF	Sociedad Hipotecaria Federal, México
SIDS	small island developing states
SOE	state-owned enterprise
SPC	Secretariat of the Pacific Community
SPREP	South Pacific Environmental Programme
SRES	IPCC Special Report on Emissions Scenarios
SSC-PoA	small-scale PoA
STT	super transformational technology

SW	saved wealth
SWH	solar water heater
tCO_2-e	tonnes CO_2 equivalent
tWh	terawatthour (1 billion kWh)
UCF	Umbrella Carbon Facility
UNDP	United Nations Development Programme
UNEP	United Nations Environment Programme
UNFCCC	United Nations Framework Convention on Climate Change
VAT	value added tax
WHO	World Health Organization
WTO	World Trade Organization

1 The Clean Development Mechanism gold rush

Axel Michaelowa and Jorund Buen

1 The CDM: from Cinderella to fairy princess

The Clean Development Mechanism (CDM) is the only market mechanism of the Kyoto Protocol that involves developing countries without emissions commitments.[1] It allows emissions mitigation projects in those countries to generate emissions credits – the so-called Certified Emission Reductions (CERs) – that can be used by industrialized countries to fulfil their Kyoto targets. After a slow start related to the set-up of the institutions required to approve projects on the international and host country levels between 1997 and 2005, the CDM has become a resounding numerical success. Since late 2003, when the first project was formally registered by the CDM Executive Board (CDM EB), over 3,000 projects have been registered. Another 3,000 projects are on their way towards registration and each month more than 100 new projects are submitted (Figure 1.1).

Since 2006, many observers have forecast an imminent downturn in the number of new projects entering the CDM pipeline. Reasons for this expectation were the reduction in pre-2013 crediting time of projects and the impact of the 2008 economic crisis; also, since the failure of the Copenhagen conference in late 2009, there has been general uncertainty about the future of international climate policy. However, the inflow of projects in the validation pipeline remains stubbornly high and has even been increasing to new peaks.

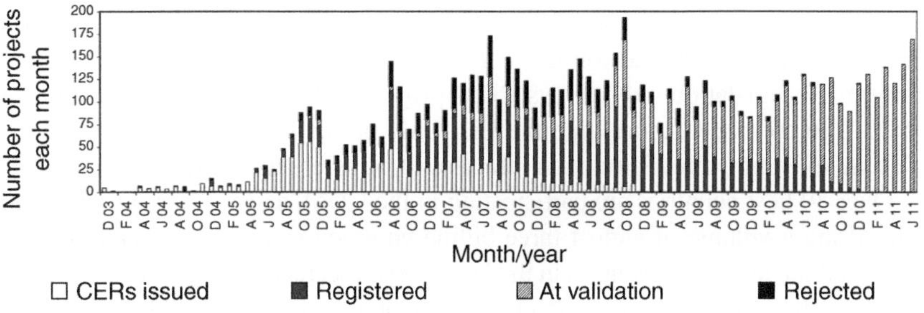

Figure 1.1 Inflow of projects in the CDM pipeline until July 2011 (numbers per month) (source: own illustration based on UNEP Riso Centre 2011a).

This resilience could be due to four main reasons, as well as two minor reasons. The first major one would be the fact that now in all large CDM host countries, there is a wealth of consultancies who have made a good living by identifying CDM projects, and who continue to 'unearth' renewables and energy-efficiency projects. While in 2005 and 2006, only a few bold and risk-loving enterprises got involved in the new markets in India, China and Brazil, in 2009 any modern entrepreneur in advanced developing countries takes the CDM seriously.

The second main trend is that China and India continue to provide attractive subsidies to renewable energy, with a continuously growing domestic manufacturing capacity, especially for wind power (see Chapter 3 for more details on wind in China). These subsidies make projects attractive but do not lead to rejections by the CDM regulators, because they do not have to be assessed in the determination of a project's 'additionality', and they can be relatively easily financed in a unilateral way (see the discussion below). We have also seen a broadening of the host countries involved. Southeast Asia is progressing well, and even the Middle East is starting to discover the benefits of the CDM together with renewable-energy promotion programmes. Generally, the good experience with the CDM has bolstered trust that it has a bright future, even after the Copenhagen shock.

Third, a CDM project can be quite economically attractive even without CDM, as long as other options can be shown to be more attractive. The test to ensure that a CDM project is not common practice excludes other CDM projects, although CDM itself has become common practice for some project types in some areas (see the discussion about additionality, below). Hence, the lack of clarity on future CER demand does not necessarily mean a termination of all projects.

Fourth, although CER revenues do make projects more financially attractive and less financially risky to implement, prospective CER revenues are in most cases not taken into account in the financing of the underlying project (more detail on this follows below, as well as in Chapter 3), as the main outputs of most CDM projects started nowadays (bar some methane-reduction projects) is power or some other product or service, not CERs. Hence, if CER demand dwindles, the project may still be financially sound.

Fifth, project owners believe in additional demand emerging from other developed countries than EU member states and Australia, and see the voluntary market as a potential outlet for their carbon credits in the meantime. The sixth, more negative, interpretation of the current trend would be that we are seeing a last-minute rush to embark on CDM projects before the EU closes the door, as current EU legislation only allows CDM projects formally registered by the end of 2012 to continue exports into the EU. Only projects in least developed countries are exempt from this rule; its effects will be assessed below in more detail.

Over 80 host countries are participating in the CDM, and registered projects are forecasting a volume of almost three billion emission credits by the end of 2012. This is all the more surprising as in the late 1990s researchers foresaw that a project-based mechanism based on reductions in developing countries would not be attractive and would be sidelined by the other Kyoto Mechanisms – Joint Implementation (JI) and International Emissions Trading (IET).[2] Some (e.g. Haites 2000) thought that zero-cost 'hot air' sold through IET would dominate the market, whereas others (e.g. Black-Arbeláez 2003) felt that the CDM would be much too risky for investors, transaction costs of the international bureaucracy required would be prohibitive and host-country governments would stifle projects due to their hostile attitude towards the mechanism. However, in contrast to the CDM, these mechanisms have languished and only recently seen some activity (Figure 1.2).

Why did the CDM transform from an unwanted Cinderella to a fairy princess? Why is it now seen as the cornerstone of the global carbon market and its continuation supported by a large majority of countries even if there is no agreement on a second commitment period of the Kyoto Protocol? Which technologies and countries have benefited the most from CDM so far? How can it be upscaled and reformed?

2 What were the reasons for the CDM gold rush?

The CDM gold rush did not only have one cause. Several levers had to be pulled before the CDM could be unleashed. This did not happen at the same time and some actions were completely unexpected.

2.1 The EU emissions trading scheme and Japan as key demand sources taking over from the World Bank and European governments

While the Kyoto Protocol specified that CERs could be used to comply with the emissions commitments of industrialized countries, initially demand was rather

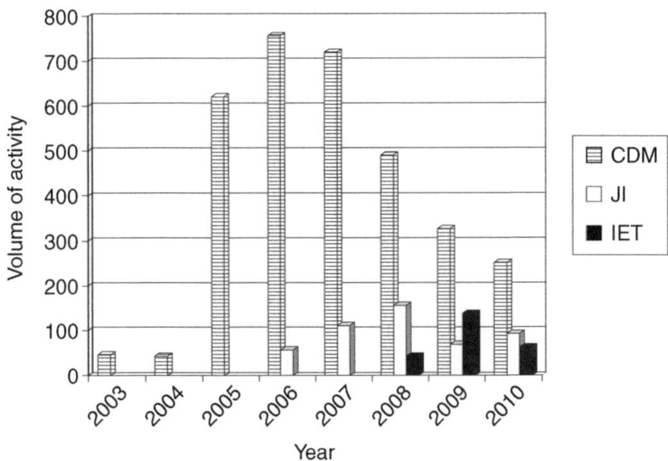

Figure 1.2 Volume of new activity in the CDM, JI and IET by the end of 2010 (source: UNEP Riso Centre 2011a, 2011b for CDM and JI; Point Carbon 2011 for IET).

Note
Million tCO_2-e pre-2013 for CDM and JI, transaction volume for IET.

sluggish. The first institution to set-up a dedicated CER acquisition programme was the World Bank. We cover this in some detail below, as it may provide important lessons for future climate finance. The World Bank set-up a 'Prototype Carbon Fund' (PCF) in 1999 with capital of US$180 million, subscribed to by six governments and 17 companies. The PCF understood itself as a trailblazer of global carbon markets and set out to develop a detailed framework for this. By October 2003, the PCF had signed seven CER purchase contracts totalling 7.8 million CERs and received 420 project ideas (PCF 2003).

The Netherlands was the first country to embark on a coordinated CER acquisition strategy to cover 50 per cent of its estimated reduction target under Kyoto, i.e. 67 million CERs. In November 2001 it established a tender programme called CERUPT, supervised by the Ministry of Housing, Spatial Planning and the Environment. This programme used the experience of the ERUPT tenders for emission credits from JI projects that had been launched in 1999. In CERUPT's terms of reference (Senter International 2001), maximum CER prices were specified and differentiated by project types. Non-biomass renewables would receive up to €5.5/CER, biomass and energy efficiency €4.4/CER and all other types €3.3/CER. The CERUPT contract also introduced the magical threshold of 100,000 CERs, from which a purchase contract would be seen as attractive. In 2002 two contracts with the World Bank Group – leading to the setting up of a dedicated carbon fund at both the World Bank and the International Finance Corporation – and one with the Andean Development Corporation CAF were signed, totalling 36 million CERs, while a contract of ten million CERs was signed with Rabobank (Netherlands Ministry of Housing, Spatial Planning and the Environment 2004). CERUPT selected 18 projects in March 2003 which were expected to generate 16 million CERs, and the World Bank contract was increased by five million CERs in 2004. CERUPT did pioneering work with respect to definition of baselines and project emissions calculation, as well as the legal form of emission reduction purchase agreements. In the wake of the Dutch acquisition programme, Finland, Austria and Sweden set-up similar, but much smaller programmes in 2003 and 2004.

The collaboration between the Netherlands and the World Bank led to a flurry of follow-up activities; between 2002 and 2005 several other Annex I countries, including Italy, Spain and Denmark followed (see Danish Energy Agency 2010 for an overview of the Danish programme). Between 2002 and 2004, the World Bank was dominating the demand side of the CDM market, and the price for CERs was actually determined by the World Bank offers, set at US$3–4/CER.

Had this situation persisted, the CDM would today probably have generated a few hundred projects and be seen as an offspring of development cooperation with limited relevance. Why did this change?

In a bold move by a small group of EU Commission officials, the attempt to introduce an EU-wide carbon tax was replaced by a move towards an EU-wide emission-trading system in 2000, with a view to get the system in place within five years. This had made surprisingly good headway by 2002 (see Skjaerseth and Wettestad 2010 for a good discussion), but industry lobbies had made it clear that they wanted a safety valve in case EU allowances were scarce. Thus, from late 2002 onwards, a 'Linking Directive' was prepared by the EU Commission, whose first draft leaked in June 2003. At that time it was already clear that the EU Emissions Trading Scheme (EU ETS) would have a first trading period from 2005 to 2007, followed by a second one covering the commitment period of the Kyoto Protocol (2008–2012). The draft did not accept CER use before 2008 and limited imports to 6 per cent of allocated EU allowances. After an outcry by industry, the final version entered into law in late 2004 (EU 2004) allowed CER use from 2005 and did not contain any quantitative import limitation. When, in 2004, the first forward prices for EU allowances were quoted at over €8, it led to an immediate upward pressure on CER prices; the further massive increase of the EU allowance price to reach up to €30 in July 2005 completely reshaped the CDM market, with companies covered by the EU ETS embarking on CER purchases. Michaelowa and Michaelowa (2010) discuss how the World Bank, due to its good relationships with developing country governments, initially could still sign CER purchase agreements below market prices. The main author of this chapter personally witnessed such a situation in Tunisia in February 2006, when the World Bank offered US$5.25/CER for a bundle of landfill gas recovery projects (ANGED and World Bank 2006) and pressurized officials to rapidly sign the contract, when the price paid by companies from the EU reached at least 50 per cent more. When asked today, the Tunisian officials regret having sold to the World Bank.

Ever since its introduction, the EU ETS has remained the key demand driver for CERs. Its introduction led to the emergence of a large number of carbon funds and other CER acquisition vehicles administered by private financial institutions. The CER price has always remained below the price for an EU allowance, except for the pre-2007 EU allowances, which could not be banked. During the February 2009 crisis, in which the EU allowance price plunged, primary CER prices for a short period remained at the same level as, or even above, the EU allowance price, but only a few CDM deals were concluded during this period. Generally, the price differential or 'spread' varies according to the perception of import possibilities and overall demand for CERs outside the EU (see Sikorski 2010 for a good discussion of the various factors influencing the spread).

The second largest demand driver after the EU ETS was Japan. Since the late 1990s, the government had lavishly subsidized more than 100 feasibility studies for offset projects in developing countries through the New Energy and Industrial Technology Development Organization (NEDO), with up to US$400,000 per study. In April 2005, the Japanese cabinet agreed to acquire at least 100 million tCO_2 through the Kyoto Mechanisms. The government acquisition programme was to be administered by NEDO. In the two financial years between March 2006 and 2008, NEDO acquired 23.1 million CERs. In 2005, the Japan Kyoto Mechanisms Acceleration Programme brought together a host of Japanese institutions to promote CDM and JI project development; the Ministry of Economy, Trade and Industry (METI) budgeted US$40 million, while the

Ministry of Environment budgeted US$22 million. The Japanese industry federation, Keidanren, allowed member companies to use CERs to comply with their emission targets specified under the voluntary agreement specified in 1996 and to be reached in 2010. In contrast to voluntary agreements in other countries, this is taken very seriously; electric utilities planned to buy 120 million CERs, and steel companies 44 million throughout the commitment period (Okamoto 2008). In December 2004, the Japanese Greenhouse Reduction Fund was set-up with a capitalization of US$140 million coming from 31 private companies. Japanese trading houses such as Marubeni, Mitsubishi and Mitsui utilized their international networks to play a key intermediary role both towards the government and the Keidanren companies, and entered many early deals on CERs from large-scale industrial gas-reduction projects.

2.2 Host countries actively promoted the mechanism

The first obstacles to a CDM take-off were host countries. As each host country needs a designated national authority (DNA) for approval of CDM projects, it could block CDM easily by just refusing to set-up a DNA (see Curnow and Hodes 2009 for a good overview of CDM host-country challenges). As many countries had opposed the principle of the CDM during the 1990s, it was unclear how many governments would embrace it. Latin America became the frontrunner, with a number of countries setting up their DNA in 2002. In 2003, key host countries such as India and China gave up their opposition to the CDM and became fervent supporters of the mechanism. This was partially due to a shift of climate policy responsibilities from foreign ministries to environment ministries or even ministries of economic affairs, which did not have ideological arguments against market mechanisms. This change in attitude was also supported by capacity-building activities supported through development collaboration. A crucial role was played by the National CDM/JI Strategy Program (NSS) of the World Bank, which supported the development of strategy documents in potential key host countries.

In India, the United States had financed a programme in which two US experts were hosted at the highly reputed Tata Energy Research Institute during 1999 to promote the CDM. They organized a study tour for Indian entrepreneurs to the United States, which included a meeting with President Clinton at the White House. Ever since, Indian industry has been pushing strongly for participation in the CDM, and eventually this pressure led to support by the Ministry of Environment and Forests.

In China, several donors financed capacity building at ministries and research institutions in Beijing from 2002 onwards. Through this, Chinese policy-makers discovered the huge potential for reduction of industrial gases that had not been on the radar earlier. From then on, Chinese government representatives became very eager to embark on the CDM, while at the same time asserting their control over the mechanism. In the 'Interim Measures for Operation and Management of Clean Development Mechanism Project in China' promulgated in the autumn of 2004, majority Chinese ownership of CDM projects in China was made mandatory and all sales contracts for CERs would have to be screened by the Chinese CDM authority.

2.3 Unilateral CDM harnesses entrepreneurial spirit in host countries

The CDM was originally seen as a mechanism by which a company from an industrialized country invests in an emissions mitigation project in a developing country and receives CERs in turn. However, already in the early 2000s, a discussion erupted regarding a 'unilateral' model in which companies from the developing countries develop CDM projects themselves and market CERs, just like any other export commodity. When the CDM EB formally gave its green light to the unilateral[3] approach in May 2005, it unleashed a wave of projects, particularly from India (Figure 1.1). Subsequently, the unilateral model dominated the CDM; for an analysis of its repercussions, see Lütken and Michaelowa (2008). Whereas companies in industrialized countries were reluctant to invest in developing countries, local entrepreneurs eagerly grasped the chance for an entirely new type of revenue – and this type of revenue could not be expropriated by greedy governments, because CERs could be held on an account at the CDM EB and sold whenever the entrepreneur was inclined to do so. Therefore, the CDM became a business for a new type of export commodity with very attractive characteristics.

2.4 Nuggets on the ground: the industrial gas projects

A key lever for the take-off of the CDM was the existence of a small set of extremely large CDM options. While some climate policy specialists had stated for several years that non-CO_2 gas reduction could be very cheap due to the high global warming potential of HFC-23, a by-product of the refrigerant HCFC-22 (11,700 times that of CO_2) and the existence of relatively straightforward technology to incinerate this gas (Blok *et al.* 1999), no one had really followed up on these reports. For example, the Global Environment Facility had not supported any non-CO_2 gas activities in developing countries. However, in early 2003, the UK company INEOS Fluor submitted a proposal for a baseline methodology on the thermal destruction of HFC-23. The accompanying project document for a plant in Korea estimated an annual emission reduction of 1.4 million tonnes CO_2 equivalent (tCO2-e). When the CDM EB approved the methodology in July 2003, international donor organizations and consultants swarmed to identify similar projects. And they found them – in China and India. Already in February 2004, the UN Environment Programme (UNEP) organized an 'International Workshop on HFC-23 Clean Development Mechanism (CDM) Project Cooperation in China', with representatives of 11 fluorochemical plants attending. At this workshop, a document bundling together 12 HCFC-22 production sites with a total annual volume of 58.5 million CERs was presented by a representative of the German Technical Cooperation (Sicars 2004). But China did not want this bonanza to fall into the hands of development cooperation people; it took its time and let the potential buyers woo the Chinese government, especially from Japan and Italy (see Schwank 2004). At the same time, a giant HFC-23 project was already getting host-country approval in India with the support of INEOS Fluor. It estimated an annual CER volume of five million at an investment cost of only a few million euros.

Chemical giant Dupont began to grasp the enormous impact of the CDM on the revenues of its competitors. In June 2004, it wrote a letter to the CDM EB arguing that the baseline HFC-23 emissions rate should be reduced from the IPCC default level of 4 per cent to the 1.37 per cent achieved by a Dupont plant in the United States. This lobbying was successful in triggering a revision of the methodology, which woke up the CDM community. In October 2004, Schwank (2004) rang the alarm bell warning that HFC-23 CDM projects would impede the phase-out of HCFC-22 agreed under the Montreal Protocol and reduce the CER price. Schneider *et al.* (2004) argued that the CDM introduced perverse incentives to increase HCFC-22 production and thus HCFC-22 plants that started construction after April 2003 should be excluded. Eventually this view prevailed and the CDM EB revised the methodology, limiting its use to plants that had operated for at least three years before the end of 2004.

In late 2004, the Chinese government embarked on a bold move, by taxing HFC-23 projects at 65 per cent of their CER revenue and N_2O projects at 30 per cent.[4] Once state revenues had been assured, the government moved swiftly to maximize these revenues, and minimize transaction costs through large contracts. As Italy had been quite pushy to get its hands on HFC-23 CERs from China since October 2003 (Russo and Lu 2005), a Sino-Italian workshop on HFC-23 projects in China was organized in January 2005, which brought together over 100 participants. While the large Italian utility ENEL and the Italian government did get a significant share of the CER bonanza, the lion's share was gobbled up by the World Bank. The Bank behaved like a hedge fund and rapidly set-up an 'Umbrella Carbon Facility' (UCF) whose sole purpose was to collect sufficient funding from private buyers to engage in a massive HFC-23 CER acquisition contract (World Bank 2006). In August 2006, the UCF spent US$737.6 million to acquire 129.3 million CERs (World Bank 2011a) from two HFC-23 projects. All other Chinese HFC-23 projects were quickly contracted and plants in other countries followed. Currently, only one eligible opportunity has not been implemented – a plant in Venezuela, where the World Bank was pushing strongly, but Venezuelan president Chavez' aversion to market mechanisms prevailed.

The second kind of CDM 'nuggets' was formed by plants reducing N_2O from adipic acid production. The situation is similar to HFC-23: large gas streams can be destroyed relatively cheaply. Here, the potential group of projects was even smaller than in the case of HFC-23. Outside China, only three eligible plants existed, two of which belonged to the French chemical company Rhodia. In May 2004, Rhodia contacted the small startup CDM consultancy Perspectives in

Germany to develop a CDM methodology for this technology. Why did Rhodia not choose an established French consultant? While its middle management thought that CDM revenues could save the company – which was close to bankruptcy at this time (see Clellant 2007 for a description of the company's situation in the mid-2000s) – the company's leaders did not believe in the CDM, and thus the middle management wanted to work in secret. The middle management prevailed; the methodology was approved quickly and both projects were registered before the end of 2005. Rhodia is the biggest CER producer worldwide, generating 14 million CERs per year from its two projects. The company's recovery would have been impossible without the related profit of €135 million in 2007 (Point Carbon 2009), rising to €158 million in 2008 (Rhodia 2010), €165 million in 2009 and €169 million in 2010 (Rhodia 2011).

Both kinds of 'nuggets' generated a backlash by NGOs and researchers. Wara (2007) prominently repeated Schneider *et al.*'s (2004) recommendation that HFC-23 projects should be excluded from the CDM due to their high rents; public funds could just finance the abatement costs. In early 2010, the NGO CDM Watch launched a campaign against HFC-23 projects, arguing that project developers had kept the HFC-23 generation level artificially high. This caused the CDM EB to put the HFC-23 methodology on hold. In autumn 2010, CDM Watch also attacked the adipic acid projects, having commissioned a study by Schneider *et al.* (2010) who argued that adipic acid production had moved from industrialized to developing countries due to the CDM. CDM Watch scored a total victory, with the EU Commission prohibiting use of CERs from HFC-23 and adipic acid projects in the EU Emissions Trading Scheme from April 2013 onwards (EU Commission 2011).

3 Which technologies and countries benefited the most?

The overall development of technologies and the role of host countries has varied considerably over time. There has not been any 'natural' champion of the CDM. This shows that the competitive nature of the CDM market has always led to the emergence of new trends.

3.1 Technology fashions

When it comes to the EB, the CDM has been a mechanism dominated by learning by doing. Regulatory decisions have frequently been the basis of a take-off of a certain project type, with 'fashions' developing. Often, the first registration of a project of a certain technology unleashes a wave of imitators. However, such fashions can also be choked off by further regulatory decisions spurred by increased knowledge of regulators regarding the drawback of the project type in question. This 'boom and bust' cycle is particularly relevant for project types whose additionality is doubtful (see the discussion on additionality below). It happened with cement blending and bagasse cogeneration and was recently repeated with wind in China (see below and Chapter 3 for more details). Project types with clear additionality exhibit a lower tendency for such cycles but are vulnerable to changed expectations regarding future CER prices and demand.

In the very first days of the CDM, methane recovery from animal waste and landfills was the preferred technology. A bold business idea was developed by the company AgCert that started to roll-out hundreds of methane recovery and flaring projects in swine and dairy farms across Mexico and Brazil. At the same time, Brazil saw the emergence of a cluster of bagasse cogeneration plants in the sugar sector, while India followed with rice husk power plants.

While the huge industrial gas projects got off the ground in 2004–2005 and triggered a wave of smaller projects reducing N_2O from nitric acid production, wind and hydro power projects made their appearance, mainly in India. First of relatively small size, they started to increase to include plants of several hundred megawatts (MW); the multi-thousand megawatt giants of the hydro sector, however, never dared to apply for CDM, probably for fear of not passing the additionality test. Similarly, waste heat recovery from cement and steel plants became a hot topic. The strengthening of the EB's rules on additionality from 2006 onwards were seen by many as a deterrent for projects in renewable energy as well as waste heat recovery, judging from the chilling effect of rejection of cement blending projects. The rejection wave of cement blending projects in early 2007 led to an abrupt decline in the development of this project type (Figure 1.3). A high rejection rate leads to a loss of reputation of a validator and thus validators try to weed out projects with a high likelihood of rejection.

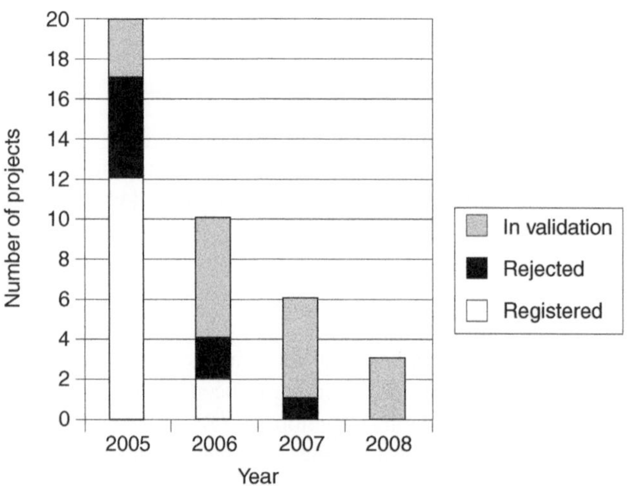

Figure 1.3 Cement blending blues (source: own illustration based on UNEP Riso Centre 2011a).

Note
The figure shows the number of projects using the cement blending methodology ACM 5 submitted for validation every year and their status in the CDM project cycle.

While some waste heat recovery, bagasse cogeneration, wind and hydro projects were rejected, in contrast to the cement case this never triggered a substantial fall in submissions. More challenging was the rejection of a number of Chinese wind projects in 2009 due to the interpretation of the CDM EB that China had reduced feed-in tariffs as a response to the availability of CER revenues (He and Morse 2010). The tariff reduction was seen as a policy that would lead to an increase of emissions, as it would reduce the attractiveness of renewable power compared to fossil power plants. This interpretation was essentially inconsistent with an earlier decision by the EB, which had specified that host-country policies giving incentives for emissions reductions would not have to be taken into account in the baseline and additionality determination if introduced after December 2001. But from late 2010 onwards, a truce was called between Chinese policy-makers and the EB, which essentially quietly buried the issue. More than 90 per cent of the massive Chinese wind expansion and the somewhat slower but still impressive Indian wind power growth have been submitted as CDM projects.

From 2009 onwards, even projects on the energy demand side started to make it into the CDM, led by replacement of incandescent lamps by compact fluorescent lamps. One sector where the CDM has disappointed to date is transport, with an exceedingly small number of projects and serious methodological problems (Grütter 2011). Likewise, the forestry sector has been unable to mobilize a significant number of projects, which is due to the limited demand for the forestry CERs – the EU ETS does not allow use of temporary CERs.

3.2 Country fashions

Host-country regulation, such as availability of DNAs or their ability to process projects, plays a crucial role in mobilizing CDM projects. Countries with a huge supply potential such as Saudi Arabia and Algeria were stymied by this factor. Even in countries with currently operational DNAs, a change in government or even single officials can lead to a blocking of new supply, as has happened in the Philippines.

The first movers in the CDM market were the Latin American countries, which set-up their CDM institutions in 2002. Brazil took the early lead in project development, benefitting from a vibrant sector of CDM consultancies. From 2004, India took over, as the high availability of domestic capital and the willingness to take risks led to a wave of unilateral projects. After the government regulation had been set-up by China, from late 2005 the country dominated the CDM market. China benefited from a massive outreach of central government to the provinces through 'CDM centres' (Schroeder 2009) and the rapid emergence of a bustling community of domestic CDM consultants. In both India and China, consultancies surveyed the country for CDM potential, mainly in heavy industries but also beyond, applying a business model where they would develop all CDM documentation at a zero financial fee, retaining only a share of the CERs. The Indian branch of the consultancy Ernst & Young is probably the most extreme example of this strategy, developing hundreds of CDM project documents almost in an assembly-line fashion. Southeast Asian countries managed to mobilize a significant project inflow from 2007 onwards, led by Thailand, which mobilized a cluster of projects in methane collection from cassava waste, while Vietnam focused on hydro power, Malaysia on methane reduction from palm oil wastes and Indonesia on a diverse array of project types.

While the distribution of CDM projects generally reflects the attractiveness of host countries for foreign direct investment, there are cases that show that a proactive and supportive CDM policy environment can overcome a bad economic and political environment. The most extreme of these cases is the Central American country of Honduras. The country is notorious for its political instability, social violence, currency devaluation and lack of relevant industries – all characteristics aptly summarized in the term 'banana republic'. Nevertheless, Honduras has been able to mobilize a significant number of CDM projects. By July 2011, 17 projects had been registered, with an estimated level of 2.1 million pre-2013 CERs; another 19 projects were also under validation. The share of Honduras in the global CDM market is 0.5 per cent in terms of projects and 0.1 per cent in terms of CER volume, while its share in global GDP reaches just 0.03 per cent (World Bank 2011b). Eight projects have been rejected by validators or the EB. Table 1.1 shows details of the Honduran CDM pipeline.

Honduras benefited from Finnish and World Bank assistance to develop the world's first registered small-scale CDM project, the Rio Blanco hydro power station, with a capacity of 13 MW. Apparently, a crucial element of the success was the existence of streamlined approval procedures and active staff at the country's DNA. Another global milestone was achieved in October 2005 when Rio Blanco and the similar La Esperanza project were the first projects to get CER issuance. However, political instability took its toll in 2005, when DNA staff were fired after a new president took office. Nevertheless, a feed-in law for renewable energy enacted in 2007 put new breath into CDM project development. While five of the early hydro projects sold their CERs to Finland, five projects from different sectors were developed by Ecosecurities. One-third of the projects in the pipeline are unilateral, which is surprising given the low domestic capital formation in Honduras.

Table 1.1 Characteristics of CDM projects in Honduras

Project type	*Total number*	*Of which registered (%)*	*Of which rejected (%)*	*Issuance success (%)*
Hydro	14	71	0	68 (8 projects)
Electricity from palm oil waste	11	36	27	139 (2 projects)
Bagasse cogeneration	7	28	43	N/A
Other	4	25	25	N/A
Total	36	47	21	75

Source: UNEP Riso Centre (2011a).

Lokey (2009) provides an interesting example of the early CDM 'Wild West days' in Honduras, in which La Esperanza turned down an offer from the Finnish Industrial Development Fund of US$1/CER and concluded a forward contract with the World Bank for US$4.5/CER, with a 30 per cent upfront payment. She sees the active renewable generators association AHPPER (Asociación Hondureña de Pequeños Productores de Energía Renovable) as crucial to dissemination of information about the CDM, through workshops and conferences.

3.3 Differences in project performance between countries and technologies[5]

Many projects that are submitted never make it to CDM issuance. Overall performance of projects that have issued CERs has remained close to 100 per cent throughout CDM history, hovering at 95–98 per cent. This, however, hides a wide imbalance between industrial gas projects that have strongly overperformed and all other project categories, some of which have seriously underperformed.

Where can underperformance come from? Figure 1.4 shows possible reasons for failure and underperformance throughout the CDM project cycle, starting from the validation process. These reasons are not limited to a specific project type.

As shown by several of the risk examples in Figure 1.4, financial problems that may lead to project failure can relate to the financing structure of the project ('equity provider pulls out'), as well as to problems with the revenue streams and costs of the project ('failure to service loan due to low biogas generation rate').

Traditionally, banks have been unwilling to lend against CER revenues. In many countries, especially those with a high share of unilateral projects, the main source of CDM financing is equity. As equity provision is often based on informal networks, it might be that completely non-technical reasons can kill a project. For example, the uncle of the project developer may not support the

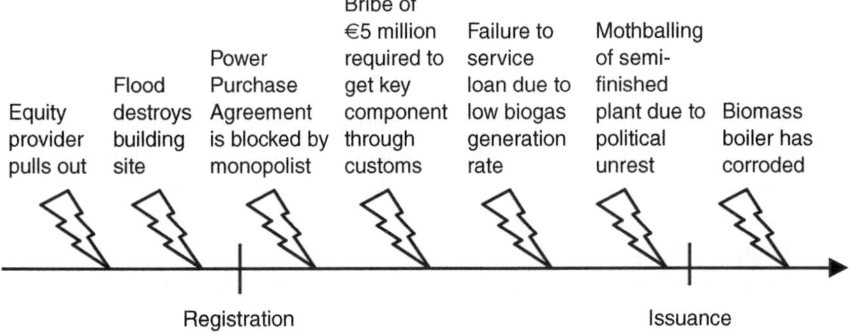

Figure 1.4 Typical project failures and underperformance throughout the CDM project cycle (source: own illustration based on UNEP Riso Centre 2011a).

project developer's choice of business partner and thus withdraws his equity investment into the project, thereby preventing its implementation. While equity providers can pull out at any time, debt-financed projects will die once their net revenues are no longer sufficient to service the debt.

Most CDM projects generate their main revenue through the sale of a product such as electricity. Risks related to that revenue stream are:

- inability to negotiate a sales contract. In many countries, electricity monopolists are unwilling to offer Power Purchase Agreements (PPAs), even if formally they are required to do so (see Figure 1.4).
- lower prices than assumed in feasibility studies. The calculation of the CER revenue stream may be based on an overestimated price level. Project developers with a partial understanding of the CDM market may have used a forecast of secondary CER prices, whereas they can only achieve a price in the primary market that is substantially discounted from secondary CER prices.
- overestimation of production due to lower resource availability (wind speed, precipitation) than projected, which can lead to the inability to repay loans. While some projects may continue to operate even after the bankruptcy of the original developer, others may be stopped. As shown by the wide distribution of CER performance both between and within specific project types, a non-negligible share of projects suffers from massive overestimation of production. Overestimation of production may be due to unavailability of data, unwillingness to carry the costs for certain measurements or lack of time for a sufficiently trustworthy production forecast. For example, wind data from meteorological stations is usually measured at a height where the wind speed is still influenced by surrounding objects (trees, houses). Data may be incomplete or sub-standard measurement equipment may have been used (see Chapter 3). Three-dimensional, numeric models require back-testing of data gained from reference wind plants. On-site measurements are expensive due to high masts and require at least a three-month measurement period.

In a similar manner, on the cost side, the assumptions regarding investment costs may be optimistic. Risks related to investment costs are:

- cost overruns of the investment due to price increases of technology providers. This can often happen if there are increases in raw material prices.
- cost overrun due to unexpected problems on the project site. For hydro projects, geological problems often increase costs for tunnelling and foundations of dams.
- cost overruns due to delays. Delays can have manifold causes:
  - incompetent management
  - regulatory bottlenecks, e.g. blocking of imported components in customs

  - infrastructural bottlenecks
  - political issues, such as changes in government
- costs for items that have not been budgeted, such as bribery requirements.

Operational risk covers the failure of the project equipment, the fact that it is not delivered on time and other related problems, as well as problems with the cooperation of the entities involved in the implementation of a project.

Particularly if it is a 'first of its kind' project – i.e. the first use of a specific technology in a specific host country – a CDM project faces the risk of technological failure. The risk differs according to the project type. Risks can be categorized as:

- unavailability of the technology as specified in the project documentation;
- malfunctions that reduce production;
- failure of the equipment.

For example, boilers that use rice husk need to have a special alloy to be resistant to abrasion and corrosion. Offshore wind turbines may not resist the marine environment. Technological risks also relate to the robustness of monitoring equipment and the ability to actually implement the monitoring plan.

Operational risk also includes an organizational component. If many entities have to work together, the complexity of communication and management structures can lead to a stalling of a project, especially if compounded by cultural differences. The more layers of actors a project has, the higher the organizational risk. Moreover, the incentives for all participants need to be sufficient to prevent sabotage. A key question is how the overall revenue from the project (including the CERs) is distributed between project participants and project owners.

The people responsible for the monitoring of emission reductions need to have a sufficiently high incentive to do this in order to deliver on this in a satisfactory manner. A key issue in the failure of many animal waste projects developed by the company AgCert was that farmers did not have an incentive to properly operate and monitor the biogas installations. For example, 58 registered animal waste projects have not received issuance four years after registration.

Political risk encompasses a wide range of events: changes in government can lead to expropriation; wars, revolts and revolutions can destroy plants or lead to prolonged shutdowns. The PanOcean gas flaring reduction project in Nigeria (UNFCCC 2011: no. 2029), now operational, was substantially delayed due to an act of sabotage against an oil pipeline, which stopped oil and gas production, and hence the gas flaring constituting the baseline of the project activity (Haugland 2011). Property rights can be interpreted differently over time. For example, the Aguan palm oil waste methane-reduction project in Honduras (UNFCCC 2011: no. 3197) has been embroiled in violent land conflicts, with militias hired by the project developer allegedly having killed a number of farmers. While so far no case of CDM-related expropriation has been reported, the risk is not negligible as shown by the recent upheavals in Tunisia and Egypt.

A CDM plant may be damaged or destroyed by a natural catastrophe, such as earthquakes, storms or floods. The Miyaluo hydro power project of Ecosecurities incurred serious damage in the Sichuan earthquake of 2008 and was never submitted for registration (UNFCCC 2011: no. 1966). In Honduras, the El Coronado project (UNFCCC 2011: no. 4560) suffered hurricane damage to its piping (Lokey 2009). Natural catastrophes may also impact the sales of a CDM project or the availability of inputs. For example, the recent flooding in Pakistan led to cement plants cutting production because of the difficulties in transporting coal from the ports. While the latter is unlikely to kill a project entirely, it may be the death knell if a project is already ailing. Project no. 1859 (UNFCCC 2011), a gas power plant in China, suffered a delay of 6–9 months of the delivery of two units as the production site of the company building these units was damaged by the Sichuan earthquake. For a less financially liquid project developer, the delay might have proven fatal for the project. Natural risks also include variations in the availability of a natural resource such as wind or runoff.

Due to the different performance risks after project registration, overall performance of countries without industrial gas projects apparently cannot reach more than two-thirds of the anticipated level. There are substantial performance differences between countries for similar technologies. With respect to power generation from biomass residue projects, India's 91 projects with issuance reach an average of just 87 per cent, whereas Brazil's 27 projects' performance is 10 per cent higher at 97 per cent. In Brazil, the sugar industry that dominates bio-power production has close to a decade of experience, so teething troubles have been weeded out. India lags behind Brazil due to the more diverse nature of the bio-power sector and the challenges linked to different fuel types. The high performance of Brazil might also be explained by a stringent process of project design document (PDD) checking before registration. This explanation gains weight due to the overperformance of Brazilian projects being replicated for river hydro power projects in which Brazil's 20 projects achieve 102 per cent compared to India's 26 projects with 86 per cent and China's 137 projects with 83 per cent.

Performance of wind projects is much better in India than in China – India's 56 projects reach 95 per cent, whereas China's 148 projects lie a full ten percentage points below, which may be due to the fact that Indian developers have an incentive to underestimate performance in order to pass the investment test. Moreover, the experience of Indian wind developers regarding the wind conditions at the key wind sites is much greater than in China, where the wind boom only started a few years ago. In China, additionality of wind plants is relatively clear (since China's preferential tariff for wind power does not need to be taken into account, according to CDM rules), hence no conservative estimate of the plant load factor is required. Moreover, the feasibility studies for government institutions tend to be on the optimistic side regarding power production level forecasts to avoid critical questions regarding project feasibility. Given the requirement to use the feasibility study parameters in the PDD, a non-conservative estimate of the plant load factor is given, which will automatically lead to an underperformance.

With regard to waste heat recovery in metal production and cement, India's 31 projects achieve 91 per cent, whereas China's 45 projects only reach 72 per cent. This huge differential may be due to the dominance of private companies in the sector in India that are likely to act more effectively than large state-owned companies in China. A similar tendency is visible with regards to improvement of power plant efficiency. Here, India's six projects have an advantage of almost 30 percentage points compared to China's 16 projects that achieve only 51 per cent.

In the animal waste sector, which has on average been a notorious underperformer, Chile's four projects show that good project management can make a difference – they achieve 102 per cent, whereas Brazil's and Mexico's 27 projects achieve 37 per cent and 30 per cent, respectively. According to Deecke (2010), who assessed 39 projects with issuance, the main reasons for underperformance are overestimated default parameters from the IPCC inventory guidelines used in the methodologies for ex-ante estimates of CERs. For three parameters, the overestimate reaches about 10–15 per cent each. If these systematic errors are excluded, the performance would improve considerably. However, Deecke also finds substantial monitoring errors.

For methane reduction from landfill gas, Brazil's 11 projects reach 58 per cent, but Argentina's four projects only 35 per cent. This is likely due to the average size of landfills in Brazil being much larger and the experience of companies implementing the projects being higher than in Argentina. Chen *et al.* (2010) discuss reasons for poor performance of landfill gas projects in China.

Even in the industrial gas sector, where the incentive to perform highly is massive, there are substantial differences between countries. In the context of HFC-23 destruction, India's five projects achieve a performance of 132 per cent compared to China's 11 projects, which reach 101 per cent. The three N_2O destruction projects in nitric acid plants in Africa reach 126 per cent and five plants in Latin America achieve 103 per cent, the ten plants in China only manage to get 74 per cent.

Generally, China underperforms compared to other host countries; this means that the overall performance of the CDM will fall as the share of Chinese issuances increases. But the small number of cases for many project types means that very project- or owner-specific reasons could be responsible for underperformance.

Summing up, to date, the projects reducing the industrial gases HFC-23 and N_2O have offset the underperformance of the other sectors due to their high share in overall CER volume and a strong overperformance. This overperformance is due to the incentive to maximize capacity utilization of the HCFC-22 and adipic acid plants because of the CER revenue. With the optimization of the industrial gas projects and regulatory efforts to reduce their overperformance as well as energy efficiency and renewable electricity projects showing a decreasing performance, average performance is likely to decline.

4 In which fields did the CDM underperform and would need reform?

The gold rush into the CDM obviously was not without serious problems. As in any gold rush, Wild West manners prevailed in the initial phase. The sheriff, i.e. the CDM EB, was initially completely helpless in stopping abuses, but over time has asserted his power. But with increased maturity of the CDM market, new challenges have arisen.

4.1 The additionality conundrum

One of the most contentious issues in the development of the CDM is the question of whether CDM projects should undergo a strict additionality test. To safeguard environmental integrity, CDM projects should be able to prove that the project is mobilized by the revenue generated through CER sales. Otherwise, global emissions increase as one CER from a non-additional project allows an industrialized country to increase its emission by 1 tCO_2-e. Regulators have fought with project developers about the interpretation of additionality, leading to a lenient interpretation of additionality until 2007 and a tightening ever since (for a detailed history of additionality regulation, see Michaelowa 2009). Repeatedly, researchers have found non-additionality of a significant share of project types (see Schneider 2009b; Haya 2010 (for projects in India and China); Partridge and Gamkhar 2010 for small hydro projects in China).

A resolution of the additionality conundrum requires understanding of why project developers engage in a project. Haya (2010) argues that this is impossible. We agree that it is difficult, but believe that it is conceptually possible.

Companies would normally be driven by a desire to maximize profits. However, this can also entail doing some projects at a loss to open new markets and test new technologies that they see as strategically relevant. If companies behave perfectly rationally, they implement all projects that generate a positive net present value at a discount rate equal to the lending rate of commercial banks. Thus, in a rational world the stringent additionality test would not lead to a reduction of CDM activities, provided that the lending rate is known. In such a world no project would be more profitable, so the most profitable alternative-additionality test would give the same result. The effect of a financial benchmark would depend on its relation to the lending rate. If it is lower than the lending rate, projects would not be implemented.

In a world of risk-averse companies, companies will use a discount rate that is higher than the lending rate. The higher the difference, the higher the volume of projects that are not implemented according to the stringent additionality test (Figure 1.5).

The additionality test looking at the most profitable alternative will reduce the volume of projects that are not implemented as the risk aversion will be reflected in the discount rate that determines the most profitable alternative. If companies

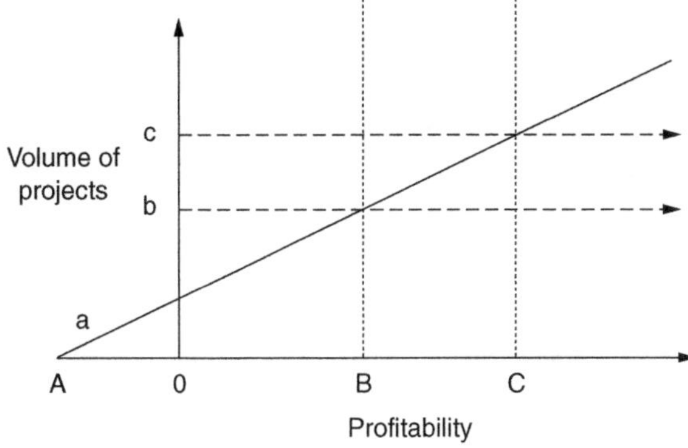

Figure 1.5 Additionality test thresholds and risk aversion (source: own illustration).

Note

Under perfect rationality and free availability of capital, companies would implement all projects from profitability of A (some projects with negative profitability for market entry and technology testing). In a rational world, they would only start at the lending rate B. In the risk-averse world, they would add the risk premium to the lending rate, increasing the profitability threshold to C. The difference c–b would be the loss of projects according to the strict additionality test.

have differing degrees of risk aversion, the situation lies between the two extremes described above.

If non-additional projects are labelled as CDM projects, the marginal cost of CER generation is zero. This leads to a downward pressure on the CER price and changes the CER revenue. The revenue change depends on the price elasticity of the CER demand; it is negative if the elasticity is larger than 1 (Figure 1.6).

With the discussion about the standardization of baselines, a discussion about simplified additionality testing has emerged. For example, additionality could be assumed in case predefined barriers exist, such as absence of feed-in tariffs for renewable energy or subsidized electricity tariffs. Capital availability constraints for energy-efficiency investments could also be accepted as such a barrier. A technology-based simplification would be achieved through a rule that all projects are additional as long as the technology penetration rate is below a predetermined threshold. The setting of this threshold would likely be contentious.

Furthermore, sector-specific rules could be developed. Additionality could be presumed for all renewable-energy technologies that have higher electricity generation costs than fossil technologies.

As discussed above, in late 2009, the EB started to question Chinese wind power projects (see also Chapter 3). This fight against (Chinese) windmills, which led to the rejection of ten projects, diverted attention from some really problematic issues and led to doubts regarding the priorities of the regulators, even among those who support high environmental stringency of the CDM.

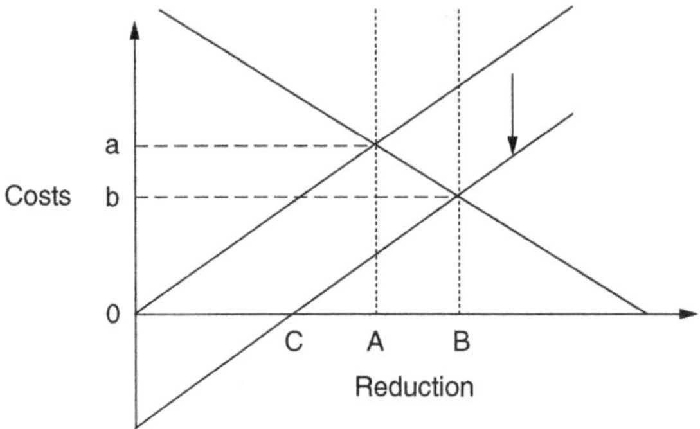

Figure 1.6 Price effects of non-additional CDM projects (source: own illustration).

Note

The supply curve of CERs is shifted downwards due to the inclusion of C reductions from non-additional projects. This increases total CER volume from A to B, but reduces CER price from a to b. Revenue changes from aA to bB. Revenue is reduced if the slope of the CER demand curve is greater than –1, i.e. price elasticity greater than 1. Even if revenue increases, there will be a crowding-out of CDM projects with costs between b and a.

With the CDM EB's decision of mid-2010 and early 2011 to assume automatic additionality for certain types of renewable-energy projects below 5 MW, energy-efficiency improvement with less than 20 GWh savings and other projects with less than 20,000 t annual reductions, a new chapter in the additionality controversy has emerged.

Given the strong incentives of a majority of stakeholders in the CDM to do away with additionality, overall the CDM EB has performed remarkably well with regards to specifying rules for additionality testing and strengthening them over time, but less with regard to actually preventing non-additional projects. Initially anything went through, as regulators were completely overwhelmed by the massive project inflow. From 2006 onwards, some smaller projects were rejected due to lack of additionality, but larger ones usually passed through. However, additionality rules may have prevented the largest hydro projects – such as the Three Gorges Dam in China – from entering the CDM pipeline.

4.2 The regulatory vicious circle due to the underperformance of validators

The original idea of the CDM regulatory system had been that independent auditors would serve as gatekeepers of the CDM, with the EB occasionally providing a Solomonic judgement on issues of generic importance. In CDM terminology, the auditors are called Designated Operational Entities (DOEs). In practice, they are often called validators or verifiers, with validation being the initial checking of project documentation, while verification is the subsequent assessment of actual project implementation.

In 2004 and 2005, the CDM EB did not check the validation reports and allowed projects to be registered automatically. When the UNFCCC Secretariat commissioned the first analyses of the portfolio of registered projects in 2006 and these analyses showed that many projects were problematic, the CDM EB started to feel outmanoeuvred by unscrupulous project developers. Thus, it developed a deep mistrust in project developers and DOEs.

The main problem related to the incentives of the DOEs. Instead of performing an in-depth check of project documentation, they were often seen as just confirming the statements of the project developers, without checking external, independent sources. Many observers argue that the main reason is that DOEs are hired by the project developers and propose that DOEs should be hired by the CDM EB (Dyck (2010) disagrees, arguing that the administrative burden would be prohibitive). However, it is often argued that a CDM-like incentive structure exists in other markets for audit services and does not generate problems.

Thus, the EB felt compelled to engage in a nitty-gritty check of each submitted project and so introduced a multi-layer system of checks and balances. The Registration and Issuance Team was introduced in spring 2006, and the UNFCCC Secretariat staff also started checking project submissions. This well-meaning endeavour led to a massive increase in processing time of registration requests. In the early days of the CDM a registration request would only require the statutory review periods, but in late 2009 the average duration of the completeness check of documents took four months, and more than half of submitted projects would be faced with a request for review that would add another two months. More than half of EB meeting time in 2009 was spent on project cases and in many cases this has held up decisions on key regulatory issues. Dyck (2010) discusses the issues related to the regulation of auditing and performance of DOEs in detail.

A key reason for the war of attrition between the DOEs and the EB was that the EB waited too long before invoking sanctions. A cat-and-mouse game ensued. In late 2008, the EB suspended DNV, the market leader in validation, sending shockwaves through the DOE community and delaying a large number of projects in the validation pipeline. This was repeated in mid-2009, when SGS, the leader in verification, was suspended. However, both DOEs were reinstated relatively quickly. The main issue leading to the suspensions was insufficient qualification of DOE staff, which frequently have to be replaced and newly trained due to poaching of experienced staff by project developers.

As CDM project developers started to face the repercussions of ever-slower registration of projects and CER issuance, adverse business consequences followed. Companies that had imprudently forward-sold large shares of their expected CER flows got into trouble, with at least one company facing bankruptcy and others suffering strong pressure on their share prices. Naturally, they stepped up pressure on the EB, threatening legal action and setting up several lobby groups.

Until 2010 relations in the regulatory process of the CDM thus became increasingly antagonistic. Since then, the situation has improved, often due to decisions taken much earlier. Recognizing that the DOE problem had a lot to do with unclear or even conflicting guidance, the EB developed a *Validation and Verification Manual*, whose first version entered into force in late 2008 (see Dyck (2010) for stakeholder views on the usefulness of the manual; he argues that a clear materiality standard is preferable to the manual in its current form). While it took some time to become effective, it has now reduced the number of contentious cases. Likewise, in the contested areas of additionality determination, clearer guidance has reduced the amount of problematic cases. A streamlined registration procedure was introduced in mid-2010, reducing the number of checks. In late 2010, a big effort involving outside consultants led to a clearing of the backlog of projects that had accumulated over time. The processing time for registration has subsequently been reduced by a factor of three.

Overall, DOE performance has improved considerably since the EB unveiled the use of suspensions, but it remains an Achilles heel of the CDM. In our view, the performance of DOEs could be improved further by providing incentives that decouple their interests from those of the project developer.

4.3 Uneven technology transfer

Over time, many studies have tried to elucidate the CDM's contribution to technology transfer (e.g. Seres *et al.* 2009). The most recent study, with the largest dataset, is UNFCCC (2010), which analyses almost 5,000 active projects. This study finds technology transfer in 40 per cent of projects, covering 59 per cent of all CERs. For simple renewable-energy technologies such as hydro and biomass with a good technology base in key host countries, the share is low, whereas for industrial gas and methane-related projects, it is close to 100 per cent (Figure 1.7).

A problem with technology transfer studies is often that they limit themselves to assessment of project documents without checking whether the statements in the documents are true. Any project developer obviously has the incentive to argue that there is technology transfer even if there is none. Wang (2010) is an exception in as much as he underpins his analyses of a large number of project documents with background interviews and a careful assessment of government policies. He finds that in all but one industrial gas project in China, technology transfer happened, but only in about one-quarter of wind and coal mine methane projects. In those, the cost differential between foreign and domestic technology reached 50–100 per cent, whereas the performance of the foreign technology was around 30 per cent better. Thus, the performance differential could not cover the cost disadvantage of the foreign technology. An extremely interesting case described by Wang (2010) is the transfer of Japanese waste heat recovery technology to a large Chinese cement producer in 1998. After successful performance of the pilot project, the cement producer applied this technology in ten other plants, of which six were submitted as CDM projects. It then set-up a joint

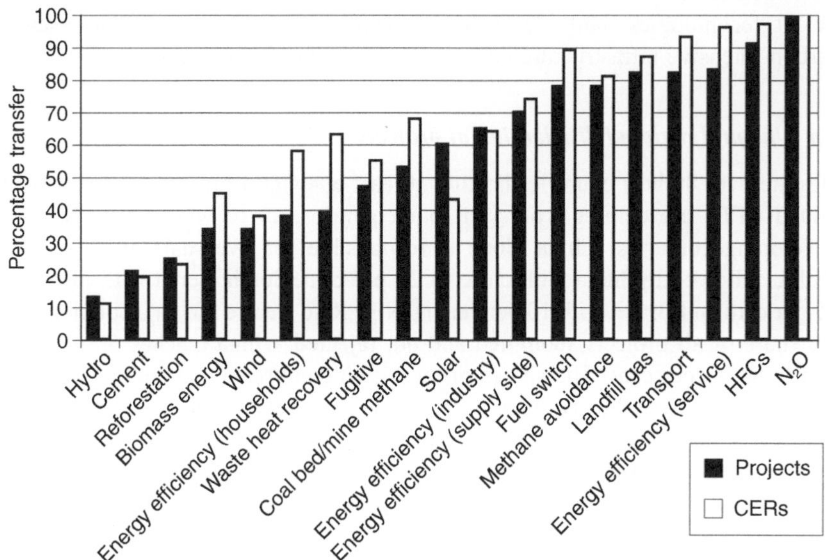

Figure 1.7 Technology transfer according to project type (%) (source: UNFCCC 2010).

Note

Only categories with over 20 projects are included. 'Fugitive' means capturing methane leaking from pipelines and methane capture from waste water.

venture with the Japanese, which reduced the costs of the technology massively to enable roll-out of another 51 projects. This case clearly shows that the CDM has contributed to technology diffusion. However, Wang notes that the structure of the CDM market limits incentives for CDM project developers to actually engage in technology transfer, as most CDM consultants have no direct links to technology producers and lack the competence to offer an integrated package.

Haya (2010) looks closely at bagasse cogeneration in India and concludes that a range of shifting barriers has impeded the development of this technology, while it principally was cost-effective. In her view, the incentive from the CER revenues alone would not have overcome these barriers.

Generally, the CDM has generated a sizeable amount of technology transfer. However, this transfer is highest for project types criticized by many stakeholders, such as industrial gas projects, and relatively limited for project types generally supported, such as renewable energy. To promote technology transfer, host countries could assert their role more strongly, as has been done by the Malaysian DNA, which rejected a number of project applications due to lacking technology transfer. Generally, CDM works reasonably well in terms of stimulating (1) renewable energy and energy-efficiency technologies that are almost competitive already; (2) more efficient applications of existing technologies. It has proven less good at (1) stimulating nascent technologies (it explicitly rejects technologies at the R&D stage); (2) helping speed up the phase-out of old, inefficient technologies; and (3) slowing down the introduction of large-scale, carbon-intensive infrastructure investment in developing countries.

4.4 Unequal regional distribution of projects

Despite over 80 host countries hosting at least one CDM project, 90 per cent of issued CERs are coming from just four countries, all of which are advanced developing countries. China alone is responsible for over half of the issued CERs, followed by India with close to 20 per cent, South Korea with just over 15 per cent and Brazil with 10 per cent (UNEP Riso Centre 2011a). Looking into the share of all projects submitted and not rejected, China reaches 50 per cent and India 20 per cent. The shares of these two countries have remained essentially constant over the last three years. However, India's share of CDM project inflow has increased and China's decreased lately.

Mirroring this trend, the shares of Africa and LDCs have remained very small, around 2.5 per cent for Africa and 1 per cent for LDCs (Figure 1.8). Since late 2007, a small upward trend is visible.

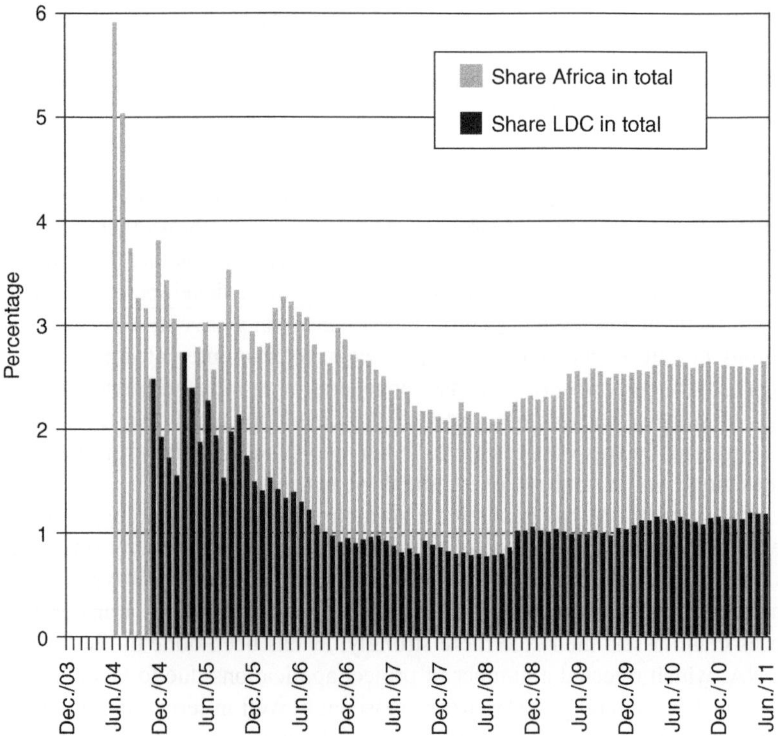

Figure 1.8 Share of Africa and LDCs in total CDM projects (source: raw data from UNEP Riso Centre 2011a, not including rejected and withdrawn projects).

The main reason for this low performance of low-income countries is the mainly unilateral nature of CDM projects underlying financing. Given that actual investment from industrialized countries is rare, project development can only happen if domestic capital is available. Domestic capital availability is limited in low-income countries and the required profit rates for investment of this capital are much higher than in emerging economies, where capital is abundant. Another issue stifling CDM in many low-income countries is the absence of data for baseline calculation. Moreover, even if data are available, there is often a lack of GHG emission sources that could be addressed under existing methodologies, or the baseline emission factor could be unattractive due to low fossil fuel use. The recent decision of the CDM EB to allow for 'suppressed demand' in baseline methodologies may improve chances for projects in the poorest countries. Likewise, the EU decision to limit imports of CERs from projects registered after the end of 2012 to LDCs may increase the LDC pipeline; it will not overcome the technical and financial barriers, though (Castro and Michaelowa 2011).

Forestry projects – which would be a possible supply source in many countries so far playing a negligible role in the CDM – have faced too many barriers so far (see Pearson *et al.* (2009) for a description of rules for forestry projects and recommendations for their design, Neeff and Henders (2007) for a good overview of the potential and barriers facing such projects, as well as Socorro *et al.* (2005) for legal issues relating to such projects).

Several actions have been taken to rebalance the distribution of CDM projects, including waiving fees for projects in LDCs, a loan scheme for projects in such countries, as well as simplified CDM modalities and procedures.

4.5 Limited contribution to sustainable development

The twin aim of the CDM to produce low-cost offsets for industrialized countries and contribute to sustainable development in the host countries has always been awkward, given that effective policy instruments normally have a single aim. Olsen (2007) has neatly summarized the early literature and did not find a significant support for sustainable development by CDM projects. Alexeew *et al.* (2010) looked at a sample of 40 registered projects in India and found a negative correlation between their additionality and contribution to sustainable development. The key reason for the lack of contribution of projects to sustainable development is that the sustainability benefits of CDM projects are to be evaluated by the DNAs, but due to competition for projects between countries, no DNA takes this task seriously. The CDM EB recently asked for public input on how to take into account projects' co-benefits as well as their negative impacts in the guidelines for CDM project documentation. Another rule meant to enhance sustainable development, the participation of local stakeholders, which has to be described in the project documentation, has all too often been emptied of substance – for example by just inviting people supportive of the project to answer a questionnaire. The CDM EB has so far never enforced it, but is reviewing its approach. Surprisingly, this problem was not addressed by NGOs, but only some academics sceptical towards markets (e.g. Lohmann 2006; Böhm and Dabhi 2009).

But the transparency of the CDM process and the possibility of anybody submitting critical comments about projects under validation theoretically make it a good field for NGOs that can develop coordinated campaigns of commenting and pointing fingers at bad projects. However, the only, one-man NGO critically assessing CDM projects, CDM Watch (CDM Watch 2004), was closed down in late 2004, just when the CDM started to gather steam. Girling (2010) discusses the timid role of NGOs in the debates about the CDM in Europe. Resuscitation of CDM Watch took many years and only in 2009 was a new CDM Watch started. However, it immediately became a strong force, editing a newsletter to influence CDM EB decisions, mobilizing NGO networks in the key CDM host countries and organizing commenting campaigns. It organized a successful campaign against industrial gas projects (see Section 2.4) and seems poised to repeat this success with regards to coal power projects.

4.6 How can the CDM be upscaled?

If we want to reach the peak of global emissions in the next decade, as would be required to reach the 2°C target endorsed by the Cancun Agreement, the stringency of emission commitments of industrialized countries needs to be increased, further countries have to take on commitments and the supply of CDM credits be enhanced, probably by an order of magnitude.

Obviously, the potential for large single projects addressing existing emission sources is beginning to be exhausted, as shown by the lack of new industrial gas project submissions. But entire regions such as the Middle East or whole sectors such as buildings (e.g. Jiang and Tovey 2010) have only been touched upon, and thus a wholesale exhaustion of the CDM will not happen, as long as demand for CERs exists. In principle, renewable energy and energy efficiency can be upscaled without limit, provided the CER incentive is large enough to close the cost gap to fossil fuels. Moreover, new technologies are constantly being developed that provide new mitigation potential.

4.7 What determines CDM potential?

The economic policy of a country and historical chance determines the actual technical potential for GHG reductions.[6] A necessary condition is a theoretical technical potential. A flat, dry country cannot have hydro power potential, while bio-energy depends on the availability of biomass residues and wind on windy areas. The potential can also shift over time as hydrology, crop growing conditions and windspeeds change over time (and due to climate change!).

Political support is required to mobilize the technical potential. This can take many forms. The most effective forms of political support are direct monetary incentives. If a country introduces credible feed-in tariffs for renewable electricity sufficient to make such activities profitable, a strong increase in renewable-energy installations will ensue.

As the slow development of wind power in China over 15 years and its sudden explosion from 2005 onwards has shown (see Lewis 2010 and Chapter 3 in this volume for overviews of CDM and wind energy in China), it is very difficult to predict the exact date and size of utilization of technical potential. Also, both sudden and creeping political events can disable/enable potential. For example, a revolution in Thailand could block the promising CDM development in that country. On the other hand, pacification of Somalia would allow access to huge wind power potential. A trustworthy government in the Democratic Republic of Congo could enable construction of the world's largest hydro power plant at the Inga site, where the plans are ready.

4.8 Waiting for Godot? Programmatic CDM

Programmatic CDM was introduced in mid-2007 to help very small projects overcome the CDM project cycle transaction cost barrier. Programmes of Activities (PoAs) allow combining a number of project activities (called CDM Programme Activities, CPAs) under a joint 'umbrella' (for detailed overviews of PoAs, see Hayashi *et al.* (2010); Beaurain and Schmidt-Traub (2010); ClimateFocus (2011)). In general, PoAs are measures that are coordinated and implemented voluntarily by private or public entities leading to GHG emission reductions. A PoA has a duration of up to 28 years and can use any approved baseline and monitoring methodology. The key difference from the possibility of 'bundling' projects, which has existed for many years, is that the number and timing of projects developed under the PoA is completely flexible. Because only the PoA umbrella needs to be registered and not the CPAs, the likelihood of obtaining upfront carbon finance for CPAs should be higher than a normal CDM project due to shorter time to market and smaller regulatory risk. Another important advantage of PoAs compared to the option of bundling projects is that small-scale methodologies can be applied without any limit on the size of the PoA. Since small-scale methodologies are much simpler and more standardized, small-scale PoAs (SSC-PoA) have a comparative advantage over large-scale PoAs. However, for over two years, PoAs did not really move forward. The main reasons were regulatory barriers such as liability of the validator for any part of the PoA that might be found faulty even years after its registration, the limitation to one baseline methodology and the debundling rules for application of small-scale methodologies (see Parhelion (2010) for an assessment of how 45 CDM stakeholders evaluated the key regulatory barriers in PoAs). Particularly, the validator liability led validators to refuse validation of PoAs. After a long regulatory tug of war, the EB removed some of the barriers in May 2009 and again in May 2011. But some liability remains, albeit at a much reduced level. In the meantime, validators had started to shift the liability to the PoA developer through a private law contract.

The first PoA – a campaign for the distribution of compact fluorescent lightbulbs in Mexico – was registered on 31 July 2009 (see McInnes (2010) for a description of the programme), but this was only communicated by the CDM EB during its meeting in early September 2009. As many CDM stakeholders had held their breath until the first PoA registration, this meant that many of them were now eager to get going, especially for activities that had already started in the past. At its forty-seventh meeting in May 2009, which had amended PoA rules, the CDM EB had also decided that PoAs which commenced validation prior to 31 December 2009 could include CPAs with a starting date between 22 June 2007 and the commencement of validation of the PoA, if a list of such specific CPAs was provided to validating DOE and the UNFCCC Secretariat prior to 31 January 2010. Thus, in the single month of December 2009 more PoAs were submitted than in 30 months before – 21 compared to 19. Since late 2010, monthly inflow has oscillated around five. By July 2011, the total number of PoAs submitted had just reached 100.

The largest PoA developer is the World Bank, which is involved in 16 per cent of PoAs in the pipeline, but its share has declined recently. The private sector and unilateral approaches are underrepresented compared to standard CDM projects, but PoAs have made inroads in areas that have been neglected by the classical project developers. The relative share of PoAs, as compared to share of standard CDM projects, is higher in LDCs than that of Africa. By July 2011, Africa's share stood at 23 per cent compared to 2.6 per cent for standard CDM. For LDCs the corresponding numbers are: 11.4 per cent compared to 1.2 per cent.

4.9 Standardization of baselines and monitoring

Baseline and monitoring methodologies are a public good and thus the incentive for project developers to spend money on methodology development is limited. This problem is exacerbated by the stubbornly high rejection rate of submitted methodologies. If project developers nevertheless embark on a methodology, they will define its applicability as narrowly as possible, because this facilitates methodology approval and at the same time limits the benefits for competitors. Several hundred methodologies have been developed and close to 200 approved (see Michaelowa (2005) for an account of the principles of baseline methodology approval). But many of these methodologies can only be used if a large amount of data is collected. Moreover, methodologies applicable for similar technologies show large conceptual differences. Finally, methodologies have been revised very often. Methodology revisions have frequently been caused by regulators understanding problematic issues that come to light after a number of projects have successfully used a methodology. Such revisions can significantly curtail the CER potential and lead to frantic efforts to submit projects before methodology expiry. In some cases, methodology revisions have blocked entire project categories for a certain time period, like the shift from approved consolidated methodology (ACM) 4 to ACM 12 with regards to waste heat recovery.

To reduce the data collection burden for project developers and increase consistency, a drive for baseline standardization started in 2010. Moreover, regulators are implementing a programme of top-down methodology development. Standardization could take the form of applying performance benchmarks. Since 2007, three methodologies have been accepted that use a benchmark, covering greenfield coal power plants, energy-efficient refrigerators and greenfield energy-efficient buildings. Key challenges in benchmark determination are the level of aggregation, the degree of stringency and the frequency of updating (see Hayashi *et al.* 2010). For project types where benchmarks are inappropriate, the increased use of default factors would be a solution to reduce the data collection burden.

5 The risk of marginalization of the CDM

While the CDM has developed at an unexpected pace, there is no guarantee that this will continue in the long run. We will discuss several forces that are likely to be barriers to further expansion or might even lead to a demise of the mechanism.

5.1 Criticism by the media

Despite its successes, the CDM has suffered from a bad reputation in the popular press ever since 2007. Ironically, this started when the CDM EB was starting to tighten up rules and rejected the first projects for being non-additional. The renowned British newspaper the *Guardian* opened the salvo with a headline article in June 2007, lambasting the CDM for being non-additional and not leading to sustainable development (Davies 2007). From then on, journalists repeatedly dug up the CDM's purported failures. US newspapers, in particular, were very strong in this (e.g. Ball 2008a, 2008b), probably motivated by the widely publicized paper of Stanford University's Wara (2008). Readers of such articles had to believe that the CDM was dominated by greedy hit-and-run entrepreneurs – Ecosecurities' Marc Stuart compared the situation to generating sub-prime housing loans, where 'You keep layering on c – until you say, "We can't do this anymore"' (cited in Ball 2008b) – sleazy auditors and an incompetent UN bureaucracy making things worse. The media campaign also reached TV and glossy magazines such as *Harper's* in the United States (Schapiro 2010) or the widely read *GEO* in Germany (Henk and Schaefer 2010). It has strongly contributed to the hostile stance of US policy-makers with regards to the CDM. From 2008 onwards, no US legislation could openly refer to the CDM as a source of offsets for US cap-and-trade systems. The ease with which the EU Commission was able to prohibit imports from the two largest project categories is also due to this generally hostile environment.

5.2 The uncertain future of the international climate policy regime

There are now two main international climate policy scenarios influencing the attractiveness of the CDM after 2012. The optimistic one would see a resuscitation of the international climate policy regime in a way akin to the revival of the

Kyoto Protocol after the failure of COP 6 in The Hague in 2000 by the Bonn and Marrakech conferences in 2001. Essentially, the Bali Action Plan would be honoured and an international, legally binding agreement negotiated. This agreement would include the CDM as a cornerstone and create a unified, large market with CERs as world currency for GHG reduction. It would generate a substantial demand; Delbosc *et al.* (2011) estimate up to 4.4 billion tCO_2 between 2008 and 2020 in case the EU increases its reduction target to 30 per cent. Supply could possibly just catch up with that demand level.

The pessimistic scenario would see a failure of the international climate negotiations and the emergence of regional climate policy systems – in the United States, the EU, Australia, and maybe Japan. Each of these systems would have its specific rules for offsets. While the CDM regulators can continue their work for many years due to the accumulated budget surplus of over US$80 million, the key challenge the CDM would face under such a system is a differentiation of demand according to specific project types.

5.3 Fragmentation of climate policy and 'à la carte mechanisms'

The EU treatment of the CDM in the third phase of the EU ETS spanning 2013–2020 is a harbinger of what will happen under a fragmented climate policy system. After the EU had generously allowed imports into the EU ETS totalling 1.4 billion CERs during 2008–2012, in the preparation for the third phase it was decided that projects registered after the end of 2012 will be allowed to export CERs to the EU ETS only if located in LDCs. Moreover, overall import thresholds for phase three are less than 200 million (Delbosc *et al.* 2011). Global demand in a fragmented scenario could just reach 2.2 billion for the 2008–2020 period (Delbosc *et al.* 2011), which would be much less than the available supply. In such a situation, the CER price would plunge, limiting CDM to the cheapest project types.

Even more dangerous is the competition of new market mechanisms with the CDM. Will we see some governments slaughtering the CDM cash cows grazing on their territory and appropriating the emissions reductions?

The EU is pushing for sectoral mechanisms to replace the CDM in all but the LDCs, unless it concludes bilateral agreements with certain host countries. Its main argument is that advanced developing countries have a disincentive to take-up emissions commitments as they would lose the revenue from CER sales. Another variant of this argument is that developing countries would use up their cheapest mitigation options, thus exhausting 'low-hanging fruit' and only having to rely on more costly abatement options when taking up commitments. Castro (2010) nicely shows that the CDM to date has not exhausted the cheap reduction options and that a large potential remains.

Moreover, the EU argues that instead of just generating offset credits, mitigation in developing countries should contribute to global emission reductions. This could be done through a sectoral baseline which is more stringent than business-as-usual (BAU). The same effect, however, can be achieved with a

CDM in which CERs are discounted according to certain parameters (Schneider 2009a; Castro and Michaelowa 2010). This allows retaining the effective incentive properties of the CDM that are unlikely to exist in the case of a sectoral mechanism (see also Chapter 6 of this volume).

If the EU strengthens its emission reduction target beyond the unilaterally declared –20 per cent, it might open up for more types of CERs.

Japan is setting up a bilateral mechanism with simplified rules because Japanese technology exporters want to get rid of additionality determination and cumbersome project documentation. Essentially, the new mechanism is to become an export subsidy.

State-level US trading schemes have their own, relatively restrictive offset criteria. Most of them only allow project-based offsets from specific countries in Latin America.

A positive sign for the CDM market has recently come from Australia, which has announced a relatively stringent trading scheme starting from the mid-2010s, which might lead to an annual CER import of close to 100 million by 2020. While industrial gas CERs will be excluded, in contrast to the EU ETS, CERs from all developing countries, not only LDCs, will be accepted.

The volatility of the regional systems is likely to be much higher than that of the international market. They could be changed at the whim of political decision-makers in each region. Private sector trust in these systems would be limited. It might be possible to convert CDM projects into offset projects for a specific region. Some consultants and developers might thrive due to arbitrage options. But in general, demand is likely to be much lower than in the optimistic case. Due to the inability of the international community to agree on a universally accepted climate policy regime with a legally binding nature, there is a realistic chance of such a fragmentation of the international climate policy system.

6 Future climate finance: key lessons from the CDM gold rush

The CDM performed much better than originally expected by analysts, due to a number of factors that generated incentives for investments, albeit in partly unexpected ways. The CDM mechanism is relatively independent of host (and investor) country bureaucracy, as opposed to, for example, bilateral aid or multilateral climate funds. CERs accrue on an internationally administered account and cannot be expropriated by governments. The project-based approach makes bottom-up private entrepreneur involvement possible on both the supply and demand side. CDM has hence provided a welcome entry point to developing country markets for lots of industrialized country companies that previously had never had any activity outside Europe, and mobilized a lot of entrepreneurial energy in developing countries, where the private sector started to generate CERs like classical export cash crops. Despite being criticized for rigidity and red tape, the CDM regulatory system is very transparent. Given today's international political and financial climate, (1) transparency, (2) sufficient barriers towards government interference and (3) sufficient private sector stimulus will likely be crucial for successful implementation of new climate finance initiatives, a fact that is seemingly not fully recognized by negotiators, whose focus has too often been on mechanisms with a bias towards government-to-government interaction.

In some aspects, the CDM was purely lucky. On the supply side, negotiators and market players alike were surprised at the emergence of industrial gas CDM project types (HFC-23, N_2O from adipic acid), which yielded very large CER volumes, had relatively short lead times and had low development costs. This helped build the liquidity needed for a secondary CER market. This, in turn, made CDM attractive for financial institutions and large power companies for trading and hedging purposes. With regard to demand, CDM prompt start rules, the acceptance of CERs and exclusion of ERUs in EU ETS's first phase (2005–2007), and Russia's slowness in getting JI approval and 'hot air' sales procedures in place, meant lots of government purchasers have engaged heavily in CDM instead of JI or IET. This CER demand growth coincided with explosive subsidy-stimulated development of the renewables industry in key supply countries, which have also set-up effective project-approval regimes. In particular, China's approval system is more effective than expected.

Paradoxically, the gradual shift from industrial gas projects – that are inherently additional – to CO_2-reduction projects in the energy and industry sector is likely to reduce environmental integrity of the mechanism as such. At current CER prices, additionality is difficult to prove, as CER revenues do not play a key role in overall project financing or cashflow of renewable-energy and energy-efficiency projects. As CDM project participants incur large costs before CERs are generated and sold, financing structures should be developed that take into account the key role of upfront cash needs and the relatively limited 'project maintenance costs' later on. This would improve additionality and lead to an upscaling of the CDM.

As illustrated in the initial part of this chapter, a key element in the CDM's success was broadening of the CDM demand side from being the playground of a very small number of multilateral and government purchasers to a large population of mostly private sector market players that were unable to coordinate their actions. While private sector participation is not a *sufficient* condition for the functioning of a new carbon market mechanism, a lesson from the CDM's early years is that it might well be a *necessary* one.

Despite its relative success, the CDM's development was severely hampered, especially in its boom years of 2005–2007, due to a severe lack of manpower on the regulatory side resulting from a lack of available funding combined with rather rigid UN staffing rules. This also had the unfortunate implication that there was no bandwidth available for dialogue with – or capacity building of – DOEs, DNAs and project developers. An obvious lesson for development of future climate financing mechanisms would be to ensure sufficient upfront funding to avoid delays and difficulties that could affect not only an initiative's environmental integrity, but also its actual effects in terms of reduced emissions. A seasoned US negotiator aptly stated that the CDM EB was at one point running a global carbon credit 'central bank' at a budget less than that of the US pilot programme for international carbon credit projects in the mid-1990s (so-called Activities Implemented Jointly). The lack of manpower on the regulatory side was mirrored by the lack of manpower on the side of the auditors, who were reluctant to build-up teams of skilled experts in a situation of uncertain long-term prospects for the mechanism. This means that new mechanisms should have a sufficiently long duration to enable development of the required skills in monitoring, reporting and verification.

7 There is life after the gold rush: how a maturing CDM can become the cornerstone of global climate policy

As we have seen, the CDM has come a long way from its early 'Wild West' days. While the gold rush has exposed a number of teething troubles, most of them can be overcome. Under a Kyoto-style post-2012 climate policy system, a maturing CDM can fulfil a role as the 'gold standard' currency of mitigation. But even in a 'pledge and review', bottom-up climate policy world, the CDM could still serve as a bridge between the different national mitigation policies, like a generally accepted means of exchange. A reformed and upscaled CDM could thus be the key element to reduce the adverse effects of fragmentation of global climate policy. But this can only be achieved if national politicians do not listen to populists attacking carbon markets, and understand that refraining from short-term gains can bring much larger benefits in the medium to long term.

Notes

1 See UNFCCC (2011) for detailed CDM modalities and procedures, or IGES (2011) for an overview.

2 Joint Implementation refers to projects implemented in countries with emissions commitments under the Kyoto Protocol, whereas International Emissions Trading has nothing to do with emission reduction projects, but allows governments of industrialized countries to sell a surplus in their emissions budget. This is only relevant for countries in transition that had a strong reduction in emissions due to the demise of their heavy industries.

3 There are different interpretations of unilateral CDM: i) the underlying investment for the project is coming from the CDM host country, ii) there is no involvement of a CER buyer before the CERs have actually been generated. We use the former definition while acknowledging that the latter issue is important; for example in China until recently almost all CDM projects had a CER buyer in an early project stage while they financed the investment through domestic sources.

4 In 2011, the tax on CER revenue from CDM projects reducing N_2O from nitric acid was reduced to 10 per cent.

5 Important parts of this section are based on Michaelowa *et al.* (2011), which is only available to paying subscribers of Point Carbon.

6 See Bakker *et al.* (2007) for an attempt at a bottom-up assessment of post-2012 carbon credit supply from developing countries.

References

Alexeew, J., Bergset, L., Meyer, K., Petersen, J., Schneider, L. and Unger, C. (2010) 'An analysis of the relationship between the additionality of CDM projects and their contribution to sustainable development', *International Environmental Agreements*, 10: 233–48.

ANGED and World Bank (2006) 'Montage d'un projet sur la gestion des déchets couplé avec une composante Mécanisme de Développement Propre MDP en Tunisie', Tunis.

Bakker, S., Arvanitakis, A., Bole, T., van de Brug, E., Doets, C. and Gilbert, A. (2007) 'Carbon credit supply potential beyond 2012: a bottom-up assessment of mitigation options'. Online. Available: www.ecn.nl/docs/library/report/2007/e07090.pdf.

Ball, J. (2008a) 'U.N. effort to curtail emissions in turmoil', *Wall Street Journal*, 12 April. Online. Available: http://online.wsj.com/article/SB120796372237309757.html (accessed 27 July 2011).

Ball, J. (2008b) 'Two carbon-market millionaires take a hit as UN clamps down', *Wall Street Journal*, 14 April. Online. Available: http://online.wsj.com/article/SB120813542203111705.html?mod=googlenews_wsj (accessed 27 July 2011).

Beaurain, F. and Schmidt-Traub, G. (2010) *Developing CDM Programmes of Activities: A Guidebook*, Zurich: South Pole.

Black-Arbeláez, T. (2003) 'The state of development of National CDM offices in Central and South America: barriers to the deployment of CDM potential'. Online. Available: www.ucd.ie/envinst/envstud/CATEP%20Webpage/Powerpoint/paris%20pres/thomas-black.pdf (accessed 26 June 2011).

Blok, K., van Brummelen, M. and Heijnes, H. (1999) 'Reduction of the emissions of HFC's, PFC's and SF6 in the European Union'. Online. Available http://ec.europa.eu/environment/enveco/climate_change/pdf/9800043sm.pdf.

Böhm, S. and Dabhi, S. (eds) (2009) *Upsetting the Offset*, London: MayFlyBooks.

Castro, P. (2010) 'Climate change mitigation in advanced developing countries: empirical analysis of the low-hanging fruit issue in the current CDM', *CIS Working Paper*, 54, Zürich: University of Zürich, ETH Zürich.

Castro, P. and Michaelowa, A. (2010) 'The impact of CER discounting on the competitiveness of different CDM host countries', *Ecological Economics*, 70: 34–42.

Castro, P. and Michaelowa, A. (2011) 'Would preferential access measures be sufficient to overcome current barriers to CDM projects in least developed countries?', *Climate and Development*, 3: 123–42.

CDM Watch (2004) 'Market failure: why the Clean Development Mechanism won't promote clean development'. Online. Available: www.commonenergy.org/documents/pearson%20-%20why%20CDM%20won%27t%20promote%20clean%20development.pdf.

CDM Watch (2010) 'UN under pressure to halt gaming and abuse of CDM'. Online. Available: www.cdm-watch.org/wordpress/wp-content/uploads/2010/06/hfc-23_press-release_gaming-and-abuse-of-cdm1.pdf (accessed 30 June 2011).

Chen, Z., Gong, H., Jiang, R., Jiang, Q. and Wu, W. (2010) 'Overview on LFG projects in China', *Waste Management*, 30: 1006–10.

Clellant, G. (2007) 'Rhodia finds the formula for revival', *Financial News*, 30 April. Online. Available: www.efinancialnews.com/story/2007-04-30/rhodia-finds-the-formula-for-revival (accessed 27 July 2011).

Climate Focus (2011) *The Handbook for Programme of Activities: Practical Guidance to Successful Implementation*, Rotterdam: Climate Focus.

Curnow, P. and Hodes, G. (2009) *Implementing CDM Projects: A Guidebook to Host Country Legal Issues*, Roskilde: UNEP Riso Centre.

Danish Energy Agency (2010) 'The Danish JI and CDM program: seven years experience with climate projects around the world'. Online. Available: www.ens.dk/Documents/Netboghandel%20-%20publikationer/2010/The_danish_ji_and_cdm_program.pdf.

Davies, N. (2007) 'Abuse and incompetence in fight against global warming: up to 20% of carbon savings in doubt as monitoring firms criticised by UN body', *Guardian*, 2 June. Online. Available: www.guardian.co.uk/environment/2007/jun/02/energy.business (accessed 26 July 2011).

Deecke, I. (2010) 'Reasons for the underperformance of Clean Development Mechanism project activities in the animal waste management sector', PhD thesis, University of Göttingen. Online. Available: d-nb.info/1007525479/34 (accessed 26 July 2011).

Delbosc, A., Stephan, N., Bellassen, V., Cormier, A. and Leguet, B. (2011) 'Assessment of supply–demand balance for Kyoto offsets (CERs and ERUs) up to 2020', *CDC Climat Research Working Paper*, 2011–10, Paris.

Dyck, T. (2010) 'Auditing emissions offsets: examining the external arm of the Clean Development Mechanism', Master's thesis, University of Stanford. Online. Available: www.law.stanford.edu/publications/dissertations_theses/diss/TyseonWDyck-ta2010.pdf (accessed 26 July 2011).

EU (2004) 'Directive 2004/101/EC of the European Parliament and the Council of 27 October 2004 amending Directive 2003/87/EC establishing a scheme for greenhouse gas emission allowance trading within the Community, in respect of the Kyoto Protocol's project mechanisms', *Official Journal of the European Union*, L338/18, Brussels.

EU Commission (2011) 'Commission regulation No 550/2011 of 7 June 2011 on determining, pursuant to Directive 2003/87/EC of the European Parliament and of the Council, certain restrictions applicable to the use of international credits from projects involving industrial gases', *Official Journal of the European Union*, L149, Brussels.

Girling, A. (2010) 'NGOs and the Clean Development Mechanism: constraints and opportunities in the discourse of EU consultations', *The Governance of Clean Development Working Paper*, 005, Norwich: University of East Anglia.

Grütter, J. (2011) 'Transport and carbon finance', presented at Practitioner Workshop on the Improvement of CDM Methodologies for Transportation, 3 March, Bonn.

Haites, E. (2000) 'Proposed rules and the size of the CDM market', in Institute of Global Environmental Strategies (ed.) *Potential and Barriers to the CDM: Proceedings of the IGES International Workshop on the Clean Development Mechanism*, 26–27 January, Hayama, pp. 133–7.

Haugland, T. (2011) 'Personal communication with T. Haughland from Carbon Limits on PanOcean project', interviewed by Jorund Buen, 24 July.

Haya, B. (2010) 'Carbon offsetting: an efficient way to reduce emissions or to avoid reducing emissions? An investigation and analysis of offsetting design and practice in India and China', PhD thesis, University of California, Berkeley. Online. Available: http://bhaya.berkeley.edu/docs/HayaDissertation.pdf (accessed 25 June 2011).

Hayashi, D., Michaelowa, A., Dransfeld, B., Niemann, M., Marr, M., Oppermann, K. and Neufeld, C. (2010a) *PoA Blueprint Book, Guidebook for PoA Coordinators Under CDM/JI*, 2nd edition, Frankfurt: KfW Bankengruppe.

Hayashi, D., Müller, N., Feige, S. and Michaelowa, A. (2010b) 'Towards a more standardised approach to baselines and additionality under the CDM', Zurich: Perspectives GmbH.

He, G. and Morse, R. (2010) 'Making carbon offsets work in the developing world: lessons from the Chinese wind controversy', *Program on Energy and Sustainable Development Working Paper*, 90, Stanford University.

Henk, M. and Schaefer, J. (2010) 'Die Luftnummer', *GEO*, December: 129–54.

IGES (2011) 'CDM in charts, Version 13.1'. Online. Available: http://enviroscope.iges.or.jp/modules/envirolib/upload/835/attach/charts.pdf (accessed 24 July 2011).

Jiang, P. and Tovey, K. (2010) 'Overcoming barriers to implementation of carbon reduction strategies in large commercial buildings in China', *Building and Environment*, 45: 856–64.

Lewis, J. (2010) 'The evolving role of carbon finance in promoting renewable energy development in China', *Energy Policy*, 38: 2875–86.

Lohmann, L. (2006) 'Carbon trading: a critical conversation on climate change, privatisation and power', *Development Dialogue*, 48.

Lokey, E. (2009) *Renewable Energy Project Development under the Clean Development Mechanism: A Guide for Latin America*, London: Earthscan.

Lütken, S. and Michaelowa, A. (2008) *Corporate Strategies and the Clean Development Mechanism*, Cheltenham: Edward Elgar.

McInnes, D. (2010) 'Red, amber and green lights', *Trading Carbon*, November: 32–4.

Michaelowa, A. (2005) 'Determination of baselines and additionality for the CDM: a crucial element of credibility of the climate regime', in F. Yamin. (ed.) *Climate Change and Carbon Markets: A Handbook of Emission Reduction Mechanisms*, Earthscan, London, pp. 289–304.

Michaelowa, A. (2009) 'Interpreting the additionality of CDM projects: changes in additionality definitions and regulatory practices over time', in D. Freestone and C. Streck (eds) *Legal Aspects of Carbon Trading*, Oxford: Oxford University Press, pp. 248–71.

Michaelowa, A. and Michaelowa, K. (2010) 'Climate business for poverty reduction? The role of the World Bank', *CIS Working Paper*, 59, Zürich: University of Zürich, ETH Zürich.

Michaelowa, A., Heimdal, C., Sørhus, I., Petit C. and Buen, J. (2011) 'Going down the drain: a typology of CDM project failure', Online. Available: www.pointcarbon.com/trading/1.1557452 (accessed 9 July 2011).

Neeff, T. and Henders, S. (2007) *Guidebook to Markets and Commercialization of Forestry CDM projects*, Turrialba: Tropical Agricultural Research and Higher Education Center (CATIE).

Netherlands Ministry of Housing, Spatial Planning and the Environment (2004) *Clean Development Mechanism (CDM): The Netherlands Approach*, The Hague: Netherlands Ministry of Housing, Spatial Planning and the Environment.

Okamato, S. (2008) 'Contribution and challenges of Kyoto Mechanisms', Online. Available: http://unfccc.meta-fusion.com/kongresse/AWG_08/downl/0401_1500_p2/Japan%20JI_CDM.pdf (accessed 21 July 2011).

Olsen, K. (2007) 'The Clean Development Mechanism's contribution to sustainable development: a review of the literature', *Climatic Change*, 84: 59–73.

Parhelion Underwriting Ltd (2010) *Programmes of Activities (PoAs): Realising the Potential*, London: Parhelion Underwriting Ltd.

Partridge, I. and Gamkhar, S. (2010) 'The role of offsets in a post-Kyoto climate agreement: the power sector in China', *Energy Policy*, 38: 4457–66.

PCF (Prototype Carbon Fund) (2003) *Annual Report 2003*, Washington: Prototype Carbon Fund.

Pearson, T., Walker, S., Chalmers, J., Swails, E. and Brown, S. (2009) *Guidebook for the Formulation of Afforestation/Reforestation and Bioenergy Projects in the Regulatory Carbon Market*, Arlington: Winrock International.

Point Carbon (2009) 'Rhodia hedges 2009 CER sales at €15.50', 25 February. Online. Available: www.pointcarbon.com/news/1.1064372 (accessed 26 July 2011).

Point Carbon (2011) 'Carbon market monitor: a review of 2010' Online subscription service.

Rhodia (2010) 'Rhodia Energy Services: overview 2010'. Online. Available: www.chaireeconomieduclimat.org/wp-content/uploads/2010/12/Rhodia-Energy-Services-OVERVIEW-Sept-2010.pdf (accessed 30 June 2011).

Rhodia (2011) 'Full year and fourth quarter 2010 results'. Online. Available: www.rhodia.com.br/en/news_center/news_releases/2010_annual_results_220211.tcm (accessed 30 June 2011).

Russo, E. and Lu, G. (2005) 'Sino-Italian HFC-23 CDM feasibility study', presented at Sino-Italian Workshop on HFC-23 projects in China, 24 January, Beijing.

Schapiro, M. (2010) 'Conning the climate: inside the carbon-trading shell game', *Harper's Magazine*, February: 31–9.

Schneider, L. (2009a) 'A Clean Development Mechanism with atmospheric benefits for a post-2012 climate regime', *International Environmental Agreements*, 9: 95–111.

Schneider, L. (2009b) 'Assessing the additionality of CDM projects: practical experiences and lessons learned', *Climate Policy*, 9: 242–54.

Schneider, L., Graichen, J. and Stricker, E. (2004) 'Submission to the CDM Executive Board on HFC-23 CDM projects', Öko-Institut.

Schneider, L., Lazarus, M. and Kollmuss, A. (2010) 'Industrial N_2O projects under the CDM: adipic acid – a case of carbon leakage'. Online. Available: http://ec.europa.eu/clima/consultations/0004/unregistered/cdm_watch_2_en.pdf.

Schroeder, M. (2009) 'The performance of hybrid actors in environmental governance in China: lessons learned from promotional centres for the Clean Development Mechanism', unpublished PhD thesis, University of Potsdam.

Schwank, O. (2004) 'Concerns about CDM projects based on decomposition of HFC-23 emissions from 22 HCFC production sites'. Online. Available: http://cdm.unfccc.int/public_inputs/inputam0001/Comment_AM0001_Schwank_081004.pdf.

Senter International (2001) 'Terms of reference CERUPT 2001', Senter International.

Seres, S., Haites, E. and Murphy, K. (2009) 'Analysis of technology transfer in CDM projects: an update', *Energy Policy*, 37: 4919–26.

Sicars, S. (2004) 'Phase-Out of HFC-23 emissions in 12 HCFC-22 production sites in China', unpublished project idea note draft.

Sikorski, T. (2010) 'Carbon wide boy', *Trading Emissions*, October: 28–30.

Skjaerseth, J. and Wettestad, J. (2010) 'Making the EU Emissions Trading System: the European Commission as an entrepreneurial epistemic leader', *Global Environmental Change*, 20: 314–21.

Socorro, M., Verheyen, R., Mackensen, J. and Scholz, G. (2005) *Legal Aspects in the Implementation of CDM Forestry Projects*, Gland and Cambridge: International Union for Conservation of Nature (IUCN).

UNEP Riso Centre (2011b) *CDM pipeline, 1 July, 2011*, Roskilde: UNEP Riso Centre. Online. Available: http://cdmpipeline.org/publications/CDMpipeline.xlsx (accessed 2 July 2011).

UNEP Riso Centre (2011b) *JI pipeline, July 1, 2011*, Roskilde: UNEP Riso Centre. Online. Available: http://cdmpipeline.org/publications/JiPipeline.xlsx (accessed 2 July 2011).

UNFCCC (2010) 'The contribution of the Clean Development Mechanism under the Kyoto Protocol to technology transfer'. Online. Available: http://cdm.unfccc.int/Reference/Reports/TTreport/TTrep10.pdf.

UNFCCC (2011) 'The CDM'. Online. Available: http://cdm.unfccc.int (accessed 26 July 2011).

Wang, B. (2010) 'Can CDM bring technology transfer to China? An empirical study of technology transfer in China's CDM projects', *Energy Policy*, 38: 2572–85.

Wara, M. (2007) 'Is the global carbon market working?', *Nature*, 445: 595–6.

World Bank (2006) 'Umbrella Carbon Facility completes allocation of first tranche'. Online. Available: www.worldbank.org/en/news/2006/08/30/umbrella-carbon-facility-completes-allocation-first-tranche (accessed 26 July 2011).

World Bank (2011a) 'GNI, PPP (current international $)'. Online. Available: http://data.worldbank.org/indicator/NY.GNP.MKTP.PP.CD (accessed 15 July 2011).

World Bank (2011b) 'Umbrella Carbon Facility T1'. Online. Available: http://wbcarbonfinance.org/Router.cfm?Page=UCF (accessed 30 June 2011).

2 Development cooperation and climate change

Political-economic determinants of adaptation aid

Katharina Michaelowa and Axel Michaelowa

1 Introduction

Ever since the Rio conference of 1992, combining development- and climate-related efforts has been an international objective, embodied in the principle of 'common but differentiated responsibilities' (CISDL 2002). Correspondingly, OECD/DAC statistics show a substantial increase in climate mitigation-related aid. However, detailed keyword searches in AidData[1] suggest that only about 25 per cent of the corresponding projects are coded correctly by the reporting donors (Roberts *et al.* 2010; Michaelowa and Michaelowa 2011a). When looking at the actual development of mitigation aid over time, the oil price turns out to be the key major determinant. This was the case before Rio, just as afterwards, with stronger support, e.g. for hydro power plants, biomass and solar energy, whenever the oil price peaked. At the same time, the econometric analysis clearly rejects any positive effect of major landmarks in international climate change negotiations (Rio, Kyoto, Kyoto ratification). Finally, green preferences of the voters seem to matter much more clearly for donors' re-labelling of aid activities than for any substantive change towards mitigation (Michaelowa and Michaelowa 2011a, 2011b).

In this chapter we will examine whether the same is true for adaptation. We will therefore examine the following questions:

- Has there been a real change in aid activities towards a greater emphasis on adaptation to climate change?
- If so, what are the major drivers of this effect? Has the change come about as a consequence of the international treaties on climate policy (by increasing the supply of adaptation projects by aid agencies, and the demand for adaptation projects by recipient countries) or, more generally, of a stronger environmental consciousness in donor countries?

It should be noted that adaptation and mitigation differ substantially with respect to key basic characteristics; mitigation is a global public good and adaptation mainly a regional/local public or even a private good. Only in a few cases such as the development of drought-resistant crops, does adaptation take the same global public good character as mitigation. In Section 2 we further discuss this conceptual distinction and its implications for development policy from a normative perspective. In Section 3 we describe the data and our coding procedure for adaptation aid. Section 4 presents the econometric analysis and Section 5 concludes.

2 Adaptation versus mitigation aid: why donors might behave differently

As we have seen above, donors pretend to respond to the challenges of climate change through a corresponding allocation of development aid, but de facto, mitigation-related aid has not increased in response to either the international climate negotiation process or the greener preferences of their electorate. Why should we expect the picture for adaptation-related aid to be any different?

Let us assume that a donor agency's prime objective is the reduction of poverty in the world. Given the high vulnerability of many poor countries, climate change mitigation certainly contributes to this objective. At the same time, other aid activities may have an even stronger impact in this respect. This raises the question of priorities (see also Michaelowa and Michaelowa 2007).

In addition, since mitigation is a global public good, by definition, it does not matter where mitigation takes place. The effect of 1 t of emission reduction is the same regardless of where it takes place. If two countries have the same needs and preferences, the benefits will be identical. Therefore, it does not matter whether a given amount of emissions is reduced in the country itself, in Switzerland, the United States or anywhere else in the world. The principle of non-excludability ensures that Mali cannot be exempted from the benefits of mitigation in the United States, and the principle of non-rivalry ensures that Mali will not benefit less if other countries benefit simultaneously. When the benefits are not higher if mitigation happens in Mali itself, why should we even speak of aid to Mali in this case? Since the location of the implementation is independent of the benefits, Mali is no more a distinct beneficiary of this measure than any other country.

Of course, there can be local benefits attached to the global public good of mitigation. For example, a reduction of fossil fuel use will reduce local pollutants such as dust and SO_2. However, usually there exist a number of cheaper alternatives for the reduction of local pollutants, e.g. filters. Generally, the local benefits are – if they exist at all – only a minor side effect which we will not consider further in our discussion.

For adaptation, the situation is different. If Bangladesh adjusts to increased flooding in its delta area, this will not help anyone in Uganda or Peru, and not even those Bangladeshis who live in other areas of the country. Clearly, for adaptation, the public good characteristics of non-excludability and non-rivalry seldom reach beyond the country's borders.

Thus, with respect to adaptation, it makes much more sense to speak of development cooperation with a particular country, and the corresponding activities can be compared to other aid activities suggested for this country and included in the ranking of development priorities. An adaptation activity should then be carried out when it appears sufficiently high on the list. Given that impacts of climate change are likely to be larger in low-latitude countries and crop yields are likely to decline at low levels of warming (Schneider *et al.* 2007), the probability that some adaptation activities will indeed be high on the list is significant. This might be reinforced by the fact that vulnerability of poor communities is typically much higher than for the population as a whole. Adaptation is thus often seen as strongly poverty-reducing (see Vernon 2008).

In contrast, with respect to mitigation, any such comparisons would have to happen at the global level. Given the magnitude of mitigation activities required to achieve a significant impact on poverty reduction, for many developing countries other activities would certainly enjoy a higher priority. Calculating this in detail would be extremely complex and, in practice, certainly go beyond the capacity of any development agency. Typically, donors first decide about their central partner countries (on the basis of poverty considerations, cultural and political relations, geostrategic reasoning or economic interests), and then determine individual activities within these countries.

A development agency faithful to its key objective of poverty reduction may thus have reasons not to engage in mitigation activities, and yet engage in adaptation. The willingness to engage in adaptation may be reinforced by the fact that, on the demand side, recipient countries will also request adaptation rather than mitigation. The reasons are the same: adaptation has a much more direct effect for the country concerned than mitigation, apart from the minor side effects mentioned above.

As a consequence, the aid agency may try to gain public support by adopting a strong climate change rhetoric, and by reporting all types of climate-related projects, but effectively only focus on adaptation.

Since the international climate negotiation process has raised the awareness of aid agencies, governments and the general public on the relevance of protecting people in poor countries from climate change-related natural hazards and disasters, we can expect this process to have had an impact on adaptation aid, even if it did not have any on mitigation aid. More specifically, following our earlier work on mitigation aid (Michaelowa and Michaelowa 2011b), we consider that there may be a direct or an indirect impact of the Rio summit and its agreement on the UN Framework Convention on Climate Change (UNFCCC) and the following (and still ongoing) international negotiations on the mitigation of climate change, which led to the signing of the Kyoto Protocol in 1997 and its entry into force in 2005. Any direct impact should be reflected in a clear difference between sectoral aid allocations before and after 1992, 1997 and 2005. An indirect effect could work via these negotiations and subsequent debates shaping public and government's preferences in donor countries. These indirect effects as well as possible lags linked to the time required to raise public awareness may of course make it more difficult to attach the effect to the individual years. Nevertheless, these years should mark structural shifts in the relevance of climate policy.

In addition, there may be an effect related to the general environmental attitudes in the donor countries, reflected in government composition or vote shares of environmental parties. We expect government and parliaments with green preferences to more closely follow the climate negotiation process and thereby to achieve stronger awareness of the adaptation problem. Therefore, we should expect changes in aid allocation for adaptation to follow changes in donor government composition, or, alternatively, in the vote share of environmental parties. Obviously, we would expect this effect to be smaller than the one for mitigation, given that mitigation contributes to preservation of the environment, whereas adaptation only reduces the negative impacts of environmental change. Yet, given that the final aid allocation is determined within the aid agencies, which according to our discussion above could have a general preference for adaptation over mitigation aid, even a somewhat milder public pressure for adaptation might have a noticeable effect.

We thus formulate the following hypotheses:

H1: With every new international climate policy agreement, donors increase aid to adaptation.

H2: Greener donor government preferences lead to higher aid for adaptation.

H3: Greener public preferences in donor countries lead to higher aid for adaptation.

The following section will present the data on the basis of which these hypotheses will be tested.

3 The data

AidData (2010) provides information for over 750,000 aid activities for 21 bilateral DAC donor countries starting in the 1970s. Our dependent variable is the share of adaptation activities in total aid. We calculate this share both in terms of project numbers and in terms of financial commitments. Detailed project descriptions enable us to specify projects according to all relevant project categories.

Our coding procedure was based on the following three steps (Michaelowa and Michaelowa 2011a: Appendix 1).

First, we decided upon a comprehensive list of keywords relevant in the context of climate change adaptation. Besides the direct use of the keyword ‘adaptation’, strengthening of resilience against and relief of impacts of meteorological extreme events was looked at with the keywords ‘flood’, ‘drought’, ‘storm’ (including cyclone, hurricane, typhoon), as well as ‘disaster’, ‘urgency’, ‘compensation’. The set-up of early warning and meteorological coordination systems was also included. Moreover, dyke/sea wall projects as well as sea-level-related projects were looked at. Resource-availability improvement and integrated rural development projects were also included if they strengthened overall resilience or led to a better management of water/agricultural resources, even if they did not have an explicit disaster-related component.[2] We purposefully chose a wide range of terms to ensure that all activities that would today be considered as adaptation would also be taken into account in earlier periods, where the adaptation vocabulary did not exist.

Second, we manually assessed the actual relevance of these aid activities to exclude those that did not contribute to adaptation. This procedure led us to delete the vast majority of aid activities because the keywords appeared in a different context. Choices were not always obvious, however. While it is simple to exclude non-meteorological disasters such as earthquakes, tsunamis or civil war, it is much more difficult to assess whether a resource-related project can be seen as a resilience-enhancing activity. Particularly regarding water resources, projects frequently relate to digging a few wells. Such projects with a limited scope were excluded; this required a subjective case-by-case decision. Another problem could be that the terminology used to describe aid projects might have changed over time so that certain projects in earlier years may have escaped our attention. However, this effect should also be limited through our effort to keep the range of keywords sufficiently large.

Finally, we double-checked the mismatches between our coding and the donors' own classification of projects when reporting to the OECD/DAC (Michaelowa and Michaelowa 2011a). We thus tried to reduce the risk that any project was omitted in our coding simply for having escaped our initial mechanical search procedure. This led us to reconsider a total of 8,854 projects which did not previously appear in our list of climate-relevant aid activities. Where necessary, our own adaptation codes were revised accordingly.

Eventually, mean values across individual aid activities were computed for all donor/year combinations to obtain the final variables, i.e. adaptation-related activities as a share of total aid activities and as a share of total commitments, by donor and year. The descriptive statistics below illustrate the composition of these variables and their variation over time.

Table 2.1 provides a breakdown of adaptation aid by type of adaptation considered (across all donors and years).

On average, the share of adaptation in total development assistance is below 1 per cent, but this average hides strong differences between countries and over time. For both 1983 and 1984, the United Kingdom's share of adaptation projects within overall aid activities is over 20 per cent. Other donor/year combinations where adaptation aid exceeds 10 per cent of either aid activities or commitments are Ireland (2008), Japan (1998, 1999) and the United Kingdom (1987).

Adaptation commitments are about evenly spread between water-related (avoided flooding, but also measures to cope with drought), resource-related and disaster-related adaptation. The latter appears much stronger in terms of aid activities, accounting for almost half of all adaptation projects. This reflects that many of the emergency activities are relatively small in terms of aid volumes.

Table 2.1 Adaptation aid by type of adaptation, 1970–2008

	Mean	*Std dev.*	*Min.*	*Max.*
Share of aid activities (%)				
Adaptation, total	0.92	1.78	0	23.39
• water related	0.29	0.64	0	7.38
• wind related	0.12	0.36	0	3.90
• resource related	0.23	0.49	0	5.95
• disaster related	0.41	1.50	0	23.39
• other	0.03	0.21	0	4.41
Share of commitments (%)				
Adaptation, total	0.72	1.24	0	13.90
• water related	0.25	0.59	0	6.53
• wind related	0.08	0.29	0	4.71
• resource related	0.24	0.63	0	9.47
• disaster related	0.22	0.74	0	13.78
• other	0.03	0.18	0	2.75

Source: authors' own coding drawn from AidData (2010).

Figure 2.1 shows the development of adaptation aid over time, both in terms of project shares and in terms of commitment shares. The data again show that so far, adaptation plays only a relatively limited role in development cooperation. However, we observe a general upward trend in adaptation aid, despite strong inter-annual variability throughout most of the observation period, with shares ranging from below 0.5 per cent to almost 3 per cent. The variability is mainly due to projects established to support victims of meteorological extreme events. For example, hurricane Mitch, which devastated Central America in 1998, led to a peak of projects in 1998–2001. The 1992 peak (most clearly visible in the commitment shares) is linked to the 1991 cyclone in Bangladesh, which killed 140,000 people, and a strong drought in Southern Africa. The 1983–1984 peak falls into the driest period of the century in the Sahel. However, since the early 2000s, a clear upward trend can be found that is not linked to specific disasters.

In this chapter we would like to examine whether, over and above the random variation related to meteorological extreme events, there is some variation that can be explained by political-economic variables related to the negotiation process as specified in our hypotheses. We therefore proceed now with the operationalization of our explanatory variables. Green public preferences in donor countries are measured as the percentage of green seats in national parliaments (Armingeon *et al.* 2008). Environmental preferences of the donor government are proxied by the index of cabinet composition developed by Schmidt (1992) and updated by Armingeon *et al.* (2008). The index takes on values from 1 (hegemony of right-wing and centre parties) to 5 (hegemony of social-democratic and other left parties). As ecological preferences are only imprecisely reflected on a left–right dimension (Knill *et al.* 2010: 304), the ideal indicator would more closely reflect party positions (e.g. the indicator based on the

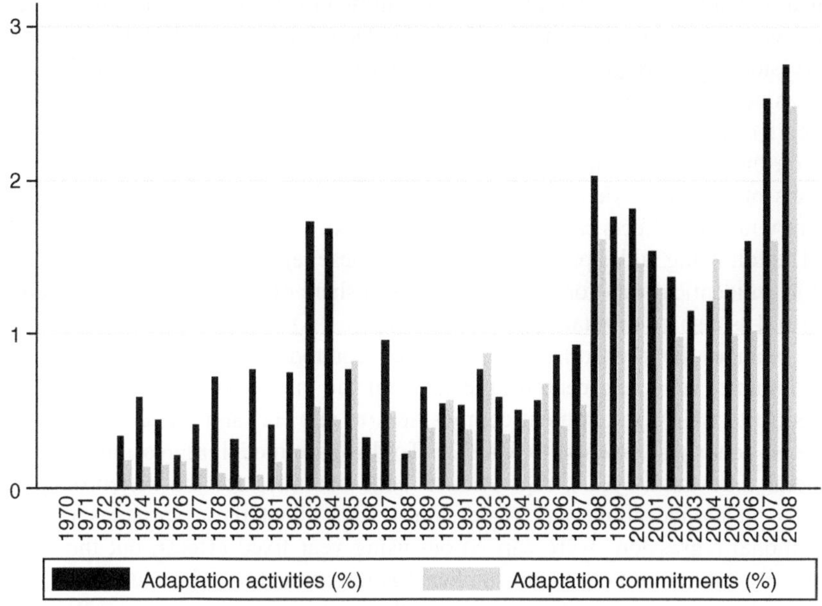

Figure 2.1 Adaptation aid as a share of total development assistance (source: authors' own coding from AidData 2010).

Note
The nil values for 1970–1972 may not be representative since the overall number of aid activities covered during these years is extremely small. The same is true for the overall volume of commitments.

assessment of party manifestos by Cusack and Engelhardt 2002), but such data is not available for the whole time period under consideration.

To reflect direct policy change in response to international agreements we construct indicator variables for the periods from 1992 (post-Rio), from 1997 (post-Kyoto) and from 2005 (post-Kyoto ratification) onwards.[3]

In addition, we will consider the use of country-fixed effects to control for any donor-specific characteristics that do not vary over time, and of time-fixed effects to control for meteorological extreme events. Moreover, we consider a general time trend. The specification of the econometric model will be discussed in more detail in the following section.

4 Econometric analysis

As there can be no negative project shares, the data are censored at zero. This suggests the use of a Tobit model. The Tobit model assumes that there should be no conceptual difference between the mechanisms determining (1) whether or not there is adaptation aid at all, and (2) if so, which share is being allocated for this purpose. On theoretical grounds, there is no reason to believe that the determinants should be different, and this is confirmed by an empirical testing of separate equations. In addition, the Tobit model might be problematic in panel regressions if we require country-fixed effects. As indicated above, such fixed effects need to be considered here, in particular since we do not control for any specific differences between donors otherwise. However, a Hausman test carried out on the basis of simple linear models consistently suggests that the country effects may be considered as random. This confirms that a Tobit model with country random effects can be used in our context.

The following tables present the results of these regressions, which are carried out in an identical way for adaptation aid as a share of total aid activities (Table 2.2) and as a share of total commitments (Table 2.3). In each table, regression 1 only includes the key explanatory variables required to test our hypotheses, i.e. the dummies reflecting central milestones of the international climate negotiations (to test H1), government composition (to test H2) and the share of green seats in donor parliaments (to test H3). To this base model, regression 2 adds a general time trend (year), regression 3 adds dummies for the meteorological events mentioned above and regression 4 adds all of these variables jointly. Additional regressions were carried out using year fixed effects, but the latter generally did not turn out to be significant in the context of aid projects, and prevented the convergence of the model in the context of commitments. We thus hope to capture the relevant year effects through the more specific controls we have included in the models.

All regressions without the general time trend provide clear support to H1. Two out of the three landmarks of international climate negotiations are significantly and positively associated with subsequent aid allocated to adaptation. According to Table 2.2, *ceteris paribus*, after the Rio conference, the share of aid activities related to adaptation increased by 0.3 percentage points (Reg1a) or 0.4 percentage points (Reg3a). After the Kyoto conference, this share increased by yet another 0.5 percentage points (Reg1a) or 0.4 percentage points (Reg3a). Also, in Reg3a the post-Kyoto ratification period adds another 0.3 percentage points (not significant in Reg1a). Given the overall share of adaptation aid, these values are substantial. Results for commitment shares in Table 2.3 look similar (see Reg1b, Reg3b).

However, when adding a general time trend in Regressions 2 and 4, it becomes clear that the effect of the negotiation milestones is difficult to disentangle from this general trend. The general upward trend towards greater shares of adaptation aid is highly significant and wipes out the significance of most of the negotiation dummies. Only the post-Kyoto period remains positively significant in Reg2a and b, suggesting an effect of the Kyoto conference over and above the general trend. Conversely, the dummy indicating the period after the ratification of the Kyoto Protocol becomes negatively significant in Reg2b, suggesting that the overall positive Kyoto effect is reduced to 0.06 percentage points (0.21–0.15) after ratification, and thus becomes hardly distinguishable from the general time trend.

Table 2.2 Tobit regressions on adaptation aid as a share of aid activities (%)

	Reg1a	*Reg2a*	*Reg3a*	*Reg4a*
Year		0.046***		0.047***
Post-Rio	0.323***	–0.213	0.419***	–0.174
Post-Kyoto	0.498***	0.213*	0.394***	0.048
Post-Kyoto ratification	0.171	–0.075	0.276**	0.071
Green seats in parliament (%)	0.033*	0.010	0.031*	0.012
Cabinet composition	–0.041*	–0.038	–0.044*	–0.043*
Hurricane Mitch (1998)			0.212*	0.311**
Cyclone in Bangladesh and drought in South Africa (1991)			0.332*	–0.126
Drought in the Sahel region (1983–1984)			0.746***	0.625***
Log likelihood	–1,123.0	–1,104.2	–1,108.1	–1,091.2
p-value for Wald test	0	0	0	0

Source: authors' own regression.

Note

The total number of observations is 780 (21 donors), out of which 355 are left-censored at 0. The table shows average marginal effects dE(adaptation|adaptation>0)/d x. Significance at the 1, 5, and 10% level is indicated by ***, **,and * respectively. All regressions are calculated with donor random effects. For details on the variables, see the Appendix.

Table 2.3 Tobit regressions on adaptation aid as a share of aid commitments (%)

	Reg1b	*Reg2b*	*Reg3b*	*Reg4b*
Year		0.028***		0.032***
Post-Rio	0.298***	0.001	0.331***	–0.034
Post-Kyoto	0.385***	0.210***	0.271***	0.037
Post-Kyoto ratification	–0.005	–0.151**	0.108	–0.028
Green seats in parliament (%)	0.005	–0.008	0.003	–0.009
Cabinet composition	–0.013	–0.007	–0.017	–0.011
Hurricane Mitch (1998)			0.241***	0.307***
Cyclone in Bangladesh and drought in South Africa (1991)			0.231*	–0.043
Drought in the Sahel region (1983–1984)			0.136	0.089
Log likelihood	–765.49	–752.28	–757.88	–743.34
p-value for Wald test	0	0	0	0

Source: authors' own regression.

Notes

The total number of observations is 626 (21 donors), out of which 201 are left-censored at 0. The table shows average marginal effects dE(adaptation|adaptation>0)/d x. Significance at the 1, 5, and 10% level is indicated by ***, ** and * respectively. All regressions are calculated with donor random effects. For details on the variables, see the Appendix.

The question is what this implies for the overall assessment of H1. Reality does not quite follow the exact stepwise increase implied by the formulation that donors increase aid to adaptation with every new international climate policy agreement. The time trend together with the dummies for different time periods (including both negotiation periods and periods with meteorological extreme events) provide a more appropriate functional form for the development of adaptation aid over time. While this is inconsistent with the idea of clear jumps related to individual milestones of the negotiation process (apart from the Kyoto conference, where this effect is significant), it is consistent with the idea that the negotiation process led to a general increase in awareness of the relevance of adaptation in developing countries, thereby leading to an increase in the share of aid allocated to adaptation. The simple dummies do not capture that it may take time for a change to set in, so that the increase is somewhat smoothed out over time. Let us take the example of the period starting with the early 2000s. In Figure 2.1 we noticed a clear upward trend unrelated to natural hazards. This coincides with a period in which adaptation played an increasingly important role as a topic within the negotiation process. This is obviously much better captured by a time trend than by a simple dummy variable for the period post-2005 (Kyoto ratification).

Thus, while H1 cannot be fully upheld in the details of its formulation, the empirical evidence is consistent with the essence of the argument that the international climate negotiation process comes along with changes in development assistance towards more aid for adaptation.

When it comes to the effect of greener public preferences as measured by the percentage of green parliamentarians (H3), we observe a similar effect, albeit only in Table 2.2. Green public preferences do not seem to matter for the share of the aid volume committed to adaptation, but they turn out to be significant for the share of aid activities (Reg1a and Reg3a). In these regressions, an increase in green seats in parliament (as an indicator of general public environmental preferences) by 10 percentage points is associated with an increase of adaptation aid by 0.3 percentage points. Given that adaptation, as opposed to mitigation, is not at the centre of environmental interest, this outcome is remarkable, even if the result is significant only in some regressions. However, again, the introduction of the time trend in Reg2a and 4a supersedes this effect. This is a problem of collinearity as green parties have improved their vote shares over time.

Thus, in a way, the time trend is able to capture national as well as international moves towards greater environmental sensitivity. Only in those models without the general trend can these developments be distinguished.

While H1 and H3 can thus be partially confirmed by the empirical evidence, this is not the case for H2, at least if left-wing governments are considered as an acceptable proxy for green donor government preferences. Surprisingly, the computed marginal effect of left-wing governments is consistently negative, and significant in most regressions in Table 2.2 (Reg1a, Reg3a and Reg4a).

This effectively implies that conservative governments tend to give a higher priority to adaptation projects within total aid. This might be explained by conservative governments being less enthusiastic regarding mitigation, while wanting to cater to global shifts in preferences. As already noted above in the context of green public preferences, for adaptation commitments (Table 2.3), national politics in the donor countries appears to be less relevant. Maybe in a small field such as adaptation aid, to please the local voters, it is initially more important to be able to name a few interventions, rather than to report their financial volumes.

5 Conclusions

Since the UN Conference on Environment and Development in Rio 1992, bilateral and multilateral donors stress that development assistance has increasingly been oriented towards climate-friendly interventions. With respect to mitigation, prior analysis indicates that this corresponds to donors' self-reporting, but finds little reflection in actual aid allocation. Mitigation aid is driven primarily by the oil price, and political-economic variables do not play any role.

Using Tobit regressions based on a self-coded panel dataset for adaptation aid, we find that the situation is different here. As opposed to mitigation aid, adaptation aid (as a share of total commitments and of total aid activities) shows a clear upward trend over time. While specific political influences on this development are difficult to disentangle from a general time trend, the evidence is consistent with the interpretation that this trend is driven by the increasing relevance of the topic at international climate negotiations. This interpretation is also consistent with the significance of the post-Rio and post-Kyoto variables, at least in those regressions in which the general time trend is not added to the explanatory variables. For adaptation aid as a share of aid activities, the increase of green preferences within donor countries also seems to contribute to the positive trend. Finally, conservative governments tend to give a higher priority to adaptation within total aid, which might be explained by their more critical stance with regard to mitigation.

We interpret this as the effect of a significantly increased awareness of climate change-related issues following the international negotiation process, which is reflected by the activities of aid agencies in the context of adaptation much more than in the context of mitigation.

While these results do not fully support our hypotheses, they show the relevance of political variables for the allocation of adaptation aid and the dynamics of adaptation aid over time. Its share has about doubled since the early 1990s, and at least tripled since the late 1970s. While at less than 3 per cent of total aid, there is no need to fear that adaptation aid may in the foreseeable future dominate development cooperation, this is a remarkable development, and totally different from what we observe for aid allocated to mitigation activities.

While the limitation of climate aid dynamics to adaptation is not in line with donors' own rhetoric, it is well in line with a development-oriented focus of bilateral aid. Adaptation is much more clearly linked to the needs of any individual recipient country and can be easily compared to alternative interventions in that country in terms of its relevance to poverty alleviation. Climate change mitigation, however, is a global public good and may be implemented, with the same effect for the developing world, in the United States, Australia or Switzerland. From a development perspective, there is thus little reason to carry out the implementation in, say, Mali, and to label this activity 'development assistance'.

While inconsistent with their rhetoric, donor behaviour thus turns out to be consistent with the central mission of their activities. They leave the provision of global public goods such as mitigation to other areas of public policy-making, and concentrate their climate change-related activities on those areas specifically relevant for their partner country.

Appendix

Table 2.4 Variable descriptions and sources

Variable	*Source*
Adaptatation, project share (%)	AidData (2010)/authors' coding
Adaptation, commitment share (%)	AidData (2010)/authors' coding
Post-Rio: dummy (=1 if year^{3} 1992; = 0 otherwise)	
Post-Kyoto: dummy (=1 if year ^{3} 1997; = 0 otherwise)	
Post-Kyoto ratification: dummy (=1 if year^{3} 2005; = 0 otherwise)	
Year (=annual trend variable, 1970–2008)	
Hurricane Mitch: dummy (=1 if year = 1998; = 0 otherwise)	
Cyclone in Bangladesh and drought in South Africa: dummy (=1 if year = 1991; = 0 otherwise)	
Drought in the Sahel region: dummy (=1 if year = 1983 or 1984; = 0 otherwise)	
Green seats (share of seats in the national parliament, %)	Armingeon *et al.* (2008)
Cabinet composition (Schmidt-index: from 1: hegemony of right-wing and centre parties; to 5: hegemony of social-democratic and other left parties)	Armingeon *et al.* (2008) following Schmidt (1992)

Notes

1 AidData is a comprehensive new aid database bringing together information from the OECD/DAC Creditor Reporting System and a variety of other sources at the level of individual aid activities ('project'-level).

2 The following adaptation-related keywords were entered into the AidData search engine: adaptation, early warning, disaster, compensation, insurance, dyke, sea wall, resource, *ressource*, relief, *urgence*, urgency, *inondation*, inundation, flood, rehabilitation, river, drought, storm, cyclone, hurricane, typhoon, dry, sea level. The list also includes some French terminology (in italics) since not all project descriptions were translated into English. As we did not do a search for all terms in all possible languages, however, some projects that only had non-English terminology are likely to have been overlooked.

3 These indicator variables are dummies taking the value of 1 for all years including and after the respective conference, and zero otherwise.

References

AidData (2010) *PLAID 1.9: Final Development Release of the PLAID Database*, AidData. Online. Available: www.AidData.org (accessed 15 February 2010).

Armingeon, K., Potolidis, P., Gerber, M. and Leimgruber, P. (2008) 'Comparative Political Data Set I (CPDS I), 1960–2007'. Online. Available: www.nsd.uib.no/macrodataguide/set.html?id=6&sub=2 (accessed 15 March 2010).

CISDL (2002) *The Principle of Common But Differentiated Responsibilities: Origins and Scope*, Montreal: Centre for International Sustainable Development Law, McGill University Faculty of Law.

Cusack, T. and Engelhardt, L. (2002) 'The PGL File Collection: File Structures and Procedures'. Online. Available: www.wzberlin.de/mp/ism/people/misc/cusack/d_sets.en.htm#data (accessed 2 May 2010).

Knill, C., Debus, M. and Heichel, S. (2010) 'Do parties matter in internationalised policy areas? The impact of political parties on environmental policy outputs in 18 OECD countries', *European Journal of Political Research*, 49 (3): 301–36.

Michaelowa, A. and Michaelowa, K. (2007) 'Climate or development: is ODA diverted from its original purpose?', *Climatic Change*, 84 (1): 5–22.

Michaelowa, A. and Michaelowa, K. (2011a) 'Coding error or statistical embellishment? The political economy of reporting climate aid', *World Development*, forthcoming.

Michaelowa, A. and Michaelowa, K. (2011b) 'Old wine in new bottles? Does climate policy determine bilateral development aid for renewable energy and energy efficiency?', *International Development Policy*, 2: 60–86.

Roberts, J.T., Weissberger, M. and Peratsakis, C. (2010) 'Trends in official climate finance: evidence from human and machine coding', unpublished paper, Brown University.

Schmidt, M.G. (1992) 'Regierungen: parteipolitische Zusammensetzung', in M.G. Schmidt (ed.) *Lexikon der Politik*, vol. 3, Munich: C.H. Beck, pp. 393–400.

Schneider, S., Semenov, S., Patwardhan, A., Burton, I., Magadza, C., Oppenheimer, M., Pittock, A., Rahman, A., Smith, J., Suarez, A. and Yamin, F. (2007) 'Assessing key vulnerabilities and the risk from climate change', in M. Parry, O. Canziani, J. Palutikof, P. van der Linden and C. Hanson (eds) *Climate Change 2007: Impacts, Adaptation and Vulnerability – Contribution of Working Group II to the Fourth Assessment Report of the Intergovernmental Panel on Climate Change*, Cambridge: Cambridge University Press, pp. 779–810.

Vernon, T. (2008) 'The economic case for pro-poor adaptation: what do we know?', *IDS Bulletin*, 39 (4): 32–41.

3 How Brazil and China have financed industry development and energy security initiatives that support mitigation objectives

Jorund Buen and Paula Castro

1 Introduction

Climate change mitigation in the South has not only been achieved through the Clean Development Mechanism (CDM) or through donor-funded projects. Even though many industrialized countries still claim that developing countries have not embarked on emission reductions, several unilateral initiatives exist, as will be shown through the cases of the Brazilian ethanol programme and China's massive wind energy expansion.

The aim of this chapter is to show, on the basis of these two cases, how financial resources have been mobilized domestically in the South to support programmes that have had a proven impact on energy systems and, by extension, on greenhouse gas (GHG) emissions. These examples provide lessons that can be used when defining financial packages for future mitigation in developing countries – either through pure unilateral means, or through a combination with international funds or carbon markets.

The chapter will also discuss the motives behind the creation of these programmes, and why the governments[1] in both countries were persuaded to mobilize resources to fund these energy sources that were, at the time of launching, not fully competitive against the conventional fossil fuels they were replacing.

The chapter will first present the cases of the Brazilian ethanol programme and the Chinese wind energy deployment, before discussing common characteristics of both cases and lessons learned in terms of the role of unilateral action and financing from the South for future climate change mitigation. Each case presentation provides a historical overview, analyses the objectives behind the initiative in question, reviews policies and incentives introduced to support it, and examines its sources of financing as well as the role of stakeholders. With regard to policies and incentives, our focus is on the latter (that is, how funds are spent to stimulate development, e.g. wind power development in China), but we also refer to the policies providing the context for these incentives. Where sufficiently detailed and chronological material has been available, we have sought to structure the cases in phases.

2 The Brazilian National Alcohol Programme ProAlcool

2.1 History

Ethanol from sugarcane has been used as a fuel in Brazil since the early twentieth century. The government promoted this use to help stabilize sugar prices and to overcome eventual oil supply shortages, especially during the World Wars (Serôa da Motta 1987). Even then, sugar mills had annexed distilleries, and research and experience in the use of ethanol–gasoline blends had been accumulated (de Araujo and Ghirardi 1987). During the First World War, ethanol use was compulsory in many areas of the country, and in 1931 a Federal Decree mandated a blend of 5 per cent ethanol in gasoline (Moreira and Goldemberg 1999). The level of consumption, production and exportation of ethanol was controlled by the federal government by means of production quotas, fixed prices and fiscal and credit policies (Serôa da Motta and da Rocha Ferreira 1988). After the war, the low international oil prices and large supply made ethanol use as fuel non-competitive (de Oliveira 1991), until oil prices started to rise in the 1970s. The official ProAlcool programme started in 1975, and has since gone through four distinct phases.

2.1.1 Phase 1 (1975–1979): the first oil crisis and ethanol for blending

When the first oil shock took place in 1973–1974, production in the first (and at the time only) Brazilian oil field had reached its peak and was expected to decline. At that time, ethanol was still more expensive than gasoline. However, the expectation that the domestic oil supply would remain limited and that the international oil price would keep rising was a key driver of the launch of the Brazilian Alcohol Programme in 1975. This, among other reasons (see Section 2.2) led the government to increase support for ethanol production and use. As international sugar prices fell sharply in 1975–1976, a massive switch to alcohol production took place (de Araujo and Ghirardi 1987; de Oliveira 1991).

The alcohol programme of 1975 had the aim of using anhydrous ethanol[2] in a 22 per cent mixture with gasoline in Brazilian cars. Such a mixture (commonly known as gasohol) had the advantages that it increased the octane of gasoline, thus eliminating the need for lead, and could be used in normal gasoline engines without modifications. Alcohol was mixed with gasoline in the refineries and the blend was distributed through the existing distribution network. Thus, the gradual replacement of pure gasoline did not significantly affect consumers or retailers, and could be started right away. The initial goal was to increase production from 0.6 to 2.5 billion litres by 1979 (de Oliveira 1991).

2.1.2 Phase 2 (1979–1985): the second oil shock and acceleration

The ethanol production target for 1979 had been achieved when the second oil shock 'drastically worsened the Brazilian balance of payments situation and also induced widespread views that oil prices would keep increasing in the future' (de Oliveira 1991: 48). This led to new policies to encourage energy conservation and stronger oil substitution, including the promotion of pure hydrated alcohol as fuel instead of the gasoline–ethanol mix. As hydrated alcohol cannot be used in gasoline engines, this decision completely changed the nature of the alcohol programme. Consumers had to be persuaded to buy alcohol-based vehicles, the car industry needed to be convinced to produce them, and a new distribution network for pure ethanol was required in parallel to the gasohol one. New alcohol distilleries, independent from existing sugar producers, were established. Thus, a completely new demand and supply network was created, making the programme much more complex than before and making state intervention even more necessary (de Oliveira 1991; Rosillo-Calle and Cortez 1998). In the words of de Araujo and Ghirardi (1987: 27): 'The programme ceased to be a reversible policy mechanism, becoming an irreversible commitment.'

Ethanol-fuelled cars exceeded 95 per cent of total Brazilian vehicle sales in 1985, with a peak fleet of 4.4 million ethanol cars in 1993 (ANFAVEA 2010; La Rovere *et al.* 2010).

2.1.3 Phase 3 (1986–2002): crisis and official end

However, ethanol production stopped growing in 1986. The Brazilian economy was in crisis, with high inflation and foreign debt. In the international market, oil prices collapsed and sugar prices rose, while domestically, producers were paid low prices for ethanol. Domestic oil exploration had been successful, resulting in a large increase in domestic production, which in 1987 covered about 55 per cent of total domestic oil consumption and was expected to match it by the mid-1990s. Under these new circumstances, the raison d'être of the alcohol programme no longer existed, as oil import substitution was no longer needed, and oil prices were expected to remain low. These circumstances led to a major ethanol supply crisis in 1989. Ethanol and methanol had to be imported in large quantities to compensate for the insufficient domestic production, and public confidence in the alcohol programme dropped (de Oliveira 1991; Rosillo-Calle and Cortez 1998; La Rovere *et al.* 2010). In 1990, only 13 per cent of new passenger cars sold were ethanol-based (ANFAVEA 2010).

An intense debate surrounded the future direction of ProAlcool in the late 1980s. Despite estimates questioning the economic viability of the alcohol programme due to low oil prices, experts still supported the continuation of the programme (Serôa da Motta 1987; Serôa da Motta and da Rocha Ferreira 1988; de Oliveira 1991). They considered that if ProAlcool 'were to be abandoned, it would be a disaster' (Serôa da Motta and da Rocha Ferreira 1988: 230), resulting in (1) losses of fixed assets in distilleries and sugarcane plantations; (2) a need to convert existing alcohol cars to gasoline; (3) unemployment; and (4) a need to relocate the labour force. The sugar and alcohol industry was at the time the third largest job provider in the agricultural sector (Serôa da Motta and da Rocha Ferreira 1988).

However, the Brazilian economy was still facing difficulties, and the public deficit (including the contribution of the alcohol programme towards it) needed to be tackled. The focus of the alcohol programme was again shifted towards ethanol–gasoline blends, and demand was maintained by increasing the mandatory blend to 24 per cent. Cost reductions and higher productivity of both sugarcane and ethanol production were expected to increase the programme's viability, and governmental intervention by means of subsidies was reduced. From 1989 onwards, local environmental benefits in urban areas and employment generation in rural ones became the main reasons to keep the programme (Rosillo-Calle and Cortez 1998; La Rovere *et al.* 2010).

The alcohol programme was officially ended in 1991, with the closure of most of its institutional framework. During the 1990s, subsidies for ethanol and regulation were gradually removed, but blending requirements were maintained (Rosillo-Calle and Cortez 1998; Hira and de Oliveira 2009). In 1997 the anhydrous ethanol market was liberalized, and in 1999 the hydrated ethanol one as well. Since then, market forces have been the main drivers of ethanol production and use. Once oil prices rose above US$30 per barrel in 2000, ethanol again became a cost-effective alternative (La Rovere *et al.* 2010).

2.1.4 Phase 4 (2003–): rebirth?

The year 2003 marked the latest phase of the Brazilian alcohol programme. The production and sale of flex-fuel vehicles started, which allow the use of any mix of hydrated ethanol and gasohol. A new and huge investment cycle has been witnessed since then, driven mainly by high international oil prices, energy security considerations and climate change concerns. While domestic demand grows again due to the flex-fuel cars, which already in 2007 represented 90 per cent of new car sales in the Brazilian market, the increasing world demand for alternative fuels is opening up export opportunities (La Rovere *et al.* 2010).

Despite the crises arising several times throughout the lifetime of ProAlcool, its overall success at establishing ethanol as a viable fuel cannot be denied. Figure 3.1 presents, for the period 1970–2009, the evolution of anhydrous and hydrated ethanol consumption, and of gasoline and ethanol-based vehicle sales in Brazil, in the context of the changing oil prices and regulatory framework.

ProAlcool allowed a rapid and massive increase in ethanol production, from 600 million litres in 1974, to 12.9 billion litres in 1991 and to 27 billion litres in 2008 (Ministério de Minas e Energia 2011). Estimations of the macroeconomic impact of the programme vary. Goldemberg (2007) calculated that over US$50 billion have been saved in petroleum imports as of 2006, and BNDES and CGEE (2008: 154) note that US$195.5 billion have been saved, of which US$69.1 billion corresponded to avoided fuel imports, and US$126.4 billion to foreign debt interests. Even though it did not manage to decentralize sugarcane production from the wealthy southeast into the poorer areas of the northeast, the programme generated about 700,000 new direct jobs and over 200,000 indirect jobs

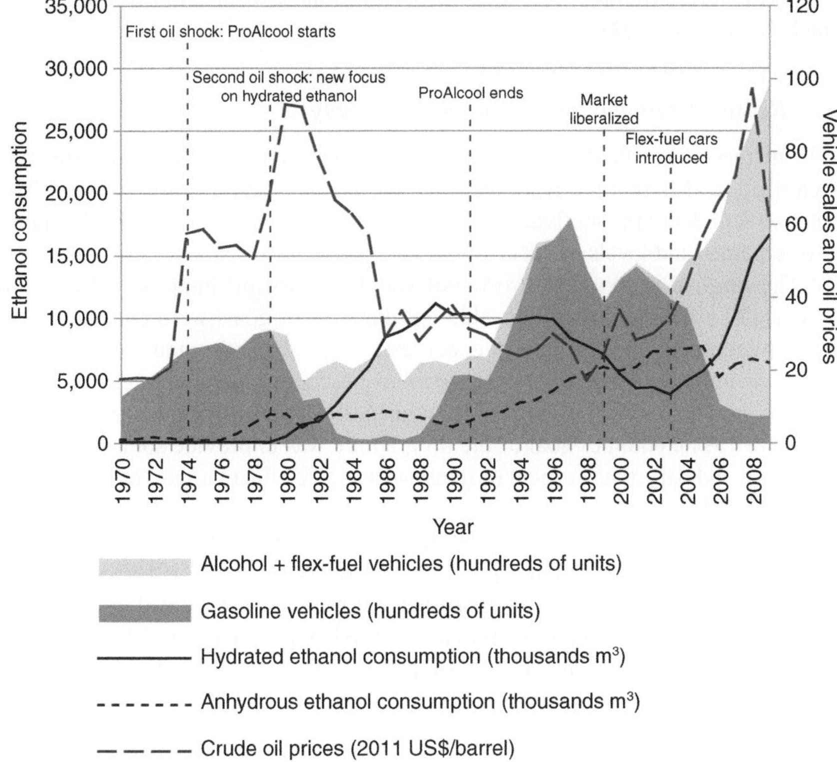

Figure 3.1 Anhydrous and hydrated ethanol consumption in Brazil and its drivers, 1970–2009 (sources: own elaboration based on ANFAVEA (2010) (vehicle sales), Ministério de Minas e Energia (2011) (ethanol consumption), US EIA (2011b) (oil prices)).

in rural areas, with wages above the Brazilian average (de Oliveira 1991; Moreira and Goldemberg 1999; Macedo and Horta Nogueira 2004).

Brazil has become a world-class technology leader in the ethanol industry, including the agricultural, transformation and combustion processes. Innovations led to a 16 per cent increase in sugarcane yield per hectare and a 23 per cent improvement in the ethanol yield per tonne of sugarcane between 1977 and 1985. Such trends allowed an overall increase in ethanol yield from 2,400 l/ha in the 1970s to 7,900 l/ha in the mid-1990s (Goldemberg and Macedo 1994; Rosillo-Calle and Cortez 1998). Production costs have equally declined, at a relatively slow pace until 1985, and more rapidly afterwards, due to a reduction in subsidies for producers (Goldemberg *et al.* 2004b).

These and other positive externalities of the alcohol programme created dynamics that eventually made it impossible to stop. Brazilian ethanol is now definitely attractive without subsidies, thanks not only to the international market situation, but also to the substantial technological improvements and increased yields achieved. In 2008, ethanol overtook gasoline as Brazil's most used engine fuel (Dias Leite 2009).

2.2 Reasons: national interests or climate change?

The history of the alcohol programme shows that its different phases were characterized by different motivations, incentive schemes and levels of success. This section will detail the motivations, and the following one will describe the incentive schemes and levels of success.

The original purpose of ProAlcool was to reduce oil imports and alleviate balance of payment difficulties, although three other goals were put forward by the government: to stimulate the domestic capital goods industry; to reduce regional imbalances by promoting alcohol production in poor regions; and to reduce income disparities by generating unskilled employment in rural areas (de Oliveira 1991). Another goal of the programme was to provide some stability to the sugar industry with respect to international price fluctuations (de Araujo and Ghirardi 1987).

After the 1979 oil shock, reducing the dependence on oil imports was emphasized as the main goal of the programme (Serôa da Motta 1987; de Oliveira 1991). Ethanol production was expanded and focused on hydrated ethanol to be used as pure fuel, instead of the previously used ethanol–gasoline blends.

However, even after the crash in oil prices in the late 1980s, ProAlcool could not be stopped due to strategic considerations (Serôa da Motta and da Rocha Ferreira 1988):

> The ProAlcool objectives went far beyond energy alone. It involved an intricate and politically difficult combination of economic policy in the agricultural and industrial sectors with incentives for smaller scale production, public investment in agricultural research and, especially in the northeast of the country, incentives for private innovation and investment.
>
> (Hall *et al.* 1992: 65)

Neither climate change nor any other environmental consideration was included among the key purposes of the programme in the 1970s–1980s. The first attempts we are aware of to estimate the benefits of the programme in terms of carbon dioxide (CO_2) emission reductions were made by Macedo (1992) and Goldemberg and Macedo (1994). Macedo (1992) estimated that the use of ethanol as a replacement for gasoline and of bagasse for energy cogeneration allowed a reduction of about 18 per cent of Brazil's total emissions from fossil fuels in 1990.

It was not until 1999 that carbon dioxide (CO_2) emission reductions were emphasized as the 'main attractiveness' of the programme, and 'as a solution for industrialized countries to fulfil their commitments' with the United Nations Framework Convention on Climate Change (UNFCCC) (Moreira and Goldemberg

1999: 229).[3] The possibility to export ethanol for climate change mitigation in developed countries emerged as an opportunity for Brazilian industry, although abatement costs, estimated at US$55 per tonne of carbon dioxide equivalent emissions (tCO_2-e) in 1999, were relatively high if other social and environmental benefits of ethanol production and use were not internalized in the cost calculations (Moreira and Goldemberg 1999).

How was this all achieved? Which policies and incentive measures did the Brazilian government implement to make the alcohol programme work? How were they financed? What actors were involved?

2.3 Policies and incentive measures

According to Puppim de Oliveira (2002), the success of the ProAlcool programme was due to an enormous effort by the state, in the form of:

- agricultural and industrial policies;
- public investment in research;
- regulation and provision of incentives for the private sector to pursue innovation and invest in alcohol-related activities;
- provision of incentives to car owners to shift to alcohol-based vehicles, generating greater demand for ethanol.

Until the 1990s, ethanol production, consumption and prices remained tightly controlled by the government. Specific supply targets were set, and their achievement was supported through different incentive measures (Serôa da Motta and da Rocha Ferreira 1988). Blending requirements with gasoline – according to Goldemberg (2007) a sort of renewable portfolio standard for fuels – were also fixed, in parallel with the policy to promote pure ethanol vehicles. While this tight control and many of the related policies have remained in place throughout the duration of ProAlcool, incentives did also change throughout the phases of the programme described above. The main supply push and demand pull measures adopted in each phase will be detailed in the following sections.

2.3.1 Phase 1

In the early years of the programme, between 1975 and 1979, the required growth in alcohol supply was supported by financing the installation of distilleries in existing sugar production plants. Investment costs of these associated distilleries were only 55 per cent of independent ones, and installation could be completed quickly. These capital investments were subsidized through the provision of government loans with negative interest rates (the interest rate was 15 per cent, at a time when inflation was over 30 per cent per year) and with substantial grace periods (Barzelay 1986; de Oliveira 1991).

The government additionally provided incentives for sugar manufacturers to diversify into alcohol production: it promised to keep alcohol prices for producers at the same level as sugar prices and, at the same time, subsidized the difference between alcohol prices for producers and for consumers (which was fixed at the level of gasoline prices). Thus, the alcohol market was free from the risk of competition with oil prices (de Oliveira 1991). In addition, importing alcohol was prohibited under normal circumstances, and entrepreneurs were guaranteed that if they invested in expanding alcohol production capacity, they would have a market for it (Puppim de Oliveira 2002). The major state-controlled fuel producer and distributor Petrobrás was required to buy a guaranteed amount of ethanol each year (Hira and de Oliveira 2009).

2.3.2 Phase 2

From 1979 onwards, the new goal was to produce hydrated ethanol for direct use in cars without mixing it with gasoline. A much more ambitious production target of 10.7 billion litres by 1985 was fixed, which meant that over two million hectares of sugarcane would have to be planted. While the supply needs of the first programme could be met with the production from existing sugar producers that diversified into alcohol, this new target needed new sugarcane producers strictly focused on alcohol production. Indeed, since 1980, most of the increase in alcohol production came from such independent distilleries (de Oliveira 1991).

Supply was incentivized further by means of capital subsidies. Between 1980 and 1985, an estimated US$2 billion in low-interest loans were offered to firms willing to produce ethanol, which amounts to 29 per cent of the total investment needed to reach the installed capacity in 1996 (Moreira and Goldemberg 1999). Provision of finance was substantially accelerated through simplified procedures and involvement of private banks. Financing was funded through an 'open account' in Brazil's monetary budget, so shortages were not to be feared. Additionally, funds collected from taxes on petroleum products and car sales were available in case resources were lacking. Furthermore, international capital was attracted to the programme. A group of nine European and American banks offered US$1 billion in loans for ProAlcool, and the World Bank agreed to a US$250 million loan (Barzelay 1986). All these assurances that funding would be available made entrepreneurs confident that the programme would be continued and resources would not be lacking. In addition to the capital subsidies, ethanol producers also received a slightly higher price for alcohol relative to sugar (Barzelay 1986).

Demand was fostered by allowing lower prices for alcohol cars and for the fuel ethanol itself, in comparison to gasoline. The value added tax (VAT) was reduced for new alcohol-based cars, and increased for gasoline-based ones, resulting in a 5 per cent differential between them. Additionally, the annual road licence fee was reduced for alcohol cars, and the period for repaying purchase loans was extended (Barzelay 1986; de Oliveira 1991).

Gasoline was, at the time, strongly taxed, and had a price about double the price in the United States. Through cross-subsidization, this tax income allowed setting the price of ethanol at the pump initially at 65 per cent of the price of gasoline and later at 59 per cent. Due to the lower calorific value of alcohol, this meant a 19 per cent and a 26 per cent saving in terms of real fuel expenses with respect to gasoline, respectively (de Oliveira 1991; Moreira and Goldemberg 1999).

As a result of the policy mix, the 1985 production target was achieved. Consumers were initially sceptical towards the pure-alcohol vehicle due to technical problems. These were later overcome, so that by 1991 over three million cars (of a seven-million-car fleet) were fully alcohol-based, and almost 95 per cent of new cars sold in Brazil were fuelled by alcohol (de Oliveira 1991).

These achievements, however, came at a cost. By the mid-1980s, not only was the ethanol production cost higher than the cost of the equivalent amount of gasoline, but the ethanol price fixed for consumers was lower than the alcohol price for producers. Oil prices had fallen again. Massive subsidies were thus required: 'In 1986 alcohol production was 52.5 million boe [barrels of oil equivalent], which means subsidies for alcohol are over 770 million US$/year' (de Oliveira 1991: 53). As gasoline was gradually being displaced in favour of alcohol, new challenges arose: first, the tax revenues from gasoline declined, reducing the funds available to subsidize alcohol; second, as the alcohol-fuelled car fleet grew and the differential prices for alcohol and gasoline subsisted, the required amount of subsidies increased (de Araujo and Ghirardi 1987).

At the same time, the installed ethanol-producing capacity was still growing fast, so that from 1983 onwards alcohol stocks were larger than needed. As a response, credits for production expansion were drastically reduced and licensing of distilleries became stricter, which did not prevent new capacity from being contracted even without subsidized loans (de Araujo and Ghirardi 1987).

2.3.3 Phase 3

These problems, coupled with the overall economic difficulties faced by the country, led the Brazilian government to reduce ethanol subsidies. The price of pure ethanol was gradually increased to 80 per cent of the gasoline price. The advantage in the VAT for cars was eliminated in 1990. To incentivize consumption, in the same year, the government launched a programme supporting cheap popular cars through a very low tax rate. These cars could not be adapted to pure alcohol rapidly enough to profit from the offered incentives. Hence, mostly gasoline cars benefited from the programme. Confidence in the supply of ethanol declined as domestic production fell in favour of sugar, and ethanol/methanol had to be imported to compensate for that. All this led to the decline of ethanol car sales from the late 1980s, falling to almost zero in 1996. The mix of 22 per cent ethanol in gasoline was not affected, as it was still required by law (Moreira and Goldemberg 1999).

2.3.4 Phase 4

From 1999 onwards, price liberalization, the resulting drop in alcohol prices and the new increase in oil prices started to raise the interest in ethanol again (Coelho *et al.* 1999), especially after the introduction of the flex-fuel car in 2003. Nowadays, ethanol is fully competitive with gasoline at current oil prices. However, flex-fuel cars are eligible for special tax breaks, and gasoline is still taxed more heavily than ethanol (as of 2006, taxes for gasoline were 58 per cent higher than for pure ethanol, and anhydrous ethanol for gasohol blends was untaxed), which shows the continued support of the government for this industry (Hira and de Oliveira 2009).

2.4 Financing of the programme

As described in Section 2.3, the alcohol programme was financed directly from the government budget; from the revenues of gasoline and car taxes; and from foreign capital. However, it is very difficult to track which amounts of money originate from which source. This is due to the frequent changes in support policies and taxing systems, as well as in the general institutional framework of the programme.

Dias Leite (2009) estimates that about US$7 billion were invested in the programme, of which US$4 billion came from the government, and the rest from private firms. Goldemberg *et al.* (2004a, 2004b) refer to an official total of US$4.92 billion (constant 2001 dollars) invested directly in the agricultural and industrial sectors of the programme between 1975 and 1989 – that is, during the whole duration of the official ProAlcool programme. De Oliveira (1991) cites an investment of about US$3.7 billion to install 450 distilleries. The estimate given by Rosillo-Calle and Cortez (1998) for total investment in the programme since 1976 is US$11.3 billion.

These figures, however, do not reflect the total picture. Goldemberg (2007) estimates that the total subsidies that flew into the programme amounted to about US$30 billion over 20 years, and La Rovere *et al.* (2010) mention, in addition to the investments in the agricultural and industrial sectors, public subsidies amounting to around US$10 billion.

None of these sources describes whether these subsidies and investments were generated from the government budget only, or whether they already include foreign loans and tax money. Indeed, as described in Section 2.3, once the programme was running and the first successes were obtained, a group of European and American banks, as well as the World Bank, offered loans. In addition, the difference between the low consumer prices for hydrated ethanol and its production costs was covered by Petrobrás from the profits made from gasoline taxes. Petrobrás also had to invest in the storage and distribution system for pure ethanol.

Finally, the important investment in R&D by Brazilian universities, research institutes and firms throughout the ethanol value chain cannot be neglected. Both at the federal and state level, the government supported research, and it is not clear whether the finance for this support is included among the reported investments in ProAlcool.

The renewed interest in ethanol as a fuel in the new century has resulted in 'an avalanche of investments that are beginning to transform the profile of the sector' (Wilkinson and Herrera 2010: 751). Not only the traditional domestic entrepreneurs, but also foreign investors including global corporations, global investment funds, and firms or government agencies from China, India and Japan are involved in planned investments in new production capacity, land purchase, and infrastructure for exporting ethanol (Wilkinson and Herrera 2010).

2.5 Stakeholders, knowledge and natural endowments

Policies and incentive measures were crucial for the success of the Brazilian alcohol programme, but were not the only factors enabling it. Puppim de Oliveira (2002) describes in detail the role of domestic stakeholders, of knowledge and of natural endowments as necessary conditions for the programme to start in the first place.

The large economic importance of the sugarcane sector in Brazil, which was facing difficulties in the 1970s due to falling sugar prices, emphasized by the mounting pressure from industry lobbyists with good political connections and from state governments in areas economically dependent on sugarcane production, was one of the drivers that moved the federal government to enact policies to promote the use of alcohol as a fuel during the first phase of the programme. Additionally, military leaders regarded the oil crisis as a threat to their key values of national sovereignty and security. Thus, the military government of the time was interested in a strategy of self-sufficiency in fuel. Economists and technocrats in the government saw alcohol as a solution to national account deficits and inflation problems, especially after the second oil shock (Puppim de Oliveira 2002). A third interest group was composed of researchers in state laboratories and universities, who pushed for the development of national technology as a way of avoiding technological dependence on industrialized countries. Their success in developing an alcohol-based engine in the early 1970s encouraged the government to invest more in research in this area, with a view of becoming technologically independent. The media also had an influence on policy-making, as it frequently showed the possible consequences of the oil crisis for Brazil, and the public was worried about fuel price increases, thus supporting an alcohol fuel policy (Puppim de Oliveira 2002). It is reported that the pride about the locally developed vehicles and fuel also drove Brazilians to prefer ethanol-based cars (Hira and de Oliveira 2009).

Still, some groups were, at least initially, sceptical towards an alcohol fuel policy. Among them were the national and multinational oil companies and car manufacturers, but also the financial agencies that were supposed to support the programme. Lack of strong leadership, barriers set-up by these opponents and lack of financing due to the slow reaction of banks resulted in a slow start of

ProAlcool (Hira and de Oliveira 2009). However, the power of the groups supporting the policy was greater, and the remaining opposition was eventually calmed after negotiations across ministries, with Petrobrás and with car manufacturers. Not only opposition to the programme, but also competition across ministries and private actors for control over ethanol production needed to be tackled (Barzelay 1986).

Additionally, Brazil already had assets that made such a programme possible: its large agricultural area, appropriate climate for sugarcane production without irrigation and the existing agricultural and industrial know-how. Sugarcane itself has several good characteristics as an energy crop, such as high yields per area and useful by-products.

A strong research tradition, coupled with the necessary incentives for public and private R&D, enabled the development of Brazil's own technology for alcohol-fuelled vehicles, the increase in sugarcane production and processing productivity, and the development of the use of by-products.

As Puppim de Oliveira (2002) describes it, the oil shocks provided the window of opportunity to start the programme, but it was enabled by the interaction between interests, values and knowledge.

3 Wind power development in China

3.1 History

Wind power development in China has gone through three phases:[4] (1) off-grid, R&D and demonstration applications (mid-1970s–1993); (2) donor-dominated development accompanied by emerging, but volatile government support (1994–2002); and (3) government use of market forces to stimulate local manufacturing (2003–present).

3.1.2 Phase 1 (mid-1970s–1993)

The first phase was initiated in the mid-1970s by (mainly domestically manufactured)[5] micro-scale wind turbines for use by herdsmen and other inhabitants in areas far from the power grid (Gamos 1999; Lew 2000).[6] While the off-grid applications were part of a concerted effort of Inner Mongolia's local government (and later the Ministry of Agriculture), the initial stages of grid-connected wind power development in China were not the result of any coordinated Chinese government initiative. Between the mid-1980s and mid-1990s, a very limited number of grid-connected pilot demonstration turbines were erected, mainly using equipment imported from donor countries financing the projects.

3.1.3 Phase 2 (1994–2002)

The second development phase (1994–2002) was still mainly characterized by imports, but following the development of domestic regulations and growth in domestic funding, a domestic industry was initiated. Although the government published its first wind power development targets (see Table 3.1), the number of installed turbines and the installed kilowatt (kW) per turbine showed a rather unstable pattern from year to year, closely linked to unclear regulations and volatility in donor funding, and did not meet targets.

Since no standardized price-setting mechanism existed, tariffs in the second phase were set on a case-by-case basis. This could either lead to hightariffsprices in cases where the wind project developer was the subsidiary of the power company purchasing the wind power (Brown 2001), or to protracted negotiations between the power producer and the grid or utility (Li *et al.* 2004). The central government's planning commission was also hesitant to approve wind projects. It even reopened existing agreements, as it questioned high tariffs in light of large supply coming online; feared lack of acceptance locally; and generally wanted to keep power prices low for socioeconomic reasons (many state-owned enterprises were on the verge of bankruptcy and could not stand higher power prices) (Li, J. 2002; Wallace 2002). It did not help that the central government commissions for planning, and economic operations and industrial policy both

Table 3.1 Selected targets for installed wind power capacity in China, 1994–2020

Agency	*Decided (year)*	*Targeted gigawatt (GW) installed capacity (achieved targets in* ***bold****)*				
		2000	*2005*	*2010*	*2015*	*2020*
MOEP[a]	1994	1.0				
SPC/SSTC/SETC[b]	1995	**0.3–0.4**		**1.0–1.1**		
MOEP	1998	0.5–0.6	1.5	**3.0**		
SPC	1998	~0.8	~3.1	**~5.1**	**~7.3**	
SETC	1998	~0.7	3.0	**4.9**	**7.0**	
SDPC	2001		1.5			
NDRC	2007			**5.0**		**30.0**
NDRC	2007			**10.0**		
NDRC	2009					100.0
NDRC (unofficial)	2010					200.0[c]

Sources: World Bank (1999), GEF (2002), Liu *et al.* (2002), Haum (2004), Lema and Ruby (2007), NDRC (2007), Cyranoski (2009), *People's Daily Online* (2009), Dewey and LeBoeuf LLP (2010), Sievert (2010).

Notes

a This ministry no longer exists (its responsibilities are shared between five power generation companies and two grid companies).

b State Planning Commission (SPC) changed its name to State Development Planning Commission (SDPC) in 1996, and to National Development Reform Commission (NDRC) in 2003. State Science and Technology Commission changed its name to Ministry of Science and Technology (MOST) in 1998. State Economic and Trade Commission (SETC) was absorbed by the NDRC in 2003.

c Other sources say 150 GW, or that new renewable energy in total should contribute 200 GW. Recently, a 30 GW target for offshore wind capacity by 2020 was decided (*People's Daily Online*, 2011) had divisions dealing with renewable energy, with resulting overlaps and conflicts, in these formative years of the Chinese wind industry (He 2002).[7] For example, in single wind power initiatives, it was difficult to differentiate between the industrialization element (e.g. domestically made wind turbines) on the one hand and infrastructure planning on the other (Liu 2002). Similarly, the commission responsible for industrialization argued against the planning commission's wish to cap wind tariffs at ¥0.5 RMB[8] (about US$0.06), as this would limit diffusion of wind equipment (Liu 2002).

All the above led the Bank of Construction, the number-one lender to wind projects at the time, to hold off from more project lending, calling for stronger government support for wind power (Brown 2001). Donor funding made Chinese buyers unwilling to pay the full cost of equipment (Lew 2000) or to implement projects with commercial financing which had higher interest rates and shorter payback periods (Brown 2001). Hence the market was limited to whatever volume of donor funding was available at any given time. Donor-funded projects also likely prevented cost reductions since aid was tied to technology from the donor country, barring local manufacturers from entering the market and hence stifling competition. Most donor projects were also so small that the relative transaction and infrastructure costs became high. Furthermore, the domestic bank loan component of such projects had such short payback periods that project owners had to increase the wind power price to be able to repay in time.

3.1.4 Phase 3 (2003–)

The third phase of China's wind power development (2003–) has seen an explosive growth of domestic manufacturing. This has been instigated by a combination of (1) favourable regulations (see Section 3.3.3); (2) low-cost labour and raw materials, plus lower transport costs to the Chinese market; (3) leading wind turbine producers establishing or expanding China-based manufacturing;[9] and (4) licensing agreements and joint ventures between Chinese and foreign manufacturers. Some joint ventures implemented earlier (through the 'Ride the Wind' initiative, see Table 3.3) bore the signs of 'forced marriages' as the partners were essentially chosen by government (Lewis 2005: 7), and were probably entered into by the European companies mainly to obtain Chinese government goodwill (Sieg 2004). The licensing agreements seemingly primarily gave access to old production lines of established manufacturers, or products from second-rate manufacturers. However, the largest domestic manufacturer, Goldwind, cooperated directly with foreign turbine designers instead of only entering a technology-licensing agreement (Liu 2006), and has in general focused substantially on quality assurance and internationalization (Yu and Wang 2002).

From 2003 China rapidly increased its share of global newly installed capacity. Between 2006 and 2009, domestic turbine manufacturers increased their share of total turbine sales in China from 40 per cent to 82 per cent, and by 2009 three domestic manufacturers (Goldwind, Sinovel and DEC) each had about twice the share of newly installed capacity of the largest foreign supplier (Vestas).

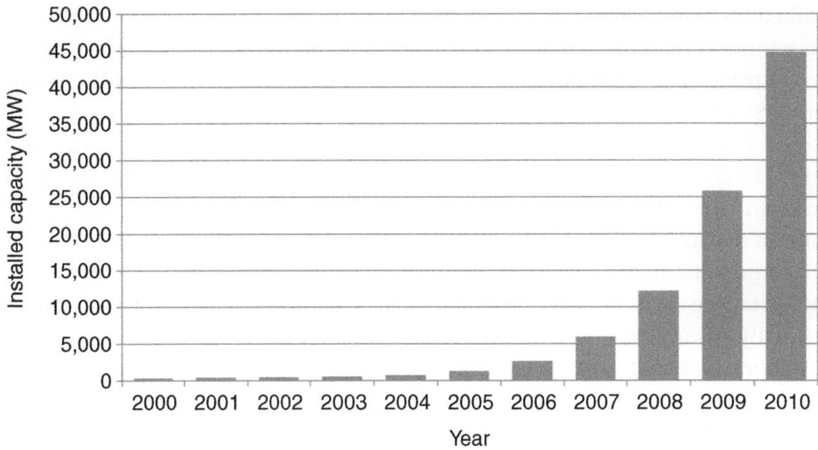

Figure 3.2 Development of China's installed wind power capacity, 2000–2010 (megawatts) (source: own illustration based on data from Shi 2011).

There has been an explosive growth in the number of turbines installed, as well as in the kilowatts per turbine. Several new, privately owned companies have been established, often as spinoffs from government-funded research institutes, and with the help of government R&D funding.[10] Since 2009, Chinese manufacturers have also begun exporting, and Goldwind has joined a joint venture in the United States (CWEI 2011).[11] The year 2010 saw the first offshore wind farm being built (Conrad and Meissner 2011). China is now the world's number-one wind turbine manufacturer, with four manufacturers – Sinovel (2), Goldwind (4), Dongfang (7) and United Power (10) – on the world's top-ten list (BTM Consult 2011) and another 80 or so manufacturers ranging from the prototype stage to aspiring top-ten candidates. Longyuan, China's leading wind developer, is now the world's third largest. It recently partnered with wind turbine manufacturer Gamesa to develop wind farms internationally (Gamesa 2011).

3.2 Reasons for China's wind power development

The early-stage micro-scale wind power applications were developed to alleviate poverty in remote areas without access to the power grid (see Lew 2000; Liu *et al.* 2002), and to support social stability and national unity (Zhang *et al.* 1999). As mentioned above, the initial phase of China's grid-connected wind power development was mainly reactive, rather than a result of any conscious strategy. Bluntly put, the main reason for the wind turbine installation in China during this period was that turbine-producing countries supported internationalization of their industries. These faced huge difficulties at the time,[12] and their governments tied bilateral aid (grants and loans) to purchase of their equipment.

Several planning documents published in the mid-1990s (cf. Table 3.1) marked the transition to the second wind industry development phase by providing a more certain outlook for wind power development, and also built a rationale for prioritizing such development (for more details, see Buen 1998a, 1998b). The first rationale was to help meet China's growing energy and power needs (Lewis 2004). The second, closely related to the first, was to diversify away from coal (Liu *et al.* 2002), oil, natural gas and hydro power (Buen 1998a; Dewey & LeBoeuf LLP 2010) in meeting such needs. Coal is a major contributor to emissions of smoke, dust and sulphur dioxide; natural gas and oil reserves are scarce; and large-scale hydro power development has increasingly met popular resistance. Starting from the late 1990s, fostering a domestic manufacturing industry gradually rose to become the perhaps primary objective of China's wind power development initiative (see more details in Section 3.3.3). China's electricity supply–demand balance (and the perception of such) has changed over the years; what seemed a rock-solid rationale for wind power in the mid-1990s was used against it in the late 1990s when the go-ahead for the giant Three Gorges hydro power project and close-down of power-intensive industry led to the perception of electricity oversupply (Shi 2002).

While local pollution such as that from sulphur dioxide and nitrogen oxide was regarded as more important at the time (Shi 2002), China ratified the UNFCCC in 1992, and its National Response Strategy (East-West Center *et al.* 1993) had a clear reference to the role of wind power. A giant study financed by the UNDP and World Bank, and involving 20 ministries and agencies on the Chinese side with the important central government planning commission in a leading role, started in 1993. It concluded that over the longer term, 'the only option for China … is to switch to non-carbon energy sources' (Johnson *et al.* 1996: ix), and mentioned wind power among the priorities (Johnson *et al.* 1996: 62–3). The Energy Ministry played an active role in formulating China's climate change policy (Economy 1994). However, wind power was not really regarded as a serious, large-scale option at the time, and its potential was severely underestimated (Buen 1998b). An example illustrates how wind power was downplayed compared to alternatives: while nuclear power (less than 2 GW) and wind power (0.2 GW) installed capacity were minuscule compared to coal in China at the time, the climate change country study completed in 1999 foresaw wind power installed capacity at 2 GW in 2020, but estimated nuclear power at 150 GW in 2010 (RTCCCCS 1999). In reality, nuclear power capacity was a meagre 10 GW in 2010 (Fang 2011; *Asia Today* 2011), compared to 44.7 GW for wind power (GWEC 2011).

3.3 Policies and incentives

3.3.1 Phase 1 (mid-1970s–1993)

During the initial phase, Inner Mongolia's local Science and Technology Commission (1986 onwards) and the Ministry of Agriculture (1990 onwards) made parallel efforts to subsidize off-grid wind (Gamos 1999; Lew 2000). From 1986, 200 RMB (US$24.2)[13] were awarded to purchasers of off-grid wind equipment; this subsidy was changed to about 100 RMB (US$12.1) per 100 W of rated capacity around the year 2000 (Lew 2000).

Domestic support measures for grid-connected wind power were limited (Table 3.2).

3.3.2 Phase 2 (1994–2002)

The second phase (1994–2002) saw the introduction of several rather limited policies and incentives. A regulation mandating utilities to purchase wind power was introduced in 1994 (Table 3.3), but met resistance in practice, for several reasons:

1 The extra cost for wind power was to be shared with the whole grid, but in practice, this became restricted to the local grid of the utility buying the wind power. As the utility had to ask the authorities for approval to raise prices, which was very cumbersome, purchasing wind power had a direct negative impact on its earnings.
2 In the late 1990s there was a perceived oversupply of power, and provinces even breached power purchase agreements when there was no longer a power shortage (Raufer and Wang 2003).

Table 3.2 China's support measures for wind power: phase 1 (mid-1970s–1993)

Policy	*Duration*	*Description*	*Type of support*	*Implementer*
Income tax exemptions	Varies year to year	Typically 2–3 years tax holiday initially, followed by a period at 50 per cent of normal tax rate	Tax incentive	Provincial tax bureaus
Import duty reductions	1980s–	Import duty exemption on request until mid-1990s, removed when China prioritized build-up of domestic industry; still granted for high-tech components; 6 per cent 1996–2003, then 8 per cent for generator, 3 per cent for components (normal is 12 per cent)	Financial incentive	Ministry of Commerce
Low-interest loans, manufacturing	1986–1990	For local industry to build up manufacturing capability	Financial incentive	Unclear (state and local governments)

Sources: expanded and updated from Dai *et al.* (1996), Lin (1998), Zhang *et al.* (1999), Lew (2000).

Note
Income tax exemptions have also been granted after phase 1.

3 It was difficult for wind project proponents to agree on a price with the local grid or utility, as both were becoming separate profit-making entities as a result of partial power sector deregulation in parallel with the development of wind power policy.

A requirement that projects should contain locally manufactured technologies was introduced, but implemented rather loosely in this phase. Domestic industry was embryonic, and there was a perception that foreign expertise and key components were needed for the industry to develop further. Furthermore, the local content requirement was at odds with donor demands that recipients purchase their manufacturers' technologies (Lewis 2005).

3.3.3 Phase 3 (2003–)

Several support policies, detailed in the subsections below, characterize this period.

BUILDING A COMPETITIVE INDUSTRY THROUGH A POLITICALLY CREATED HOME MARKET

As seen in the previous section, the focus on creating a domestic wind industry increased during the second development phase. However, the 'localization' of wind power and wind equipment industry development in China completely changed gears from 2003 onwards. Since then, Chinese authorities have consciously nurtured a strategic niche market (Kemp *et al.* 1998; Christiansen and Buen 2002; Buen 2006) for domestic equipment manufacturers and developers through protecting the home market from external competitors.

The combination of competitive bidding, a local content requirement and a near lack of requirements relating to track record or lifetime turbine performance provided the intended stimulus to local manufacturers and developers.

WIND POWER CONCESSIONS

The Chinese government initiated a wind power concession programme in 2003. The main components were (1) competitive bidding for development of large (100 MW) projects with minimum 600 kW turbines; (2) a requirement that a minimum share of the equipment used be domestically manufactured (initially 50 per cent, later increased to 70 per cent and made valid for non-concession projects as well; in practice measured by the fraction of locally sourced expenses (Lewis 2007)); (3) a government guarantee that produced power would be bought at the winning price; (4) government financial support for grid extension and access roads; (5) a guaranteed 25-year power purchase agreement; and (6) preferential loan and tax conditions.

In addition to the support China's manufacturers obtained through concessions and local content requirements, the government established a Special Fund

Table 3.3 China's support measures for wind power: phase 2 (1994–2002)

Policy	*Duration*	*Description*	*Type of support*	*Implementer*
Provisions for grid-connected wind farm management	1994	Mandated provincial electric power authorities to give priority to wind power in purchasing electricity	Financial incentive	MOEP[a]
National debt wind power programme	1996	Low-interest loans to protect owners willing to take the risk of using locally made wind turbines (80 MW)	Financial incentive	SETC
Lower-interest loans, wind farm development	1996, 1999	Loans with up to 50 per cent lower interest rates for wind farm developers; 'encouraged' local content	Financial incentive	SDPC, SETC
'Ride the Wind'	1997	Encouraged joint ventures between Chinese and foreign wind equipment manufacturers; funded large-scale turbine R&D; subsidies for pilot projects for domestic wind turbine production	R&D; local content recommendation	SDPC
'Double Increase'	1997	Double (1) the 80 MW wind capacity then installed, and (2) the share of local manufacture by 2000, through no-/low-interest loans	Financial incentive	SDPC/SETC
Renewable energy fund	1996–2000	Development of 600 kW turbines	R&D	MOST
Directive on wind power pricing	1999	Set wind power pricing at a level that would repay capital cost with interest plus a reasonable profit	Financial incentive	State Council NDRC/MOST
Local content requirement	2000–2009	40 per cent local content requirement for all new wind power projects, later increased (see Table 3.4)	Local content requirement	SDPC
836 Wind Programme	2001	Funded Chinese turbine manufacturers to develop technologies for MW-size wind turbines; encouraged technologies for variable-pitch rotors and variable-speed generators	R&D	MOST
VAT reduction	2001	VAT on wind power reduced from 17 per cent to 8.5 per cent	Financial incentive	MOF,[b] State Duty Bureau

Sources: expanded and updated from Dai *et al.* (1996), Lin (1998), Zhang *et al.* (1999), Lew (2000), Li, B. (2002).

Notes

a See Table 3.1 for explanations of abbreviations.

b Ministry of Finance.

for Wind Power Manufacturing in 2008, again with comprehensive local content requirements, whose subsidies reportedly contributed up to 10 per cent of turbine cost (OUSTR 2010). To qualify, the applicant has had to document that critical components of the turbines were bought in China.

Several large wind concessions were awarded until mid-2009. The final ones provided part of China's economic stimulus package after the financial crisis starting in 2007. Province-level price discovery took place first through such competitive auctions (Martinot 2010). Developers may have had an incentive to underbid as the projects were low-risk but high-profile, and hence were a nice showcase for later (more profitable) assignments. Furthermore, county governments have competed against each other by offering upfront economic support for project owners in their geographic area, with the hope of obtaining tax revenues if their bid is successful (Wu 2006). A final reason why tariffs in the first tenders were very low could have been that many bidders were state-owned companies, which wanted to prepare for an expected mandated market share of renewable energy (see the following section).

MANDATED MARKET SHARE

China gradually left the concession approach after 2007 to make way for policies providing for lower transaction costs and more regulatory transparency. That year, the Chinese government decided that renewable-energy sources other than hydro power should contribute 1 per cent of total power generation in the whole grid by 2010, and 3 per cent by 2020. It required power generators with installed capacity of more than 5 GW to have 3 per cent renewable-energy sources other than hydro power installed by 2010 and 8 per cent by 2020. As wind power is the non-hydro renewable-energy technology closest to commercialization, it has obtained the lion's share of this increase.

STANDARDIZED FEED-IN TARIFFS

The Renewable Energy Law (2006) reinstated the policy of mandated grid connection of wind power and sharing of extra costs of wind power among all grid participants, and introduced a minor renewable-energy surcharge for all consumers (see Table 3.4). However, to the surprise and disappointment of foreign investors, the law stopped short of introducing standardized national feed-in tariffs for wind power, and instead confirmed the concession approach.

China revised the law in 2009, improving the market conditions for wind power in several ways. First, it further clarified utilities' obligation to purchase *all* renewable electricity produced during a project's lifetime; previously they could, in practice, opt out in case there was no power demand, and only purchase a defined number of load hours. Second, it clarified that the extra cost was to be shared with consumers country-wide rather than in the specific local grid, and that in case of no local demand the extra power could be sold to the national grid. Third, deadlines and penalties added teeth to the above provisions (Buen

2010; Martinot 2010). The above-mentioned surcharge was increased, and revenues were estimated at 4.5 billion RMB (about US$697 million) in 2009 (Shi 2009).

In August 2009 a national regulation specifying four standardized regional feed-in tariffs was established. They vary from 0.51 RMB (US$0.079) per kilowatt-hour in the regions with the best wind resources to 0.61 RMB (US$0.094) per kilowatt-hour in areas with the least suitable wind resources. This marked the end of the concession approach on the mainland. It will only be used offshore from now on. The new tariffs are for the full lifetime of the project. This makes it easier for investors to calculate financial returns than before, when preferential tariffs were only for the first 30,000 load hours (Shi 2009).

As part of its commitment to reducing carbon intensity (tonnes of carbon dioxide emitted per unit of gross domestic product) by 40–45 per cent from 2005 levels until 2020, China has committed to increase the share of non-fossil fuels (renewable and nuclear) in energy consumption to 15 per cent (compared to about 10 per cent today). Since fossil fuel installed power generation capacity increases rapidly, this is such a major undertaking that additional comprehensive policies and incentives will be needed.

THE ROLE OF THE CDM

Since the first Chinese wind power Clean Development Mechanism (CDM) project obtained a domestic letter of approval in 2002, a rapidly increasing number of them have sought additional funding through selling Certified Emission Reductions (CERs) to buyers from industrialized countries through the CDM. Wind power is among the CDM project types given priority by China.

Chinese authorities have introduced an unofficial price floor for CERs of the RMB equivalent of €8 per CER, which adds some revenue certainty for wind project owners. Adjusting to differences on the demand side, the authorities have later adjusted the price floor for specific project types, including wind power. The unofficial wind power price floor has long been €10.50. Chinese letters of approval (LoAs) for the CDM list a maximum CER volume; it is not fully clear whether projects exceeding this volume can apply for another LoA. Nor is it clear whether or not the authorities accept emission reduction purchase agreements with floating prices post-2012 that can end up below the €8 price floor.

Yang *et al.* (2010) find that the price floor only limits investor risk to a limited extent, and the uncertainty about the CDM's future limits its contribution to net present value. While important for project economics on the margin, in practice the CDM has rarely played a key role in the actual financing of wind power projects in China (Li *et al.* 2010; Lewis 2010). There are several reasons for this. Until now, Chinese banks have not been willing to accept CERs as collateral because:

- they are not familiar with the mechanism;

- projects may be rejected by the UN (for example, until the Chinese government issued a clarification recently (CDM EB 2011), wind projects whose tariffs had been reduced during the project development process were faced with the impossible task of proving this was not part of a policy to stimulate more GHG-intensive alternatives, and had not been manipulated to ensure that the projects qualified under the CDM (CDWEDPO and CREIA 2009; Buen and Røine 2010; He and Morse 2010);
- the amount of CERs actually generated by a registered project is uncertain;
- the future role of the CDM in China is not fully clear.[14]

Since projects normally reach financial closure prior to CDM registration, and revenues from power sales dwarf CER revenues, financing is most commonly based on a combination of the project owner's own equity and loans from domestic banks, based on projected power sales revenues. That said, for the large majority of wind projects that have indeed been registered, CER revenues constitute up to 10 per cent of overall revenues. Almost 80 per cent of China's installed wind power generation capacity is submitted or registered as a CDM project (Castro *et al.* 2011).

OTHER SUPPORT

During the last few years, China has more actively supported exports of renewable-energy technology, including wind turbines, through its Export Product Research and Development Fund, and export credits from China's Export–Import Bank (the world's largest of its kind).

3.3.4 Financing China's wind development

During the first phase of China's wind industry development, funding for the grid-connected demonstration plants came mainly from European countries such as Denmark and the Netherlands, through loans and grants conditional on the purchase of their industries' equipment.

The local government and utility initially provided 5 million RMB (about US$0.6 million) per year each for Inner Mongolia's part of the off-grid wind subsidy (Lew 2000). Gamos (1999) estimated the total off-grid wind subsidy in Inner Mongolia until that time at 30 million RMB (US$3.6 million),[15] while Zhang *et al.* (1999) put the subsidy at 25 million RMB (US$3 million) in the period 1986–1996.

As mentioned in Section 3.1, the second phase was characterized by a rather volatile – and limited – combination of donor and government funding, with little room for private sector involvement and use of market mechanisms.

Liu *et al.* (2002) estimated that over 90 per cent of total investment in Chinese wind power until then had come from either government loans and subsidies or foreign grants/loans, and the rest from foreign private investors. They found a precise breakdown of funding sources very difficult to calculate, as neither Chinese

Table 3.4 China's support measures for wind power: phase 3 (2003–)

Policy	*Duration*	*Description*	*Type of support*	*Implementer*
Wind concessions	2003–2009, (still ongoing for special projects, e.g. offshore wind)	Government auction for development of selected wind sites. Initially 50 per cent local content, later 70 per cent	Government auction; local content requirement	NDRC[a]
Renewable Energy Law	2006	Government-guided prices for wind power; 0.4 RMB (US$0.062) per kWh surcharge on all electricity sales to cover national renewable energy project investments and feed-in tariff costs.	Financial incentive	NDRC
973 Program	2006–2010	Exploration of utility-scale wind power	R&D	MOST
International Science and Technology Cooperation Program in Renewable Energy	2007	International R&D cooperation for multi-MW/ offshore wind turbines	R&D	MOST/NDRC
Mandated market share	2007	Renewables to form 1 per cent of power of total generation in grid 2010, 3 per cent 2020 (more for large power generators)	Mandated market share	NDRC
Special Fund for Wind Power Manufacturing	2008–2011	Grant of 600 RMB (US$92.9) per kW for first 50 units, to domestic wind turbine manufacturers	Financial incentive	MOF
Revised Renewable Energy Law	2009	Fines for non-connection of wind; sharing of *all* costs with whole grid	Financial incentive	NDRC

Sources: expanded and updated from Lewis (2005), NREL (2004), Martinot (2010: 5), Dewey and LeBoeuf LLP (2010), ChinaFAQs (2010).

Notes

a See Tables 3.1 and 3.3 for explanations of abbreviations.

government agencies nor donor countries had statistics on wind investments and because unit costs had varied considerably over the long time period in question.

The same authors cited a total initial wind farm investment cost in 1998 of US$1000/kW. Applied to the cumulative installed capacity up until 2002, this would yield a rough figure of US$425 million of domestic government plus donor funding, and US$45 million of foreign private sector investment. A report compiled in 2001 (GTZ 2002: 64) estimated 'more than US$500 million' in international donor funding for wind projects. For Inner Mongolia, Zhang *et al.* (1999) found that 57 per cent of funding for wind power had come from the central government until that date, 13 per cent from lower levels of government and 30 per cent from foreign donors. However, the latter figures probably include micro-turbine funding, while the former do not. Furthermore, Vaupen's (1999) and Dai *et al.*'s (1996) overview indicate a more limited Chinese government role. Extrapolating from Dai *et al.*'s (1996) project-level data, it can be estimated that out of the assumed US$425 million of financing by 2002, roughly 15 per cent (US$64 million) were funded by the Chinese government.

After 2002, during the third phase, foreign aid has played a negligible role in the funding of Chinese wind power, while a combination of direct Chinese government investment and subsidies to manufacturers and developers has emerged.

China Renewable Energy Industries Association recently said current wind farm investments average US$764,000 per megawatt (Castano 2011). Given China's 44.7 GW of total installed capacity as of the end of 2010, this would imply a total wind project investment since the start of China's wind development initiative in the mid-1970s of roughly US$34 billion so far. However, the average investment per megawatt has gone down significantly over the last 3–4 years; it probably averaged US$1 million/MW before that (Liu *et al.* 2002). Hence, a rough total wind project investment cost estimate of US$40 billion seems realistic.

As for actual power generation cost (in particular depreciation, operating cost, interest payments), Liu *et al.* (2002) estimate the dynamic costs over the lifetime at 2–5 per cent of initial investment. Using this as a very rough guidepost, power generation cost would add another US$800 million to US$2 billion to the estimated investment cost, making US$1 billion a reasonably conservative estimate.

How large a part of this bill has the Chinese government footed? It seems clear that other funding sources have been negligible. The Global Wind Energy Council (GWEC) cited total wind investment in China in 2006 at 16.27 billion RMB, noting that no private sector or foreign investor had won any tenders (Li *et al.* 2007). For 2009 GWEC indicates that private sector and foreign investor participation is well below 10 per cent (Li *et al.* 2010). The almost full state ownership of the Chinese power sector also means the recent mandated market share policy has been almost completely government-funded.

Adding up the estimated investment and power generation cost, and assuming a 90 per cent Chinese government share of investment,[16] yields a very rough estimate of some US$37 billion in Chinese government investment in wind projects and their actual operation (Castano 2011).

The government (and arguably also the non-government portion of the) implicit subsidies provided to cover the costs throughout the whole grid of wind generation through sharing of extra cost for grid-connected wind power compared to conventional power generation between 2003 and now should be added to the sum above, to the extent that this subsidy also covers a reasonable profit in addition to actual costs. We estimate the subsidy as the difference between an (assumed) weighted average wind power tariff (0.55 RMB (US$0.085) per kilowatt-hour, excluding tax) and an (assumed) weighted average conventional power tariff (0.3 RMB (US$0.046) per kilowatt-hour) over the period, multiplied by the net generation per year (see Table 3.5).

NREL (2004) estimated the overhead (operating) expenses for China's central government renewable-energy agencies related to management, R&D, training, equipment certification and inspection at US$181 million based on an estimated 100,000 staff and average 1998 salary levels. While this describes the situation during the second phase, it is also relevant for the two other phases (we have not been able to find more updated estimates). It seems reasonable to assume that almost all such costs would be covered by the government. Wind power is only part of this, but it probably had a decent share, and the estimate did not include all administrative costs at all levels of government.

Outlays for dedicated infrastructure and R&D costs exclusive of personnel costs would come in addition to the above, and would probably also have limited contribution from foreign investors. However, the Chinese government made use of bilateral and multilateral aid to build-up R&D, planning and policy-making capabilities in the mid-1990s (Lema and Ruby 2007). Regarding grid connection costs, the government-owned State Grid Corporation has spent 42 billion RMB (US$6.5 billion) on power lines for wind projects, and plans smart grid investments – where wind power is a priority – of two trillion RMB (US$310 billion) in both the current five-year plan and the next (Schwartz 2011; ResearchViews 2011). It recently promised at least 90GW of wind power by 2015 and 150GW by 2020 (Wang 2011).

Table 3.5 Estimated Chinese wind power subsidy 2003–2009

Year	*Wind electricity net generation (billion kWh)*	*Subsidy (billion RMB (US$))*
2003	0.99	0.25 (0.04)
2004	1.27	0.32 (0.05)
2005	1.93	0.48 (0.07)
2006	3.67	0.92 (0.14)
2007	5.42	1.36 (0.21)
2008	12.43	3.11 (0.48)
2009	25.00	6.25 (0.97)
Total	50.71	12.69 (1.9)

Source: US EIA (2011a).

Notes
Difference between total and sum of individual years of subsidy in dollars is due to rounding.

Starting in 2010, the leading Chinese developers (e.g. Longyuan, Datang, Huaneng, Huadian) and manufacturers (e.g. Sinovel, Goldwind) have been – or are in the process of being – listed on stock exchanges (Tong 2011; Rahman 2011). This allows them to fund further domestic and international expansion, but also opens them for non-Chinese ownership. However, most companies have floated only a minor portion of their shares. This means that though the share of Chinese government investment could be reduced in relative terms, it will likely increase in absolute terms, and government control will remain.

3.3.5 Stakeholders, knowledge and natural endowments

China's electric power grid is operated by two state-owned enterprises (SOEs); about 90 per cent of wind power is generated by the renewable-energy subsidiaries of five SOEs plus other SOEs; and most of China's wind power generation and transmission equipment is produced by SOEs (Dewey & LeBoeuf LLP 2010). These enterprises enjoy much better relations with banks than (foreign) private sector players, can accept less profitable projects and can justify investments on other grounds than pure profitability. In contrast, private sector involvement in China's wind sector has been hampered by regulatory and investment risks, long payback times, low profit margins and lack of long-term loans with low interest rates (Lin 1998). Exceptions are purchasers of carbon credits from wind projects, as well as selected developers and manufacturers.

Given that almost all funding for China's wind development comes from the government, some might think there have been no diverging interests and no internal conflicts in the process. However, we have already mentioned internal infighting between different bureaucracies for power and prestige related to a quickly growing wind industry; utilities' and grid companies' disincentive to accept to connect wind power; and the problem of fragmented grid authority.

The central government and provincial governments have had reasonably aligned incentives, as the former's wish for domestic production and more supply matches the latter's wish for lower wind power tariffs and more wind power investments (be they central government or foreign) (Lewis 2004). Local governments have an incentive to support manufacturers and developers based there, but have had little incentive to lower wind power tariffs, as they tax a percentage of the power tariff.

With regards to changes over time, it seems clear that stakeholders are better coordinated and incentives more aligned in the current development phase than the two previous ones. For example, the bureaucracies dealing with wind power have been merged; there is a clearer division between grid companies and project development companies; and there is a clearer incentive for grid companies and utilities to connect wind power plants. However, manufacturing is the exception to the rule. It is characterized by an overly large number of new entrants, supported by county governments hoping for tax revenue, trying to use skill sets developed in other fields (e.g. aviation and machine industry) to gain market share.

China has very significant wind resources, but has only to a rather limited extent been able to map and analyse them systematically. This is valid both at a general and site-specific level. Wind resource data, and tools used to optimize wind project locations, are sub-standard (Wallace *et al.* 2006). Wind measurements have been done at too low heights and in irrelevant places, and the most commonly used micro-siting tools do not seem adapted to Chinese conditions. This likely results in suboptimal siting, making projects less profitable than expected. It has likely also hampered development because decision-makers have not been aware of the potential for growth in installed wind power capacity. Li (Li, J. 2009), noting major differences between others' projections, recently estimated the realistically achievable onshore wind capacity at 600–1,000 GW, plus 100–200 GW offshore wind capacity. Throughout the first two phases, China's wind resources were often estimated at 253 GW.

4 Lessons for financing emission reduction initiatives in developing countries

4.1 Positive lessons

Both cases analysed in this chapter highlight lessons with potential generic validity for financing of GHG emission reductions in developing countries.

The first is to consciously link the financing of emission reduction initiatives with the gradual build-up of a local industry supplying the products and services needed for the reduction initiative in question. In Brazil, the industry existed already and was improved and expanded; in China, it was almost built from scratch. Industrial development is more likely to secure continued political support in the host country because it yields tax revenue and produces a local constituency. Furthermore, supply of products and services will in many cases reduce costs substantially compared to imports. The first reason for this is shorter transport distances, lack of custom duties, and lower labour and material costs locally. The second is that the link between donor funding and imported technology can provide a disincentive for cost reductions through (domestic or international) competition. The guidelines for funding should nevertheless ensure that entities from foreign countries are able to establish themselves in the host country and compete on equal terms with domestic players.

Second, finance has to reflect needs. In Brazil, the subsidies for ethanol are no longer needed, as the technology has become competitive on its own. A key question is when to phase-out subsidies. In Brazil, it was almost a lucky coincidence that, after market liberalization, oil prices started to rise again, and that the flex-fuel motors emerged. In China, the planning authorities tried to define a maximum price at a time when the industry was not mature enough for cost-cutting, resulting in stagnation. Similarly, the wind concessions initiative led to unsustainable underbidding – the prices bid in the 2007 round were at the same level or higher than the prices bid in 2003, despite the equipment cost reductions in the meantime. Wind power will still need subsidies in China for many years, especially if its 2020 carbon intensity target is to be met, but subsidies may nevertheless be possible to phase out gradually, especially if the price of conventional coal power keeps on rising.

4.2 Replicability of support and financial strategy

While it might be too early to conclude in the case of China, in terms of finance and support, Brazil's ethanol programme and China's wind power development effort seem to have several features in common:

- Through a combination of public funding and policy instruments well-adapted to the characteristics of the domestic industry, the government has provided a relatively protected strategic niche market for that industry.
- In line with the idea of dynamic efficiency (Christiansen 2002), public funding and policy instruments have (1) supported both supply and demand over a long time period, and (2) stimulated *both* R&D, strategic niche market introduction *and* diffusion into a domestic and international mass market.
- A mandated market share has been introduced for the new entrant technology, with extra tough requirements put on major SOEs (electricity utilities in China, fuel producer and distributor Petrobrás in Brazil).
- The government has set realistic mid- and long-term targets.
- When the domestic industry is ready for exports to a mass market, the support adapted specifically to the needs of that industry is toned down or phased out.

The feasibility of a domestically centred, government-dominated strategy for a particular mitigation initiative in a particular developing country, such as that followed by Brazil and China in the cases examined in this chapter, likely rests on at least the following preconditions:

- The country in question is large enough to muster large and sustained domestic demand.
- The domestic market for the technology at play is protected (either through measures such as minimum content requirements or high import tariffs, or because the technology itself is still not mature, so that no important foreign competitors are there).
- The country's government must have significant administrative capacity and financial muscle.
- The country must have natural endowments making it suitable for developing the initiative.

Few developing countries match all, or even most, of the above criteria, and combinations of suitable countries and initiatives would be even more limited. But there seems to be an alternative to China's and Brazil's strategies, namely targeting regional or global niche markets. Lewis and Wiser (2007: 1848) conclude that 'in the early years of a wind company's development … the home market is likely to make up the majority of that company's market share; more mature wind power companies tend to export a large share of their wind turbines, especially once they have saturated the domestic market'. However, there are countries with limited domestic demand and/or natural endowments that have managed to become renewable-energy leaders. For example, long-time global wind industry leader Denmark's wind resources are not extraordinary, and export markets have played a crucial role in its development.[17] Furthermore, Norway has fostered one of the leading solar companies with an almost non-existent home market for solar photovoltaics (Christiansen and Buen 2002).

4.3 Challenges

4.3.1 Transparency and sustainability

The GHG mitigation initiatives in developing countries envisaged in the discussion about nationally appropriate mitigation actions (NAMAs[18]), are large-scale and long-term. The case studies in this chapter – each spanning 30-plus years – faced the same two institutional challenges. First, there has been very limited transparency on the amount, duration, source and precise coverage of finance provided. Different sources of information consulted for this chapter quite often provided different figures. Perhaps more information was available at the time, in local languages, or perhaps nobody saw the need for it. However, such clarifications are required for future detailed guidelines for NAMAs, as otherwise monitoring, reporting and verification (MRV) of their funding will be an impossible task over the timeframe of such a programme.

Second, the government agencies involved in the two initiatives merged, were closed down, changed their responsibilities or changed their name – several times. The same could happen with the mitigation initiatives themselves. In the case of China, calling its wind power effort a unitary programme would be a stretch. This problem is unlikely to be less prevalent in countries whose government structures are far less developed than those of Brazil and China. Developing country mitigation finance guidelines should hence be carefully designed to promote programme stability and consistency over time, but should also provide for adjustments underway.

Even if appropriate institutions, support policies and sources of funding are established, the long-term sustainability of the programmes can be affected by external shocks that the host country is not able to influence. In the Brazilian case, the peaks and troughs of the alcohol programme were closely linked to the evolution of oil and sugar prices in the international market. However, the government and the industry were able to respond to these challenges and adapt to them. In addition, when the domestic industry was established, it became an important political player, so that support for the programme became unstoppable. While reducing the dependency on international oil prices due to oil imports has been a driver behind China's wind power thrust, it is less clear that oil price changes have influenced industry growth. China was also able to shrug off the financial crisis with only a few bruises. The almost full government ownership of the sector is the main reason; hence, smaller countries with less government involvement in the sector in question could face more difficulties than China.

4.3.2 Misaligned incentives and unexpected consequences

Large-scale programmes can also become the victims of their own success, which can be seen in both cases described in this chapter. In the 1980s, the Brazilian ethanol programme suffered a severe funding crisis due to its rapid growth. As described above, as the ethanol price was being subsidized from the taxes charged on gasoline, the gradual shift in demand from gasoline to ethanol meant that the source of funding was being depleted. As a result, subsidies had to be scaled down. In the case of wind power development in China, problems are arising for several reasons. First, it faces severe grid connection constraints. The main reason is that wind power tends to be produced in remote areas where the grid is the weakest, but the problems also stem from lack of transparency on planned wind energy development (Liu, Yuanyuan 2011).[19] Until early 2011, wind projects below 50 MW did not require central planning authorities' approval (from this year on the energy planning authorities need to approve them (*China Daily* 2011)). As a consequence, lots of wind projects are 49.5 MW, and larger projects are split into 49.5 MW modules. CWEI (2010) estimated that 30 per cent of China's installed capacity had yet to be grid-connected, and that power purchase agreements put this risk on developers.[20] Furthermore, there is a lag in the development of the storage capacity (e.g. through new hydro power) needed to balance the huge increase in the inflow of intermittent wind power (Martinot 2010).

There are two other reasons why the Chinese government funding has been ineffective in terms of actual wind power output, and which will likely require further government investments in R&D and quality assurance institutions. The first is wind resource data quality, mentioned in Section 3.3.5. The second is that Chinese equipment still has not had the same quality over its lifetime as foreign equipment.[21] China's decision-makers increasingly worry that the wind turbines currently being installed in large numbers in its desert areas will have a too short lifespan to give a proper return on investment (Zhang 2010).

4.3.3 International competition

The host country's eagerness to support local manufacturers and developers might result in disputes and challenges in the international sphere. Recently, China removed subsidies awarded to manufacturers using local equipment by closing down the 'Ride the Wind' programme and the Special Fund for Wind Power Manufacturing (Tables 3.3 and 3.4) (Liu, Yiyi 2011). One reason was probably that the US Trade Representative had started investigation into a petition from the powerful organization United Steelworkers (OUSTR 2010, 2011), claiming that China violated its World Trade Organization (WTO) accession agreement by: (1) imposing export restraints on rare earths used in wind turbines; (2) favouring domestic manufacturers through domestic content requirements; (3) providing illegal export subsidies to wind manufacturers; and (4) preventing non-Chinese firms from accessing CERs due to the rule that CER sellers shall be majority-owned Chinese companies.

Similarly, the Brazilian industry has been growing strongly in recent years with the prospects to expand into the export market. It has therefore attracted significant foreign capital and joint ventures, both for production and infrastructure development. Still, it faces barriers: even if a WTO dispute is not likely here, because the industry is no longer subsidized, important potential ethanol buyers have large domestic subsidies to protect their own industries from cheaper Brazilian ethanol.

In the case of NAMAs, especially those seeking international support and funding, such increasing competition between the host country's own industry and potential donors' may become an issue.

5 Concluding remarks

Our assessment of the motivations and driving forces behind the two initiatives analysed in this chapter shows that it is debatable whether they can purely be regarded as climate change mitigation programmes. Both Brazil and China had interests other than climate change when they launched their respective programmes: energy security; industrial development and competitiveness; and rural development. From this point of view, it can be argued that climate change mitigation was a side benefit of programmes that were rather driven by domestic interest politics.

Future climate change mitigation in the South will need to learn from these experiences and mobilize domestic interests in developing countries, so that they receive the necessary local support for implementation, not only from the financial point of view, but also in terms of political, institutional and legal support, private sector involvement and ownership by the public. Only this can ensure long-term sustainability of such programmes.

Acknowledgements

The wind power case study is partly based on field work and interviews conducted in the period 2001–2009. Jørund Buen wishes to thank Shi Pengfei for providing historical data on Chinese wind turbine installations, and Ida Bjørkum for help in mapping research on Chinese wind power policy.

Notes

1 We purposefully have tried to avoid extensive use of acronyms for government agencies, as the numerous changes that have taken place over the period in question would confuse the reader. For more details on organizational and institutional aspects, see Barzelay (1986), Hira and de Oliveira (2009) and Puerto Rico *et al.* (2010) (Brazil), as well as Yeh and Lewis (2004) and Lema and Ruby (2007) (China).

2 Throughout this chapter, the terms 'alcohol' and 'ethanol' will be used interchangeably to denote ethylic alcohol for use as fuel. Note that in order to be blended with gasoline, ethanol can only have a maximum of 0.4 per cent of water content; this ethanol is thus called anhydrous. If used as fuel in pure form (without blending with gasoline), ethanol can have up to 5 per cent water content, thus being called hydrated ethanol.

3 Even since then the emission reduction impact of the programme has been debated, due to indirect land-use effects of expanding sugarcane plantations (Sparovek *et al.* 2009; Pacca and Moreira 2009; Lapola *et al.* 2010).

4 Similarly, CDWEDPO and CREIA (2009) distinguish between initial demonstration (1986–1993), industrialization (1994–2003) and scale-up and turbine localization (2003–); Lema and Ruby (2007) divide the period into an initial phase (1986–1993), an incremental phase (1994–1999) and a coordinated phase (2000–2006).

5 However, the dominant micro wind turbine is an adapted version of a turbine licensed from a Swedish company in 1988 (Lew 2000).

6 This section also builds on interviews with Qi (2002) and Huade New Technology Company representatives (2002).

7 'We have tried to bring [the economic operations and planning bureaucracies] together, but have failed' (He 2002).

8 RMB stands for Renminbi ('peoples' money').

9 Vestas has even customized a new wind turbine to Chinese conditions (Hille 2009).

10 'We are a private company but we seek to obtain government funding for research for a new control system' (New Image Electric representative 2006). 'The company is privately owned, and financed by investments from investment companies from China.... We were previously a research institute under CAS [Chinese Academy of Sciences]' (Zhongke Hengyuan Energy Technology Co. Ltd representative 2006).

11 Goldwind recently claimed sales of 200 turbines abroad, of which 80 were to the United States (Liu, Yiyi 2011). Micro wind turbines have been exported to other Asian countries since the 1980s (Lew 2000).

12 See Buen (2006) for insights into the case of the Danish wind turbine industry.

13 Where no conversion from yuan (RMB) to US dollars is available in the source consulted, the historical annual exchange rate listed by the State Administration of Foreign Exchange of the People's Republic of China and People's Bank of China cited in Chinability (2010) for the publication year of the source in question is used. For data that is still valid, the current exchange rate is used.

14 It is not yet clear how large the demand will be for CERs post-2012, and hence the future CER price is uncertain (see Chapter 1). It is also possible that China will restrict its post-2012 CER exports.

15 Gamos (1999) cites studies indicating Inner Mongolia had an off-grid wind market share of 75–80 per cent in the early and mid-1990s, suggesting additional subsidies have been awarded by other provinces. The amount does not seem to have been adjusted for inflation.

16 This is in line with Shi (2009), who estimated that 70 per cent of financing prior to that time had come from the central government and 20 per cent from local governments.

17 When California removed tax rebates for wind power in the mid-1980s, almost all Danish wind manufacturers went bankrupt (Buen 2006), which at least does not signal full dependence on the home market.

18 'Nationally appropriate mitigation actions' is a concept coined in the international climate negotiations referring to GHG emission reduction activities that are to take place in developing countries in accordance with their national circumstances. Discussions are under way on how they should be financed – either domestically, with international support, and/or through the carbon market. See Chapter 7 for a detailed discussion of the concept.

19 That said, Xinjiang Wind Energy Company representatives (2002) referred to a study suggesting that the maximum feasible share of wind power in the grid should be 4 per cent.
20 Bloomberg has cited sources claiming 40 per cent of capacity lies idle (Ying and Bi 2010).
21 'We have technical problems and less quality than the foreign products' (Chongqing Chongchi Wind Power Gearbox Ltd representative 2006). 'The main difficulties with the technology [from Chinese manufacturers] is that it is not precise enough; that it is not really the capacity announced; or that it is taking more time to produce' (Beiyu International Ltd representative 2006).

References

ANFAVEA (2010) *Anuário da Indústria Automobilística Brasileira 2010*, São Paulo: Associaçao Nacional dos Fabricantes de Veículos Automotores (ANFAVEA). Online. Available: http://anfavea2010.virapagina.com.br/anfavea2010/ (accessed 22 June 2011).

Asia Today (2011) 'China's installed nuclear power capacity to reach 70 GW in 2020', *Asia Today*. Online. Available: http://asiatoday.com/pressrelease/chinas-installed-nuclear-power-capacity-reach-70-gw-2020 (accessed 9 July 2011).

Barzelay, M. (1986) *The Politicized Market Economy: Alcohol in Brazil's Energy Strategy*, Berkeley and Los Angeles: University of California Press.

Beiyu International Ltd representative (2006) 'Interview', interviewed by Jorund Buen, at Great Wall World Renewable Energy Forum, Beijing, 24 October.

BNDES and CGEE (2008) *Sugarcane-based Bioethanol: Energy for Sustainable Development*, Rio de Janeiro: Banco Nacional de Desenvolvimento Econômico e Social (BNDES) and Centro de Gestão e Estudos Estratégicos (CGEE).

Brown, C.-A. (2001) 'Wind power in China: current status and implications for the international community', *Refocus*, 2 (3): 24–8.

BTM Consult (2011) 'International wind energy development: World Market Update 2010', AltEnergyMag.com. Online. Available: www.altenergymag.com/emagazine/2011/05/international-wind-energy-development-world-market-update-2010/1713 (accessed 1 July 2011).

Buen, J. (1998a) 'China's energy-environmental dilemma: strategies and framework conditions', *Forum for Development Studies*, 1: 163–203.

Buen, J. (1998b) 'China's new renewable energy policy: political priorities and market potential', *FNI Report 1–1998*, Lysaker: The Fridtjof Nansen Institute.

Buen, J. (2006) 'Danish and Norwegian wind industry: the relationship between policy instruments, innovation and diffusion', *Energy Policy*, 34 (18): 3887–97.

Buen, J. (2010) 'Amendments to China's Renewable Energy Law: increased certainty for CDM developers?', *Analyst Update 11 January*, Oslo: Point Carbon.

Buen, J. and Røine, K. (2010) 'Understanding E+/E– policy: some pluses, lots of minuses', *Analyst Update 20 September*, Oslo: Point Carbon.

Castano, I. (2011) 'China installing wind-power capacity as fast as it can', Renewable Energy World. Online. Available: www.renewableenergyworld.com/rea/news/print/article/2011/04/china-installing-wind-power-capacity-as-fast-as-it-can (accessed 30 June 2011).

Castro, P., Hayashi, D., Kristiansen, K.-O., Michaelowa, A. and Stadelmann, M. (2011) 'Scoping study: 'Linking RE promotion policies with international carbon trade (LINK)', International Energy Agency – Renewable Energy Technology Deployment (IEA-RETD). Online. Available: www.iea-retd.org/page.aspx?idsection=109 (accessed 24 July 2011).

CDM EB (2011) 'Meeting report, 61st Meeting, 3 June', Clean Development Mechanism Executive Board, United Nations Framework Convention on Climate Change.

CDWEDPO and CREIA (2009) 'Study report on development of policy of Chinese wind power tariff'. Online. Available: http://cdm.ccchina.gov.cn/WebSite/CDM/UpFile/File2364.doc.

Chinability (2010) Renminbi (Chinese yuan) exchange rates 1969–2010. Online. Available: www.chinability.com/Rmb.htm (accessed 30 June 2011).

China Daily (2011) 'China drafting new rules for small wind farm projects'. Online. Available: www.chinadaily.com.cn/bizchina/2011-04/11/content_12302327.htm (accessed 14 October 2011).

ChinaFAQs (2010) 'An emerging revolution: clean technology research, development and innovation in China'. Online. Available: www.chinafaqs.org/library/chinafaqs-emerging-revolution-clean-technology-research-development-and-innovation-china (accessed 9 July 2011).

Chongqing Chongchi Wind Power Gearbox Ltd representative (2006) 'Interview', interviewed by Jorund Buen, at Great Wall World Renewable Energy Forum, Beijing, 24 October.

Christiansen, A. (2002) 'Promoting environmental innovation in the energy sector: an analytical framework for dynamic efficiency assessments', *Energy & Environment*, 13 (6): 813–32.

Christiansen, A. and Buen, J. (2002) 'Managing environmental innovation in the energy sector: the case of photovoltaic and wave power development in Norway', *International Journal of Innovation Management*, 6 (3): 233–56.

Coelho, S., Bolognini, M. and Machado Paletta, C. (1999) *The Current Situation of PROALCOOL the Brazilian Alcohol Program*, Sao Paulo: The National Reference Center on Biomass.

Conrad, B. and Meissner, M. (2011) 'Catching a second wind: changing the logic of international cooperation in China's wind energy sector', *GPPi Policy Paper*, 12, Global Public Policy Institute.

CWEI (2010) 'China's wind energy sector in 2009 managed to surprise even many optimists'. Online. Available: www.cwei.org.cn/windpowerfor/News_Content.aspx?ID=3537&Type=2 (accessed 23 June 2011).

CWEI (2011) 'China's wind-energy facing slowdown', Online. Available: www.cwei.org.cn/windpowerfor/News_Content.aspx?ID=4061&Type=2 (accessed 23 June 2011).

Cyranoski, D. (2009) 'Renewable energy: Beijing's windy bet', *Nature*, 457: 372–4.

Dai, H., Chen, S., Wu, X. and Cai, J. (1996) 'Grid connected wind power in China: development, problems and solutions', paper presented at the International Conference on Energy Efficiency Improvements: Coal and Renewables, Beijing, 3–4 December.

de Araujo, J. and Ghirardi, A. (1987) 'Substitution of petroleum products in Brazil: urgent issues', *Energy Policy*, 15 (1): 22–39.

de Oliveira, A. (1991) 'Reassessing the Brazilian alcohol programme', *Energy Policy*, 19 (1): 47–55.

Dewey & LeBoeuf LLP (2010) 'China's promotion of the renewable electric power equipment industry: hydro, wind, solar, biomass', National Foreign Trade Council (NFTC). Online. Available: www.nftc.org/default/Press%20Release/2010/China%20Renewable%20Energy.pdf.

Dias Leite, A. (2009) *Energy in Brazil: Towards a Renewable Energy Dominated System*, London: Earthscan.

East-West Center, Argonne National Laboratory and State Science and Technology Commission (1993) 'National response strategy for climate change: People's Republic of China – Draft final report', Office of Environment, Asian Development Bank (ADB).

Economy, E. (1994) 'Negotiating the terrain of global climate change policy in the Soviet Union and China: linking international and domestic decisionmaking pathways', unpublished thesis, University of Michigan.

Fang, T. (2011) 'To develop nuclear power in advance of ensuring security', State Grid Energy Research Institute (SGERI) Viewpoints. Online. Available: www.sgeri.sgcc.com.cn/english/Center/Viewpoints/97998.shtml (accessed 7 July 2011).

Gamesa (2011) 'Gamesa signs MoUs for 900 MW of turbine capacity with 3 Chinese companies: to support Longyuan's "Go Global" effort in joint international wind farm development'.

Gamos Ltd (1999) 'Evaluating the impact of wind generators in Inner Mongolia: project technical report', UK Department for International Development, Gamos.

GEF (2002) 'Final project brief: wind power development project in the People's Republic of China (PRC)'.

Goldemberg, J. (2007) 'Ethanol for a sustainable energy future', *Science*, 315: 808–10.

Goldemberg, J. and Macedo, I.C. (1994) 'Brazilian alcohol program: an overview', *Energy for Sustainable Development*, 1 (1): 17–22.

Goldemberg, J., Coelho, S. and Lucon, O. (2004a) 'How adequate policies can push renewables', *Energy Policy*, 32 (9): 1141–6.

Goldemberg, J., Coelho, S., Nastari, P. and Lucon, O. (2004b) 'Ethanol learning curve: the Brazilian experience', *Biomass & Bioenergy*, 26 (3): 301–4.

GTZ (2002) 'Producing electricity from renewable energy sources: energy sector framework in 15 countries in Asia, Africa and Latin America, 2002 edition', Gesellschaft für Technische Zusammenarbeit (GTZ).

GWEC (Global Wind Energy Council) (2011) 'China adds 18.9 GW of new wind power capacity in 2010'. Online. Available: www.gwec.net/index.php?id=30&no_cache=1&tx_ttnews%5Btt_news%5D=287&tx_ttnews%5BbackPid%5D=4&cHash=c5a5b5659f (accessed 9 July 2011).

Hall, D., Rosillo-Calle, F. and de Groot, P. (1992) 'Biomass energy: lessons from case studies in developing countries', *Energy Policy*, 20 (1): 62–73.

Haum, R. (2004) 'Technology transfer under the Clean Development Mechanism: a case study of conflict and cooperation between Germany and China in wind energy', *Schriftenreihe des Instituts für Ökologische Wirtschaftsforschung* (IÖW), 175/*04*, IÖW.

He, P. (2002) 'Interview', interviewed by Jorund Buen, at UNDP offices, Beijing, 9 October.

He, G. and Morse, R. (2010) 'Making carbon offsets work in the developing world: lessons from the Chinese wind controversy', *Program on Energy and Sustainable Development Working Paper*, 90, Stanford University.

Hille, K. (2009) 'Vestas blows new life into Chinese energy', *Financial Times*. Online. Available: http://cachef.ft.com/cms/s/0/e169786a-2aa9–11de-8415–00144feabdc0.html#axzz1RPAcdANe (accessed 7 July 2011).

Hira, A. and de Oliveira, L.G. (2009) 'No substitute for oil? How Brazil developed its ethanol industry', *Energy Policy*, 37 (6): 2450–6.

Huade New Technology Company representatives (2002) 'Interview', interviewed by Jorund Buen, at Huade New Technology Company offices, Hohhot, China, 22 October.

Johnson, T., Li, J., Jiang, Z. and Taylor, R. (eds) (1996) *China: Issues and Options in Greenhouse Gas Emissions Control*, Washington, DC: World Bank.

Kemp, R., Schot, J. and Hoogma, R. (1998) 'Regime shifts to sustainability through processes of niche formation: the approach of Strategic Niche Management', *Technology Analysis & Strategic Management*, 10: 175–95.

Lapola, D., Schaldach, R., Alcamo, J., Bondeau, A., Koch, J., Koelking, C. and Priess, J. (2010) 'Indirect land-use changes can overcome carbon savings from biofuels in Brazil', *Proceedings of the National Academy of Sciences*, 107 (8): 3388–93.

La Rovere, E., Pereira, A. and Simões, A. (2010) 'Biofuels and sustainable energy development in Brazil', *World Development*, 39 (6): 1026–36.

Lema, A. and Ruby, K. (2007) 'Between fragmented authoritarianism and policy coordination: creating a Chinese market for wind energy', *Energy Policy*, 35 (7): 3879–90.

Lew, D. (2000) 'Alternatives to coal and candles: wind power in China', *Energy Policy*, 28: 271–86.

Lewis, J. (2004) 'Conceding too much? Conflicts between the government and developers in promoting the China "Wind Concession" project model', paper presented at the World Renewable Energy Congress VIII, Denver, 29 August–3 September.

Lewis, J. (2005) 'Part of the climate change problem ... and the solution? Chinese-made wind power technology and opportunities for dissemination', paper presented at the Breslauer Symposium, University of California International and Area Studies.

Lewis, J. (2007) 'A review of the potential international trade implications of key wind power industry policies in China', Energy Foundation, China Sustainable Energy Program. Online. Available: www.resource-solutions.org/pub_pdfs/China.wind.policy.and.intl.trade.law.Oct.07.pdf.

Lewis, J. (2010) 'The evolving role of carbon finance in promoting renewable energy development in China', *Energy Policy*, 38: 2875–86.

Lewis, J. and Wiser, R. (2007) 'Fostering a renewable energy technology industry: an international comparison of wind industry policy support mechanisms', *Energy Policy*, 35 (3): 1844–57.

Li, Baoshan (2002) 'Interview', interviewed by Jorund Buen, at MOST offices, Beijing, 18 October.

Li, J. (2002) 'Interview', interviewed by Jorund Buen, at China Renewable Energy Industry Association offices, Beijing, 9 October.

Li, J. (2009) 'The development and perspective of China wind power', paper presented at a workshop on sustainable energy, DTU Campus, Lyngby, 14–15 January.

Li, J., Song, Y. and Hu, X. (2004) 'A renewable energy development plan and strategy for China', *EETIC InfoPoint*, 3 (4): 4–6.

Li, J., Gao, H., Shi, P., Shi, J., Ma, L., Qin, H., and Song, Y. (2007) 'China wind power report 2007'. Online. Available: www.greenpeace.org/raw/content/eastasia/press/reports/wind-power-report.pdf.

Li, J., Shi, P. and Gao, H. (2010) 'China wind power outlook 2010', Renewable Energy Industries Association, Global Wind Energy Council, Greenpeace. Online. Available: www.greenpeace.org/eastasia/Global/eastasia/publications/reports/climate-energy/2010/2010-china-wind-power-outlook.pdf.

Lin, G. (1998) 'Wind energy development and dissemination in China: prospects and constraints in an institutional context', *CICERO Working Paper 1998*, 7, Center for International Climate and Environmental Research.

Liu, H. (2002) 'Interview', interviewed by Jorund Buen, at SETC offices, Beijing, 14 October.

Liu, W., Gan, L. and Zhang, X. (2002) 'Cost-competitive incentives for wind energy development in China: institutional dynamics and policy changes', *Energy Policy*, 30: 753–65.

Liu, Yingling (2006) 'Made in China, or made *by* China? Chinese wind turbine manufacturers struggle to enter own market', WorldWatch Institute. Online. Available: www.worldwatch.org/node/3931 (accessed 24 June 2011).

Liu, Yiyi (2011) 'China to halt wind turbine subsidies', *China Daily*. Online. Available: www.chinadaily.com.cn/cndy/2011–06/08/content_12654114.htm (accessed 21 June 2011).

Liu, Yuanyuan (2011) 'China seeks big wind in a push to standardize project size', *Renewable Energy World*. Online. Available: www.renewableenergyworld.com/rea/news/article/2011/05/china-to-standardize-wind-power-projects (accessed 9 July 2011).

Macedo, I. and Horta Nogueira, L. (2004) *Cadernos NAE: Biocombustíveis*, Brasilia: Núcleo de Assuntos Estratégicos da Presidência da República.

Martinot, E. (2010) 'Renewable power for China: past, present, and future', *Frontiers of Energy and Power Engineering in China*, 4 (3): 287–94.

Ministério de Minas e Energia (2011) 'Balanço Energético Nacional, Séries Completas, Capítulo 2: Oferta e Demanda de Energia por Fonte 1970–2009'. Online. Available: https://ben.epe.gov.br/BENSeriesCompletas.aspx (accessed 22 June 2011).

Moreira, J. and Goldemberg, J. (1999) 'The alcohol program', *Energy Policy*, 27 (4): 229–45.

NDRC (2007) 'Medium and long-term development plan for renewable energy in China', abbreviated Version, English Draft, National Development Reform Commission (NDRC).

New Image Electric representative (2006), 'Interview', interviewed by Jorund Buen, at Great Wall World Renewable Energy Forum, Beijing, 24 October.

NREL (2004) 'Renewable energy policy in China: financial incentives', National Renewable Energy Laboratory. Online. Available: www.nrel.gov/docs/fy04osti/36045.pdf.

OUSTR (2010) 'Petition for relief under Section 301 of the Trade Act of 1974, as amended: China's policies affecting trade and investment in green technology' Office of the US Trade Representative, On behalf of United Steel Workers, 1 (9).

OUSTR (2011) 'China ends wind power equipment subsidies challenged by the United States in WTO dispute', Office of the US Trade Representative. Online. Available: www.ustr.gov/about-us/press-office/press-releases/2011/june/china-ends-wind-power-equipment-subsidies-challenged (accessed 13 July 2011).

Pacca, S. and Moreira, J. (2009) 'Historical carbon budget of the Brazilian ethanol program', *Energy Policy*, 37 (11): 4863–73.

People's Daily Online (2009) 'China to have 100 GW wind power energy capacity by 2020', *People's Daily Online*. Online. Available: http://english.people.com.cn/90001/90778/90857/90860/6650353.html (accessed 9 July 2011).

People's Daily Online (2011) 'China to boost offshore wind power to 30 gigawatts by 2020', *People's Daily Online*. Online. Available: http://cdm.ccchina.gov.cn/english/NewsInfo.asp?NewsId=5436 (accessed 1 July 2011).

Puerto Rico, J., Mercedes, S. and Sauer, I. (2010) 'Genesis and consolidation of the Brazilian bioethanol: a review of policies and incentive mechanisms', *Renewable & Sustainable Energy Reviews*, 14 (7): 1874–87.

Puppim de Oliveira, J. (2002) 'The policymaking process for creating competitive assets for the use of biomass energy: the Brazilian alcohol programme', *Renewable & Sustainable Energy Reviews*, 6 (1–2): 129–40.

Qi, L. (2002) 'Interview', interviewed by Jorund Buen, at Inner Mongolia Wind Power Development Company offices, Hohhot, China, 21 October.

Rahman (2011) 'China's wind sector steps on the accelerator', Eco Periodicals. Online. Available: http://ecoperiodicals.com/2010/03/17/china%E2%80%99s-wind-sector-steps-on-the-accelerator (accessed 9 July 2011).

Raufer, R. and Wang, S. (2003) 'Navigating the policy path for support of wind power in China', *China Environment Series*, 6: 37–53.

ResearchViews (2011) 'SGCC to expand smart grid application in developing electric-charging stations and wind-power installations in 2011', ResearchViews. Online. Available: www.researchviews.com/energy/oilandgas/energyefficiency/NewsReport.aspx?ArticleID=437634§or=energy%20efficiency (accessed 9 July 2011).

Rosillo-Calle, F. and Cortez, L. (1998) 'Towards ProAlcool II: a review of the Brazilian bioethanol programme', *Biomass and Bioenergy*, 14 (2): 115–24.

RTCCCCS (Research Team of China Climate Change Country Study) (1999) *China Climate Change Country Study*, Beijing: Tsinghua University Press, supported by the US Department of Energy and State Science and Technology Commission.

Schwartz, L. (2011) 'The power grid and the wind industry in China: an update', *Renewable Energy World*. Online. Available: www.renewableenergyworld.com/rea/news/article/2011/05/the-power-grid-and-the-wind-industry-in-china-an-update (accessed 9 July 2011).

Serôa da Motta, R. (1987) 'The social viability of ethanol production in Brazil', *Energy Economics*, 9 (3): 176–82.

Serôa da Motta, R. and da Rocha Ferreira, L. (1988) 'The Brazilian National Alcohol Programme: an economic reappraisal and adjustments', *Energy Economics*, 10 (3): 229–34.

Shi, P. (2002) 'Interview with Shi Pengfei, Vice President, China Wind Energy Association', interviewed by Jorund Buen, at China Hydropower Planning General Institute offices, Beijing, 11 October.

Shi, P. (2009) 'Interview with Shi Pengfei, Vice President, China Wind Energy Association', interviewed by Jorund Buen, at China Hydropower Planning General Institute offices, Beijing, 14 September.

Shi, P. (2011) Data file containing installed wind power capacity in China 1985–2011, sent to Jorund Buen.

Sieg, K. (2004) 'Riding the wind', *New Energy*, 4 (4): 44. Online. Available: www.new-energy.info/index.php?id=848 (accessed 1 July 2011).

Sievert, T. (2010) 'China: wind power installed capacity to hit 200 GW by 2020'. Online. Available: www.windfair.net/press/8002.html (accessed 11 July 2011).

Sparovek, G., Barretto, A., Berndes, G., Martins, S. and Maule, R. (2009) 'Environmental, land-use and economic implications of Brazilian sugarcane expansion 1996–2006', *Mitigation and Adaptation Strategies for Global Change*, 14 (3): 285–98.

Tong, X. (2011) 'Huadian's new energy unit seeks public listing in 2011', Xinhuanet.com. Online. Available: http://news.xinhuanet.com/english2010/business/2011–02/06/c_13720638.htm (accessed 9 July 2011).

US EIA (2011a) 'Statistics on wind electricity net generation (billion kilowatthours)', US Energy Information Administration. Online. Available: www.eia.gov/cfapps/ipdbproject/iedindex3.cfm?tid=6&pid=37&aid=12&cid=CH,&syid=1980&eyid=2009&unit=BKWH (accessed 11 July 2011).

US EIA (2011b) 'Short-term energy outlook: real energy prices', US Energy Information Administration. Online. Available: www.eia.gov/emeu/steo/realprices/index.cfm (accessed 30 June 2011).

Vaupen, S.B. (1999) *Renewable Energy Markets in China: An Analysis of Renewable Energy Markets in Guangdong, Jiangxi, Jilin, and Yunnan Provinces, with Updated*

Information from Beijing, Golden, CO: National Renewable Energy Laboratory (NREL).

Wallace, W. (2002) 'Interview', interviewed by Jorund Buen, at CREIA offices, Beijing, 9 October.

Wallace, W., Wang, Z. and Liu, S. (2006) 'Support for wind resource assessment and wind farm development in China', paper presented at the Great Wall World Renewable Energy Forum, Beijing, 24–26 October.

Wang, D. (2011) 'State grid releases White Paper on wind power development', State Grid Corporation of China. Online. Available: www.sgcc.com.cn/ywlm/mediacenter/corporatenews/04/245999.shtml (accessed 9 July 2011).

Wilkinson, J. and Herrera, S. (2010) 'Biofuels in Brazil: debates and impacts', *The Journal of Peasant Studies*, 37 (4): 749–68.

World Bank (1999) 'Project implementation plan windfarm development component: China Renewable Energy Development Project', Online. Available: http://siteresources.worldbank.org/EXTRENENERGYTK/Resources/5138246–1237906527727/5950705–1239137586151/Project0Implem10Development0Project.pdf (accessed 7 July 2011).

Wu, Y. (2006) 'Interview with representative from Windey', interviewed by Jorund Buen, at Great Wall World Renewable Energy Forum, Beijing, 25 October.

Xinjiang Wind Energy Company (XWEC) representatives (2002) 'Interview', interviewed by Jorund Buen, at XWEC offices, Urumqi, China, 23 October.

Yang, M., Nguyen, F., De T'Serclaes, P. and Buchner, B. (2010) 'Wind farm investment risks under uncertain CDM benefit in China', *Energy Policy*, 38: 1436–47.

Yeh, E. and Lewis, J. (2004) 'State power and the logic of reform in China's electricity sector', *Pacific Affairs*, 77 (3): 437–66.

Ying, W. and Bi, W. (2010) 'China idles 40% of windpower turbine output capacity', *Bloomberg News*. Online. Available: www.bloomberg.com/apps/news?pid=newsarchive&sid=awwKSAHcRTHY (accessed 7 July 2011).

Yu, W. and Wang, L. (2002) 'Interview', interviewed by Jorund Buen, at Goldwind factory, Urumqi, China, 24 October.

Zhang, J. (2010) 'Wind power factories called "image projects"', *China Daily*. Online. Available: www.chinadaily.com.cn/china/2010–03/10/content_9567436.htm (accessed 13 July 2011).

Zhang, X., Lin, G., Gu, S. and Liu, W. (1999) 'Wind energy technology development and diffusion: a case study of Inner Mongolia, China', *CICERO Working Paper 1999*, 5, Center for International Climate and Environmental Research (CICERO).

Zhongke Hengyuan Energy Technology Co. Ltd representative (2006) 'Interview', interviewed by Jorund Buen, at Great Wall World Renewable Energy Forum, Beijing, 24 October.

4 The Adaptation Fund

Towards resilient economies in the developing world

Izabela Ratajczak-Juszko

1 Introduction

Climate change governance issues are still very much in the formative stages at both international and national levels in developed and developing countries. Consequently, they fail to address climate change adaptation needs adequately. Current international and national mitigation efforts are unlikely to meet the goal of limiting the average global temperature increase to 2°C, agreed at the Cancun COP (UNFCCC 2010). This means that adaptation to climate change impacts is unavoidable. According to the Third Assessment Report of the Intergovernmental Panel on Climate Change (IPCC), adaptation depends greatly on the adaptive capacity or adaptability of an affected system, region or community to cope with the impacts and risks of climate change (McCarthy *et al.* 2001). Adaptation to climate change impacts has become widely accepted in science, and climate policy as an inevitable social process in need of extensive funding (Stern 2006; Pielke *et al.* 2007). As Jerneck and Olsson (2010) argue, for adaptation to be successful the local level must be bridged in an effective way with the global level, at which the funds and mechanisms are available. Adaptation not only requires vast amounts of money, but also capacity and effective governance structures. The Australian *Garnaut Climate Change Review* (2008: 13) on issues related to reduction of costs of climate change through effective adaptation concluded that adaptation requires 'a strong applied science base; good markets for relocation of resources, goods and services; and capital for investment in defensive structures and new productive capacity that is more suitable to the new environment'. Therefore, challenges for researchers and policy-makers are the development of participatory knowledge-based adaptation based on local experience and priorities, as well as mobilization of sufficient global funds accessible for local needs.

This chapter presents the Adaptation Fund of the Kyoto Protocol as an innovative policy instrument. It could be a model for other international forms of 'intergovernmental grant systems' mandated to finance climate change in developing countries such as the Green Climate Fund.[1] The following sections will provide background on evolution of climate change finance and on economics of climate change adaptation. Section 2 will provide an introduction to the

Adaptation Fund while focusing on new concepts and its funding decisions. Reviewing in detail the Fund's evolution over the past three years since its inception offers insight into its future. Yet it is also apparent, as I lay out in this chapter, that the Adaptation Fund has potential as a model for adaptation finance in the post-2012 UNFCCC era.

2 The UN Framework Convention on Climate Change and Kyoto Protocol provisions on adaptation

As Fermann (1997) argues, the primary obligation in the UNFCCC can be divided into two groups. The first one concerns the actual abatement of greenhouse gases (GHG) (mitigation) while the second one relates to the need of financial resources and technology in developing countries. Adaptation to adverse effects of climate change has been recognized as an important element of the international climate change regime since its inception. However, limited availability of funding as well as limited capacity in developing countries to undertake vulnerability assessments impeded implementation of the UNFCCC's adaptation provisions (Yamin and Deplegde 2004).

The outcomes of UN climate change negotiations in recent years contributed to a paradigm shift in international climate policy. Climate change adaptation was recognized as equally important to climate change mitigation, which is formally the primary objective of the UNFCCC. However, explicit consideration of adaptation under the international regime is still in its infancy, and international policy fails to address the needs of developing countries (Stern 2006; Pielke *et al.* 2007; Müller 2008a; Ayers *et al.* 2010). Moreover, despite a slowly growing literature on adaptation policy, still relatively little information is available to support policy integration of adaptation and mitigation.

Huq and Toulmin (2006) suggest that adaptation discourse went through 'three eras' towards gaining gradual prominence on the international political arena. The first era was marked by the first IPCC assessment report published in 1990, which established the global climate change problem as a global, long-term environmental problem that requires urgent action. The second era of adaptation discourse was marked by the third assessment report of the IPCC in 2001, which recognized climate change as a development problem. This was translated into policy at the Seventh Conference of the Parties to the UNFCCC in Marrakech in 2001. The Marrakech Accord established four new funds focused on support of concrete adaptation projects and programmes in developing countries, particularly addressing food security, water resources, disaster preparedness and health in the least developed countries (LDCs). The third era was shaped by the IPCC's Fourth Assessment Report of 2007, which was based not only on predictions, but also on observations over the last ten years. As a result, the Fourth Assessment Report showed that climate change is already happening.

How does the international climate regime frame climate change adaptation? The UNFCCC and the Protocol do not contain a definition of adaptation or related terms such as 'adaptive capacity' and 'vulnerability' (Yamin and

Depledge 2004). Thus, the most commonly deployed definitions of adaptation are those from the IPCC's Third Assessment Report, where adaptation is defined as 'adjustment in practices, process, or structures [which] can moderate or offset the potential for damage or take advantage of opportunities created by a given change in climate' (McCarthy *et al.* 2001: 89). Or, in terms of the Fourth Assessment Report, 'actions that help human and natural systems to adjust to climate change' (Fisher *et al.* 2007: 225). This particular framing of adaptation has often resulted in technology-based adaptation measures that are based on specific knowledge. The policy lesson is that the international climate regime treats adaptation in the narrowest sense (Klein 2008; Ayers and Dodman 2010). For a definition of climate vulnerability, see McCarthy *et al.* (2001: 21), who state:

> The degree to which a system is susceptible to, or unable to cope with, adverse effects of climate change.... Vulnerability is a function of the character, magnitude, and rate of climate variation to which a system is exposed, its sensitivity, and its adaptive capacity.

Arguably, multilateral climate adaptation finance, building on several existing mechanisms, has been one of the most dynamic and transformational elements within the whole international climate regime. Like in most multilateral environmental agreements, the international climate regime follows the pathway of evolution towards more and more complex architecture through establishment of new institutions and mechanisms. Climate finance contributes to this complexity.

Yamin and Depledge (2004) explain the UNFCCC and Kyoto Protocol rules, institutional and procedural features that have a particular bearing on adaptation financing. A key starting point of this discussion is the general understanding that industrialized countries (as a group) historically are the main source of GHGs and thus have an increased accountability for climate change. Thus, industrialized countries formally are obliged to provide funding for adaptation-related activities in developing countries as stated in Articles 4.3 and 4.4 of the Convention (UNFCCC 1994). However, this obligation is generic and not underpinned by quantitative targets or mechanisms. Thus, not a lot of adaptation finance has been actually delivered by industrialized countries. Combined with declining official development assistance (ODA) levels, 'frustration at the bottleneck in provision of adaptation funding through the Convention's financial mechanism' (Yamin and Depledge 2004) led developing countries to push for unconventional sources of adaptation finance. In the Marrakech Accords of 2001, a levy on the Clean Development Mechanism (CDM, see Chapter 1) under the Kyoto Protocol was agreed to fund adaptation projects.

3 Financial needs for adaptation in developing countries

How much money is needed for climate change adaptation in developing countries as a group? As Yamin and Depledge (2004) argue, estimating the cost of climate change, sometimes also known as the benefits of avoided climate change, is an important strand in adaptation-related policy discussions. However, estimates are still very vague (Müller 2008a). The UNFCCC Secretariat analysis (UNFCCC 2007c) estimated additional investment and financial flows for adaptation in 2030 at US$28–67 billion. These estimates are rather modest in comparison with other analyses. The World Bank (2009) estimates both public and private adaptation funding needs at US$75–100 billion per year. However, Parry *et al.* (2009) criticized the UNFCCC estimate for probably being an underestimate by a factor of 2–3.

4 The Adaptation Fund under the Kyoto Protocol

The Adaptation Fund under the Kyoto Protocol is the first multilateral policy instrument to promote adaptation in developing countries by providing grants for adaptation projects and programmes driven by host-country ownership. With its innovative features, such as alternative sources of revenue, recipient-country-driven process, as well as transparent governance process, the Adaptation Fund is well positioned to deal with adaptation challenges in vulnerable countries and communities.

The Adaptation Fund is a self-standing institution established under decision 10/CP.7 (UNFCCC 2001c). The legal framework of the Fund was established at the 2008 UN climate negotiations in Poznań, Poland, where the parties agreed that the Adaptation Fund should begin to operate as soon as possible. The Adaptation Fund as an 'intergovernmental grant system' is mandated to finance concrete adaptation projects and programmes (see Ratajczak-Juszko and Feaver 2011). Besides the proceeds from the levy on CDM projects, which by April 2011 made up US$153.9 million, the Adaptation Fund had received US$85.8 million in voluntary contributions from donor countries (AFB 2011).

The Adaptation Fund has been operational since late 2010 when the Adaptation Fund Board (AFB) sent out its first call for proposals of projects. The advantages of the Adaptation Fund over traditional bilateral climate finance could be greater transparency, recipient-country ownership, independence, increased democratic control and efficiency, depending on whether its procedures manage to achieve these aims. Its effectiveness depends, however, on three main elements:

- adequate resources to meet adaptation needs in developing countries, allowing access in an equal manner;
- a governance structure that will allow developing countries to access resources when required;
- funding decisions driven by principles of equity and efficiency assessment.

In terms of assessment indicators, the guidelines used by the Adaptation Fund's Project and Programme Review Committee (PPRC) entail multiple, general criteria for the assessment of projects, such as economic, social and environmental benefits, meeting national standards, cost-effectiveness and arrangements for management and monitoring (AFB 2010d). However, the approach adopted by the Adaptation Fund does not allow comparing the concrete adaptation effect of project proposals using an objective set of indicators as proposed by Stadelmann *et al.* (2011). As a result, lack of such methodology poses the risk of maladaptation. Obviously, introduction of the impact indicators requires highly challenging data collection exercises.

4.1 Governance structure of the Adaptation Fund

The transparent governance structure of the Adaptation Fund differs from other existing funds for climate adaptation – the Least Developed Countries Fund, Special Climate Change Fund and GEF Trust Fund for Climate Change (Chandani *et al.* 2009). The process of obtaining endorsement for funding decisions under the Adaptation Fund is much shorter.

The Adaptation Fund is supervised and managed by the AFB, which is composed of 16 members and 16 alternates and meets every four months. Members serve for a term of two years (UNFCCC 2007a). The terms as members do not count towards the terms as alternate members, and terms as alternate members do not count towards the terms as members, allowing an eternal rotation (UNFCCC 2007b). The Adaptation Fund is based on the 'principle of ownership' for developing countries (Chandani *et al.* 2009), which is embedded by giving them the majority of seats on the AFB. This principle ensures that countries most affected by climate change impacts remain reassured that funds will be allocated in a transparent and effectively grounded manner. The AFB is responsible for strategic oversight of projects and programmes. The Ethics and Finance Committee (EFC) monitors the Adaptation Fund's portfolio of projects and programmes.

The Global Environment Facility (GEF) provides secretariat services to the AFB and the World Bank serves as trustee of the Adaptation Fund; both of these act on an interim basis. The World Bank sells the CERs that accrue to the Adaptation Fund in order to generate revenue.

The Adaptation Fund's definition of 'concrete adaptation' actions is rather vague. A concrete adaptation project is defined as

> a set of activities aimed at addressing the adverse impacts of and risks posed by climate change. Adaptation projects can be implemented at the community, national, and transboundary level. Projects concern discrete activities with a collective objective(s) and concrete outcomes and outputs that are more narrowly defined in scope, space, and time.
>
> (AFB 2009: 4)

This is not surprising, as none of the legal instruments of the UNFCCC provide a clear definition of what constitutes adaptation actions (Yamin and Depledge 2004; Ratajczak-Juszko and Feaver 2011). The closest to such a definition is provided by Paragraph 8 a–d, of decision 5/CP.7 (UNFCCC 2001a):

> Prompt implementation of adaptation activities, where sufficient information is available to warrant such activities, inter alia in the areas of water resources management, land management, agriculture, health, infrastructure development, fragile ecosystems and integrated coastal zone management. Improving monitoring of disease and vectors affected by climate change, and related forecasting and early warning systems, and in this context improving disease control and prevention. Supporting capacity-building, including institutional capacity for preventive measures, planning, preparedness and management of disasters relating to climate change, including contingency planning, in particular for droughts and floods in areas prone to extreme weather events and strengthening existing and, where needed, establishing national and regional centres and information networks for rapid responses to extreme weather events, utilising information technology as much as possible.

Adaptation Fund governance principles include sound financial management, including the use of international fiduciary standards and a direct access approach. There are two categories of projects. The first is small-sized projects and programmes defined as project proposals requesting up to US$1 million. The second is regular-sized projects and programmes above that level (AFB 2009).

4.2 A unique funding mechanism: the Adaptation Levy

The Adaptation Levy is a unique funding mechanism. The rule that gave birth to this innovative approach to international climate finance is embedded in Article 12.8 of the Kyoto Protocol relating to the CDM. The Article provides that a 'share of the proceeds from certified project activities undertaken by Annex I Parties to the Protocol is to be used to fund adaptation in vulnerable developing country Parties' (UNFCCC 1997). COP 7 in Marrakech agreed that the share of proceeds 'shall be two per cent of Certified Emission Reductions (CERs) issued for all CDM project activities except for activities registered in LDCs which are exempt from this' (UNFCCC 2001d).

As the CDM has mobilized a large number of projects (see Chapter 1), the inflow of CERs from the Adaptation Levy has been substantial. But a key problem is that the monetary volume of the levy depends on the CER market price and overall market activity. The impact of CER price fluctuations is limited by selling CERs into the market in small batches. But surprises are not unknown. For example, the World Bank could not sell in early 2011 due to the temporary closure of the BlueNext carbon market and the Swiss national registry. Table 4.1 shows the revenues from CER sales over time.

Compared to the requirements for adaptation discussed above, the revenue from the Adaptation Levy is two orders of magnitude too low. But bilateral financing is forthcoming only slowly. Article 11.2 of the Kyoto Protocol (UNFCCC 1997) specifies that Annex-II (i.e. OECD) countries shall provide 'new and additional financial resources' to developing countries. This rule

Table 4.1 Revenues from sales of CERs received as Adaptation Levy

Year	*Month*	*CER stock*	*CERs sold*	*Revenue (million US$)*
2009	June		520,000	8.26
	July		10,000	0.15
	August	5,386,295	–	–
	September	5,232,601	70,000	1.37
	October	5,070,883	480,000	9.01
	November	5,167,718	240,000	4.64
	December	5,225,632	130,000	2.42
2010	January	5,217,023	160,000	2.63
	February	5,063,241	430,000	6.81
	March	4,161,678	1,130,000	18.51
	April	3,140,433	1,230,000	20.20
	May	2,756,268	595,000	11.41
	June	2,174,188	640,000	10.23
	July	1,815,084	410,000	6.55
	August	1,650,637	310,000	5.14
	September	1,306,693	520,000	9.23
	October	1,320,841	200,000	3.72
	November	1,626,218	180,000	3.01
	December	1,888,232	180,000	2.79
2011	January	2,771,383	120,000	1.82
	February	2,849,129	60,000	0.93
	March	3,005,041	300,000	5.44
	April	3,086,613	500,000	9.36
Total			8,415,000	143.63

Source: AFB (2011).

intended to ensure that existing, scarce ODA funds would not count as adaptation finance. However, this rule has never triggered relevant funding streams. Even the formal, quantitative pledge of Annex-II countries at COP 7 in Marrakech to provide US$410 million annually by 2005 for the Adaptation Fund (see Yamin and Depledge 2004) has not been honoured.

Because of the degree of uncertainty on the amount of financing from CDM, the COP 7 agreed that a group of Annex-II countries will mobilize new and additional finances for adaptation in developing countries (Yamin and Depledge 2004). As of April 2011, only Germany, Monaco, Spain and Sweden have provided grants. Other countries – Australia, Denmark, Finland, France, Japan, the Netherlands, Norway, Switzerland and the United Kingdom – provided loans to the Adaptation Fund when it did not yet have a secure budget. The issue arises of the predictability of future revenues as a result of such analysis. While it is possible to some extent to predict revenues from CER sales, it is difficult to forecast the exact amount of pledges by donor countries.

Concluding this section, it is important to emphasize that in recent years there have been many debates aimed at tackling the main problem of a financial mechanism: lack of adequate finance. This governance challenge raises the potential political and legal concerns related to equity requirements embedded in the UNFCCC and their impacts on the disbursement of funds by the AF.

The COP has highlighted the need of two particular groups of countries: LDCs and small island developing states (SIDS) in decision 6/CP.7 paragraph 1 (UNFCCC 2001b). Decision 2/CP.15 highlights the attention required in assisting developing countries with adaptation to adverse effects of climate change and the potential impacts of response measures. Paragraph 3 of the decision set out that 'enhanced action and international cooperation on adaptation is urgently required to ensure implementation of adaptation actions aimed at reducing vulnerability and building resilience in developing countries, especially those that are particularly vulnerable especially LDCs, SIDS and Africa' (UNFCCC 2009). The latter decision enlarges the group of countries highlighted by the COP as particularly vulnerable. Nevertheless, the first sentence of paragraph 3 of decision 2/CP.15 argues that all countries face challenges of adaptation to the adverse effects of climate change and the potential impacts of response measures. Thus, the situation remains unclear.

Formally, Article 3.1 of the UNFCCC (UNFCCC 1994) imposes an obligation directed towards developed countries to 'take the lead' in combating climate change and its adverse effects. The latter requirement is contained in the preamble to decision 5/CMP.2 (UNFCCC 2006) and is reinforced by a more specific equity obligation in Article 1 (b), which provides that 'the Adaptation Fund shall be guided by the following principles: … (b) Access to the fund in a balanced and equitable manner for eligible countries.' In conclusion, the above-mentioned requirements provide the basis of the legal obligations imposed on the Adaptation Fund, having both Fund design and operational implications. One could argue that cost-efficient adaptation is especially crucial due to the absence of adequate finance. Implementing project prioritization based on certain adaptation effectiveness assessment indicators is required.

4.3 Direct access approach

The direct access approach to the Adaptation Fund is an important, new feature available to developing countries. In recent times there has been a significant policy shift within global climate governance towards 'enabling' developing countries (Chandani *et al.* 2009); for them to be in the 'driver's seat' and fully accountable for development of the institutional capacity necessary to meet the fiduciary standards of the Adaptation Fund.

The resources from the Adaptation Fund can be accessed through two different channels: either directly, through an accredited national implementing entity (NIE), or using the services of an accredited multilateral implementing entity (MIE) (AFB 2009).

How is direct access operationalized? In order to use this option, a recipient country needs to nominate a domestic institution for accreditation as a national implementing entity, which has to meet certain standards established by the AFB.

The nominated NIE could be an academic institution, a civil society organization or a government department (Transitional Committee 2011). Once the accreditation process of NIE by the AFB is completed and its project proposal approved, the NIE enters into legal agreements with the AFB and receives the grant directly from the Adaptation Fund.

The definition of direct access is institutionalized by decision 1/CMP.3 paragraph 29 as follows:

> Eligible Parties shall be able to submit their project proposals directly to the Adaptation Fund Board and implementing or executing entities chosen by governments that are able to implement the projects funded under the Adaptation Fund may also approach the Adaptation Fund Board directly.
>
> (UNFCCC 2007a)

In other words, direct access can be defined as a funding modality in which domestic entities with legal personality have the main implementing status within the project or programme cycle and ensure fiduciary standards. A direct access approach stands in contrast with the traditional, indirect funding approach, in the sense that it does not require intermediary 'implementing entities' such as multilateral institutions to apply for and access financial resources.

Decision 5/CP.7 paragraphs 1 and 2 confirm the importance of a country-driven approach to adaptation planning, allowing 'specific activities most appropriate to their unique national circumstances'. At the same time the rule insists that

> action related adaptation follow an assessment and evaluation process, based on national communication and or other relevant information, as to prevent maladaptation and to ensure that adaptation actions are environmentally sound and will produce real benefits in support of sustainable development. This particular rule, arguably, provides a basis for direct access approach and a degree of assurance that funding proposals are based on information that is a sound and possible.
>
> (UNFCCC 2001a)

The direct access approach, if implemented accordingly to fiduciary standards, could offer benefits such as better harmonization with national climate adaptation plans and governance structure of a recipient country. Moreover, as the adaptation needs of recipient countries are high and require immediate implementation of adaptation actions, direct access can help increase the speed of delivery of desired outcomes. The additional benefit of such a decentralized approach is a lower transaction cost to the Adaptation Fund management side by transferring design, implementation and evaluation responsibilities to NIEs. The potential drawback is that NIEs have insufficient management capacity and thus are unable to implement the project as planned; then the funding would have been wasted. In the worst case, the money can just vanish through corruption.

Thus it is imperative that NIEs are enabled to actually perform in project implementation and there are incentives for good performance.

This approach seeks to ensure country ownership and allow developing country recipient countries to be in the 'driver's seat' when it comes to national adaptation programmes and projects. At the early stage of operationalization of the direct access approach there has been little evidence of practical experiences of utilizing this innovative element of the Adaptation Fund.

Direct access to financial resources for concrete climate adaptation programmes and projects has raised considerable interest among NGOs as an innovative element of the Adaptation Fund's governance structure (Sharma 2010). Some focused on 'multiple interests' involved in climate finance as reaffirming the importance of ensuring that the future finance architecture addresses the needs and concerns of poor and marginalized communities. According to Craeynest (2010), the direct access modality can provide more efficient and effective delivery of financial support to developing countries than indirect access modalities as it promotes a more balanced partnership between contributors and recipients, streamlines access and reduces the arbitrary nature of finance flow.

NGOs follow developments of the AFB closely through an Adaptation Fund NGO network. The aim of the network is to strengthen involvement of civil society from developing countries in the AFB meetings. For the successful implementation and to ensure the accountability of the implementers it will be important that civil society stakeholders can observe and accompany the implementation of projects.

In order to support the process of accreditation of implementing entities to the Adaptation Fund, in early 2010 the AFB established an Accreditation Panel. However, in practice, mobilization of direct access turned out to be rather challenging. As of May 2011, only three countries worldwide successfully obtained an accredited NIE status. The first three NIEs are: (1) the Planning Institute of Jamaica (PIJ); (2) the Centre de Suivi Ecologique from Senegal; (3) the Agencia Naçional de Investigaçión e Innovaçión (ANII) from Uruguay.

The major concern of developing countries in terms of mobilizing national efforts to meet the fiduciary standards of the AF is lack of institutional and human capacity. Tuvalu's Minister for Foreign Affairs, Enele Sopoaga, urged the AFB to assist with greater capacity building:

> In order for entities to be accredited as National Implementing Agencies they have to prove capacity for sound financial management and sound reporting practices among others – many of our small island countries don't have that capacity because of our limited human capacity, and also our limited infrastructure.
>
> (Simpson 2010)

But this problem cannot be resolved through the Adaptation Fund alone.

4.4 Insights from Adaptation Fund operations: project proposals

Approval of the first projects during the tenth meeting of the AFB marks the beginning of the implementation phase. As Harmeling and Kaloga (2010) argue, the success of this phase is dependent on many factors and actors, in particular within developing countries. Unfortunately, the early experiences of the Adaptation Fund in terms of entering into a legal partnership with national entities present only a few successful results (as listed in Section 4.3). However, there have also been difficulties in addressing project eligibility criteria while submitting proposals by implementing agencies. Considering those the successful and less successful cases, the following section presents the Senegalese adaptation project, submitted by the NIE that managed to obtain AFB approval and the Egyptian project, submitted by an MIE, that was rejected. For comparison, the following section presents also the Adaptation Fund project review criteria (Table 4.2) and a summary of projects proposals by Senegal and Egypt (Boxes 4.1 and 4.1) to illustrate the discussion.

Box 4.1 illustrates the Senegalese adaptation project summary submitted by the CSE as the NIE and successfully approved by the AFB.

Box 4.2 illustrates an Egyptian adaptation project that was initially rejected, submitted by the UNDP acting as the MIE.

Box 4.1 The Senegalese project 'Adaptation to coastal erosion in vulnerable areas'

The project was proposed by the NIE Centre de Suivi Ecologique (CSE), which will also implement the project. The project total cost is US$8.2 million. The management fee charged by the NIE is 5.1 per cent. The project's overall objective is to contribute to the implementation of Senegal's NAPA in the areas of Rufisque, Saly and Joal. It consists of five components.

Component 1: Rufisque (US$2.7 million)

The expected outcome of this component is the protection of people, houses and economic and cultural infrastructures in the region against coastal erosion. This would include an update on the detailed technical feasibility studies for the design of coastal protection facilities and the achievements of those tasks. The subcomponents include the validation of the feasibility studies, achievement of the infrastructure of protection and the cleaning up of canals and connection with the sea.

Component 2: Saly (US$2.8 million)

The expected outcome of this component is the protection of people, houses, economic and cultural infrastructures in the region against coastal erosion. This includes the setting up of protection facilities in the vulnerable areas covering the hotels, people and poor villages, as well as fishing docks. The sub-components include the development of the infrastructure to protect the region of Saly, and the support for the fitting out of the fishing dock and the fish-processing area.

Component 3: Joal (US$2 million)

The expected outcomes of this component include the protection against salination in the rice-growing areas, a built coastal infrastructure for processing activities, a rational and effective waste management system and the monitoring of the implemented Environmental and Social Management plan. Sub-components include the validation of feasibility studies and achievement of the anti-salt barrier, strengthening of protection and development of the beach and fish smoke kilns.

Component 4: Regulations (US$0.2 million)

The expected outcomes of this component are the development of regulations that cover all areas, the revision of the environmental code, the adoption of the law on the littoral and the development of a good communication effort. Sub-components include the development, strengthening and implementation of the regulations on coastal protection and adaptation and the development of the communication regarding these regulations.

Component 5: Information/sensitization/training/communication (US$0.5 million)

The expected outcome of this component is the sensitization of locals regarding adaptation techniques to climate change in coastal areas and the respect of the regulations on the management of the littoral zones. Sub-components include the training of the various target groups on the new regulations and the development of communication tools.

Source: AFB (2010c).

Box 4.2 The Egyptian project 'Promoting mariculture as an adaptation strategy to sea level rise in Nile Delta'

The project was proposed by the UNDP and shall be implemented by the Ministry of Water Resources and Irrigation, Coastal Research Institute and the National Water Research Center. It has a total cost of US$5.7 million and management costs reach 16 per cent. The project's objective is to introduce mariculture as an adaptation technology in an area severely hit by coastal erosion in the Nile Delta.

Component 1: Technical design and socioeconomic feasibility of mariculture development (US$0.5 million)

The expected outcome of this component is to develop the technical capacity for scientifically sound and socioeconomically feasible mariculture development in the Rosetta area of the Nile Delta. This component's outputs include the generation of models to determine potential climate change impacts on spawning migration and availability of juveniles for pond farming, a field-based study to identify the most appropriate native fish species for changed climate conditions, the completion of bathymetric surveys and the collection of data of available wind, wave, sea level and current. Other outputs include the technical engineering design and drawings for the fish-pond embankments and cages as sea defence systems, scientific design of the mariculture system and the development of a mariculture business plan with participation of local companies and community groups.

Component 2: Policy and regulatory framework for mariculture development (US$0.35 million)

The expected outcome of this component is to establish a regulatory framework for mariculture development and operations. The component's outputs include a revised region-based integrated coastal zone management to include mariculture as part of the framework, the formulation and adoption of legislative adjustments, sub-laws and code of conduct regulating climate-resilient mariculture development in compliance with social and environmental standards, and the establishment of private sector licensing and incentive measures for mariculture business development with direct involvement of vulnerable coastal communities.

Component 3: On-the-ground concrete adaptation actions for mariculture establishment (US$3.35 million)

The expected outcome is to design and build the sustainable mariculture in an area covering 50,000 m^2. The component's outputs include the installation of onshore and offshore mariculture to protect the coasts and facilitate local livelihood development, the establishment of an artificial spawning laboratory and the support of 5,000 communities to establish alternative livelihood ventures.

Component 4: Coastal monitoring capacity (US$0.6 million)

The expected outcome of this component is to establish continuous monitoring capabilities to monitor coastal stabilization trends. The component's outcomes include establishing the continuous monitoring programme for a warning system against sea-level rise and climatic change impacts on the sea parameters, such as wave height and direction, tide, erosion and storm surges. Also included is the definition of quality control and assurance procedures, the design and delivery of training for coastal monitoring and quality control system, the deployment of selected equipment in selected locations to measure sea level and the establishment of participatory monitoring mechanisms.

Source: AFB (2010d).

The project proposal put forward by Senegal, through its NIE, focuses on combating coastal erosion exacerbated by climate change and rising sea levels in three regions in Senegal: Joal, Rufisque and Saly. The Senegalese project stands out in terms of transparency and participation of local, vulnerable people in the decision-making. In addition, the management fee is only half of that charged by multilaterals.

The proposal by Egypt, submitted by the UNDP, aimed at promoting mariculture as an adaptation strategy to sea-level rise in the Nile Delta. The AFB decided to defer consideration of the Egyptian proposal based on a conclusion that the project did not explain how concrete adaptation objectives would be met. Also, a request to ensure that the proposed project did not duplicate activities financed by other sources of funding was put forward by the AFB. The implementing entity acting on behalf of Egypt, the UNDP, was provided

Table 4.2 Adaptation Fund Project Review Criteria

Adaptation Fund project review criteria	
Country eligibility	Is the country party to the Kyoto Protocol? Is the country a developing country particularly vulnerable to the adverse effects of climate change?
Project eligibility	Has the government endorsed the project? Does the project/programme support concrete adaptation actions to assist the country in addressing the adverse effects of climate change? Does the project provide economic, social and environmental benefits, with particular reference to the most vulnerable communities? Is the project cost-effective? Is the project consistent with national sustainable development strategies, national development plans, poverty reduction strategies, national communications or adaptation programmes of action, or other relevant instruments? Does the project meet the relevant national technical standards, where applicable? Is there duplication of the project with other funding sources? Does the project have a learning- and knowledge-management component to capture and feedback lessons? Has the project provided justification for the funding requested on the basis of the full cost of adaptation?
Resource availability	Is the requested project funding within the cap of the country?
Eligibility of NIE/MIE	Is the project submitted through an eligible NIE/MIE that has been accredited by the AFB?
Implementation arrangement	Is there adequate arrangement for project management? Are there measures for financial and project risk management? Are arrangements for monitoring and evaluation clearly defined, including a budgeted M&E plan?

Source: AFB (2011).

with the observations made by the PPRC with the request to transmit the comments together with the technical review sheet to the government of Egypt (AFB 2010b).

4.5 Funding decisions

There are five review criteria of Adaptation Fund projects: country eligibility, project eligibility, resource availability, eligibility of implementing entity and implementation arrangement (AFB 2009; UNFCCC 2010). The first criterion is defined by a COP decision, while the remaining four were developed by the AFB (see also AFB 2010a). The outlined review criteria for Adaptation Fund projects are applicable to both the small-size projects and regular projects under the single-approval process. As of 30 April 2011, there have been seven funding decisions made by the AFB since inception. The funding per accepted project and implementing entities is presented in Table 4.3. The average project grant is US$6.04 million.

During AFB meetings in 2010 and 2011, the governance structure was challenged by resource availability and the need to develop an initial priority funding approach. One of the reasons why the challenge emerged was a lack of a clear definition of particularly vulnerable countries. Prioritizing SIDS and LDCs as Adaptation Fund recipients would have cut the number of eligible countries by almost two-thirds. However, as of March 2011, the AFB decided to cap the maximum amount of funding per country at US$10 million. If by the end of 2012 about 1 billion CERs have been issued, the AF will have received 20 million CERs that, at the prices for which CERs were sold in the past and current market, would yield a revenue of US$300 million. Adding the voluntary contributions, the Adaptation Fund's total resources will reach about US$400 million. If every country tries to capture the available funding up to the threshold, this means that about 40–50 countries out of the 149 eligible might eventually receive funding. The country-specific cap means, in effect, that 'equal' distribution between countries is seen as a more important criteria than others, such as levels of vulnerability, targeting of vulnerable communities within a country, benefits attained and cost-effectiveness (Persson 2010).

What role do multilateral agencies play in distributing Adaptation Fund finance? There is no doubt that the multilateral option to access adaptation finance strengthens recipient countries' ability to address pressing adaptation needs. Using existing institutions and their experiences often removes governance challenges facing developing countries. However, there are some long-term disadvantages if the multilateral approach leads to perpetuation of lack of capacity to utilize the direct access approach, as national institutions that could administer future international climate finance streams would not be able to compete with the multilateral ones. In other words, this could lead to an ongoing dependency of developing countries on multilateral agencies in terms of administrative assistance to design and implement projects.

Table 4.3 illustrates this argument, as 12 of 15 proposals to the Adaptation Fund were submitted by one MIE (UNDP) on behalf of recipient countries.

The vast majority of countries submitting proposals has chosen the multilateral access modality. Their choice arguably reflects a perceived lack of institutional capacity and lack of sound fiduciary management, which are essential to the integrity of direct access, as well as the fear of being left behind if they first build-up an NIE before submitting a proposal.

Considering the lack of adequate financial resources and the current first-come, first-serve principle for funding allocation that does not take into account vulnerability and adaptive needs, the next challenge for the Adaptation Fund is to arrive at a simple formula to determine where a country may fall with respect to its vulnerability and adaptability to climate change (Ratajczak-Juszko and Feaver 2011). The derivation of a suitable formula is theoretically simple but practically and politically not easy.

Table 4.3 Proposals endorsed by the Adaptation Fund for funding or awaiting final decisions

	Recipient country	*Status of proposal*	*Implementing entity*	*Amount in US$ (million)*
1	Honduras	Funding approved	MIE/UNDP	5.62
2	Nicaragua	Funding approved	MIE/UNDP	5.50
3	Pakistan	Funding approved	MIE/UNDP	3.91
4	Senegal	Funding approved	NIE/CSE	8.62
5	Ecuador	Funding approved	MIE/WFP	7.45
6	Eritrea	Funding approved	MIE/UNDP	6.52
7	Solomon Islands	Funding approved	MIE/UNDP	5.53
8	Cook Islands	Project concepts endorsed	MIE/UNDP	4.99
9	El Salvador	Project concepts endorsed	MIE/UNDP	5.43
10	Georgia	Project concepts endorsed	MIE/UNDP	5.32
11	Guatemala	Project concepts endorsed	MIE/UNDP	5.50
12	Madagascar	Project concepts endorsed	MIE/UNDP	4.51
13	Maldives	Project concepts endorsed	MIE/UNDP	8.99
14	Mongolia	Project concepts endorsed	MIE/UNDP	5.50
15	Uruguay	Project concepts endorsed	NIE/ANII	7.35
Total amount allocated				90.74

Source: own calculation based on data in AFB (2011).

5 The importance of capacity building and enabling conditions

As was mentioned in the earlier section, aligning global mechanisms and funds with local needs of communities in developing countries in an effective way remains a major challenge for policy-makers. The transformational structure of the Adaptation Fund can play a role as *agent of change*, leading towards robust adaptation governance. The structural changes that slowly emerge at national levels, driven by climate change policy, could contribute to building institutions for global governance. However, some countries more then others will face difficulties in implementing those structural changes. Nevertheless, in order to enable the Adaptation Fund to act as an agent of change not only needs adequate amounts of money to be available, but also capacity building to achieve enabling conditions in the most disadvantaged countries. The Adaptation Fund cannot itself provide technical assistance and capacity support to countries wishing to establish NIEs, because the COP/MOP decided the Adaptation Fund should finance only concrete adaptation projects and programmes. Even if the Adaptation Fund had formally been able to provide capacity building, it would not have been able to do so as it was fully occupied with setting up its own structure and disbursement procedures under strong international scrutiny. Promoting equitable access to multilateral climate finance and avoiding restricted access for developing countries that have special circumstances remains a key challenge.

There is no doubt that the national implementation modality could lead to sustainable building of institutions in developing countries. Unfortunately, as experiences of the Adaptation Fund show, the national implementation approach is used only where there has been a lot of previous capacity building (as in the case of Senegal, where the NIE was essentially developed under a previous development assistance project), or where, due to an already advanced level of development, there is adequate capacity in the national authorities (Uruguay). In other words, most developing countries lack technical and administrative capacity to efficiently administer adaptation funding. This limited institutional experience is arguably the main barrier to substantial evolution of institutional reform underpinned by principles of accountability and transparency.

Most interesting is an assessment of fiduciary standards of NIE candidates, especially those rejected. For example, at the fourteenth AFB meeting, the candidate 'NIE 1' was rejected by the Accreditation Panel of the AFB. The term 'NIE 1' is used because applicant NIEs are treated anonymously until they are recommended for accreditation to avoid 'naming and blaming'. What would be interesting to know is the conditions of 'NIE 1' that resulted in a recommendation for non-approval.

What has happened to date with regards to capacity building? The Adaptation Fund secretariat has published an online tool kit on its website for countries interested in submitting a project proposal. The UNFCCC Secretariat, at the request of the COP/MOP and in cooperation with the AFB and its secretariat, are organizing regional workshops to further potential NIE understanding of the accreditation process from July 2011. The funding for the workshops will not come from the Adaptation Fund budget.

6 Regional approach to access modality

The Alliance of Small Island States (AOSIS) is particularly disadvantaged in terms of institutional capacity to meet Adaptation Fund standards. Another group of countries facing similar institutional challenges is the LDCs. Alternatives for these groups of primarily small countries to the current national implementation modality could involve regional approaches administered through Regional Implementing Entities. For example, as mentioned by Maclellan (2011), sub-regional institutions such as the South Pacific Environmental Programme (SPREP), the Secretariat of the Pacific Community (SPC) or the Melanesian Spearhead Group (MSG) may be the best institutions to support Pacific islands. The use of such regional organizations would harness economies of scale for small countries such as members of AOSIS.

7 The challenge of defining most vulnerable countries

Who is most vulnerable to impacts of climate change and how does the international climate regime recognize vulnerability? Defining particularly vulnerable countries has been a political dilemma within the UNFCCC for many years and remains unresolved (Klein 2008; Klein and Möhner 2011). The Preamble of the UNFCCC explicitly mentions low-lying and other small island countries, countries with low-lying coastal, arid and semi-arid areas or areas liable to floods, drought and desertification, and developing countries with fragile mountainous ecosystems. According to Verheyen (2005) and others (UN 1969; Yamin 1998), this text can only be used as an interpretative aid. The discussion on the interpretation commenced at COP 1 in 1995 in Berlin. Regarding a financial mechanism and climate change adaptation, the first session of the COP provided initial guidelines on policies, programmes, priorities and eligibility criteria (UNFCCC 1995). The COP agreed that 'adaptation to adverse effects of climate change will require short, medium and long term strategies which should be cost effective, take into account important socioeconomic implications and should be implemented on stage-by stage basis' (UNFCCC 1995: 36–7). The COP envisaged three stages:

> Stage I – Planning, which includes studies of possible impacts of climate change, to identify particularly vulnerable countries or regions and policy options for adaptation and appropriate capacity building.
>
> Stage II – Measures in the countries identified in Stage I, including further capacity building.
>
> Stage III – Measures to facilitate adequate adaptation, including insurance, and other adaptation measures (UNFCCC 1995).

There has been a discussion about an IPCC-entrusted role of developing objective scientific indicators (Verheyen 2005) based on the outputs of the Stage I studies, as well as other relevant scientific and technical studies, and any emerging evidence of the adverse effects of climate change.

Yamin (1998) has suggested that the list of vulnerable countries should be negotiated, but it is worth mentioning that such an approach has not been demanded by the group of G77 and China (Verheyen 2005), arguably to avoid conflicts on funding prioritization within the group. The unsolved problem remains the extent of funding to be provided, with the potential that a lack of policy definition may lead to political conflicts. However, at Marrakech, the COP has highlighted the needs of two particular groups of countries: LDCs and SIDS, in decision 6/CP.7 paragraph 1 (UNFCCC 2001b).

Given this stalemate, the decision on the Adaptation Fund (UNFCCC 2006: 28) does not address the issue and declares that 'access to the fund [is to be] in a balanced and equitable manner for eligible countries'. Paragraph 3 of decision 2/CP.15 (UNFCCC 2009: 6) specifies that 'enhanced action and international cooperation on adaptation is urgently required to ensure implementation of adaptation actions aimed at reducing vulnerability and building resilience in developing countries, especially those that are particularly vulnerable especially LDCs, SIDS and Africa'. Thus the African region as a whole is added to the two groups of countries highlighted by the Marrakech COP as being particularly vulnerable.

8 Lessons learned from the Adaptation Fund and policy implications for the Green Climate Fund

In the Copenhagen Accord of 2009 (UNFCCC 2009), and confirmed by the Cancun Agreement of 2010 (UNFCCC 2010), industrialized countries set a goal of mobilizing US$100 billion per year by 2020 to support mitigation and adaptation activities in developing countries. While at Cancun a Green Climate Fund (GCF) was formally endorsed to administer a part of these resources, it remains unclear how these funds are to be mobilized. In 2010, the UN Secretary-General established a High-level Advisory Group on Climate Change Financing, with the task of elaborating on innovative ways to mobilize additional financial resources, especially at a time when many governments were experiencing fiscal and budgetary constraints. The report of the Advisory Group recommended that carbon markets should be further strengthened and developed, while ensuring environmental integrity based on the conclusion that carbon markets offer important opportunities for supporting new technologies and leveraging private investment in developing countries (UN 2010). Moreover, the report recommended that funding for adaptation should focus on the most vulnerable developing countries, such as the LDCs, SIDS and Africa.

The squabble about reporting on the disbursement of the US$30 billion 'fast-track finance' to be provided by industrialized countries between 2010 and 2012 shows the critical elements of climate finance: donors are unwilling to relinquish control over funding decisions to international entities, and there is a tendency to shirk on commitments by re-labelling previously allocated funds. Measuring the new and additional resources thus remains so far technically and politically challenging due to difficulties in collecting the financial data and the problem of tracking finances through various bilateral and multilateral channels (see Chapter 5).

Processing climate change mitigation and adaptation projects and programmes will require large financial and administrative resources to support the transition process in developing countries. The alternative to the centralized decision-making model of traditional funds plays a crucial role in the analysis of the operational modalities of multilateral finance.

Which lessons could be drawn from the three years' experience of the Adaptation Fund for the adaptation component of the Green Climate Fund? While the GCF faces much greater challenges than the Adaptation Fund in terms of the scale of its finance and its complex thematic scope, there are some elements of the Adaptation Fund model that may be particularly useful for the design of operational guidelines and policies of the GCF. The Adaptation Fund uses two main ways of raising adaptation finance: the 2 per cent Adaptation Levy on CERs from the CDM; and voluntary contributions from developed countries. While the levy works well and provides significant resources, the voluntary contributions remain limited and haphazard. So the GCF would have to build either on mandatory contributions by industrialized countries, or on a strongly upscaled levy covering all market mechanisms, not only the CDM. The latter approach will only work if demand for credits from the market mechanisms is strong, leading to a high credit price as well as a high volume of credits generated.

Despite being hailed as a major innovation, so far the direct access option of the Adaptation Fund has not been widely used, probably due to the fear of recipient countries of missing out in the first-come, first-serve process of funding allocation. Therefore, the funding allocation should be much more criteria-based and should check whether real host-country ownership exists, which is most likely if an NIE has developed the proposal. Having said this, it is important also to emphasize that the GCF should earmark an adequate budget for capacity-building activities to support mobilization of the NIEs. The rationale behind this view is that bottom-up funding decisions (to the country level) would increase the effectiveness of climate finance. It would also address the requirement agreed by the COP with regards to developing country ownership over the decisions. The direct access approach is essential if the funding is to be mainstreamed into domestic policies of recipient countries, and not just seen as an 'add on'.

A further innovation that so far has not been tested in practice is the Adaptation Fund's 'throughput' model in which the consolidated funds are disbursed to National Funding Entities which are tasked with administration and funding decisions responsibilities. So far, NIEs have not been allowed to take a certain funding volume and distribute it according to their own criteria.

9 Conclusions

Any upscaled climate finance requires strengthening capacity to address barriers and constraints currently preventing climate adaptation and mitigation in developing countries. Only then could significantly increased financial resources be effectively disbursed, taking into account country ownership, effective use and allocation of resources to ensure that the money reaches the most vulnerable countries and communities (Schalatek and Bird 2010).

From a geopolitical perspective the promotion of adaptation is a step towards overcoming political tensions between a focus on mitigation in richer countries vis-à-vis a focus on adaptation in poorer countries (Jerneck and Olsson 2010). In this context, between 2007 and 2010 the UN climate negotiations made a major step forward. Decisions were taken that developing countries should be compensated for the costs of climate adaptation (UNFCCC 1994) and that adaptation should be addressed in an integrated and comprehensive manner to enhance and achieve the full, effective and sustained implementation of the Convention, now, up to and beyond 2012 (Decision CP.16, Paragraph 1 of the Shared Vision, LCA, UNFCCC 2010).

The Adaptation Fund is a fascinating laboratory to test allocation of adaptation funding before a major upscaling of funding takes place. Progress made on the development of a transparent set of operational guidelines by the AFB requires recognition. The Adaptation Fund is the most transparent and democratic climate finance vehicle yet devised. However, so far insufficient lessons have been drawn from its operations to clearly indicate which innovations should be retained when climate finance is upscaled. The lack of adequate institutional capacity to meet fiduciary standards is probably the most alarming lesson, as it undermines hopes that the direct access mode may revolutionize climate finance. Unfortunately, so far cost-effectiveness of adaptation has not yet played a relevant role in Adaptation Fund decision-making. Considering governance mechanisms for project prioritization based on certain 'adaptation efficiency indicators' may play a particularly important role.

Developing countries are the 'canary in the coalmine' of climate change – they will be the first ones to face the consequences, and the least able to ward off adverse impacts. Therefore, we need credible and effective institutions to support these countries in their struggle to adapt. The Adaptation Fund is only the first step on a long, long journey.

Note

1 The Green Climate Fund (GCF) was established by the Parties to the UNFCCC at COP 16 in Cancun, December 2010. The COP, in its decision 1/CP.16 set-up the Transitional Committee for design of the GCF to develop and recommend operational documents for approval at its seventeenth session (UNFCCC 2010).

References

AFB (2009) ‘Operational policies and guidelines for parties to access resources from the Adaptation Fund’. Online. Available: http://adaptation-fund.org/system/files/file/AFB_Operational%20Policies%20and%20Guidelines.pdf.

AFB (2010a) ‘Project and Programme Review Committee. First Meeting. Bonn, June 14, 2010. Agenda item 3’. Online. Available: www.adaptation-fund.org/sites/default/files/AFB.PPRC_.1.11.Rev_.1%20Report%20by%20the%20secretariat%20on%20project%20review.final_.pdf.

AFB (2010b) ‘Report of the tenth meeting of the Adaptation Fund Board’. Online. Available: www.adaptation-fund.org/sites/default/files/AFB%2010%20Rev.1%20final%20report_9_7_10.pdf (accessed 25 May 2011).

AFB (2010c) ‘Project/programme proposal for Senegal’. Online. Available: http://adaptation-fund.org/system/files/AFB.PPRC_.1.3%20Technical%20Review%20of%20Project%20Concept%20AFB_NIE_Coastal_2010_1_Senegal.pdf (accessed 25 July 2010).

AFB (2010d) ‘Proposal for Egypt, September 15’. Online. Available: http://adaptation-fund.org/system/files/AFB.PPRC_.2.5%20Proposal%20for%20Egypt.pdf (accessed 25 July 2011).

AFB (2011) ‘Document AFB/EFC.5/8’. Online. Available: www.adaptation-fund.org/sites/default/files/AFB.EFC_.5.8%20AF%20Trustee%20Report_1.pdf (accessed 26 July 2011).

Ayers, J. and Dodman, D. (2010) ‘Climate change adaptation and development: the state of the debate’, *Progress in Development Studies*, 10 (2): 161–8.

Ayers, J., Alam, M. and Huq, S. (2010) ‘Global adaptation governance beyond 2012: developing country perspective’, in F. Biermann, P. Pattberg and F. Zelli (eds) *Global Climate Governance Beyond 2012: Architecture, Agency and Adaptation*, Cambridge: Cambridge University Press, pp. 270–85.

Chandani, A., Huq, S. and Kaloga, A.O. (2009) ‘The Adaptation Fund: a model for the future?’, *IIED briefing August 2009*, London: International Institute for Environment and Development.

Craeynest, L. (2010) ‘Business as unusual: Direct Access – giving power back to the poor?’, Caritas Internationalis, CIDSE. Online. Available: www.cidse.org/uploadedFiles/Publications/Publication_repository/CIDSE-CARITAS%20INTERNATIONALIS%20DISCUSSION%20PAPER%20ON%20DIRECT%20ACCESS.pdf.

Fermann, G. (1997) *International Politics of Climate Change*, Oslo: Skandinavien University Press.

Fisher, B., Nakicenovic, N., Alfsen, K., Corfee-Morlot, J., de la Chesnaye, F., Hourcade, J.-Ch., Jiang, K., Kainuma, M., La Rovere, E., Matysek, A., Rana, A., Riahi, K., Richels, R., Rose, S., van Vuuren, D. and Warren, R. (2007) ‘Issues related to mitigation in the long term context’, in B. Metz, O. Davidson, P. Bosch, R. Dave and L. Meyer (eds) *Climate Change 2007: Mitigation – Contribution of Working Group III to the Fourth Assessment Report of the Intergovernmental Panel on Climate Change*, Cambridge and New York: Cambridge University Press, pp. 169–250.

Garnaut Climate Change Review (2008) *The Garnaut Climate Change Review: Final Report*, Cambridge: Cambridge University Press.

Harmeling, S. and Kaloga, A. (2010) ‘Adaptation Fund under the KP: mature for concrete implementation of projects and direct access’, *ECBI Policy Brief*, Oxford: European Capacity Building Initiative.

Huq, S. and Toulmin, C. (2006) 'Three eras of climate change', *IIED Sustainable Development Opinion October 2006*, London: International Institute for Environment and Development.

Jerneck, A. and Olsson, L. (2010) 'Shaping future adaptation governance: perspectives from the poorest of the poor', in F. Biermann, P. Pattberg and F. Zelli (eds) *Global Climate Governance Beyond 2012: Architecture, Agency and Adaptation*, Cambridge: Cambridge University Press, pp. 286–305.

Klein, N. (2008) 'Mainstreaming climate adaptation into development policies and programmes: a European perspective', in C. Bursi (ed.) *Financing Climate Change Policies in Developing Countries*, Directorate-General Internal Policies, Brussels: European Parliament, pp. 38–51.

Klein, R. (2009) 'Identifying countries that are particularly vulnerable to the adverse effects of climate change: an academic or a political challenge?', *Carbon & Climate Law Review*, 3 (3): 284–91.

Klein, R.J.T. and Möhner, A. (2011) 'The political dimension of vulnerability: implications for the Green Climate Fund', *IDS Bulletin* 42 (3): 15–22.

McCarthy, J.J., Canziani, O.V., Leary, N.A., Dokken, D.J. and Kasey, S.W. (eds) (2001) *Climate Change 2001: Impacts, Adaptation, and Vulnerability – Contribution of Working Group II to the Third Assessment Report of the Intergovernmental Panel on Climate Change*, Cambridge and New York: Cambridge University Press.

Maclellan, N. (2011) 'Improving Access to Climate Financing for the Pacific Islands', Lowy Institute for International Policy. Online. Available: http://kms1.isn.ethz.ch/serviceengine/Files/ISN/132565/ipublicationdocument_singledocument/4327139f-20ef-429d-aa2c-ff6bef2ade10/en/Maclellan%2C+Improving+access+to+climate+financing_web.pdf.

Müller, B. (2008a) 'International adaptation finance: the need for an innovative and strategic approach', Oxford Institute for Energy Studies. Online. Available: www.eed.de/fix/files/doc/2008_BMueller_int_adapatation_finance.pdf (accessed 12 April 2011).

Müller, B. (2008b) 'International Air Passenger Adaptation Levy (IAPAL): a proposal by the group of least developed countries (LDCs) within the framework of the Bali Action Plan. Submitted to the UNFCCC AWC-LCA on 12 December 2008', *ECBI Policy Brief*, Oxford: European Capacity Building Initiative.

Parry, M., Arnell, N., Berry, P., Dodman, D., Fankhauser, S., Hope, C., Kovats, S., Nicholls, R., Satterthwaite, D., Tiffin, R. and Wheeler, T. (2009) 'Assessing the costs of adaptation to climate change: a review of the UNFCCC and other recent estimates', London: Imperial College, Grantham Institute for Climate Change, International Institute for Environment and Development.

Persson, Å. (2010) 'Governance of international climate change adaptation finance: early experiences of the UNFCCC Adaptation Fund', Stockholm Resilience Centre, Stockholm Environment Institute.

Pielke, R.G.P., Rayner, S. and Sarewitz, D. (2007) 'Climate change 2007: lifting the taboo on adaptation', *Nature*, 445: 597–8.

Ratajczak-Juszko, I. and Feaver, D. (2011) 'International climate finance: the equitable allocation of adaptation funding', Discussion Paper, RMIT University.

Schalatek, L. and Bird, N. (2010) 'A normative framework for climate finance', *Climate Finance Fundamentals* 1, Washingtion, DC and London: Heinrich Böll Foundation North America, Overseas Development Institute.

Sharma, A. (2010) 'The reformed financial mechanism of the UNFCCC: renegotiating the role of civil society in the governance of climate change', Oxford Institute for Energy Studies.

Simpson, S. (2010) 'Tuvalu urges Adaptation Fund Board to provide greater capacity building for islands', *Solomon Times Online*. Online. Available: www.solomontimes.com/news.aspx?nwID=5745 (accessed 12 June 2011).

Stadelmann, M., Michaelowa, A., Butzengeiger-Geyer, S. and Köhler, M. (2011) 'Universal metrics to compare the effectiveness of climate change adaptation projects'. Online. Available: http://cc2011.earthsystemgovernance.org/pdf/2011Colora_0126.pdf (accessed 22 July 2011).

Stern, N. (2006) *The Economics of Climate Change: The Stern Review*, Cambridge: Cambridge University Press. Online. Available: http://webarchive.nationalarchives.gov.uk/+/www.hm-treasury.gov.uk/stern_review_report.htm (accessed 22 July 2011).

Transitional Committee (2011) *Technical Workshop in Japan. Workstream II: Governance and Institutional Arrangements. Workstream III: Operational Modalities*, Tokyo: Transitional Committee for the Green Climate Fund. Online. Available: http://unfccc.int/files/cancun_agreements/green_climate_fund/application/pdf/tc2_ws3_2_290611.pdf (accessed 18 July 2011).

UN (1969) 'Vienna Convention on the Law of Treaties. 23 May 1969', Article 31.

UN (2010) 'Report of the Secretary-General's High-level Advisory Group on Climate Change Financing'. Online. Available: www.un.org/wcm/webdav/site/climatechange/shared/Documents/AGF_reports/AGF_Final_Report.pdf (accessed 20 April 2011).

UNFCCC (1994) 'United Nations Framework Convention on Climate Change'.

UNFCCC (1995) 'FCCC/CP/1995/7/Add1 Report of the Conference of the Parties on its first session, held at Berlin from 28 March to 7 April 1995'. Online. Available: http://unfccc.int/resource/docs/cop1/07a01.pdf (accessed 26 July 2011).

UNFCCC (1997) 'Kyoto Protocol to the United Nations Framework Convention on Climate Change'.

UNFCCC (2001a) 'Decision 5/CP.7 Implementation of Article 4, paragraphs 8 and 9, of the Convention (decision 3/CP.3 and Article 2, paragraph 3, and Article 3, paragraph 14, of the Kyoto Protocol)'. Online. Available: http://unfccc.int/resource/docs/cop7/13a01.pdf#page=32 (accessed 22 July 2011).

UNFCCC (2001b) 'Decision 6/CP.7 Additional guidance to an operating entity of the financial mechanism'. Online. Available: http://unfccc.int/resource/docs/cop7/13a01.pdf#page=40 (accessed 22 July 2011).

UNFCCC (2001c) 'Decision 10/CP.7 Funding under the Kyoto Protocol'. Online. Available: http://unfccc.int/resource/docs/cop7/13a01.pdf#page=52 (accessed 22 July 2011).

UNFCCC (2001d) 'Decision 17/CP.7 Modalities and procedures for a clean development mechanism as defined in Article 12 of the Kyoto Protocol'. Online. Available: http://unfccc.int/resource/docs/cop7/13a02.pdf#page=20 (accessed 22 July 2011).

UNFCCC (2006) 'Decision 5/CMP.2 Adaptation Fund'. Online. Available: http://unfccc.int/resource/docs/2006/cmp2/eng/10a01.pdf#page=28 (accessed 22 July 2011).

UNFCCC (2007a) 'Decision 1/CMP.3 Adaptation Fund'. Online. Available: http://unfccc.int/resource/docs/2007/cmp3/eng/09a01.pdf#page=3 (accessed 22 July 2011).

UNFCCC (2007b) 'Decision 1/CMP.3 Adaptation Fund'. Online. Available: http://unfccc.int/resource/docs/2008/cmp4/eng/11a02.pdf#page=1 (accessed 22 July 2011).

UNFCCC (2007c) 'Report on the analysis of existing and potential investment and financial flows relevant to the development of an effective and appropriate international response to climate change'. Online. Available: http://unfccc.int/files/cooperation_and_support/financial_mechanism/financial_mechanism_gef/application/pdf/dialogue_working_paper_8.pdf (accessed 22 July 2011).

UNFCCC (2009) 'Decision 2/CP.15 Copenhagen Accord'. Online. Available: http://unfccc.int/resource/docs/2009/cop15/eng/11a01.pdf#page=4 (accessed 22 July 2011).

UNFCCC (2010) 'FCCC/CP/2010/7/Add.1. Report of the Conference of the Parties on its sixteenth session, held in Cancun from 29 November to 10 December 2010'. Online. Available: http://unfccc.int/resource/docs/2010/cop16/eng/07a01.pdf (accessed 15 March 2011).

Verheyen, R. (2005) *Climate Change Damage and International Law: Prevention Duties and State Responsibility*, Leiden and Boston, MA: Martinus Nijhoff Publishers.

World Bank (2009) 'Economics of adaption to climate: change synthesis report'. Online. Available: http://climatechange.worldbank.org/sites/default/files/documents/EACC-SynthesisReport.pdf.

Yamin, F. (1998) 'The Clean Development Mechanism and adaptation: paper for the FCCC Secretariat Capacity Building Workshop', *FIELD Working Paper*, 19, Foundation for International Environmental Law and Development.

Yamin, F. and Depledge, J. (2004) *The International Climate Change Regime: A Guide to Rules, Institutions and Procedures*, Cambridge: Cambridge University Press.

5 Fast-start finance

Scattered governance, information and programmes

Martin Stadelmann, Jessica Brown and Lena Hörnlein

1 Introduction: how fast-start finance has emerged

The 2009 Copenhagen Accord includes a collective pledge by industrialized countries to provide 'new and additional resources, including forestry and investments through international institutions, approaching US$30 billion for the period 2010–2012 with balanced allocation between adaptation and mitigation' (UNFCCC 2009). These resources are commonly called 'fast-start finance' (FSF). As fast-start finance is seen as a testing ground for longer-term arrangements for climate finance, we will explore in this chapter how this funding has been used to date and what lessons should be drawn for the future.

To start with, what is the purpose of FSF? The US$30 billion is serving three implicit goals: (1) meeting the financing needs of developing countries to address climate change; (2) sharing the global burden of addressing climate change; and (3) reaching an international climate policy agreement for the post-2012 period.

The first goal of FSF is a contribution to cover the high costs of financing mitigation and adaptation in the developing world. On the one hand, mitigation of climate change may cost developing countries US$140–175 billion annually by 2030[1] under a scenario to limit global warming to 2°C[2] (World Bank 2009). On the other hand, adaptation to climate change may cost them US$75–100 billion per year (on average, 2010–2050)[3] under this scenario (World Bank 2010). The slow process of international climate negotiations and the current low ambition of national mitigation policies make it very unlikely that the 2°C target will be met, and thus, adaptation costs are likely to be higher, while mitigation costs would be lower than the numbers given here.

The second goal of FSF is burden sharing. In article 3.1 of the UNFCCC (1992), the principle of common but differentiated responsibilities and respective capabilities has been defined. Developing countries have a lower responsibility for climate change than industrialized countries (if measured by historical CO_2 emissions or current per capita emissions) and are also less capable of adapting and paying for mitigation and adaptation (Dellink *et al.* 2009; Müller *et al.* 2009). Furthermore, developing countries will probably face larger climate change-related losses relative to their income than the North and their capacity to cope with climate change is on average lower as well (Parry *et al.* 2007). Therefore, the climate financing needs of developing countries are partly to be met by payments from industrialized countries.[4]

The third goal of FSF is a contribution to reach an ambitious international climate agreement. As part of a post-2012 deal, industrialized countries want developing countries to undertake their own mitigation policies and measures. Many developing countries, however, are only willing to commit to such actions if they receive financial and technological support for both mitigation and adaptation measures.[5] While the Copenhagen climate summit in December 2009 did not result in the ambitious legally binding emissions reduction agreement many had hoped for, it resulted in the promise of longer-term finance (up to US$100 billion by 2020) and of FSF. The sum of US$30 billion of FSF over three years is an order of magnitude below developing countries' funding needs, but it is nevertheless ambitious as it implies a doubling of international climate-specific public financial flows.[6] FSF is therefore seen as a testing ground for future climate finance, especially for the longer-term US$100 billion of 'public and private' funding to be provided annually by 2020 (UNFCCC 2009).

This chapter will take a closer look at how the FSF promises have been implemented in practice. The discussion here provides a literature and policy document review to analyse the following questions: is the collective US$30 billion pledge really being met? Is there a balance between funds for mitigation and adaptation? What is the share of investment flows (loans, equity) and funding through international institutions? Are the important principles of transparency[7] and effectiveness[8] fulfilled?

The first part of this chapter will provide an overview of the knowledge on FSF as of June 2011, equating to roughly halfway through the 2010–2012 period. We analyse funding volumes, the mitigation–adaptation balance, the grant–loan share and the share of multilateral and bilateral channels. In the second part of the chapter, we deal with governance, transparency and the three different steps of delivering climate finance. These steps consist of, first, sourcing 'new and additional' funds by industrialized countries, either through their general budgets or new sources; second, channelling of the funding to developing countries, either through bilateral or multilateral institutions; and third, the use for adaptation or mitigation measures in developing countries (Figure 5.1). Depending on the way it is used, climate finance will be effective in mitigating climate change and adapting to its adverse effects or not. Effectiveness is also indirectly dependent on how much funding is sourced and how (fast) it is channelled.

2 Fast-start finance: overview of current knowledge

What do we currently know about the form, shape and size of FSF? FSF has no specific structure or form, and it has no direct legal implications. FSF is simply a tool to demonstrate an upscaling and support towards immediate climate change activities in developing countries. FSF does not create new funds or initiatives,

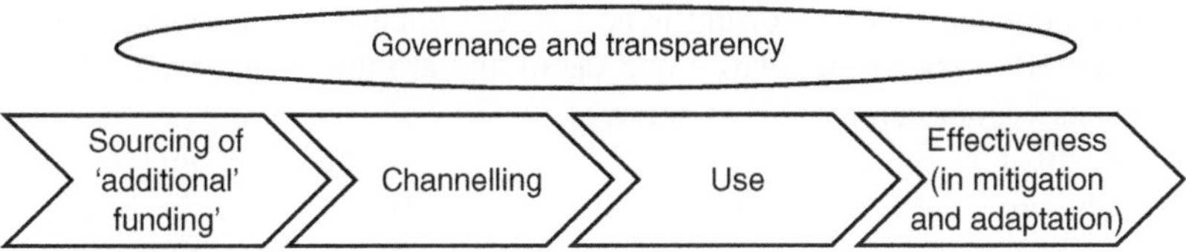

Figure 5.1 Steps and criteria for delivery of fast-start finance.

but rather uses existing channels of delivery and disbursement. Therefore, trying to track FSF and separate out what is counted as FSF alongside existing flows is rather difficult, given that most funding channels overlap. For example, Australia, Belgium, Norway, Spain, Sweden, Switzerland and the United States consider funding to the Global Environment Facility (GEF) to be part of their FSF pledges; others (Canada,[9] Finland,[10] France and the United Kingdom) partly count it; while some – for example Denmark and Germany – do not count it at all.

Hence, separating out FSF as a financial flow is rather difficult and has only limited application. Analysing the amount of 'new and additional' FSF gives some indications of whether climate funds have been stepped up since Copenhagen, but FSF is – apart from its requirement to be 'new and additional' – not any different from other public climate finance flows.

As is the case for other public funding between industrialized and developing countries, FSF can be split into the following phases:

- *Pledges* – represents finance pledged by an industrialized country to a developing country made through a political statement (either oral or written commitment).
- *Commitments* – represents funding that has been firmly obligated within the contributor country for FSF (e.g. earmarked within a national budget).[11]
- *Allocations* – represents funding that has been earmarked to a specific climate initiative or fund; or for specific projects/programmes in recipient countries.
- *Disbursements* – represents those funds that have been spent, either through administrative means, payment to a fund or directly to an implementation programme or project, with proof of spending.

2.1 Data sources for the fast-start finance overview

www.faststartfinance.org (Faststartfinance.org 2011) was the first government-initiated and supported reporting initiative collecting data on FSF. This website, initiated by the Netherlands and supported by other contributor governments as well as international organizations, came online in mid-2010 and provides information on the funding that individual developed countries are providing, as well as on funding the recipient countries are reporting as having received from FSF commitments. Since reporting is ad hoc and voluntary, individual country funding reports vary in granularity and detail and are thus neither complete or comprehensive, nor comparable in nature.

Before this governmental website was set-up, some NGOs had analysed fast-start funds, with the World Resources Institute (WRI 2011) website being the most encompassing and most regularly updated one. As the WRI takes a critical view on the information provided on www.faststartfinance.org, and also includes some additional data, we will also partly use this information.

Most Annex-I countries reported on their FSF programmes in May–June 2011; as in the Cancun Agreement, all Annex-I countries to the UNFCCC are invited to report annually on their fast-start activities by May 2011, 2012 and 2013 (UNFCCC 2010). These reports provide even less comparable data than the above-mentioned sources, but include some updated information we will use.

The data we present below are based on the following sources:

- Pledged amounts come from the Faststartfinance.org (2011) website, which provides the same data for pledged funds as WRI. If allocations as reported in the 2011 fast-start reports (UNFCCC 2011) were higher than these pledges, then the pledges were updated.
- Committed amounts are taken from two sources. First, we take commitments from Faststartfinance.org (2011) showing the figures reported by the countries themselves. These data have a quasi-official status but, unfortunately, there is no agreed definition of 'commitments' across reporting countries and the figures may not be comparable. Therefore, we also show the committed-requested amounts from WRI (2011), which defines this category as 'actions taken by either the executive and/or legislative bodies of the country to make the resources pledged available to developing countries'. The WRI figures includes some funding not reported as 'committed' on Faststartfinance.org (2011) – either funds that are requested but not committed or funds where parties have forgotten to inscribe the commitments on the website – but it excludes funds where the reported 'commitment' is doubtful, as it has not yet resulted in any legislative action.
- Allocated amounts are taken from the data presented on individual projects, programmes and funds included in the contributing country reports on Faststartfinance.org (2011) and accompanying links to websites providing country-specific information, while some figures are updated with data from the 2011 fast-start reports submitted to the UNFCCC (2011).

The main challenge is to ensure comparability, which is aggravated by at least two issues: exchange rate and additionality. First, exchange rates will change over time. Therefore, a certain comparison is just valid for one moment in time. We used exchange rates in June 2011 from Oanda (2011). Second, countries use different baselines for justifying that their funding is 'new and additional' (Brown *et al.* 2010; Stadelmann *et al.* 2011c). Therefore, some countries may provide totally fresh resources while others just re-label already-promised pledges. We do not control for the 'additionality' of individual countries' FSF because of the methodological challenges involved, but we will discuss overall additionality of FSF below.

Table 5.1 shows the amounts reported as pledged, committed and allocated to FSF. While 94 per cent of the promised US$30 billion has been pledged, only 21–45 per cent has been 'committed-requested', and an even lower 29 per cent has been allocated to specific projects. The volume of allocated funds can be higher than the committed funds, as some countries may plan spending funds for specific programmes and funds without it being approved by the legislative bodies in charge. The pledges range from around US$1 million (Iceland, Liechtenstein and Malta) to Japan's US$15 billion, of which US$4 billion is private funding. Relative to GNI, we see some countries pledging more than 0.2 per cent of their 2009 GNI for FSF (Japan, Norway and Sweden), while the average is 0.07 per cent. The comparability between country data is so low that we can only conclude that the promise of US$30 billion is almost met by pledges but far less has been yet committed and allocated.

2.2 Thematic focus of fast-start finance

For the FSF pledges and allocations which specify the thematic focus of finance, there appears to be a greater focus on mitigation (including avoided deforestation (REDD)) than on adaptation – 67 per cent has been pledged or allocated to mitigation (which includes 17 per cent to REDD), and only 21 per cent to adaptation, with 11 per cent going to a multiple or unknown focus (Figure 5.2). These

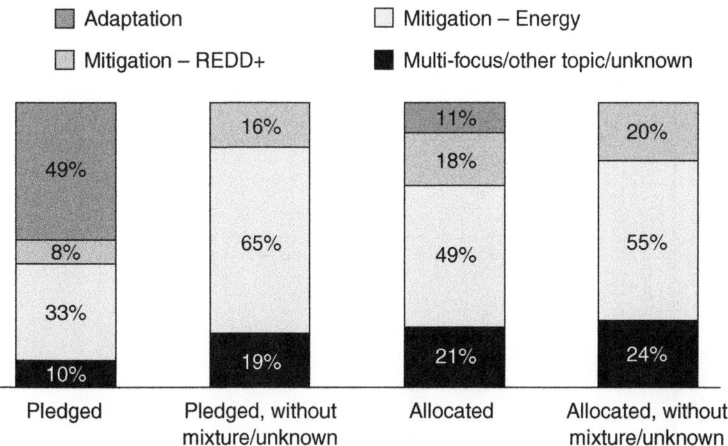

Figure 5.2 Share of mitigation and adaptation in FSF (source: own graphs based on Faststartfinance.org 2011; WRI 2011).

Table 5.1 Pledged, committed and allocated fast-start finance by June 2011

Country	*Amount pledged (US$ million)*[a]	*Pledge/GNI (%) (2009)*[b]	*Amount requested-committed (US$ million)*[c]	*Amount committed (US$ million)*[d]	*Amount allocated to projects/funds (US$ million)*[e]
EU Commission	214.7		71.6	71.6	71.6
Australia	641.1	0.07	641.1	0.0	641.1
Austria	58.0	0.01	–	–	58.0
Belgium	214.7	0.04	60.1	60.1	60.1
Canada	409.5	0.03	409.5	0.0	409.5
Cyprus	0.9	0.00	–	0.0	0.9
Czech Republic	2.4	0.00	–	0.0	2.4
Denmark	229.9	0.07	59.0	59.0	7.9
Finland	157.4	0.06	143.1	0.0	32.9
France	1,803.5	0.07	601.2	1,803.5	609.6
Germany	1,803.5	0.05	509.6	417.8	442.7
Greece	6.3	0.00	–	–	6.3
Hungary	1.4	0.00	–	–	1.4
Iceland	1.0	0.01	1.0	0.0	1.0
Ireland	143.1	0.07	–	–	34.7
Italy	386.2	0.02	–	–	426.1
Japan	15,000.0	0.31	7,200.0	0.0	1,958.7
Liechtenstein	1.2	0.02	–	1.2	1.2

Luxemburg	12.9	0.03	4.3	12.9	4.3
Malta	1.1	0.02	0.2	0.2	0.2
Netherlands	443.7	0.06	–	443.7	432.6
New Zealand	72.8	0.06	308.8	308.8	382.8
Norway	1,000.0	0.24	382.0	382.0	473.5
Poland	4.6	0.00	–	0.0	4.6
Portugal	51.5	0.02	17.2	17.2	30.4
Slovakia	1.5	0.00	–	0.0	1.5
Slovenia	11.5	0.02	11.5	0.0	0.1
Spain	536.8	0.04	191.8	0.0	184.8
Sweden	1,145.1	0.25	164.6	–	159.4
Switzerland	164.7	0.03	–	0.0	17.7
UK	2,475.6	0.10	937.4	937.4	1,044.1
US	1,704.0	0.01	1,704.0	1,700.0	1,083.7
Total	28,700.5	0.07	13,418.0	6,215.4	8,585.5
% of pledge	100%		47%	22%	30%
% of US$30 billion	96%		45%	21%	29%

Source: own table from data sources: a = Faststartfinance.org (2011), UNFCCC (2011); b = World Bank (2011); c = WRI (2011); d = Faststartfinance.org (2011); e = Faststartfinance.org (2011), UNFCCC (2011)

overall figures hide some important differences between individual donors: Australia and the EU Commission are providing an equal share of their resources to both mitigation and adaptation, while Japan has allocated a mere 10 per cent towards adaptation.

Many civil society organizations and developing countries in need of immediate support for adaptation argue that a 'balanced' allocation between mitigation and adaptation that developed countries have committed to in the Copenhagen Accord requires an equal split in resources being allocated to adaptation and mitigation. Others argue that a 'balanced' allocation can be interpreted in a variety of ways, and that an increased investment in mitigation today means lower emissions and hence less need for adaptation tomorrow, and thereby justifies prioritizing mitigation finance in the immediate term.

2.3 Bilateral versus multilateral channels of fast-start finance

In terms of delivery channels, some countries do not report on whether FSF funding will be delivered through bilateral or multilateral channels. For those that do, it appears there is a fairly close split between the two – roughly 41 per cent has been allocated to multilateral delivery channels, 51 per cent bilateral, and 8 per cent unknown (Figure 5.3). This means that FSF is rather more channelled through multilateral channels than past development and climate funds. In 2008 and 2009 multilateral channels only represented 30–45 per cent of both general and climate-marked official development assistance (ODA) and other financial flows (OOF), with OOF representing flows not concessional enough to be counted as ODA (OECD 2011b). Still, even more may have been expected to be channelled through multilateral funds given the recent proliferation in multilateral funds. The split in FSF spending between bilateral and multilateral indicates that many donors are interested in preserving their bilateral control over climate finance.[12]

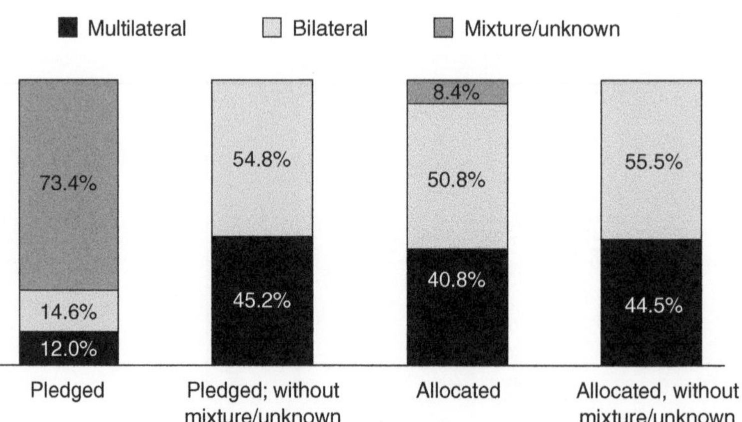

Figure 5.3 Share of bilateral and multilateral channels in FSF (source: own graphs from Faststartfinance.org 2011; WRI 2011).

2.4 Grants vs loans

The Copenhagen Accord states that FSF includes 'investments through international institutions'. While 'investments' is not clearly defined, it may be understood that it also includes loans. Indeed, roughly one-third of fast-start funds, for which the grant–loan share is known, is paid as loans or as capital contribution (Figure 5.4). Capital contributions differ from one-time loans in the way that funds receiving capital contribution can reinvest the money once loans are repaid (DECC and DFID 2010).

Is this inclusion of loans beneficial? There are two sides to the coin. On the one hand, many developing countries and some NGOs are not pleased that loans are included as this may lead to higher Southern debts, and is also inconsistent with the view that funds for adaptation represents some kind of 'compensation' for damages. In fact a high share of one-time loans would mean that the actual net-disbursed level will be below US$30 billion, as funds have to be paid back later on. On the other hand, there may also be benefits of loans – in the case of capital contributions, loans are re-invested when paid back, which increases the grant-equivalence over time. Furthermore, some studies have found that loans are more beneficial than grants for more developed, less-indebted countries with good fiscal policies, and in cases of low-risk revenue-generating projects (Cordella and Ulku 2004; Baudienville *et al.* 2009).

2.5 The status of disbursed funds

Perhaps most importantly, there is almost no data on the extent to which funds have been disbursed or delivered to specific projects, programmes and countries. This is problematic, as understanding how FSF is being implemented requires understanding how the finance committed by donor countries is actually being delivered on the ground.

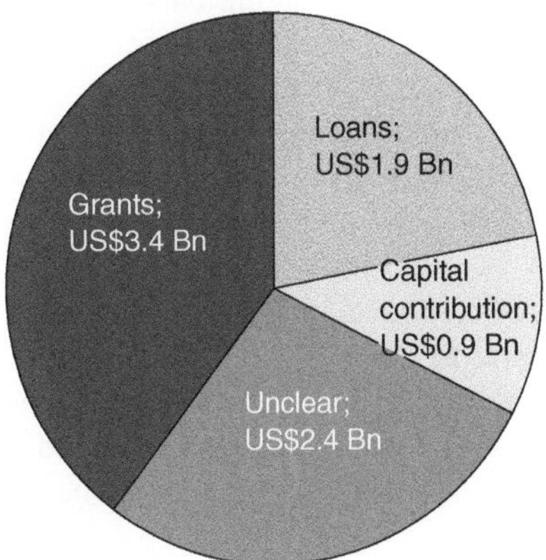

Figure 5.4 Share of grants/loans in allocated FSF (source: own graph based on Faststartfinance.org 2011; WRI 2011).

Some countries use wordings in their fast-start reports that suggest disbursements. The newest EU report on FSF (EU 2011) provides 2010 finance numbers under the heading 'delivering on our commitments', but again there is no agreed definition of what 'delivered' actually means, and it most likely refers to activities that have been approved or where money has been allocated, but not actually spent. Similarly, Australia (Australian government 2011) says that one-third of the fast-start package has been 'provided' to countries, regions and multilateral initiatives, which seems to be one step further than commitments. But again, the term 'provided' is not clearly defined.

In fairness, the actual delivery and disbursement of finance is often hard to measure given the nature and complexity of how finance is channelled (see the discussion on channels below). International public finance flows from North to South tend to pass through several intermediary channels before reaching the end user, making the actual flow and delivery of finance hard to follow. Because of the intermediary steps through which the finance passes, a donor may consider the money disbursed without the project receiving any money at all, because from the donor's perspective funds have been 'disbursed' from their accounts to another (implementing agency's) account.

In part because of this complexity, FSF and climate finance more generally tends to be rather slow in its disbursement, getting caught up in intermediary institutions and channels. Multilateral funds often give a particular role to international implementing organizations with complex sign-off procedures (e.g. the GEF and its implementing agencies, the World Bank, UN Development Programme (UNDP), UN Environment Programme (UNEP) and others). International climate funds also tend to have lengthy project approval procedures, which can cause severe delays in project delivery. Moreover, projects can be easily conceptualized and budgets created, but actual implementation of complex activities takes time and delays are common, particularly given the fact that addressing adaptation is a new issue where experience and proficiency is lacking.

There are a few important takeaway points regarding our current knowledge of FSF:

- FSF represents financial commitments made in a political context, and does not represent the creation of any new fund or institution. Rather FSF will be delivered through existing channels within the established international climate finance architecture.
- While pledges almost reach the promised level of US$30 billion, commitments and allocations are much lower by June 2011, while there is hardly any information on FSF disbursements. In any case, it appears that funds are slow to get out of the door and, although funding may be committed within the period of 2010–2012, it is unlikely that funds committed will be spent in this timeframe (see below).
- Although countries are committed to a 'balanced' allocation of climate finance between adaptation and mitigation, FSF appears to heavily prioritize mitigation investments.

- Bilateral and multilateral support seems to be fairly split, but in many cases contributor countries have not reported on their intended FSF delivery channels.

3 Governance and transparency of fast-start finance

FSF has had a decentralized governance structure from the beginning: the UNFCCC just provides an arena for loose, non-institutionalized exchange of information (e.g. within side events at UNFCCC conferences). Contributors decide themselves on the amount, timing, channels and spending (in countries and to programmes) of their funding. Recipients do not have any firm obligations either. The decentralized structure certainly complicates coordination, but it may also have its benefits in terms of flexibility of timing, channels and programmes, which allows for testing.

Given that decentralized governance also means lack of official and verified information, transparency of FSF has become a hotly debated topic. Transparency is important to build trust that funding is provided and wisely spent (WRI 2011c; Roberts *et al.* 2010; Schalatek *et al.* 2010; Transparency International 2011). While NGOs and scholars often call for transparency on the provision and channelling of FSF, transparency may be equally important on the spending side to assure effective use of funding and avoid corruption (see Box 5.1).

Box 5.1 Climate finance and corruption

One of the challenges related to transparency is the high corruption which exists in many of the countries to which climate finance will flow (Transparency International 2011). Most scholars agree that corruption, on average, decreases economic development and reduces aid effectiveness (Wei 1998; Collier and Dollar 2004; Aidt 2009). These lessons may also apply to climate finance, but few related studies exist (e.g. Buen and Michaelowa 2009).

Apart from the currently available sources (Faststartfinance.org, WRI and fast-start reports by June 2011), two additional sources will be available after the fast-start period of 2010–2012. First, information submitted to UNFCCC will be available, consisting of both the non-reviewed voluntary fast-start reports (May 2012, 2013) and the obligatory and reviewed national communications of Annex-I parties, in which all provided financial resources have to be reported. Second, the OECD DAC data on aid flows will provide information on the level of development and climate flows, around two years after the disbursement. Then the 2010–2012 disbursements can be compared with the pre-Copenhagen years 2007–2009 to assess whether climate funds have increased by US$10 billion per year without decreasing non-climate ODA.[13] Full UN documents and OECD data will probably not be available before 2014. Therefore, policy-makers and researchers will have to rely on scattered, diverse and non-reviewed sources of information for the next two years.

Table 5.2 shows for which parameters information is currently given and will probably be available by 2014. We will probably still miss information on baselines for 'new and additional' as well as programme features, and little will be known about effectiveness.

The current low-level of transparency will limit the scope of our following analysis on sources, channelling, use and effectiveness.

4 Sourcing of 'new and additional' fast-start finance

Even if US$30 billion will be delivered, this does not automatically mean that the Copenhagen promises have been fulfilled. The remaining question is whether the US$30 billion is really 'new and additional'.

Most contributor countries claim that their funding is 'new and additional' but in fact this is not obvious. The major problem is that while 'new and additional' has been a criterion for all UN climate finance since Rio in 1992, its baseline has never been properly defined. The most commonly used definitions for 'new and additional' are referring to funds beyond '0.7% of GNI spent for ODA' or 'beyond existing funds', and the latter definition may refer to climate or development, and past or promised funds (Brown *et al.* 2010; Stadelmann *et al.* 2011c). Given the lack of a definition, it is not possible to exactly assess novelty and additionality. Comparing funding and pledges made before Copenhagen with data on FSF (Faststartfinance.org 2011; WRI 2011) we estimate that around half of fast-start funds have been promised or planned before Copenhagen.

Linked to the issue of 'new and additional' is the sourcing of FSF because the current dependence on governmental budgets will make it difficult to upscale and secure 'new and additional' climate funds. FSF has – with the exception of Germany, who also used auctioning of emission allowances – been sourced from the general budgets of industrialized countries. General budgets are always subject to domestic pressure groups and suffer from decreased income in times of economic downturns, as just experienced in the years 2008–2009. Therefore, climate funds from general budgets are subject to budget cuts. For instance, US climate finance has been decreased from 2010 to 2011 due to fiscal constraints (Volvovici 2011) and the FSF proposed by the Swiss government was almost cut by its parliament. Another issue with general budgets is the risk that classic development funds are diverted; instead of using fresh climate sources, governments just re-channel money planned for development to climate issues. This diversion is not visible to the public, as climate finance is in most cases also accounted as ODA. Providing reliable, predictable funds beyond FSF will require new sources, preferably instruments putting a price on carbon emissions, such as international transport levies or auctioning of emission allowances (UN 2010). Another interesting source, which is not pricing emissions but rather taxing emission reductions, are carbon market levies such as the existing 2 per cent levy on CDM credits, used as the main funding source of the Adaptation Fund (see also the detailed discussion in Chapter 4).

Table 5.2 Transparency in FSF in the short- and long-term

Parameter	*Current information*		*Possible information by 2014*	
	Sources	*Transparency level*	*Sources*	*Transparency level*
Sources of funding	FSF reports, FSF website	+(+)	NC, FSF reports, FSF website	++?
Level, pledged	FSF reports, FSF website, WRI	++	NC, FSF reports, FSF website	++?
Level, disbursed	FSF reports	(+)	OECD, NC	+(+)?
Baseline for 'new and additional'	FSF reports, website, WRI	(+)	NC, FSF reports, FSF website	(+)?
Grants, loans or capital contribution	FSF reports, FSF website	+	NC, FSF reports, FSF website	+(+)?
Channel: bilateral vs multilateral	FSF reports, FSF website	+	NC, FSF reports, OECD, FSF website	+(+)?
Use: adaptation vs mitigation	FSF reports, FSF website	+	NC, FSF reports, OECD, FSF website	+(+)?
Use: recipient	FSF reports, FSF website	+	NC, FSF reports, OECD, FSF website	+(+)?
Use: programme features	FSF reports, FSF website	(+)	NC, FSF reports, FSF website	+?
Use: effectiveness	–	0	?	0?

Notes
++ fully transparent/comparable, + partly transparent/comparable, 0 not transparent/comparable.
FSF reports: voluntary FSF reports; FSF website: Faststartfinance.org; WRI: World Resources Institute; NC: national communications; OECD: OECD DAC statistics.

5 Channelling of fast-start funding: decentralized structures

As seen above, FSF is channelled through different bilateral and multilateral channels. These channels have different features regarding donor coordination, transparency, decision power and speed.

5.1 Donor coordination

In development assistance, proliferation of donors and fragmentation of their funds has led to increased costs and lower bureaucratic quality in recipient countries (Acharya *et al.* 2006; Knack and Rahman 2007). As a consequence, donors undertook efforts to increase harmonization by adopting the Paris Declaration on Aid Effectiveness (OECD 2008). Coordination has also become a problem within the climate regime. While in the 1990s most multilateral funding was channelled through the GEF Trust Fund, a wide range of multilateral and bilateral funding channels has emerged in the last few years (HBS/ODI 2011), a problem that has already been discussed by Greene (2004). There is some evidence that duplication is happening – for example, by funding several adaptation strategies in one country.[14]

Multilateral funding has the potential to increase coordination, but the proliferation of multilateral climate funds (see HBS/ODI 2011) limits coordination: e.g. multilateral adaptation funding is spent by GEF funds, the Adaptation Fund, EU funds, UNDP programmes and the Climate Investment Funds (CIF)'s Pilot Programme for Climate Resilience (PPCR), with all of them having differing governing boards and secretariats. Bilateral funding channels often meant fragmentation of funds in the past, but the commitment to 'donor harmonization' has led to increased coordination efforts in the last few years, while the outcome of this process is difficult to evaluate (see below).

5.2 Transparency

Multilateral climate funds have been quite transparent in the past, showing project documents and current status online (AFB 2011; CIF 2011b; CIF 2011c; GEF 2011). The GEF has also been transparent on the formula for allocation of funding (GEF 2010a, 2010b) and project evaluations (GEF 2011). Bilateral agencies have been less transparent, reporting only a little information (e.g. amount of funding, project title, short description and recipients) to the OECD (2011b), but not displaying the project documents. Some recent initiatives have been made to increase transparency (e.g. BMU 2011; DFID 2011; IATI 2011), but the level of information given by the multilateral channels, especially the GEF, has not yet been reached.

5.3 Decision power

Most multilateral channels incorporate balanced decision power between contributors and recipients. Of all multilateral channels, the Adaptation Fund is the only one where developing countries have a clear majority in decision-making. In the GEF's Council, developing countries have half of the votes, while developed and transition countries have the other. Also the CIFs, administered by the World Bank, which are often criticized as donor-driven, actually split the votes equally between developing and developed countries, which is no different from the governing system chosen for the new Green Climate Fund (GCF) in Cancun.

Within bilateral channels, contributors have traditionally been more dominant in decision-making. However, since the end of the Cold War, aid allocation criteria have shifted away from donor interests towards recipient needs and quality of policies (Berthelemy and Tichit 2004; Claessens *et al.* 2009), while the degree to which donors follow their own interests does vary a lot among countries (Berthelemy 2006). There may have been a further shift towards recipient needs following the Paris Declaration on Aid Effectiveness, but no statistical evaluation has been undertaken so far. Some development NGOs criticize country (and democratic) ownership is still far from being assured (Reality of Aid 2010). In climate finance, some recent examples show increased recipient ownership: some contributors support National Climate Trust Funds in developing countries (e.g. Bangladesh Climate Resilience Fund, Indonesia Climate Change Trust Fund), which means that recipient authorities decide on details of spending.

5.4 Speed

Multilateral funds often need more time for channelling, given the rigorous decision-making structures of multilateral institutions and the added steps in the delivery chain (Figure 5.5). While bilateral funds can be directly channelled to national implementing agencies, multilateral finance is, normally, first paid to a fund before it is channelled to national agencies.

In most cases, there is even another step between the multilateral fund and the national institutions: GEF funds are flowing through multilateral implementing agencies (mainly the UNDP and the World Bank), while funding of the CIFs is mainly flowing through multilateral development banks (MDBs). With the introduction of 'direct access', recipients can now also access funding directly from

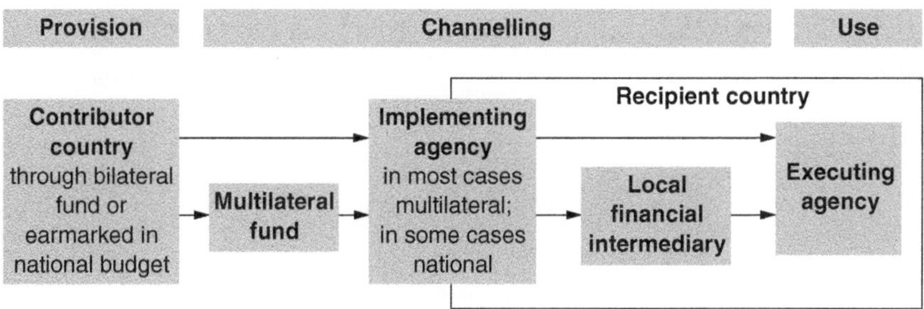

Figure 5.5 The climate finance supply chain.

the Adaptation Fund through accredited National Implementing Entities (NIEs), which may speed up delivery compared to the CIFs' and GEF's procedures (see the discussion in Chapter 4).

Generally, the GEF is the slowest multilateral disbursement channel due to the double approval by the GEF itself and its agencies.[15] But even the CIFs, thought to benefit from the faster decision process within the World Bank, have not been very fast in disbursing funds: of the US$4.5 billion pledged for the CIFs' Clean Technology Fund in 2008, only US$2.5 billion had been deposited at the World Bank by end of March 2011; just US$217 million had been transferred to the MDBs and US$116 million (or 2.5 per cent of the pledges) had been disbursed to the recipients by December 2010 (CIF 2011a).

Figure 5.6 shows the decision power, the level of coordination, transparency and the speed for different channels. The multilateral channels, responsible for more than half of FSF channelling, have in most cases higher transparency and increased donor coordination, while coordination is hampered by the proliferation of multilateral funds. On the other hand, bilateral channels are often quicker in disbursing funds and they may also be more flexible in terms of adapting programmes and responding to recipient countries' needs.[16]

6 Spending fast-start finance: scattered programmes and unknown effectiveness

While governance, transparency, sourcing and channelling of fast-start and long-term climate finance are often discussed (e.g. Müller *et al.* 2010; Roberts *et al.* 2010; Schalatek *et al.* 2010; Transparency International 2011; WRI 2011), the way money is spent is less often analysed.

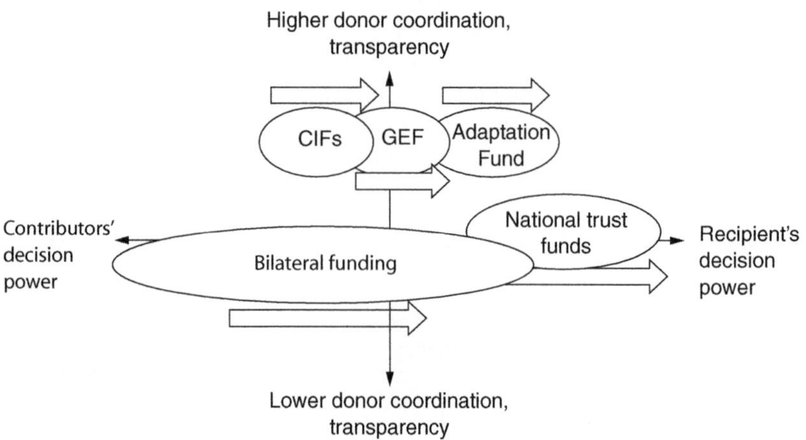

Figure 5.6 Speed, coordination and decision power within fast-start channels.

Note
Longer arrows mean faster channelling.

Regarding spending of FSF, there are two big questions. First, will the funds really be provided by 2012? Assuming an average time span of 2–4 years between pledge and disbursement,[17] some FSF will not be delivered by the end of 2012. This, however, is not necessarily a disadvantage, as delivering all FSF by 2012 would probably mean that some funds have already been committed before Copenhagen, making it questionable whether they are 'new and additional'.[18]

Second, is FSF effective? Assessment of effectiveness starts by defining the indicators, which can both be found at the outcome and the process level.

6.1 Outcome-based indicators to measure effectiveness

The outcome is what we are finally interested in: do funded actions and programmes result in mitigation and adaptation to climate change? Little has been written about the desired outcomes of FSF as a policy instrument for at least three reasons.

First, in the case of adaptation, universal indicators have never been agreed; this in contrast to mitigation, where the agreed indicator is GHG reductions or storage. For instance, the Adaptation Fund and the GEF both use a large set of indicators for adaptation projects, while there is not even comparability between different project documents (see Stadelmann *et al.* 2011b).

Second, outcomes are difficult to measure and uncertain as they may only show up after some years. This long-term measurement problem especially exists in the case of adaptation funding, where benefits are often not immediate. Limiting outcomes to the first years after project implementation would mean that only short-term measures are seen as effective.

Third, and probably related to the other two issues, it has never been politically decided that the outcome of FSF should be measured. Given the uncertainty and the missing agreement on indicators for adaptation, the hesitation to measure outcomes is understandable. However, this should not prevent policymakers from beginning to learn about outcome indicators.

In the long run, the missing knowledge about the impact of climate finance may not be accepted by the broader public. The CDM, with its established monitoring, reporting and verification system, may provide an interesting start for assessing outcome indicators. In the case of mitigation, the challenge is to move from the hard technology perspective of the CDM to a programme/policy perspective including 'softer' instruments. In the case of adaptation, as a first step, general outcome indicators have to be defined (Butzengeiger *et al.* 2011).

6.2 Process-based indicators to measure effectiveness

As the outcome of FSF is difficult to measure, it is useful to assess *process* indicators. Process indicators are meant to measure whether certain projects and programmes incorporate or have led to processes that should finally result in the desired outcomes.[19] Rather than assessing which process indicators for FSF are best at incentivizing adaptation and mitigation, we will pick some common process indicators and assess how well FSF performs on them.

As process indicators, we may use the process-based principles outlined by the Paris Declaration of Aid Effectiveness (OECD 2008): ownership, alignment, donor harmonization, mutual accountability and managing for results. While climate funds have different drivers than development assistance – mitigation funds target a global environmental good and adaptation funds are often seen as compensation rather than aid – the actors and institutions are similar. Therefore, the following analysis may provide useful insights regarding the effectiveness of FSF.

6.2.1 Ownership

Ownership is understood here as the leadership of developing countries in formulating climate and development strategies as well as in coordinating the incoming development and (in our context) climate funds. According to the Paris Declaration the role of industrialized countries is to respect Southern leadership and help build capacity for ownership.

Regarding formulation of climate strategies, several larger countries have established their own climate change strategies in the past few years (e.g. Brazil, China, India, Mexico and South Africa; see Fransen *et al.* 2011). Some small developing countries do not have a national climate plan of action (see annex of Clapp *et al.* 2010). Several existing national climate strategies (also called low-carbon development or emission strategies) are supported by international organizations and contributors (see also the discussion in Chapter 7). While such strategies are important, their development, in the case of smaller developing countries, is sometimes driven by international consultants and industrialized countries.[20] As low-carbon development strategies remain voluntary after the Cancun Agreements (UNFCCC 2010), a significant share of FSF will flow to countries without a clear climate strategy.

Incoming FSF is not fully coordinated by recipients, as parts of the funds are directly invested in projects without special consideration of national plans. However, some progress is made with National Climate Trust Funds, which are managed by recipients. Furthermore, some industrialized countries support capacity building for developing national climate strategies and NAMAs (e.g. Germany through the International Climate Initiative – see Chapter 7). Such capacity-building initiatives should enhance ownership of FSF in the long term. Summing up, full ownership is not achieved by FSF, but some progress is made.

6.2.2 Alignment with national plans

According to the Paris Declaration, donors should 'base their overall support on partner countries' national development strategies, institutions and procedures' (OECD 2008), which is subsumed under 'alignment'. In the case of FSF, alignment mainly means that funding programmes are aligned to priorities in national climate strategies.[21] First of all, such alignment is not possible in the cases of smaller countries where no climate strategies exist. Furthermore, there are single examples where FSF is not aligned with the national climate strategy, such as in the case of a French climate-related loan to the Philippines (ABS-CBN 2011). An overall judgement of whether alignment is achieved would, however, require further analysis.

6.2.3 Donor harmonization

Donor harmonization has already been touched upon in the section on channelling. Unfortunately, the diversity and proliferation of funds hampers the ability of donors to coordinate. On the side of bilateral programmes, which have been very fragmented in the past (Acharya *et al.* 2006; Thiele *et al.* 2010), there are few official signs for harmonization in the case of FSF. Only the EU may have internally coordinated its activities as it has been able to present a common fast-start report by the end of 2010 (EU 2010).

As official reports on donor harmonization are missing, can we externally measure harmonization of FSF? Some practitioners and scholars (Acharya *et al.* 2006; Thiele *et al.* 2010) argue that fewer but larger funds in the form of general or sectoral budget support can help decrease fragmentation. This can also allow governments to only deal with a few donor counterparts instead of trying to manage several donors with different funding cycles and requirements.

Using programme size and contributors per recipient as indicators, we can argue that fragmentation of FSF has not been fully avoided. Analysing the information of the nine contributors who provide it on project or programme level on Faststartfinance.org (2011), we see that while two contributors have project sizes above €50 million (France and Netherlands), the other countries have small project sizes (below US$4 million per project on average). Regarding counterparties per recipient, some recipients are targeted by the majority of contributors (e.g. Indonesia with 66 per cent of contributors, and Kenya with 55 per cent of contributors), while most recipients are not targeted by any donor (Figure 5.7). Interestingly, even Nepal, as a small country, receives funds from almost every second contributor.

While this analysis points to fragmentation, we also see some positive signs such as thematic specialization: while Norway focuses its FSF on REDD, the EU and Australia invest around half in adaptation, and Japan heavily relies on mitigation measures. Summing up, we have some signs for fragmentation of FSF, which is an indicator for non-perfect harmonization.

6.2.4 Mutual accountability

By 'mutual accountability' we mean that both contributors and recipients are accountable for development (and in our case climate) results. This implies that both sides would have to report on their contributions and achievements related to FSF. We have already assessed that the current information on provision and channels of fast-start funds is difficult to analyse; information on the spending of FSF is even more opaque.

While there are no specific rules on reporting of FSF, all countries have to report on finance in their national communications; industrialized countries on provided, and recipient countries on received. However, the finance data is hardly standardized and may need substantial improvement (Buchner *et al.* 2011). This has also been acknowledged by the decision to establish better reporting procedures in the Cancun Agreements.

Given the missing reports, we judge the criterion of mutual accountability hardly to be fulfilled in the case of FSF, especially relating to the use of finance.

6.2.5 Managing for results

Managing for results consists of three steps. First, desired results (and indicators) are clarified before the interventions; second, the results are measured; and third, the evaluations are used to improve future programmes. This 'result-based management' has become the norm in most development agencies over the past 10–15 years (Hulme 2007; UNDP 2007).

First, regarding definition of results and indicators before interventions, consistency is hardly given in the case of FSF. As we have already assessed above, outcome indicators are neither defined nor assessed and process indicators are very diverse, and often specific for each project. Furthermore, the validity of some process indicators is controversial (see Box 5.2 for an example).

Box 5.2 Leveraging investments as indicator of effectiveness?

One (rather process-based) indicator that has received a lot of attention is the leveraging of private funds. Leveraging funds is seen as a positive achievement of public climate finance. While private investment will be very important for reaching a 2°C target (World Bank 2009) and understanding the risks faced by the private sector will be key to mitigating climate change (Hamilton 2010; Ward 2010: Brown and Jacobs 2011), recent work has questioned if 'leveraged funds' is a meaningful indicator for efficiency in CO_2 mitigation (Stadelmann *et al.* 2011a).

Second, the issue of measuring, reporting and verification (MRV) of mitigation actions (and financial reports) has been heavily discussed since Bali 2007. In spite of many weeks of negotiations, no common MRV framework was available when FSF started in 2010. Therefore, various approaches for 'measuring' achievements of FSF are used, while 'reporting' is only happening in a few cases and 'verification' has been almost absent.

Third, learning from results is complicated due to a lack of indicators and lack of an agreed MRV system. Furthermore, there is no institutionalized learning process. Learning is mostly decentralized in individual organizations, while some new initiatives for knowledge sharing have been set-up, e.g. a joint website by the World Bank and UNDP (World Bank and UNDP 2011).

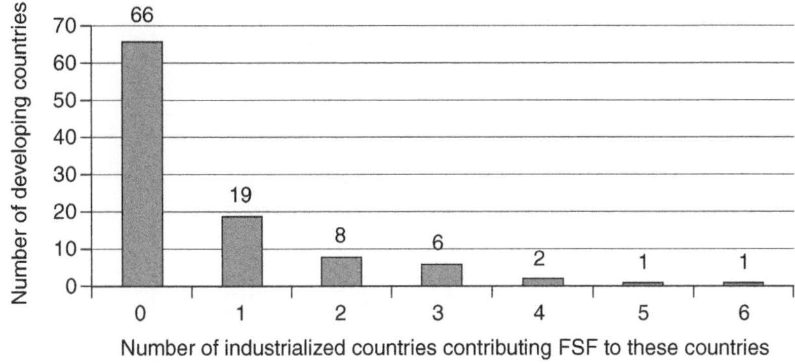

Figure 5.7 Fast-start contributors per recipient (source: own graph based on Faststart-finance.org 2011).

In conclusion, common result indicators and procedures for MRV are missing, while learning is decentralized. Some needed improvements are the work on result indicators, international coordination of MRV, inclusion of adaptation in MRV frameworks and increased exchange on the effectiveness of different instruments. To sum up, we see the criterion of 'managing for results' as hardly fulfilled, due to a disagreement on indicators, MRV procedures and missing learning platforms.

Table 5.3 summarizes how well FSF meets the different principles of the Paris Declaration. None of the process principles are fully achieved, while the largest uncertainty exists regarding the outcome measures, as neither the desired outcome nor the way of measuring it is defined.

7 Conclusions

It is not yet possible to assess if the US$30 billion FSF promised in Copenhagen will be completely and effectively delivered. While the collective pledge by developed countries almost meet this figure, less than half of the money has been committed or allocated to projects, and even less has been disbursed by June 2011. Given the long procedures of different channels, a part will – if at all – be delivered after 2012. Even when countries report to have the money delivered, it is not certain that those resources will be new and additional to ODA and existing pledges. Most FSF will be counted as ODA and around half of the funding had already been planned before Copenhagen. Furthermore, it is likely that some funds planned for development purposes have been redirected to climate finance. In order to avoid this diversion of funding and assure independence from the general budget, which is subject to short-term political pressure and economic cycles, new sources of climate finance will be needed. Within FSF, only Germany has sourced some funds from new sources. Much more of such sources (e.g. carbon taxes, auctioning of emission allowances) will be needed to secure an upscaling of funding.

Table 5.3 Fast-start finance and the principles of the Paris Declaration on Aid Effectiveness

	Process measures					*Outcome measures*
Principles in Paris Declaration	Ownership	Alignment	Donor harmonization	Mutual Accountability	Managing for results	
Indicator to assess FSF	Existence of national climate and development plans	Fast-start funds compatible with plans	Fewer and larger projects, sectoral and geographical specialization	Reports on delivery from both sides	Definitions of indicators, measuring, learning	Achieved CO_2 reductions, adaptive benefits
Assessment of FSF	*Partly achieved*: larger countries have strategies, while some smaller countries receive capacity building. Some strategies are externally driven.	*Difficult to assess*: in many cases, no national strategies exist so alignment is not possible; some evidence of non-alignment.	*Partly achieved*: some larger programmes and thematic specialization, but proliferation of funds; some countries are targeted by many countries while many are left out.	*Hardly achieved*: only voluntary reports by contributors, no reports by recipients; information especially missing related to spending.	*Hardly achieved*: Each fund/channel has its own indicators, but there is no agreement on international MRV; hardly any platform for learning.	*Difficult to assess*: CO_2 reductions unknown, no agreed indicator for the 'adaptive benefit'

Governance of FSF has been decentralized, with various multilateral and bilateral channels. While this decentralized system helps to increase flexibility, it raises questions regarding accountability and transparency. For instance, common reporting standards are missing. Some information on sources and channels of FSF are available but little is known regarding effectiveness. For measuring effectiveness, indicators developed in the context of the Paris Declaration may be used: ownership, alignment and harmonization, which are only partly given according to our assessment, and mutual accountability and management for results, which are hardly achieved because of a lack of agreed indicators, reporting formats and platforms for learning.

Learning from FSF, the transparency of providing climate finance can certainly be improved. Enhanced transparency could be achieved in two ways. First, a central system for tracking climate finance could be established, either by improving the current OECD system or creating a new UN system (e.g. by extending the planned NAMA registry to adaptation). Besides official data from both contributors and recipients, third-party sources from non-governmental actors may also be included (crowd-sourcing) (see AidData 2011). Second, transparency could also be improved by strengthening the existing reporting requirements under the UNFCCC and associated definitions of climate finance (Buchner *et al.* 2011). The decisions adopted by the international community in Cancun (improved reporting, voluntary fast-start reports, establishing a NAMA registry) are first steps to more transparency, and they give the UNFCCC the mandate to act on this issue (UNFCCC 2010).

Apart from enhancing transparency and MRV systems, longer-term climate finance should also aim at coordination of donor organizations, the measurement of results and improvements in procedures for learning.

Notes

1 This figure just represents the incremental costs. Even higher is the amount of needed investment, which is estimated to be US$250–550 billion per year by 2030 (World Bank 2009).

2 The World Bank refers to a scenario of stabilizing the GHG concentration at 450 ppm CO_2-e, which we treat here as equal to a 2°C scenario, being aware that there is uncertainty whether a 450 ppm scenario will stop global warming at 2°C.

3 The UNFCCC estimated US$28–67 billion for 2030 (UNFCCC 2008), but these costs may be underestimated (Parry *et al.* 2009).

4 Certainly, responsibility for emissions and capacity to adapt differs within industrialized and developing countries. While some very advanced developing countries should become net contributors to international climate finance from an equity point of view, the poorer developing countries will remain net recipients for at least several decades. One may also argue that richer citizens in poor countries should become net contributors to climate finance (Baer *et al.* 2007).

5 National climate change policies and measures have gradually become mainstreamed in many developing countries. Indeed, national governments worldwide recognize impacts of climate change as a serious challenge undermining their development agenda and posing threats to their citizens. However, many among small developing countries, such as small island developing states (SIDS) and least developed countries (LDCs), find

committing to a global goal of tackling climate change a challenge. This is mainly due to a lack of adequate national budgets and human resources to design and implement climate change adaptation and mitigation measures. Furthermore, even more advanced developing countries made their pledges under the Copenhagen Accord officially conditional on provision of finance and technology by industrialized countries.

6 In 2009, roughly US$9 billion of ODA and OOF was reported to be climate-related in 2009 (OECD 2011a). On one hand, this number may be too high as funds have been misreported (Michaelowa and Michaelowa 2011). Furthermore, funds where climate change is not the 'principal' but only a 'significant' object are included. On the other hand, this number may also be too low, as the marker for climate change only refers to mitigation and not to adaptation. However, adaptation funds have only reached US$0.1 billion per year across 2000–2006 (Roberts *et al.* 2008) and many adaptation programmes are wrongly coded as climate change mitigation (Michaelowa and Michaelowa 2011). See also the discussion in Chapter 2.

7 Transparency, not only on the provision but also on the recipient side, will be crucial to create trust and increase effectiveness of climate finance (Rudyk 2009; Schalatek *et al.* 2010; Stadelmann *et al.* 2011c; Transparency International 2011).

8 The effectiveness of climate finance, for both market and public flows, has been widely studied (Eberhard *et al.* 2004; Schneider 2007; Wara 2007; Okubo and Michaelowa 2010; Zerriffi and Wilson 2010) and major room for improvement has been identified. Furthermore, the IPCC sees environmental effectiveness as a major policy criteria (Gupta *et al.* 2007).

9 Canada counts its increase in funding as compared to the fourth GEF replenishment (US$18.5 million) towards the FSF pledge, not its entire GEF contribution (US$238.4 million) (Faststartfinance.org 2011).

10

> Finland's fast start support for the GEF, 11.6 million €, is calculated from the growth of the total contribution using the climate change focal area allocation percentage presented in the GEF's Annual Report 2008 (32 per cent). Finland's total contribution for GEF5 is around 84 per cent higher than for GEF4. Total contribution for GEF is 57.3 million € during the 5th Replenishment Period.
>
> (Faststartfinance.org 2011)

11 This is slightly different from the OECD definition, which sees commitments as 'a firm obligation, expressed in writing and backed by the necessary funds, undertaken by an official donor to provide specified assistance to a recipient country or a multilateral organization' (OECD 2011b). While the term 'commitment' in the FSF context is used to imply a commitment that the contributing country has made to provide resources to FSF generically, OECD takes it a step further to imply a commitment from the contributing country to a recipient country for specified activities.

12 The push to work bilaterally may come out of a sense that recent funds (such as the CIFs of the World Bank) have been slow to take shape and to spend, and also lack the tools (and in some countries the institutional credibility) to bring about lasting governance reform (personal communication with DFID associate).

13 The problem with climate vs non-climate ODA is that coding by donors has been of low quality and subject to political interests (see Michaelowa and Michaelowa 2011). Given the recent debates and more public scrutiny, an improvement can, however, be expected.

14 E.g., according to data from HBS/ODI (2011), Mozambique has received multilateral funding for the NAPA from the LDC fund and for 'environment mainstreaming and adaptation to climate change' from the MDG Achievement Fund, while funding for mainstreaming is planned by both the PPRC and the EU's Global Climate Change Alliance. Further past funds came from the Special Climate Change Fund (SCCF) and the Strategic Priority on Adaptation (GEF). On top of that, five bilateral agencies funded adaptation projects in Mozambique in 2009, while seven other multilateral/

bilateral organizations funded disaster risk management with obvious links to adaptation in 2009 (analysing data from OECD 2011a). The average size of all 19 funding occurrences is US$2.4 million.

15 However, speed of GEF disbursements has increased in the last year, and one may argue that quality may be improved by the double approval from GEF and the (multilateral) implementing agencies.

16 Bilateral channels also suffer less from principal–agent problems as there is a shorter chain of delegation from voters to decision-makers than in the case of multilateral funds (Vaubel 2006).

17 This may be even longer for multilateral funds – e.g. the GEF never disburses all resources available for a certain period (e.g. 2006–2010), and carries over the residual funds to the next period. For instance, around 15 per cent of the fifth replenishment was carried-over funds (GEF 2010c: 132).

18 For instance, Switzerland has only begun to plan FSF after Copenhagen, and parliamentary approval was only achieved in early 2011. Therefore, first disbursements will only take place in late 2011 and some funds may not be delivered by 2013. While other nations may be able to deliver funds much earlier, they do not achieve the same level of additionality.

19 Here, the importance of learning about outcomes becomes clear: without knowing the link between process and outcomes indicators, the relevance of certain 'process' indicators will always be in doubt.

20 As evidenced when developing a climate strategy for an African country (personal communication with external consultant).

21 Alignment does in a broader sense also include the set-up, improvement and use of in-country public financial management and procurement systems, strengthening of capacity by avoiding parallel implementation structures, increasing predictability of aid flows and the share of untied aid (OECD 2008).

References

ABS-CBN (2011) 'Misappropriated' climate fund a setback – Alvarez', ABS-CBN Corporation. Online. Available: www.abs-cbnnews.com/nation/07/19/10/%E2%80%98misappropriated%E2%80%99-climate-fund-setback-%E2%80%93-alvarez (accessed 10 June 2011).

Acharya, A., de Lima, A. and Moore, M. (2006) 'Proliferation and fragmentation: transactions costs and the value of aid', *Journal of Development Studies*, 42 (1): 1–21.

AFB (2011) 'Project and programme proposals'. Online. Available: http://adaptation-fund.org/projectprogrammeproposals (accessed 25 February 2011).

Aidt, T. (2009) 'Corruption, institutions, and economic development', *Oxford Review of Economic Policy*, 25 (2): 271–91.

Australian government (2011) 'Australia's fast-start finance update report: May 2011'. Online. Available: http://unfccc.int/files/cooperation_and_support/financial_mechanism/financial_mechanism_gef/application/pdf/australia--fast-start_update_report_may_2011_and_progress_report_dec_2010.pdf.

Baer, P., Athanasiou, T. and Kartha, S. (2007) 'The right to development in a climate constrained world: the greenhouse development rights framework', Heinrich Böll Foundation, Christian Aid, EcoEquity, Stockholm Environment Institute. Online. Available: www.ecoequity.org/docs/TheGDRsFramework.pdf.

Baudienville, G., Brown, J., Clay, E. and Te Velde, D. (2009) 'Assessing the comparative suitability of loans and grants for climate finance in developing countries', report for DFID, Overseas Development Institute.

Berthelemy, J. (2006) 'Bilateral donors' interest vs. recipients' development motives in aid allocation: do all donors behave the same?', *Review of Development Economics*, 10 (2): 179–94.

Berthelemy, J. and Tichit, A. (2004) 'Bilateral donors' aid allocation decisions: a three-dimensional panel analysis', *International Review of Economics & Finance*, 13 (3): 253–74.

BMU (2011) 'Project database of the International Climate Initiative', Berlin: Bundesministerium für Umwelt, Naturschutz und Reaktorsicherheit. Online. Available: www.bmu-klimaschutzinitiative.de/en/projects (accessed 8 June 2011).

Brown, J. and Jacobs, M. (2011) 'Leveraging private investment: the role of public sector finance, ODI Background Note', Overseas Development Institute. Online. Available: www.odi.org.uk/resources/download/5701.pdf.

Brown, J., Bird, N. and Schalatek, L. (2010) 'Climate finance additionality: emerging definitions and their implications', *Climate Finance Policy Brief*, 2, Heinrich Böll Foundation North America, Overseas Development Institute.

Buchner, B., Brown, J. and Corfee-Morlot, J. (2011) 'Monitoring and Tracking Long-Term Finance to Support Climate Action', OECD. Online. Available: www.oecd.org/dataoecd/57/57/48073739.pdf.

Buen, J. and Michaelowa, A. (2009) 'View from the inside: markets for carbon credits to fight climate change – addressing corruption risks proactively', in D. Zinnbauer, R. Dobson and K. Despota, *Global Corruption Report 2009: Corruption and the Private Sector*, Cambridge: Cambridge University Press, pp. 41–5.

Butzengeiger-Geyer, S., Michaelowa, A., Köhler, M. and Stadelmann, M. (2011) 'Policy instruments for climate change adaptation: lessons from mitigation and preconditions for introduction of market mechanisms for adaptation', paper presented at the Colorado Conference on Earth System Governance, 17–19 May, Colorado State University.

CIF (2011a) 'Trustee report on the financial status of the Clean Technology Fund: CTF Trust Fund Committee meeting – Wednesday, June 22, 2011, CTF/TFC.7/4', Climate Investment Fund Admin Unit, World Bank.

CIF (2011b) 'Country and regional investment plans', Climate Investment Fund Admin Unit, World Bank. Online. Available: www.climateinvestmentfunds.org/cif/Country%20Investment%20Plans (accessed 8 April 2011).

CIF (2011c) 'Projects', Climate Investment Fund Admin Unit, World Bank. Online. Available: www.climateinvestmentfunds.org/cif/current_information_documents (accessed 8 June 2011).

Claessens, S., Cassimon, D. and Van Campenhout, B. (2009) 'Evidence on changes in aid allocation criteria', *World Bank Economic Review*, 23 (2): 185–208.

Clapp, C., Briner, G. and Karousakis, K. (2010) 'Low Emission Development Strategies (LEDS): technical, institutional and policy lessons', OECD. Online. Available at: www.oecd.org/dataoecd/32/58/46553489.pdf.

Collier, P. and Dollar, D. (2004) 'Development effectiveness: what have we learnt?', *Economic Journal*, 114 (496): 244–71.

Cordella, T. and Ulku, H. (2004) 'Grants versus loans', *IMF Working Paper*, WP/04/161, International Monetary Fund.

DECC and DFID (2010) 'UK fast start climate change finance', Department for Energy and Climate Change, Department for International Development. Online. Available: www.dfid.gov.uk/Documents/BROCHURE%20UK%20FAST%20START.pdf.

DFID (2011) 'Project search', Department for International Development. Online. Available: http://projects.dfid.gov.uk (accessed 8 June 2011).

Eberhard, A., Tokle, S., Vigh, A., Del Monaco, A., Winkler, H. and Danyo, S. (2004) 'GEF Climate Change Program Study 2004', Global Environmental Facility. Online. Available: www.thegef.org/gef/sites/thegef.org/files/documents/Climate%20Change%20Program%20Study%202004%20English.pdf.

EU (2011) 'EU fast start finance report to the UNFCCC Secretariat: submission by Hungary and the European Commission on behalf of the European Union and its Member States. Budapest, 11 May 2011', Hungary/European Commission. Online. Available: http://unfccc.int/files/adaptation/application/pdf/hu-05-11-11_fsf_corr.pdf.

EU (2010) 'EU fast start finance report for Cancun', Council of the European Union.

Faststartfinance.org (2011) 'Fast start finance: contributing countries', Ministry of Housing, Spatial Planning and the Environment. Online. Available: www.faststartfinance.org/content/contributing-countries (accessed 26 April 2011).

Fransen, T., Nakhooda, S., Chu, E. and McGray, H. (2011) 'Comparative analysis of national climate change strategies in developing countries', World Resources Institute. Online. Available: www.wri.org/publication/developing-country-actions (accessed 1 June 2011).

GEF (2010a) 'Resource allocation framework'. Online. Available: www.thegef.org/gef/node/1738 (accessed 18 October 2010).

GEF (2010b) 'GEF-5 initial STAR allocations, GEF council meeting, June 29–July 2, GEF/C.38/Inf.8/Rev.1, 2010', Global Environment Facility.

GEF (2010c) 'Summary of negotiations: Fifth Replenishment of the GEF Trust Fund. Prepared by the GEF secretariat & the World Bank as Trustee', Global Environment Facility.

GEF (2011) 'GEF project database', Global Environment Facility. Online. Available: www.gefonline.org (accessed 1 June 2011).

Gomez-Echeverri, L. (2010) 'National funding entities. their role in the transition to a new paradigm of global cooperation on climate change', ECBI policy report, European Capacity Building Initiative.

Greene, W. (2004) 'Aid fragmentation and proliferation: can donors improve the delivery of climate finance?', *IDS Bulletin*, 35 (3): 66–75.

Gupta, S., Tirpak D.A., Burger, N., Gupta, J., Höhne, N., Boncheva, A.I., Kanoan, G.M., Kolstad, C., Kruger, J.A., Michaelowa, A., Murase, S., Pershing, J., Saijo, T. and Sari, A. (2007) 'Policies, instruments and co-operative arrangements', in B. Metz, O. Davidson, P. Bosch, R. Dave and L. Meyer (eds) *Climate Change 2007: Mitigation – Contribution of Working Group III to the Fourth Assessment Report of the Intergovernmental Panel on Climate Change*, Cambridge: Cambridge University Press, pp. 745–807.

Hamilton, K. (2010) 'Scaling up renewable energy in developing countries: finance and investment perspectives', Energy, Environment and Resource Governance Programme. Online. Available: www.chathamhouse.org/sites/default/files/public/Research/Energy,%20Environment%20and%20Development/0410pp_hamilton.pdf.

HBS/ODI (2011) 'Climate Funds', Heinrich Böll Foundation, Overseas Development Institute. Online. Available: www.climatefundsupdate.org/listing (accessed 26 February 2011).

Hulme, D. (2007) 'The making of the Millennium Development Goals: human development meets results-based management in an imperfect world', *Brooks World Poverty Institute Working Paper*, 16, University of Manchester.

IATI (2011) 'IATI registry', DFID, World Bank. Online. Available: http://iatiregistry.org (accessed 8 June 2011).

Knack, S. and Rahman, A. (2007) 'Donor fragmentation and bureaucratic quality in aid recipients', *Journal of Development Economics*, 83 (1): 176–97.

Michaelowa, A. and Michaelowa, K. (2011) 'Coding error or statistical embellishment? The political economy of reporting climate aid', *World Development*, 39 (11): 1010–20.

Müller, B., Höhne, N. and Ellermann, C. (2009) 'Differentiating (historic) responsibilities for climate change', *Climate Policy*, 9 (6): 593–611.

Müller, B., Sharma, A., Gomez-Echeverri, L., Rook, D.P. and Chandani, A. (2010) 'The reformed financial mechanism of the UNFCC: Part II – the question of oversight', Post Copenhagen Synthesis Report, 52, Oxford Institute for Energy Studies.

Oanda (2011) 'Oanda: currency converter'. Online. Available: www.oanda.com/lang/de/currency/converter (accessed 30 May 2011).

OECD (2008) 'The Paris Declaration on Aid Effectiveness and the Accra Agenda for Action', OECD.

OECD (2011a) 'OECD. StatExtracts. Creditor Reporting System _Full'. Online. Available: http://stats.oecd.org/Index.aspx (accessed 18 March 2011).

OECD (2011b) 'DAC glossary of key terms and concepts'. Online. Available: www.oecd.org/document/32/0,3746,en_2649_33721_42632800_1_1_1_1,00.html#Commitment (accessed 3 June 2011).

Okubo, Y. and Michaelowa, A. (2010) 'Effectiveness of subsidies for the Clean Development Mechanism: past experiences with capacity building in Africa and LDCs', *Climate and Development*, 2 (1): 30–49.

Parry, M.L., Canziani, O.F., Palutikof, J.P. and Hanson, C.E. (2007) *Climate Change 2007: Impacts, Adaptation and Vulnerability: Contribution of Working Group II to the Fourth Assessment Report of the Intergovernmental Panel on Climate Change*, Cambridge and New York: Cambridge University Press.

Parry, M., Arnell, N., Berry, P., Dodman, D., Fankhauser, S., Hope, C., Kovats, S. and Nicholls, R. (2009) 'Assessing the costs of adaptation to climate change: a review of the UNFCCC and other recent estimates', International Institute for Environment and Development. Online. Available: http://pubs.iied.org/pdfs/11501IIED.pdf.

Reality of Aid (2010) 'Aid and development effectiveness: towards human rights, social justice and democracy', Reality of Aid 2010 report. Online. Available: www.realityofaid.org/roa-reports/download/file/UHZwUGdaZ0RNMjdraGdxT1dlbDArbzhBZ3lMS0s3N-lhsZGhnbWQ3ZU9pTVJxTis5dkI1K3hWMFRVaE43VldBeE5iYkZLcFdXN-3JoZk04empGdGVORkE9PQ/sec/2/part/1.

Roberts, J.T., Stadelmann, M. and Huq, S. (2010) 'Copenhagen's climate finance promise: six key questions', *IIED Briefing February 2010*, London: International Institute for Environment and Development.

Roberts, J.T., Starr, K., Jones, T. and Abdel-Fattah, D. (2008) 'The reality of official climate aid', *Oxford Energy and Environment Comment*, Oxford: Oxford Institute of Energy Studies.

Schalatek, L., Bird, N. and Brown, J. (2010) 'Where's the money? The status of climate finance post Copenhagen – The Copenhagen Accord, UNFCCC negotiations and a look at the way forward', Heinrich Böll Foundation North America, Overseas Development Institute. Online. Available: www.boell.org/downloads/HBF-ODI_ClimateFinace_Post-Copenhagen_WhereIsTheMoney.pdf.

Schneider, L. (2007) 'Is the CDM fulfilling its environmental and sustainable development objectives? An evaluation of the CDM and options for improvement', report prepared for the WWF. Online. Available: www.oeko.de/oekodoc/622/2007-162-en.pdf.

Stadelmann, M., Castro, P. and Michaelowa, A. (2011a) 'Is there a leverage paradox in climate finance?' Climate Strategies. Online. Available: www.climatestrategies.org/component/reports/category/71/324.html (accessed 31 July 2011).

Stadelmann, M., Butzengeiger-Geyer, S., Michaelowa, A. and Köhler, M. (2011b) 'Universal metrics to compare the effectiveness of climate change adaptation projects', paper presented at the Colorado Conference on Earth System Governance, 17–19 May, Colorado State University.

Stadelmann, M., Roberts, J.T. and Michaelowa, A. (2011c) 'New and additional to what? Options for baselines to assess "new and additional" climate finance', *Climate and Development*, 3(3); 175–92

Thiele, R., Aldasoro, I. and Nunnenkamp, P. (2010) 'Less aid proliferation and more donor coordination? The wide gap between words and deeds', *Journal of International Development*, 22 (7): 920–40.

Transparency International (2011) *Global Corruption Report: Climate Change*, London: Earthscan.

UN (2010) 'Report of the Secretary-General's High-level Advisory Group on Climate Change Financing'. Online. Available: www.un.org/wcm/webdav/site/climatechange/shared/Documents/AGF_reports/AGF_Final_Report.pdf (accessed 20 April 2011).

UNFCCC (2008) 'Investment and financial flows to address climate change: an update'. Online. Available: http://unfccc.int/resource/docs/2008/tp/07.pdf (accessed 26 July 2011).

UNFCCC (2009) 'Copenhagen Accord: advance unedited version'.

UNFCCC (2010) 'FCCC/CP/2010/7/Add.1 The Cancun Agreements: Outcome of the work of the Ad hoc Working Group on Long-term Cooperative Action under the Convention'. Online. Available: http://unfccc.int/files/na/application/pdf/07a01–1.pdf (accessed 14 June 2011).

UNFCCC (2011) 'Fast-start finance'. Online. Available: http://unfccc.int/cooperation_support/financial_mechanism/fast_start_finance/items/5646.php (accessed 1 June 2011).

Vaubel, R. (2006) 'Principal–agent problems in international organizations', *Review of International Organizations*, 1 (2): 125–38.

Volvovici, V. (2011) 'Clinton defends climate spend in State Dept. budget', Point Carbon. Online. Available: www.pointcarbon.com/1.1511718 (accessed 26 May 2011).

Wara, M. (2007) 'Is the global carbon market working?', *Nature*, 445: 595–6.

Ward, M. (2010) 'Engaging private sector capital at scale in financing low-carbon infrastructure in developing countries', draft report June 2010. Private Sector Investment Project, GtripleC.

Wei, S.-J. (1998) 'Corruption in economic development: beneficial grease, minor annoyance, or major obstacle?', *World Bank Policy Research Working Paper*, 2048.

World Bank (2009) *World Development Report 2010: Development and Climate Change*, Washington, DC: World Bank.

World Bank (2010) 'Economics of adaptation to climate change study: a synthesis report – final consultation draft, August 2010'. Online. Available: http://siteresources.worldbank.org/EXTCC/Resources/EACC_FinalSynthesisReport0803_2010.pdf.

World Bank (2011) 'GNI, Atlas method (current US$)'. Online. Available: http://data.worldbank.org/indicator/NY.GDP.PCAP.CD (accessed 21 April 2011).

World Bank and UNDP (2011) 'Climate fnance options'. Online. Available: www.climatefinanceoptions.org (accessed 1 June 2011).

WRI (2011) 'Summary of developed country "fast-start" climate finance pledges'. Online. Available: www.wri.org/publication/summary-of-developed-country-fast-start-climate-finance-pledges (accessed 26 April 2011).

Zerriffi, H. and Wilson, E. (2010) 'Leapfrogging over development? Promoting rural renewables for climate change mitigation', *Energy Policy*, 38 (4): 1689–700.

6 New market mechanisms for mitigation

Getting the incentives right

Sonja Butzengeiger, Björn Dransfeld, Martin Cames, Axel Michaelowa and Sean Healy

1 Introduction

The project-based mechanisms of the Kyoto Protocol, i.e. the Clean Development Mechanism (CDM) and Joint Implementation (JI), are – in combination with the EU Emissions Trading Scheme (EU ETS) – the backbone of the international carbon market. In particular, the CDM has proven to be *the* instrument incentivizing the private sector in its search for greenhouse gas (GHG) mitigation opportunities worldwide (see Chapter 1).

While the end of the first commitment period of the Kyoto Protocol has entered its home stretch, policy-makers have started negotiating potential new market-based mechanisms as potential elements of an international post-2012 climate policy regime. At the 13th Conference of the Parties (COP) in Bali, the 'Bali Action Plan' (UNFCCC 2007) called under Item 1b (iv) for the consideration of 'various approaches, including opportunities for using markets, to enhance the cost-effectiveness, and to promote, mitigation actions, bearing in mind different circumstances of developed and developing countries'.

The concepts underlying the discussion of these new market-based mechanisms are essentially 'trading' and 'crediting'. Crediting does not impose mandatory targets on a sector or country, but rather works with a 'no-lose' character, meaning that a developing country is not punished when not meeting the target. The mechanism provides an incentive to harvest low-cost, hitherto non-mobilized emission reduction potential by using credits below the no-lose target as the 'carrot'. Trading, on the other hand, is based on the concept of emissions trading and imposes a mandatory reduction target on a certain sector or scheme, making it a compliance mechanism. The target can be – but does not have to be – an international commitment by the host country.

Important reasons for new market mechanisms are, inter alia:

- upscaling global investments in GHG reduction activities;
- providing a bridge for the transition towards a global carbon market and for the transition from a non-Annex-I to an Annex-I country;
- overcoming the flaws of project-based mechanisms such as (1) high transaction costs due to necessary registration, monitoring and verification

procedures; (2) lack of environmental integrity due to a high risk of carbon leakage and/or inflated baselines; and (3) limitations in the mitigation potentials which could be addressed by them (e.g. closure of activities without replacement at the same site) (see also the discussion on the shortcomings of the CDM in Chapter 1).

Since the focus of new market-based mechanisms is on upscaling mitigation, they address broader segments of the economy, such as sectoral activities or even mitigation programmes on a national level, rather than standalone projects. The political and scientific debate has reflected these instruments, mainly to be implemented on a sectoral level ('sectoral trading' and 'sectoral crediting'). However, the crediting of emissions reductions is also discussed for nationally appropriate mitigation actions (NAMAs) of non-Annex-I countries ('NAMA crediting').[1] NAMAs were initially mentioned in the Bali Action Plan and address voluntary activities of GHG emissions mitigation in developing countries that can be supported by industrialized countries in the form of financing, technology transfer or capacity building (see the discussion of NAMAs in Chapter 7). Under the subsequent discussion of new market mechanisms, the concepts of crediting and trading are discussed from a technical viewpoint, but do not necessarily preclude a sectoral or national scope.

All concepts have in common that their targets are set at a governmental level. The governments are then free to choose from various means to reduce GHG emissions at the sector level in order to reach the targets. These means may comprise, inter alia:

- voluntary actions to reduce emissions for reputational reasons;
- governmental 'carrots' (e.g. feed-in tariffs, subsidies, training programmes);
- governmental regulation (e.g. efficiency or performance standards for single technologies);
- governmental 'sticks' (e.g. carbon taxes/other taxes);
- domestic emissions trading schemes.

The establishment of new market mechanisms would also change the role of emitters (e.g. private entities) and the government compared to the situation with project-based mechanisms. Under the latter, the host government's role is essentially limited to initial project approval. In practice, some governments have actively encouraged the establishment of CDM projects. However, the responsibility for the actual implementation of the project and the achievement of the projected emission reductions remains entirely with the project developer or project owner. Under a new market mechanism, the host-country government would have a more active role and would have to ensure that the emission reductions are actually achieved, because otherwise no revenues to cover additional cost for GHG mitigation measures would be received.

Against this background this chapter scrutinizes whether the shift in responsibility from emitters or investors to host-country governments would limit or even eliminate emitters' incentives to engage in seeking mitigation options and, if so, by which means such an outcome could be avoided or limited to the extent possible. It should be noted that emitters may have a different legal character – public, public–private or solely private. However, it is assumed that the strongest incentives in this respect are required for private entities; hence we concentrate on the private sector.

In the following sections we describe how new market mechanisms could work and the challenge which may arise from the responsibility structure, in particular under a crediting mechanism. Based on this assessment we discuss the extent to which potential policy instruments and measures can provide the required incentive to seek cost-effective GHG mitigation options. We then complement these considerations with a summary of views of selected actors on this issue and with a synopsis of experiences gained so far. Finally, we draw conclusions and derive implications for the concept of new market mechanisms.

2 Functioning of new market mechanisms

2.1 Crediting mechanisms

Under a crediting mechanism, a country agrees to a reduction target, which is set below a business-as-usual (BAU) scenario. Due to the fact that most developing countries are not willing to accept firm commitments, this reduction target is assumed to have no binding character (a no-lose target).

The no-lose target can either be of absolute nature (i.e. total amount of CO_2-e) or be intensity-based (i.e. the amount of CO_2-e per unit of output). The performance of the emission sources covered by the mechanism will be monitored over the accounting period in order to compare the actual emissions to the baseline level. Here, the monitoring, reporting and verification (MRV) requirements depend on the policy instruments implemented by the host country.

In the case of overperformance against the no-lose target, the emission reductions below the no-lose target will be credited, ex-post (see Figure 6.1). In the case of non-compliance, no sanctions apply. Credits will be tradeable on the international carbon market and hence provide international finance for mitigation. The idea is that the host country initially contributes to mitigation through domestic measures, potentially supported by international finance and technology (see Schmidt *et al.* 2006), below the BAU scenario but above the no-lose target (essentially the ones with the lowest abatement costs, so-called 'low-hanging fruits') but can obtain international carbon finance for activities that address reductions beyond the no-lose target (so-called 'higher-hanging fruits'). However, the incentive for the government to meet or even over-achieve the no-lose target is clearly weaker than under a trading mechanism with a mandatory goal.

2.2 Trading mechanisms

A trading mechanism implies an absolute commitment to reduce GHG emissions of a certain sector for the host country. In cases of non-compliance with the target, sanctions will apply to the host country. An amount of allowances

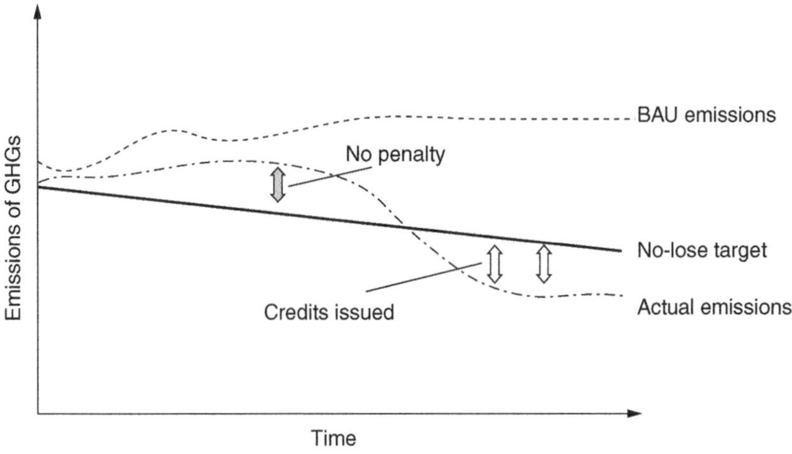

Figure 6.1 Crediting mechanism with a no-lose target.

corresponding to the target will be allocated to the sector (or country) ex-ante. Given the binding nature of this mechanism, the government will very likely implement rather strict policy measures, e.g. setting up a domestic/sectoral emissions trading scheme or by imposing mandatory measures. It needs to be acknowledged that at the UN level, no details of mandatory sectoral trading have been discussed, so there is no clarity yet on procedures and responsibilities of the involved actors. However, one option is described in the following.

The government of a host country defines a national emissions target ('cap') for a given sector over a certain compliance period, e.g. based on verified historical data. This target has to be approved by an international body such as the COP to the UNFCCC. Before each compliance period, the respective country will be allocated the amount of emission allowances equivalent to the cap. These allowances can be traded on the international carbon market. Within the compliance period, the emissions of the respective sector will be monitored. At the end of the compliance period the country has to surrender an amount of allowances for the respective sector that is equivalent to the aggregate sectoral emissions in that period. This means that the host country's government will be liable to ensure that the sectoral cap is met. The decision of which measures to take for reducing the sector's GHG emissions would be the sole decision of the government or respective authority responsible for the sector. If the country is not in compliance with its target, sanctions such as penalty fees or the cancellation of additional allowances would need to be imposed by the international authority supervising the mechanism. The government may also decide to pass the liability for compliance to the respective sector by introducing a domestic installation-based sectoral trading scheme. However, under the current state of the negotiations such binding targets appear rather unrealistic. Figure 6.2 visualizes a sectoral trading mechanism with an absolute target and the cap below the BAU emission trend for the sector.

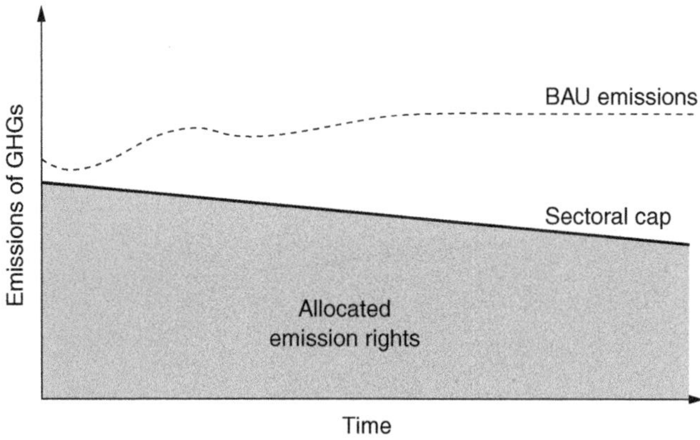

Figure 6.2 Sectoral trading with an absolute target.

2.3 Differences of new market mechanisms compared to project-based mechanisms

The market mechanisms described above are in many aspects fundamentally different to project-based mechanisms such as the CDM. However, two aspects are central with regard to the different incentive structure of new market mechanisms compared to the CDM:

- coverage of all activities or installations within a certain boundary; and
- requirements for governments to play a different role.

Under a project-based mechanism, only selected activities or installations will be subject to mitigation measures. Under the new market mechanism, in contrast, all installations within an ex-ante determined boundary will be covered. This shift will increase the mitigation potential that can be addressed; enhance the portfolio of technical mitigation measures that can be taken, especially if the boundary is wide and includes various activity types; increase environmental integrity by reducing the risk of leakage since output cannot be transferred to uncovered activities; and reduce transaction costs because a number of requirements under a project-based approach such as registration and determination of a baseline only have to be done once and not per project activity. New market mechanisms will also enable a transition to advanced or integrated mitigation technologies if the boundaries are defined adequately.

In addition, the responsibility for the emissions reduction would be shifted from the project owner or project developer to the host-country government. Currently, governments only need to approve during the registration process that a CDM project complies with their sustainability criteria; they do not face any responsibility if the project does not generate the revenues required to recover the mitigation costs. The economic risk of a mitigation project is exclusively borne by the project owner.

Under new market mechanisms, private entities cannot take the responsibility for an entire scheme including sectoral activities. Therefore, the host-country government needs to take that responsibility and needs to ensure that the envisaged GHG mitigation is actually achieved.

In this regard, new market mechanisms are much closer to international emissions trading pursuant to Article 17 of the Kyoto Protocol, which entitles industrialized countries to trade emission allowances among themselves. Governments are not required to, but may, directly involve emitting entities in the trading of internationally recognized emission allowances. The same would apply to new market mechanisms. Host-country governments would, possibly after consultations with business representatives of the covered actors or sectors, submit a proposal for the implementation of a new market mechanism scheme to the respective international authority (e.g. the COP to the UNFCCC). This proposal would include a clear definition of the sector(s), BAU projections of the scheme's threshold, a target (absolute or no-lose) including the country's own contributions and potentially a detailed description of how the target should be achieved. After approval of the proposal, the host-country government needs to ensure that the projected GHG reductions are achieved. As with international emissions trading, the government will trade excess allowances or generated reduction credits to cover the cost of incentives for the covered activities or installations in their country.

3 Incentivizing actors under new market mechanisms

3.1 Role of actors

As described above, the roles of the involved actors will change under new market mechanisms compared to project-based offset activities. The focus will shift to the government as the administrative authority, while the private sector is (1) the emitter and (2) the source of private finance. To assess the incentives, as discussed above, all emitters are regarded as private here.

3.1.1 The role of governments

Quite evidently, governments, in particular host-country governments, need to take a different role with more responsibilities under a new market mechanism.

In contrast to project-based mechanisms, where project owners or project developers, i.e. private entities, develop and implement a project, under new market mechanisms the host-country government would have the leading role in establishing mitigation efforts in their country. Initially, it would develop a proposal for the implementation of a mitigation scheme that would include

- a clear definition of the scheme's boundary, including an enumeration of activities which would not be covered, i.e. a clear definition of the scope in geographical and sectoral regards;
- a BAU projection which will be used to determine the level of ambition;
- an absolute or a no-lose target over a clear timeframe (5, 10, 15 years, etc.), which includes a certain degree of own contributions;
- a detailed description of how the necessary mitigation measures are incentivized;
- a projection of the impact of these incentives on the covered GHG emissions; and
- a reliable monitoring plan.

After a review by a supervising entity (e.g. a body charged by the COP), the proposal would be approved and could then be implemented by the government.

In the case of a mandatory target (sectoral trading), the host-country government would receive allowances corresponding to their target. At the end of the timeframe or after ex-ante agreed periods, the host-country government needs to submit an inventory for the scheme and surrender the corresponding amount of allowances. The excess allowances – the amount of which can be estimated ex-ante from the difference between the threshold and the projected emissions using sectoral incentives – can be sold on the global carbon market to recover the financial resources which are needed to provide the mitigation incentives. However, the host-country government would have to purchase additional allowances if the actual emissions turn out to be higher than the remaining allowances.

Provided the units established under the market mechanism are fully fungible with allowances under international emissions trading, the host-country government could trade these national/sectoral allowances with all parties participating in international or sectoral emissions trading. In addition, the host-country government could also trade these allowances with private entities of those countries if the governments provide for such direct involvement of the private sector.

With a no-lose target (under a crediting mechanism), the host-country government can participate in trading efforts only after credits have been issued. However, host-country governments could try to establish agreements similar to the so-called emission reduction purchase agreements (ERPAs) under the CDM. Under such an agreement, the host-country government and countries or private entities which need to purchase credits would agree ex-ante to trade credits at a certain price once they were issued. These agreements at times include upfront payments by the purchasers, which result in a respective rebate on the agreed credits price. The host-country government can also mobilize upfront financial resources to recover parts of the costs of those incentives or measures which are planned to achieve the promised emission reduction in their countries. It needs to be acknowledged, however, that at least in the CDM, upfront payments typically are not sufficient to cover significant parts of the required incremental investment.

Moreover, for crediting schemes, host-country governments need to guarantee investors the financial incentives for each tonne actually reduced, even if the agreed target is not met. Hence, host-country governments might therefore propose rather unambitious targets. Private investors will scrutinize publically available documents of any specific mitigation action under the scheme. If they basically agree with the proposal, they will check whether investing in GHG emission reductions will be economically attractive or not.

Finally, the host country's government may change during the economic lifetime of mitigation measures and the new government may withdraw the incentive. This would certainly result in mistrust against the new government and the country in general, and this mistrust would most likely not be limited to mitigation investments, but would affect any foreign investment. Such regulatory risk can therefore not be entirely denied, but seems to be small because it would cause consequences not just for mitigation investments but for the entire host-country economy.

3.1.2 The role of the private sector

The private sector is involved as (1) the emitting entity that is required to reduce emissions in the host country, but also (2) as the provider of private investments in order to finance mitigation actions.

Regarding the latter it shall be noted that climate policy relies on substantial financial amounts within the next decade in order to be effective. As per the Copenhagen Accord (UNFCCC 2009b) and the Cancun Agreements (UNFCCC 2010a, 2010b), parties have pledged huge amounts for financing adaptation and mitigation actions through fast-start finance (FSF) (see Chapter 5). Nevertheless, the final financing architecture is still under negotiation. But what has become clear so far is that money available from public donors (either through ODA or through multilateral players such as the World Bank) will have to leverage large-scale investments to limit global warming to 2°C, as aimed for in the Cancun Agreement. Probably, public finance will not be large enough to leverage the needed private investments in developing countries (up to US$500 billion per year by 2030 – see IEA 2009). Thus, further incentives are required, which can be accessed through the use of new market mechanisms. The CDM in this respect has nicely shown how the private sector responds to incentives (see Chapter 1).

On the role of the private sector as emitting entities within the host country, these can either be involved directly, indirectly or not at all in the global carbon market. It is at the host country's discretion how to provide incentives to private entities. Whichever option is selected, it is important that planned emission reductions are finally achieved. Otherwise, no credits can be issued whose revenues could be used to recover the cost of incentives or measures. Even worse, if the host country has agreed to an ERPA, the government might even be forced to pay for non-delivery of credits unless such non-delivery risks are not covered by respective insurances.

Emitters covered under the scheme would at least to the extent be involved that they need to decide whether the provided incentive would make any mitigation measures economically viable. If that is the case they may implement such measures themselves or task project developers with the implementation of such measures. Greenfield projects such as renewable-energy projects may be implemented by emitters or by project developers with specific experience in the respective field. The extent to which project developers will be involved may depend on how the incentives to reduce emissions are provided to the covered actors.

3.2 Challenges for private investors under new market mechanisms

While any new market mechanism aims to trigger investments in mitigation activities, a crucial question is how these investments are going to be incentivized. Incentives can either be of negative nature ('sticks' such as taxes or standards), forcing the emitter to act in a certain way, or of positive nature ('carrots'), rewarding action that reduces emissions. The willingness of investors to invest in certain activities depends on several parameters, such as the mechanism applied (trading or crediting), the detailed design of the scheme or country- and sector-specific parameters.

As described above, the host-country government agrees on an absolute or voluntary (no-lose) target for a certain domestic sector and is free to choose the most appropriate and economic means to keep the emissions below the targets.

In order to do so, a domestic framework that urges the emitters of the respective scheme to act in line with the governmental specifications has to be set-up. Key parameters for successful implementation of any mitigation action are thus (1) the design of the policy framework; (2) the ability of the government to implement or even enforce action under this framework; and (3) the respective emitters that have to reduce emissions.

The design of the policy framework determines instruments and measures that can or must be applied to achieve respective reductions and specifies rules and procedures for the application of these measures – for instance, responsibilities of actors, monitoring and verification or a sanctioning regime. These potential measures will differ depending on whether a trading or crediting mechanism is installed and depending on the nature of the target (absolute/no-lose).

The ability of a government to implement mitigation action under the policy framework is certainly dependent on many factors, such as the form of governance or the government's capability of asserting its positions against lobby groups. De facto dictatorships may find it easier to enforce action, while democracies strive to adopt rather balanced, consensus-orientated solutions. On the other hand, policies implemented in a democratic environment are likely to be more stable under changing governments.

Moreover, the success of any policy will be influenced by the differing legal character of emitters that can be state-owned companies, public–private entities or private businesses (either purely domestic or joint ventures with foreign shareholders). In the first place, the different forms of entities follow different intrinsic motivations to act and will do this in a more or less economic manner. While public institutions tend to operate inefficiently, private companies are first of all profit-maximizing entities and thus required to manage their resources efficiently. Second, governments may simply decide that public actors apply certain mitigation measures, whereas private emitters will usually require specific positive or negative incentives to act in any way other than the most profitable one.

Thus the question arises of whether a shift of responsibilities towards the governmental level would limit or eliminate incentives for investments. This is most relevant for a scheme that is predominantly characterized by private entities and has been featured with a no-lose crediting mechanism. It is not so much relevant for policy-based actions that focus on small emitters such as households or the transport sector. Whether the following hypothetical challenges and their potential solutions actually apply or not will be discussed further below (see also Figure 6.3):

- *Principal–agent dilemma*: emission reductions are caused by action at the emitters level; thus under this set-up any action to reduce emissions requires investments by private entities. However, the overarching incentive to reduce emissions is provided by credits that will be issued by an international body (such as the UNFCCC) and be transferred ex-post to the host-country government – but not directly to the emitters responsible for the reduction. Of course, emitters can be forced through negative incentives to reach a certain target. But if the no-lose target applies to the emitters as well, then only if the government directly forwards the credits or an equivalent of the investment to the investor, would mitigation be ensured through the emitters.
- *Free riding*: the entire scheme (i.e. aggregated emissions) has to comply with a no-lose target. If the scheme misses the no-lose target, no sanctions will apply. If it over-achieves the target, credits will be issued. If the no-lose target is transferred to the emitter level, for a single emitter the question arises whether all of his competitors will reduce, do nothing or even increase their emissions. The character of the no-lose target triggers the ‘do nothing’ option, i.e. ‘free riding behaviour’, since missing the target implies no sanctions and uncertainty about the activities of competitors prevails.
- *Lacking guarantees in the case of scheme-wide underperformance*: besides the opportunity costs that come along with this delayed payback, investors may face a lack of guarantees that they will actually receive an equivalent to their investment in the case of scheme-wide underperformance – unless the government guarantees individual crediting to every installation that exceeds its target.[2] This is particularly true for foreign investors from Annex-I countries. Unlike the CDM, a new mechanism lacks experiences and credibility and investors will therefore act rather cautiously.
- *Ex-ante investments/ex-post credits*: investments to bring down the scheme’s emissions are required prior to the start of a crediting period. But only once the abatement has been conducted, monitored at installation level and verified can credits be issued.

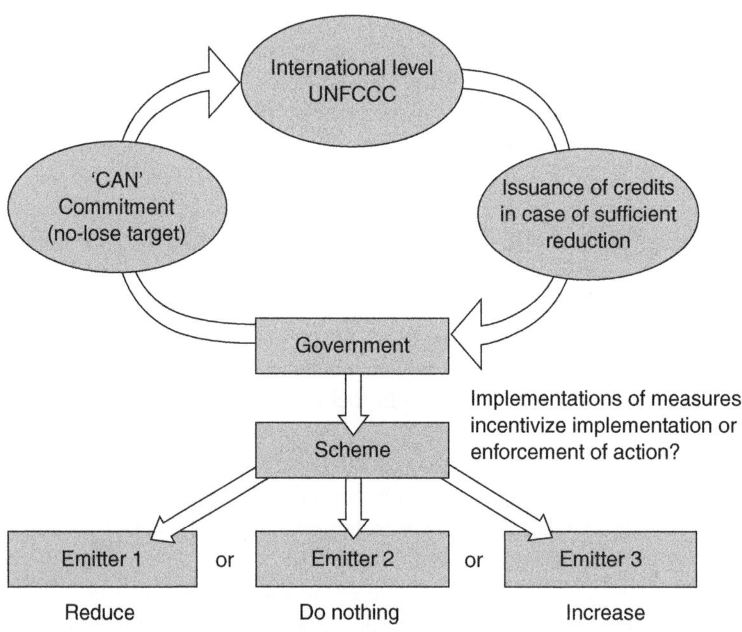

Figure 6.3 Implementation of measures under a crediting mechanism.

Compared to other baseline-and-credit schemes such as the CDM, private entities facing a no-lose target initially lack incentives and guarantees to invest in emission reduction technology. In order to overcome these challenges, the government could either impose mandatory measures to stay at least within the BAU scenario or provide incentives and guarantees for emitters to implement the respective mitigation actions.

4 Incentives: instruments and measures

Obviously, host-country governments would have strong interests in ensuring that the targets of a national or sectoral mitigation agreement are in fact achieved. Therefore, they would need to establish effective regulation, which provides sufficient incentives to the private entities in their country to reduce GHG emissions, and they would have to enforce that regulation adequately.

Incentives can be maintained for private companies through several options described below. The discussion assumes that the national or sectoral target can be allocated to emitters in the form of an installation-specific baseline; this target level will be called 'baseline level'. The first section of the following discusses incentives directly related to the emissions credits; the second part policy instruments that serve as an incentive to mitigate and thus indirectly create emissions credits.

4.1 Guaranteed sectoral credit revenues

A host-country government could guarantee each company that reduces emissions below the threshold level to receive internationally tradeable credits as per the reductions achieved and monitored. This would expose the government to the risk of having to import Certified Emissions Reductions (CERs) or Emission Reduction Units (ERUs) to cover the shortfall caused by companies emitting above the threshold level. The government could reduce the risk by introducing policy instruments that penalize emissions above the threshold level (see Sections 4.8–4.9).

4.2 Carbon funds with shared risks

All private companies in the scheme would be organized in the form of a carbon fund that pays dividends to its shareholders pro rata to the achieved and monetized reduction credits. While this approach would reduce the government-related risk, it cannot address the free-riding problem, unless the management of the carbon fund were able to introduce policy instruments that penalize emissions above the threshold level.

4.3 Revenue split

A contract between the private companies and the government would specify a revenue split from the emission credit sales. The government could retain a portion (2–5 per cent) to cover the costs for administration of the scheme while the rest would be allocated proportionally to the reductions achieved. This approach would have the same free-riding problems as the one described in Section 4.2.

4.4 Domestic mandatory emissions trading scheme

Under a mandatory emissions trading scheme there would be a clear incentive to reduce emissions as those companies with a lack of allowances would need to acquire allowances to cover their shortfall, provided the compliance regime is sufficiently stringent and enforced. The system could be designed as follows. The overall cap of the scheme could be set at the level of the threshold. This would ensure that the crediting threshold is exactly met. The host country could then allow entities in the scheme to exchange national emission allowances against future national/sectoral credits. The exchanged national emission allowances would need to be surrendered in a national cancellation account and could hence not be used on the national market. This would ensure that each exchanged allowance results in an emission reduction below the crediting threshold (Schneider and Cames 2009). To prevent the domestic carbon price exceeding the price of the global carbon market if it turns out that too many domestic allowances have been exchanged, the host-country government should also accept internationally recognized units for compliance under the national trading system.[3] Covered entities would have an incentive to swap domestic allowances against national or sectoral credits as long as the price of credits is higher than the price of allowances. Such a mechanism would interlink the national GHG emissions trading scheme with the global carbon market. Host-country governments may, however, see this approach as the first step on the slippery slope towards legally binding commitments and thus be reluctant to accept it.

4.5 Tradeable intensity standard

As many developing countries fear an approach based on absolute emissions, Whitesell and Helme (2009) have proposed a tradeable intensity standard. The host-country government would set an intensity standard in the form of a domestic benchmark equal to the threshold level for the scheme that can be set below BAU.[4] Installations which beat the benchmark would receive an internationally recognized credit for each tonne below the benchmark from the host-country government. Companies whose emissions exceed the benchmark would have to purchase internationally recognized credits from domestic installations that beat the benchmark or on the global carbon market. For each tonne below the threshold the host-country government would receive an internationally recognized sectoral credit from the respective issuing body. In addition, the host-country government would receive compliance credits from installations which exceed the benchmark. Both amounts together would be exactly equivalent to the amount required to reward the installations whose emissions are below the benchmark. However, this approach does not necessarily result in absolute environmental benefits since the crediting can be possible despite not decreasing absolute emissions.

4.6 CO_2-intensity trading

The concept discussed below aims to offer a solution to how a crediting approach based on CO_2-intensities can be designed in an environmentally sound way. In addition, the approach could make a domestic emissions trading scheme more acceptable to non-Annex-I countries and then create strong direct incentives for domestic emitters to deliver emission reductions. Hence, although this concept does not include the definition of a sector target, it can be an initial step in this direction, with the potential to upscale the system in the mid-term.

The basic concept of the proposal is that single installations/emitters of selected sectors may opt-in to International Emissions Trading (IET)[5] on the basis of a CO_2-intensity target. This target is transformed so that in the end only absolute emission reductions are credited.

In order to achieve this, an installation-specific 'Efficiency Target Factor' (ETF) needs to be defined for each participating installation/emitter. The ETF defines the maximum CO_2-intensity that an installation must beat in order to generate credits. The ETF should be lower than the actual CO_2-intensity, and consider autonomous efficiency increases over time – e.g. by assuming an increase of *x*% efficiency per year or crediting period.

Second, one needs to define the 'output baseline', i.e. the maximum output that can be applied for calculating emission reduction credits in a given year or crediting period. As an example, this might be average output of the past 3–5 years. The output baseline is defined to avoid over-crediting. The no-lose absolute target for the installation can be calculated ex-post, taking into consideration its effective output and actual CO_2-intensity. Credits will only be awarded if the actual CO_2-intensity is lower than the ETF.

4.7 Feed-in tariffs and subsidies

If a market mechanism is introduced in the electricity sector, the government could introduce a feed-in tariff for renewable electricity. If the tariff is sufficiently high to make renewables commercially attractive, the increasing renewable electricity production will generate sectoral credits, as long as other external effects such as new coal power plants do not outperform the emission reductions achieved. These credits will accrue to the government and could cover part of the cost of the feed-in tariff. The disadvantage of this approach is that the incentive based on the feed-in tariff depends on the credibility of the government, which has to sustain the tariff for a substantial time period.

Subsidies could be granted for many sectors and technology types, especially when it comes to energy-efficiency improvements (procurement programmes, scrapping schemes for old devices, etc.). The challenge with subsidies is to avoid that they 'fossilize' over time and support inefficient abatement options.

4.8 Taxes and subsidy reductions

There are different ways to use taxes as an incentive for a crediting mechanism. A win–win approach for the national economy would be the reduction of fossil fuel subsidies accruing to the companies covered by the scheme. The reduction of the subsidies would trigger emission reductions and the accrual of credits to companies reducing emissions would at least partially offset the monetary losses of the companies.

The simplest way of taxation would be to tax revenues from sales of sectoral credits that could be re-invested to buy international credits to cover emissions increases from some companies. From an incentive point of view, such an approach would be too complex and highly problematic as it reduces the incentives for reduction and actually encourages free riding.

A much more incentive-compatible way of taxation would be an emissions tax for emissions above the threshold. As a disadvantage, this approach would require determining baseline emissions at the installation level, which may result in high transaction costs and trigger lobbying activities. Proceeds from this tax could be used by the government to buy emissions credits to cover the shortfall due to the excess emissions; ideally the tax would thus be set at a level equal to the market price for international credits. Due to the variability of these prices, the tax level should probably be set higher to avoid frequent changes.

In a probably less-complex manner, the host-country government could also tax fossil fuel use entirely to incentivize energy efficiency and make renewable fuels commercially attractive. The tax level would have to be set at a level sufficiently high to lead to an emission reduction below the threshold. If the introduction of the tax increases the awareness of energy-efficiency improvements, the tax level could remain quite low and still harness a significant amount of credits that should accrue to the companies directly. The government could then redistribute the revenue from the tax in a way that does not disincentivize further emission reductions.

All tax-related options require good governance and a will to provide mitigation incentives, as well as the trust of the companies regarding the government's ability to implement and enforce such policies.

4.9 Standards and regulation

A mandatory requirement to install emissions mitigation equipment to reach the threshold could be coupled with a direct allocation of credits to the companies that reduce emissions below the baseline. The host-country government guarantees the purchase of international credits to cover emissions of companies with potential excess emissions. This approach requires willingness of developing countries to enforce the abatement mandates. Governments might slap penalties on installations that do not comply with the mandate and use the revenues to buy credits to cover the shortfall.

4.10 Result

In order to provide sufficient mitigation incentives for private investors, the host-country government would have to introduce policy instruments such as a mandatory regulation sufficient to achieve the threshold, a tax for excess emissions or a combination of several instruments, because then emission reductions will not be 'eaten up' by emissions remaining above the target level. The credibility of such an approach rests on the trustworthiness of the government to enforce regulations or to collect a surplus emissions tax. Such policy combinations would allow the government to directly collect the funding for acquisition of international credits in order to reach the scheme's target level.

5 Views of selected actors

Baron *et al.* (2009) discuss how sectoral crediting can be implemented in the host country and how emitters and other actors can be incentivized to invest in mitigation technology. They discuss options 'ranging from a separation from the price signal (credit revenues go to the government) to an attempt at a full link (with full liability assumed by the government in case of overselling)' (Baron *et al.* 2009: 27). They conclude that for 'some of the implementation options [...] the government would also have more liability compared to the CDM' (Baron *et al.* 2009: 28) and that 'the carbon market incentive to individual investors in mitigation may be less direct, and therefore weaker than that under a single project configuration like the CDM' (Baron *et al.* 2009: 6). Despite the fact that the implementation of sectoral agreements requires a significant policy effort on the part of the host-country government, they agree that incentives for private entities can basically be established.

Whitesell and Helme (2009) analyse various approaches to how the price signal of the global carbon market can be fully passed through to the entities covered by sectoral agreements. They discuss 'Sector Programs and NAMAs', 'Cap-and-Trade in Developing Countries', 'No-lose Sector Crediting' and 'Tradable Intensity Standards' and find that in each of the approaches mitigation incentives can be established which are more or less directly linked to the global carbon markets. Cap-and-trade and a tradeable intensity standard (Section 4.5) may, however, provide the most direct incentives since they would be based on internationally recognized units and do not require the establishment of national units.

IETA (2010) also scrutinizes how private sector entities could be incentivized to establish GHG mitigation measures under sectoral mechanisms. They analyse three options – 'Central Coordination of Mitigation and Crediting', 'Domestic Sectoral Emissions Trading System' and 'Installation-Level Mitigation and Crediting' – with respect to their abilities to provide such incentives to the private sector and conclude that certain design options 'would entail risks to investment that could severely curtail the ability of private finance to play a significant role', but 'that various options also exist that could incentivize scale up, achieve mitigation objectives, and still meet the needs of private investors' (IETA 2010: 15).

For developed or developing countries incentives for the private sector do not seem to be an issue at all. Earlier this year, 22 countries submitted their views on new marked-based mechanisms including sectoral mechanisms (UNFCCC 2011). Many highlighted that markets in general provide incentives for the innovation and diffusion of low-carbon technologies, but only Papua New Guinea touched on the issue of incentives for the private sector. However, even Papua New Guinea does not question that incentives for the private sector can be maintained and calls only for an implementation which provides incentives for the business sector at national and international levels.

6 Selected experiences

6.1 Guaranteeing the credibility of a mechanism: lessons of the Kyoto Mechanisms

The CDM was initially seen as the least attractive of the Kyoto Mechanisms due to the risk of investing in emissions mitigation in developing countries and the huge bureaucracy required to check whether projects were actually additional and whether emissions reductions were real. International emissions trading was seen as having much lower transaction costs and Joint Implementation (JI) would benefit from the good investment climate in transition countries.

Nevertheless, the CDM became the most successful of the Kyoto Mechanisms (see Chapter 1 for discussion of the reasons for this success). The high expectations regarding JI were shattered when host-country governments bickered for years about rules on how to allocate ERUs and were unclear about the approval rules. International emissions trading suffered from high-profile corruption cases when government officials sold AAUs at prices well below market value.

The lessons to be learned from the Kyoto Mechanisms are thus that the availability of a transparent incentive for private companies on the international level which cannot be taken away by governments of low credibility can mobilize significant mitigation action. This means that sectoral crediting mechanisms should be designed in a way that minimizes involvement of host-country governments other than in the prevention of free riding.

6.2 Examples of successful policies in developing countries

The transition from a project-based to a sectoral mechanism will require an enhanced role for government actors. However, successful policies in developing countries have already been implemented in the past and provide important lessons for how private entities can be incentivized to reduce their emissions under a sectoral approach in the future. The following two case studies from developing countries demonstrate how different combinations of incentive instruments and measures can be adopted in order to encourage emission reductions. Chapter 3 provides two further examples – the ethanol programme in Brazil and wind power expansion in China. Chapter 7 gives an example of a NAMA in the Mexican building sector.

6.2.1 The eleventh Five Year Plan in China

In China, the target of a 20 per cent reduction in energy intensity was set for the country's eleventh Five Year Plan (2006–2010). A combination of financial incentives and mandatory regulations ensured that by 2010 the country achieved a 19.1 per cent reduction in energy intensity (Hannon *et al.* 2011). Although it was necessary for the government to intervene and close small, inefficient plants in 2010 to meet the energy-intensity target, which was both socially and economically disruptive, various policies incentivizing emission reductions also made an important contribution. In particular, the Top 1,000 Energy Consuming Enterprise Programme and the Ten Key Projects Energy Efficiency Programme delivered primary energy savings of 84 Mtoe (well above the target of 70 Mtoe) and 70 Mtoe, respectively, in 2006–2008 (Hannon *et al.* 2011). The former programme covered China's 1,000 largest state-owned enterprises (SOEs). Every company participating in the programme was required to develop an energy-efficiency action plan showing how the target would be achieved. It was expected that these action plans would include measures to improve the reporting of energy consumption, conduct energy audits and identify and invest in energy-efficiency improvements. In addition to setting the energy-saving target, the Chinese government instructed local authorities to supervise and monitor the participating companies in the implementation of their energy-efficiency action plans.

Given that the programme was rapidly implemented, there was insufficient time for a detailed assessment to determine the energy-saving target of each company. As a consequence, it may be argued that the energy-saving target for the Top 1,000 Programme (i.e. 15 per cent of the total energy savings required in the eleventh Five Year Plan) was not ambitious enough (Price *et al.* 2010). Therefore, it is important to acknowledge that target setting needs to reflect actual abatement potential. In addition, many companies experienced difficulties in completing energy audits due to the lack of qualified auditing personnel. Capacity building in auditing and monitoring thus remains essential to the effectiveness of energy-efficiency programmes. However, although lessons need to be learned, the Top 1,000 Programme is generally considered a success and demonstrates how private entities can be incentivized through the setting and monitoring of top-down targets by government actors.

The aim of the Ten Key Projects Energy Efficiency Programme was to deliver an energy saving of 175 Mtoe[6] during the eleventh Five Year Period by allocating targeted funding (approximately US$1 billion) to energy-efficiency projects (WRI 2010). For example, one objective of the programme was to increase the efficiency of coal-burning boilers and kilns by five and two percentage points (*Energy Bulletin* 2006). The renovation of medium- and small-sized boilers with advanced techniques such as pulverized-coal firing were incentivized by allowing companies to apply for funding from China's Ministry of Finance. After a comprehensive energy audit, and following accounting and management system checks, an eligible company would receive 60 per cent of the project's capital cost upfront, with the remaining 40 per cent provided after the technology was installed and subject to an evaluation of the energy savings (WRI 2010). Such a payment structure 'rewarded' companies that successfully completed energy-saving projects. Based upon the data for 2006–2008, it is expected that the programme achieved its target energy saving (Price *et al.* 2010).

6.2.2 Energy-efficiency programme in Thailand

During the 1990s electricity demand in Thailand increased rapidly, with lighting representing 25 per cent of national electricity use in the country (Birner 2000). As a consequence, a comprehensive five-year demand-side management (DSM) programme was set-up by the Thai national electric power utility (EGAT) in 1993. The new DSM office implemented several market interventions for energy efficiency, which did not rely on the use of subsidies. Instead, EGAT encouraged energy-efficiency improvements through various collaborations with manufacturers and public promotions (Birner and Martinot 2003). The switching from thick (T-12) to thin (T-8) fluorescent tubes provides an example of how the DSM programme successfully intervened in the market. By financing an US$8 million consumer information campaign highlighting that the T-8 tubes provided the same quality of lighting as the T-12 tubes while consuming less energy, EGAT secured an agreement with the importers and manufactures of T-12 tubes to switch to T-8 tubes. As a consequence of this market intervention, the market share of T-8 tubes increased from 40 per cent in 1994 to 100 per cent by the end of 1995 (Birner and Martinot 2003).

The introduction of energy-efficiency labelling was another effective market intervention by EGAT in the manufacture of refrigerators. EGAT negotiated a voluntary labelling scheme for refrigerators based upon efficiency performance. This was again supported by an advertising campaign to promote the energy-efficiency standard to consumers, and EGAT ensured that there was sufficient capacity to audit refrigerator models by partnering with a technical standards institute to test the refrigerators. The scheme was subsequently made mandatory, with an increase in the energy-efficiency requirements for the labelling scheme. The impact of the programme was impressive. In 1994 only one single-door model and 2 per cent of double-door models qualified for the highest energy-efficiency level. By 2000 all single-door models and 60 per cent of double-door models qualified for the highest efficiency level (Birner and Martinot 2003). The experience in Thailand demonstrates that voluntary agreements can be effective when industry has confidence in government policies to transform the market. The empowerment of consumer choice, through the introduction of energy-efficiency labelling and information, can also facilitate necessary market transformations.

7 Implications for the concept of new market mechanisms

New market mechanisms strive to trigger investments in national and sectoral GHG mitigation activities. In particular, under the scenario of a scheme with mainly private-owned emitters that face a no-lose target, incentives to invest in mitigation might be low if investors do not get guarantees to receive an equivalent for their investment, e.g. in the form of credits. Therefore, the implementation of a crediting mechanism should be designed in such a way that prevents free riding and provides guaranteed performance-based revenues to investors. Otherwise, private investments will be alienated by the lack of credibility.

As the lessons of a decade of the CDM show (see Chapter 1), the availability of a clear incentive is the key pillar of success. Thus, new market mechanisms will only be successful if private companies see such an incentive that has a fair chance of surviving in the long run. The discussion about the role of government has shown that the increased responsibility of the government under a new market mechanism requires strong governance of the implementation of domestic mitigation policies. Therefore, crediting mechanisms may initially be implemented only in selected, advanced developing countries. However, examples of successful climate mitigation policies illustrate that several important countries have a good track record in implementing such policies and that a number of developing countries would be eligible for establishing crediting mechanisms.

In terms of measures, host-country governments should concentrate on providing policy instruments that prevent free riding, such as standards, taxes or emissions trading schemes. The fact that a crediting threshold generates no pain for the country as a whole does not necessarily imply that the implementation of the mechanism within the country needs to be painless as well.

Emissions above the threshold could be penalized by a mandatory regulation or an emissions tax, which would provide a clear message that emissions reductions achieved by one company are not diluted by the non-action of its competitor. Alternatively, subsidies such as feed-in tariffs could be used to provide a clear monetary incentive to the private sector. These incentives would, however, not be directly linked to the global carbon market. The credits would just serve to reduce the government's budgetary burden in the case of a subsidy or to increase revenues in the case of an emission tax. Last, but not least, new market mechanisms can also be implemented domestically as a mandatory emissions trading scheme. Such an approach would establish a direct link to the carbon market and provide strong mitigation incentives at the activity level.

However, each host country and each sector is different. Investors, in particular those from industrialized countries, will only invest if (1) they have trust in the respective government and (2) believe the implementation of the mechanism is credible enough. In order to build confidence in this regard, pilot schemes should be set-up sooner rather than later. Many concerns about the lack of incentive structures of new market mechanisms will disappear once the new market-based approach has become as established as the CDM now is.

Acknowledgement

Elements of this chapter build on a paper written for the German Federal Environment Agency (UBA) as part of the project 'Design of the post-2012 climate regime: sectoral approaches for greenhouse gas mitigation'. The contents of this publication solely reflect the view of the authors and are not necessarily the official opinion of the UBA.

Notes

1 The Cancun Agreements (UNFCCC 2010a, 2010b) define market mechanisms as complementary funding source for NAMAs.

2 Note that this requires the government to take over responsibility in case that sector as a whole does not meet the target. The question of course is whether any government is willing to take this responsibility if it is linked to financial obligations such as compensation payments.

3 It may be noted that in the current political context it is not likely that non-Annex-I countries would agree to a system where they buy offsets credits from Annex-I countries.
4 This may require some unit conversion if the baseline level is not defined in the form of a benchmark.
5 Alternatively, a mandatory selection of complete sectors by the host country may be considered.
6 250Mtce (China prefers to use coal equivalents due to the prevalence of coal in its energy system).

References

Baron, R., Buchner, B. and Ellis, J. (2009) 'Sectoral approaches and the carbon market', OECD, IEA. Online. Available: www.oecd.org/dataoecd/8/7/42875080.pdf.

Birner, S. (2000) 'How Thailand washed away wasteful lighting', *IAEEL newsletter 1–2/00*, International Institute for Energy Conservation. Online. Available: www.iaeel.org/iaeel/newsl/2000/Etttva2000/PrN_a_1–2_00.html (accessed 27 July 2011).

Birner, S. and Martinot, E. (2003) 'Market transformation for energy efficient products: lessons from programs in developing countries', unpublished paper. Online. Available: http://keionline.org/misc-docs/Birner_Martinot_EP.pdf (accessed 27 July 2011).

Energy Bulletin (2006) 'China outlines ten programs for energy efficiency'. Online. Available: www.energybulletin.net/print/3566 (accessed 27 July 2011).

Hannon, A., Ying, L., Walker, J. and Changhua, W. (2011) 'Delivering low carbon growth: a guide to China's 12th Five Year Plan', The Climate Group. Online. Available: www.theclimategroup.org/_assets/files/FINAL_14Mar11_-TCG_DELIVERING-LOW-CARBON-GROWTH-V3.pdf.

IEA (2009) *World Energy Outlook*, Paris: IEA.

IETA (2010) 'Thinking through the design possibilities for a sectoral crediting mechanism: three options to encourage discussion'. Online. Available: www.ieta.org/index.php?option=com_content&view=article&id=126:thinking-through-the-design-possibilities-for-a-sectoral-crediting-mechanism&catid=26:reports&Itemid=93.

Price, L., Levine, M., Zhoua, N., Fridleya, D., Adena, N., Lua, H., McNeila, M., Zhenga, N., Qina, N. and Yowargana, P. (2010) 'Assessment of China's energy-saving and emission reduction accomplishments and opportunities during the 11th Five Year Plan', *Energy Policy*, 39 (4): 2165–78.

Schmidt, J., Helme, N., Lee, J. and Houdashelt, M. (2006) 'Sector based approach to post 2012 climate change policy architecture', Center for Clean Air Policy (CCAP). Online. Available: http://citeseerx.ist.psu.edu/viewdoc/download?doi=10.1.1.169.3542&rep=rep1&type=pdf.

Schneider, L. and Cames, M. (2009) 'A framework for a sectoral crediting mechanism in a post-2012 climate regime', Report for the GWEC (Global Wind Energy Council), Öko-Institut. Online. Available: www.oeko.de/oekodoc/904/2009-022-en.pdf.

UNFCCC (2007) 'Decision 1/CP.13. Bali Action Plan'. Online. Available: http://unfccc.int/resource/docs/2007/cop13/eng/06a01.pdf#page=3 (accessed 27 July 2011).

UNFCCC (2009a) 'Document FCCC/AWGLCA/2009/INF.1, Revised negotiating text of the Ad hoc Working Group on Long-term Cooperative Action under the Convention'. Online. Available: http://unfccc.int/resource/docs/2009/awglca6/eng/inf01.pdf (accessed 27 July 2011).

UNFCCC (2009b) 'Decision 2/CP.15 Copenhagen Accord'. Online. Available: http://unfccc.int/resource/docs/2009/cop15/eng/11a01.pdf#page=4 (accessed 22 July 2011).

UNFCCC (2010a) 'Decision 1/CMP.6 The Cancun Agreements: Outcome of the work of the Ad hoc Working Group on Further Commitments for Annex I Parties under the Kyoto Protocol at its fifteenth session'. Online. Available: http://unfccc.int/resource/docs/2010/cmp6/eng/12a01.pdf#page=3 (accessed 27 July 2011).

UNFCCC (2010b) 'Decision 1/CP.16 The Cancun Agreements: Outcome of the work of the Ad hoc Working Group on Long-term Cooperative Action under the Convention'. Online. Available: http://unfccc.int/resource/docs/2010/cop16/eng/07a01.pdf#page=2 (accessed 27 July 2011).

UNFCCC (2011) 'Document FCCC/AWGLCA/2011/MISC.2 Views on the elaboration of market-based mechanisms, Submissions from Parties'. Online. Available: http://unfccc.int/resource/docs/2011/awglca14/eng/misc02.pdf (accessed 27 July 2011).

Whitesell, W. and Helme, N. (2009) 'A tradable intensity standard for sector crediting', unpublished manuscript, Center for Clean Air Policy (CCAP).

WRI (2010) 'China's ten key energy efficiency projects'. *ChinaFAQs – the network for Climate and Energy Information* World Resource Institute. Online. Available: www.chinafaqs.org/files/chinainfo/ChinaFAQs_China's_Ten_Key_Energy_Efficiency_Projects.pdf (accessed 27 July 2011).

7 Mobilizing mitigation policies in the South through a financing mix

Daisuke Hayashi and Stefan Wehner

1 Introduction

Nationally appropriate mitigation actions (NAMAs) represent a promising concept for delivering, financing and recognizing emission reductions by developing countries in a post-2012 climate regime (Levina and Helme 2009). The concept was first introduced in the Bali Action Plan under the United Nations Framework Convention on Climate Change (UNFCCC), which was adopted at the Thirteenth Conference of the Parties (COP 13) in 2007. The key breakthrough of the Bali Action Plan was the acceptance of 'NAMAs by developing country Parties in the context of sustainable development, supported and enabled by technology, financing and capacity building, in a measurable, reportable and verifiable manner' (UNFCCC 2007: Art. 1 b, ii).

A key strength of NAMAs lies in their potential to channel industrialized countries' support to policy-based mitigation actions by developing countries (Okubo *et al.* 2010). The Clean Development Mechanism (CDM) has so far been the key financial instrument for developing countries' mitigation efforts. The CDM has been successful at delivering a vast amount of emission reductions in key developing countries around the world (see Chapter 1). However, one of the CDM's key limitations is that it can only support individual mitigation projects and programmes, but not the implementation of mitigation policies. This has made it difficult to achieve large-scale market transformation towards low-carbon development. NAMAs are expected to bridge this gap in the existing climate finance instruments by enhancing policy-wide emission reductions in developing countries (Levina and Helme 2009; Okubo *et al.* 2011).

The aim of this chapter is to examine how a NAMA can be structured in a way that it harnesses different streams of finance in an optimal combination. Section 2 provides an overview of the current status of the international negotiation on NAMAs and introduces key issues relating to the design of NAMAs. In Section 3, we analyse how a NAMA can be designed with a mix of domestic and international finance streams, using a residential building programme in Mexico as our case study. Section 4 concludes by highlighting major lessons from the Mexican case study and summarizing key issues for the future development of NAMAs.

2 Where do we stand with NAMAs?

2.1 Current status of the international negotiation on NAMAs

In general, three types of NAMAs are considered in the international negotiation: (1) mitigation actions financed and implemented domestically by developing countries without any external support (unilateral NAMAs); (2) mitigation actions implemented with financial, technological and/or capacity-building support from industrialized countries (supported NAMAs); and (3) mitigation actions implemented with financing from carbon credits generated for the amount of emission reductions achieved (credited NAMAs) (Jung *et al.* 2010; Wehner *et al.* 2010; Okubo *et al.* 2011). Supported NAMAs provide upfront finance to governments, while credited NAMAs provide carbon credits to companies after emission reductions are achieved (Helme 2010). The current international negotiation does not preclude any of the three types of NAMAs. However, there has been a debate on whether credited NAMAs should be eligible (Levina and Helme 2009; UNFCCC 2010a). Consequently, unilateral and supported NAMAs have become more prominent options (UNFCCC 2010b).

COP 16 in 2010 decided to establish a registry to record NAMAs seeking international support, and to facilitate matching of finance, technology and capacity-building support to these actions. The NAMA registry will regularly update information on NAMAs seeking support, along with their estimated costs, emission reductions and the anticipated timeframe for implementation. It will also update information on support available from industrialized countries, and support provided for NAMAs in developing countries (UNFCCC 2010b).

The most contentious issue for NAMAs in the international negotiation is how to design a framework for monitoring, reporting and verification (MRV) of NAMAs implemented in developing countries. Developing countries generally prefer a voluntary, domestic MRV scheme, while industrialized countries insist on MRV by international experts. The decision adopted by the COP 16 in 2010 struck a balance between the two positions by requiring only domestic MRV for unilateral NAMAs while making supported NAMAs subject to international MRV (UNFCCC 2010b).

The COP 16 decision also requires developing countries to submit biennial reports containing updates of national greenhouse gas (GHG) inventories, information on NAMAs and international support received. The extent of the biennial reporting depends on the developing countries' capabilities and the level of support provided for reporting. The biennial reports are subject to international consultations and analysis (ICA) that are to be carried out in a manner that is 'non-intrusive, non-punitive and respectful of national sovereignty' (UNFCCC 2010b: Art. 63). It is explicitly mentioned in the decision text that the appropriateness of NAMAs shall not be part of the ICA process, showing the developing countries' emphasis on the sovereignty principle (UNFCCC 2010b). The detailed rules for the MRV, biennial reporting and ICA procedures are still under discussion. But many countries have stressed the importance of a tiered approach to accommodate different levels of capability and to provide flexibility where necessary (UNFCCC 2011a).

2.2 Natural niches of different types of NAMAs

Where do NAMAs find their natural niches? We argue below that marginal abatement costs (MACs), and causality and timeframe of GHG impacts are key determinants of natural niches of the different types of NAMAs.

With regard to the MAC consideration, we think that unilateral NAMAs should target mitigation actions with negative to very low MACs (e.g. efficient air conditioners), credited NAMAs should focus on ones with moderate MACs (e.g. wind power) and supported NAMAs should address ones with either low MAC, e.g. small hydro power, or very high MAC, e.g. photovoltaic (PV) (Figure 7.1). It should be borne in mind that some of the negative- to very low-cost mitigation actions face significant market barriers such as high upfront costs, e.g. light emitting diodes. Supported NAMAs can also be instrumental in promoting such mitigation actions as these are not necessarily going to be addressed by the carbon market (Kim *et al.* 2009).

This approach would ensure that the 'low-hanging fruit' emission reductions are not taken away by industrialized countries through the use of carbon credits. It could also help justify that carbon credits sold to the industrialized countries are 'additional' emission reductions, following the current concept of additionality applied under the CDM (see Chapter 1). By focusing on the higher-cost segments, supported and credited NAMAs would have a better basis for additionality demonstration.

Furthermore, the criticism could be addressed that the CDM has paid a too high price for low-cost mitigation projects, especially, for projects destroying HFC-23 and N_2O from adipic acid (see the detailed discussion of this project type in Chapter 1). These projects have MACs of less than €1/tCO_2-e. The CDM rewards project developers on the basis of market prices for CERs, which are currently about €10/tCO2-e in the secondary market. As shown in the HFC-23 and N_2O projects, the CER prices can be well above MACs of low-cost CDM

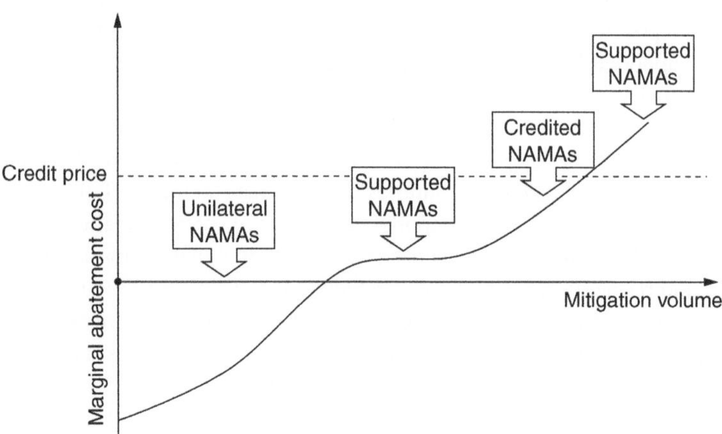

Figure 7.1 Different tiers of NAMAs.

projects, creating a large amount of economic rents to the project developers and financial intermediaries. This is a natural outcome of a market mechanism, but can be a relevant issue when the funds available to pay for emission reductions are limited (Hepburn 2009).

In addition to the MAC consideration, it is important to take into account causality and timeframe of GHG emission reductions achieved by NAMAs. The causality shows how directly or indirectly one can account for GHG impacts of mitigation actions, while the timeframe tells when the emission reductions occur. The causality has an important implication for the nature of MRV, and the timeframe for revenue streams of NAMAs. Figure 7.2 illustrates GHG impacts of some exemplary NAMAs. The impacts are evaluated as to whether the NAMAs result in direct or indirect emission reductions, and how long it takes to generate emission reductions (Jung *et al.* 2010).

The causality of GHG impacts plays a decisive role in the nature of MRV. In order to generate carbon credits, it is necessary to carry out MRV of NAMAs in an emission reduction metric (Okubo *et al.* 2011). As NAMAs with direct GHG impacts are more amenable to establishing clear causality between mitigation actions and achieved emission reductions, they serve as the best basis for credited NAMAs. Supported NAMAs are likely to require a reasonable degree of accuracy in the emission reduction calculation. This is because they are subject to international MRV and donors have expressed a desire to know how effectively their money has been spent on mitigation actions. However, supported NAMAs may apply MRV indicators other than emission reductions as they do not generate carbon credits. Alternative indicators could be based on inputs to mitigation actions, e.g. the amount of funding provided to a green building programme, or intermediate outputs, such as the number of green buildings constructed. In such a way, supported NAMAs could accommodate mitigation actions with indirect GHG impacts as well. Unilateral NAMAs have the greatest

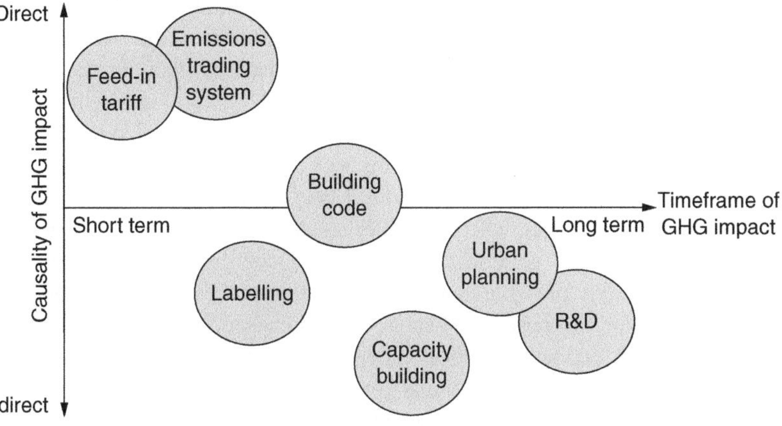

Figure 7.2 Causality and timeframe of GHG impacts of NAMAs (source: adapted from Jung *et al.* 2010).

discretion in the choice of MRV because they are subject to domestic MRV only. Therefore, unilateral NAMAs are least concerned with the causality of GHG impacts.

As for the timeframe of GHG emission reductions, short-term GHG impacts are the most important condition to credited NAMAs because private investors tend to appreciate a short-term, efficient return on investment, as demonstrated by CDM projects that have first concentrated on industrial gas projects that offer cheap, quick emission reductions (Hepburn and Stern 2009; Jung *et al.* 2010; see also Chapter 1). Supported NAMAs can include NAMAs with both short- and long-term GHG impacts because their finance does not depend on when emission reductions occur, unless donors put strict conditionality on the provision of support based on emission reductions achievement. Unilateral NAMAs are most flexible in the timeframe of GHG impacts as they are solely implemented by developing countries.

In summary, credited NAMAs will likely find their natural niche in moderate-cost mitigation actions that have direct, short-term GHG impacts. Supported NAMAs are most amenable to mitigation actions with low or very high costs and relatively direct GHG impacts. But they could also support negative- to very low-cost mitigation actions that face significant market barriers. The timeframe of GHG impacts will not likely be a concern unless donors require otherwise. Unilateral NAMAs work best for negative- to very low-cost mitigation actions, regardless of the causality and timeframe of GHG impacts.

2.3 Financing opportunities through NAMAs

2.3.1 Supported NAMAs

Several industrialized countries and multilateral organizations have already given support for preparation of pilot NAMAs (Table 7.1). However, the current processes for NAMA support matching are ad hoc, making it difficult to maintain an overview of NAMA support needs and opportunities. The NAMA registry is expected to play a key role in increasing transparency in the NAMA support matching processes.

The international negotiation has yet to elaborate on detailed procedures for NAMA support matching. Thus, it remains to be seen how the NAMA support matching process will develop in the future. Many developing countries want the support through direct access, where priorities are decided domestically by developing countries and money is allocated by a central coordinating body. However, donor countries usually prefer a competitive selection process, where NAMAs are evaluated on certain criteria and the best NAMA is chosen for support (Levina and Helme 2009). This echoes the developments in allocation of fast-start finance (FSF), as discussed in Chapter 5. Several governance options could be envisaged to channel support to mitigation actions. Centralized governance could be structured with a few multilateral funds providing support, while a decentralized one would consist of a greater number of bilateral and multilateral funds (Kim *et al.* 2009).

Table 7.1 Selected list of supported NAMAs

Host	*Mitigation action*	*Donor*
Brazil	Urban transport (roadway improvements, bus rapid transit, metro expansion, etc.)	Inter-American Development Bank
Indonesia	Peatland management (avoidance of aerobic decomposition of peat by raising water table in the peat layer)	Japan
	Urban transport (electronic road pricing, parking restraint, bus rapid transit)	Asian Development Bank
Lao PDR	Urban transport (roadway improvements, public transport systems including bus rapid transit and light rail transit, transport demand management, etc.)	Japan
Mexico	Building efficiency (lighting, solar water heaters, gas boilers, thermal insulation, water-saving appliances, etc.)	Germany
	Urban transport (optimization of conventional bus routes, including route design, concession management, operational design)	Netherlands, Inter-American Development Bank
Thailand	Waste and wastewater management (semi-aerobic treatment of municipal solid waste, composting of organic waste, anaerobic digestion of organic wastewater)	Japan
Tunisia	Renewable energies (PV, wind, etc.)	Germany
	Waste management (composting and/or anaerobic digestion of communal bio-waste, waste from agroindustry, sludge from wastewater treatment plants, etc.)	Germany

Note
The list includes supported NAMAs that have published detailed implementation plans.

In the coming years, NAMA support will mainly be channelled through bilateral agreements between host and donor countries, and through existing multilateral funds (e.g. the Climate Investment Funds, the Global Environment Facility). These are the most likely channels given the absence of UNFCCC-agreed rules on multilateral financing of NAMAs (see the detailed discussion in Chapter 5).

2.3.2 Credited NAMAs

Credited NAMAs will generate carbon credits in a way similar to the CDM. Emission reductions of a mitigation action are evaluated against a baseline, a counter-factual scenario that would happen in the absence of the mitigation action. By beating the baseline emission level and demonstrating additionality, the mitigation action will produce carbon credits that developing countries can sell to industrialized countries. However, these credited NAMAs and the CDM differ in two key aspects. First, credited NAMAs will likely be more comprehensive and of a larger scale. As opposed to CDM projects that mostly focus on single mitigation measures (Broekhoff 2007), policies implemented under credited NAMAs will likely involve a combination of measures (see Table 7.1). Thus, MRV of credited NAMAs should move from the CDM's technology-specific approach towards a more holistic one. Also, due to the broader coverage of policy-based mitigation actions, credited NAMAs would require much more capacity in implementing mitigation actions and carrying out MRV.

Second, carbon credits for credited NAMAs may first go to governments because they would play a central role in the implementation of mitigation policies. This could create an incentive problem to private investors because they get only indirect carbon price signals through governments and their revenue is dependent on the performance of other entities that may as well be competitors (see the detailed discussion of this issue and possible solutions through dedicated policy instruments in Chapter 6).

2.3.3 Combination of supported and credited NAMAs

It may also be possible to combine supported and credited NAMAs. The mix of public and private finance could be synergetic in mobilizing mitigation actions that have different characteristics in MACs, and causality and timeframe of GHG impacts.

Such a combination requires a careful governance structure so that credited NAMAs will not simply take away low-cost mitigation options from developing countries. Levina and Helme (2009) propose that the governance structure of supported and credited NAMAs should be clearly aligned to ensure that developing countries can keep low-cost mitigation options through supported NAMAs and offer only higher-cost mitigation options to industrialized countries through credited NAMAs.

However, Kim *et al.* (2009) argue that it is not straightforward to minimize the overlap between supported and credited NAMAs, unless the UNFCCC process decides to explicitly exclude certain mitigation actions from the market mechanism. If credited NAMAs were allowed without such eligibility restrictions, the private sector would likely seek out low-cost mitigation options as this is the unique advantage of a market mechanism (Kim *et al.* 2009).

2.4 Relationship between NAMAs and the CDM

Financing to be provided for supported and credited NAMAs might be double-counted if CDM projects co-exist with the NAMA (Jung *et al.* 2010). Effects of policies implemented under NAMAs might overlap with mitigation efforts of CDM projects; for example, consider a wind CDM project mobilized by a feed-in tariff whose costs are subsidized by an industrialized country. Thus, the co-existence of NAMAs and CDM projects could result in a situation where industrialized countries pay twice for the same emission reductions, if not properly accounted for.

It would be straightforward to declare that no individual CDM projects can be proposed in a policy area covered by supported or credited NAMAs. However, as there are more than 6,000 CDM projects in the pipeline, the complete displacement of the CDM projects is not very realistic. The private sector would argue that the investment made into registered CDM projects must be protected. Also, the complete displacement would create political pressure in developing countries not to propose NAMAs in sectors where a number of CDM projects are being developed (Levina and Helme 2009). Thus, the introduction of NAMAs needs to account for the interests of the CDM stakeholders, while ensuring that CDM projects and NAMAs do not result in double-counting of emission reductions.

A possible solution could be to fully account for emission reductions from already registered CDM projects, but to use a NAMA-financed emission level as the baseline for future CDM projects. In other words, baselines of the future CDM projects would have to be adjusted for the impact of mitigation policies implemented under supported or credited NAMAs. This way, emission reductions achieved by the mitigation policies would be accounted for under the supported or credited NAMAs, while the baseline emissions of the future CDM projects would be reduced by the amount of emission reductions that the mitigation policies have induced in the CDM projects.

At first sight, the approach appears to run against the so-called E+/E– rule of the CDM. The implementation of mitigation policies results in a lower level of emissions. If a CDM project were to use this emission level as its baseline, the mitigation policies would make the CDM project less attractive because the lower level of baseline emissions would result in a lower amount of CERs. This could potentially give perverse incentives to host countries not to implement mitigation policies. Thus, the E+/E– rule stipulates that mitigation policies implemented since the adoption of the Marrakech Accords on 11 November 2001 do not need to be taken into account in baselines of CDM projects.

The perverse incentive is a valid concern if the implementation of mitigation policies only generates costs to developing countries (i.e. reduction of CER revenues from CDM projects). With NAMAs in place, however, the implementation of mitigation policies can receive international support through supported and/or credited NAMAs. Therefore, it would become an issue of a balance between the carrots given to NAMAs and the sticks against CDM projects. Given NAMAs' potential of supporting mitigation actions larger than CDM projects, we would argue that the carrots could be larger than the sticks, and so the risk of perverse incentives would be alleviated. By providing a comparable advantage to NAMAs over future CDM projects, the approach could also give an incentive to transit from the project-based mechanism to the policy-based one, which is important for upscaling mitigation efforts in developing countries.

3 Supported NAMA for a residential building programme in Mexico

Using a supported NAMA designed for a residential building programme in Mexico as our case study, we explain how a NAMA can be designed with an optimal mix of domestic and international finance streams. The concept was developed in 2010 for the Mexican Environment Ministry (SEMARNAT) and the Mexican National Housing Commission (CONAVI) with support of the German Federal Ministry for the Environment, Nature Conservation and Nuclear Safety. Unless otherwise noted, the analysis in this section is based on the unpublished paper Wehner *et al.* (2010).

3.1 Relevance of the residential building programme in Mexico

Mexico has a considerable challenge to address. On the one hand, the country's population growth and demographic change creates pressure to rapidly expand housing construction. In the last 20 years the housing sector in Mexico has grown by 17 per cent annually (Hirata 2009). This rapid growth was achieved mainly by a mortgage programme created by the government. CONAVI estimates Mexico's current housing stock at 27 million houses, and expects the demand for new houses to reach 20 million for the period from 2010 to 2030. This corresponds to approximately 576,000 houses per year until 2020 (CONAVI 2010).

On the other hand, the country has committed to reduce its GHG emissions by 51 million tonnes of CO_2 equivalent (CO_2-e) by 2012, of which 5.5 million tonnes are attributed to the residential, commercial and municipal sectors. To date the residential sector represents approximately 32 per cent of Mexico's energy consumption. GHG emissions from the residential and commercial buildings in 2006 were estimated at 75 million tCO_2-e (Odón de Buen 2009). This means that buildings represented about 12 per cent of total present CO_2-e emissions in Mexico in that year.

In August 2009, Mexico formulated its Special Climate Change Programme (PECC) that defines more than 100 mitigation actions comprising a set of NAMAs to be undertaken in all relevant sectors (UNFCCC 2011c). PECC includes the 'Efficient housing and green mortgages' programme, which has been designed by CONAVI and is implemented by the National Workers' Housing Fund (INFONAVIT). The programme is expected to contribute 2.4 per cent of emissions reductions to the PECC 2012 goal. Mexico sees supported NAMAs as an important means for achieving the goals laid out in the PECC.

Mexico already has a comprehensive building code for the residential sector and a number of energy-efficiency norms for electrical appliances. However, the enforcement of the building code and norms is voluntary and delegated to local authorities that are often unable to supervise the implementation of the standards. Hence, in practice, the ambitious building standards are not implemented or enforced. At present, the code developed by CONAVI is only a model;

CONAVI cannot enforce its implementation at the federal level as building standards are established by state authorities.

As effective enforcement and periodical updates are essential for the successful implementation of building codes, Mexico is seeking international support for the enforcement and further enhancement of their existing regulations. Hence, Mexico and Germany have initiated a concept study on the 'Supported NAMA design concept for energy-efficiency measures in the Mexican residential building sector'. It explores how a supported NAMA could be designed to enhance the 'Efficient housing and green mortgages' programme of the PECC.

Since building codes are not easily implementable due to the federal and legal structure in Mexico, it is essential for the supported NAMA to build on the key existing programmes addressing the residential building sector. The next section provides an overview of the key residential building programmes in Mexico.

3.2 Existing residential building programs: 'This is Your House' and 'Green Mortgage'

The 'This is Your House' ('Ésta es tu casa') programme is a subsidy programme created by CONAVI in 2007 to meet the housing demand of the low-income population and to enhance uptake of energy-efficient technology in the residences. In doing so, CONAVI has established a set of minimum energy-efficiency criteria that need to be followed by housing developers when designing new houses or refurbishing existing houses for the low-income population. There are different criteria for single-family houses and multi-family houses. But the main energy-efficient technology requirements are broadly the same: compact fluorescent lamps (CFLs), solar water heaters (SWHs), water-saving appliances and thermal insulation.

In order to receive the subsidy, house owners need to purchase houses from registered housing developers that incorporate the minimum set of energy-efficiency requirements defined by CONAVI. The subsidy provided under the programme is granted by executive agencies authorized by the government. The subsidy amount varies according to the price of the house the subsidy recipient wants to acquire. The subsidy programme has been very successful since its initiation. In 2010, 211,102 housing units had been supported through different institutions. This represents a 32 per cent increase from 2009 (CONAVI 2011).

The 'Green Mortgage' ('Hipoteca Verde') programme was initiated in 2007. It provides an extra credit line on top of the original mortgage to low-income, state-aided house buyers. These buyers need to be members of INFONAVIT, one of the social-security institutions and by far the largest mortgage provider in Mexico, with a market share of 80 per cent of 400,000 annual mortgages. The purchased houses need to fulfil the minimum set of sustainable and energy-efficient technology requirements, such as using CFLs, SWHs, water-saving appliances and thermal insulation. The minimum set of technology requirements for the Green Mortgage programme is the same as the one in the This is Your House programme. According to the climate zone in which the house is located, the housing developer will choose an appropriate package of technologies to be incorporated in the housing design.

The Green Mortgage and CONAVI's This is Your House programmes are strongly related to each other, in that most of the green mortgages provided by INFONAVIT are complemented by the subsidy. In 2010, 151,777 houses were financed by the Green Mortgage scheme (Table 7.2); 55 per cent of the houses were also granted the subsidy under the This is Your House programme.

Taking into account CONAVI's plan to serve the future housing demand with the Green Mortgage and subsidy programmes, the total number of houses to be supported by CONAVI and INFONAVIT would represent 6.1 per cent of the total housing stock in 2020. If we compare the total number of 'sustainable houses' with the number of new houses to be constructed, it means that 35 per cent of the new housing stock by 2020 will be supported by one of these programmes.

3.3 NAMA design for the Mexican residential building sector

The NAMA concept developed by Wehner *et al.* (2010) aims to upscale the existing Green Mortgage and This is Your House programmes. It proposes an extended scope of mitigation actions, reliable MRV, baseline and additionality approaches, and a financial structure to effectively leverage domestic and international finance streams.

3.3.1 Scope of the NAMA

The current roll-out plan of the Green Mortgage and This is Your House programmes would address only about 35 per cent of the new houses built until 2020. On the other hand, the current CONAVI's catalogue of minimum energy-efficiency requirements would still allow significant potential of technological upscaling. This could be achieved, for example, by requiring more ambitious minimum efficiency levels for the technologies included in the current catalogue and by mandating the use of technologies that are currently not covered in the list.

Table 7.2 Green mortgages provided by INFONAVIT from 2007 to 2010

2007	*2008*	*2009*	*2010*
647	1,131	105,104	151,777

Source: CONAVI (2010).

Note
64 per cent of the mortgages provided in 2009 and 55 per cent provided in September 2010 also received CONAVI's subsidy under the This is Your House programme.

In order to address the barriers to energy efficiency in the residential building sector to tap its large mitigation potential, single measures alone will not be sufficient. Rather, a holistic approach is necessary, where stakeholders have the freedom to choose from different mitigation measures. The current design of the Green Mortgage and This is Your House programmes follows this approach. Given the number of barriers that need to be addressed, it is also important to include measures such as awareness raising and capacity building.

The scope of the NAMA developed by Wehner *et al.* (2010) is summarized in Table 7.3. Its goal is to upscale the Green Mortgage and This is Your House programmes through increased penetration (more houses covered, i.e. up to 100 per cent of eligible, newly built houses until 2020) and/or technology upscaling (more ambitious efficiency standards and/or inclusion of additional technologies, such as air conditioning, efficient refrigerators and PV). These measures should be backed by supportive actions to transform the programmes into a holistic urban planning process. These measures should be undertaken during the

Table 7.3 Scope of the supported NAMA for a residential building programme in Mexico

Item	*Description*
Sector	Building sector
Sub-sector	New residential buildings
NAMA boundary	Entire country
Measures with direct impacts on GHG emission reduction	Substantial upscaling of the Green mortgage and This is Your House programmes through increased subsidies and more ambitious efficiency standards
Measures with indirect impacts on GHG emission reduction	Supportive actions for transformation of the Green Mortgage and This is Your House programmes into a holistic urban planning process: • Building-code pilot in one federal state • Promotion and enforcement of building codes across federal states over time • Capacity building • Extension of urban planning criteria and inclusion in the holistic framework
NAMA timeframe	
• Implementation	2011–2012
• Operation	2013–2020
NAMA implementation and operation costs	Incremental costs required for the upscaling of actions until 2020
NAMA type	Supported NAMA (with a possibility of credited NAMA for parts of the actions)
Type of support required under the NAMA	Financial, technical and capacity building

implementation phase (2011–2012) and operation phase (2013–2020) of the NAMA. During the implementation phase, they mainly comprise the institutional set-up and NAMA administration, as well as the design of an MRV, baseline and additionality framework. As a main supportive action, the enforcement of mandatory building codes is proposed. CONAVI expects the NAMA to facilitate the enforcement of building codes at the level of federal states, starting with a 'pilot' state to demonstrate the feasibility and advantages of the enforcement in order to incentivize other states to follow the example.

The NAMA's long-term objective is the transformation of the Green Mortgage programme into a country-wide holistic urban planning process. The integration of urban planning criteria would have an indirect positive impact on the potential emission reduction under the NAMA, e.g. through avoided transportation needs. The NAMA could pave the way for this process by providing support for investigating possibilities to integrate urban planning and the Green Mortgage programme into a single holistic urban planning and sustainable housing concept for Mexico. Additionally, capacity building and information campaigns should be carried out to achieve a considerable upscaling of the Green Mortgage and a broader participation in the scheme.

The continuation of the existing This is Your House and Green Mortgage programmes should be seen as a unilateral component and Mexican contribution towards the NAMA. The upscaling of the building programme requires additional financial resources until 2020. This incremental finance requirement could be sourced from different bilateral or multilateral sources for supported or credited elements of the NAMA.

3.3.2 MRV, baselines and additionality

Considering the objective of the NAMA to significantly upscale the existing programmes with large-scale support from donors, and if appropriate, carbon credits, it is reasonable to carry out MRV based on monitoring of GHG emission reductions. This is because potential donors will be interested in a robust assessment of the effectiveness of their support and the credited NAMA will require MRV with regards to emission reduction. Thus, the challenge is how to design a robust, yet streamlined MRV framework that can serve the purposes of supported and credited NAMAs.

The size and complexity of a mitigation programme determine MRV approaches. The following three broad categories of MRV approaches are available for building efficiency programmes: (1) deemed savings approach; (2) large-scale data analysis approach; and (3) measurement and verification (M&V) approach (NAPEE 2007). The deemed savings approach estimates energy savings based on default values designed for specific energy-efficiency measures. It is most commonly used for programmes that involve simple energy-efficiency measures with well-defined applications, e.g. give-away of CFLs. This approach is only valid for projects with fixed operating conditions and well-known, documented stipulation values (NAPEE 2007). The large-scale data analysis approach conducts a statistical analysis on energy consumption data, e.g. utility records, for all or most of the participants and possibly non-participants in the programme. It is primarily used for residential building programmes with many, relatively homogeneous participants and measures, e.g. residential building weatherization programmes (NAPEE 2007). The M&V approach conducts direct MRV of the building energy consumption. Because it is more expensive on a per-project basis than the other two approaches, it is generally applied only to a sample of buildings. It is the most common approach used for programmes involving non-residential buildings, in which a wide variety of factors determine energy savings, e.g. performance-contracting programme (NAPEE 2007).

The Mexican NAMA is a residential building efficiency programme with relatively homogeneous measures applied to a number of buildings. Thus, the large-scale data analysis is the most relevant MRV approach. The NAMA plans to implement a range of mitigation measures following the set of energy-efficiency requirements. Therefore, a whole-building approach is required to assess the energy performance of an entire building. The energy performance can be expressed in energy consumption per floor area (kWh/m^2), which can reflect the improvement in specific energy consumption of houses built under the NAMA. A benchmark level of building energy performance can be used to define a baseline level, which is established by comparing the energy performance of a cohort of residential buildings that are in similar circumstances. The approach has a strong advantage in streamlining MRV procedures because it allows MRV of building energy performance in a holistic manner, without looking into every single measure implemented in the buildings.

The benchmarking approach has also proven instrumental in demonstrating additionality of CDM building projects. With this approach, all the emission reductions achieved from energy savings beyond an energy performance benchmark can be issued CERs (for a recently approved CDM methodology using this approach, see UNFCCC 2011b). This avoids the conventional way of demonstrating additionality (see Chapter 1), which is not easily applicable to building programmes. Commonly, such programmes involve a range of mitigation measures whose implementation will be spread over the duration of the crediting period. However, the standard additionality test would require the project developer to know in advance exactly what measures will be implemented at what point in time. The benchmarking approach does not require such ex-ante knowledge. As a benchmark can be updated over time, mitigation measures can be added during the course of programme implementation. Furthermore, the approach allows for holistic additionality assessment of mitigation measures, because the energy savings contributions of each measure are reflected in the whole-building energy performance indicator. This is more advantageous than the conventional way of assessing additionality of each measure, which can be prohibitively difficult if there is a wide range of mitigation measures implemented in combination.

In order to optimize the flow of public and private finance to the NAMA, differentiated baselines will be applied to unilateral, supported and credited

NAMAs (Figure 7.3). First, a business-as-usual (BAU) level of building energy performance should serve as a baseline for unilateral NAMAs, which improves the energy performance from a common practice level in Mexico. Second, a baseline for a supported NAMA should represent the energy performance level that is adjusted for future performance improvements achieved by existing building programmes. The supported NAMA aims to go beyond the energy performance level of the existing building programmes by implementing the mandatory minimum performance standards. Third, the emission level of the supported NAMA should serve as a baseline for a credited NAMA that goes beyond the minimum efficiency requirement of the supported NAMA. This means that the supported NAMA and its minimum standards would set a new baseline for future CDM projects as well. Only emission reductions under the credited NAMA or future CDM projects that will exceed the established standards would be eligible for generating carbon credits. These baselines may be established for different building categories, which could be differentiated by building types, climate zones, etc. Importantly, the baselines need to be made more stringent over time in order to account for autonomous improvement of the building energy performance (e.g. by adoption of efficient appliances over time).

In order to avoid double-counting of emission reductions with the NAMA, future CDM projects implemented in the residential building sector would need to apply the emission level of the supported NAMA as their baselines. Any CDM project registered before the implementation of the NAMA will not be harmed for the current crediting period, but will have to take the new baseline into account at potential renewal of its crediting period. Emission reductions achieved by the NAMA should not be claimed for crediting by the future CDM

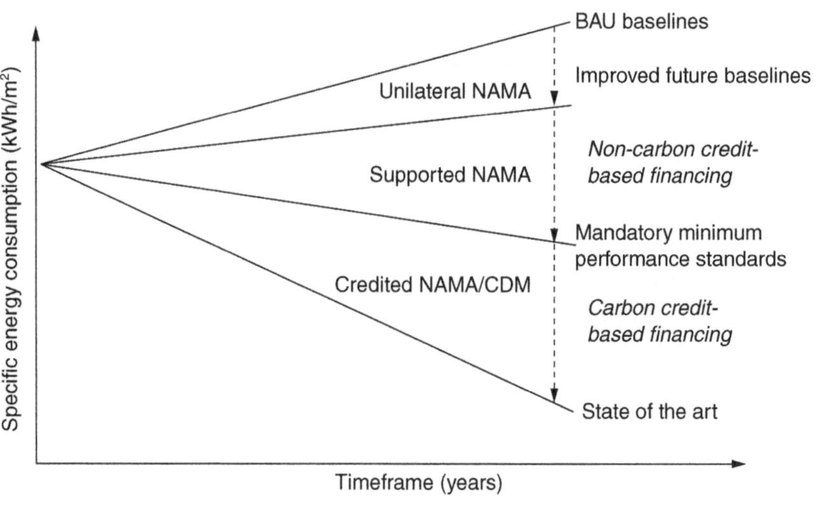

Figure 7.3 Minimum performance standards and their effect on the baselines (source: adapted from Cheng and Zhu 2009).

projects. As discussed above, such an approach can provide developing countries with the incentive to move from the CDM to NAMAs. Although the approach deviates from the E+/E– rule of the CDM, recently approved CDM methodologies for building projects do require mandatory, enforced regulations to be taken into account in the baseline setting (UNFCCC 2009, 2011b). As such, the proposed approach works in line with the recent regulatory trend of the CDM.

3.3.3 Financing structure

There are several financing mechanisms and stakeholders involved in this NAMA. In order to combine the different mechanisms and engage all the participants, Wehner *et al.* (2010) propose the creation of a revolving NAMA fund. This will centralize all the financial resources received from donors, the private sector and the Mexican government. Such a fund could be supported by soft loans from international donors and/or climate funds until the break-even is achieved. In addition, the fund would allocate the resources to the associated financial institutions that are responsible for the distribution of the loans to housing developers. The model builds on the current structure already in place for the implementation of the Green Mortgage and This is Your House programmes. An overview of the NAMA fund is provided in Figure 7.4.

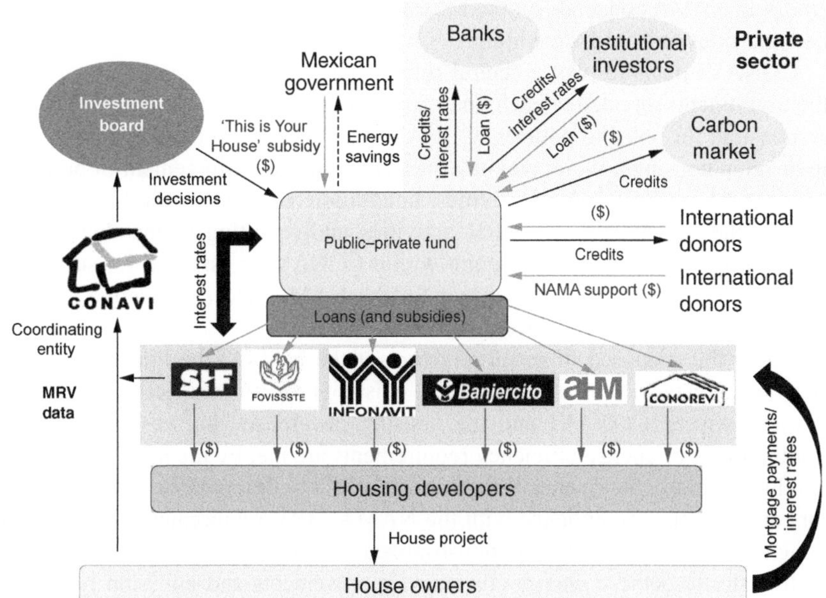

Figure 7.4 Overview of the revolving NAMA fund and finance structure.

An investment board is composed of CONAVI, the private sector and representatives from industrialized countries. The board will decide on the resource allocation and the interest rates provided to each financing institution (INFONAVIT and others). Under the fund structure, the NAMA resources (financial support or credit revenues) should be allocated to the financing institutions at favourable interest rates in order to enable distribution of the subsidy to the housing developers. The NAMA fund will provide access to untapped resources from the private sector, such as banks, institutional investors and the carbon market. They will be able to participate in the NAMA fund by providing loans and funds while receiving interests or credits in return. The NAMA fund will hence increase the number of loans that can be provided. The large potential for upscaling the Green Mortgage programme (it is projected to reach up to four million new houses by 2020 under the NAMA) will attract private investors interested in low-risk, low-return investments that can reach high volumes. If a crediting NAMA were established in the future, the private sector could also channel its funds through the carbon market.

Private investors could also mobilize low-cost finance to support the development of sustainable housing by providing loans to the NAMA fund on commercial terms. The fund structure is likely to attract pension funds and asset managers interested in guaranteed low-risk investments. The investment returns would be guaranteed by the financing institutions, and the payback backed by the energy savings generated from the households. On the other hand, credited NAMAs could provide additional incentives to the private investors who want to participate in the NAMA through the carbon market. However, a decision on crediting NAMAs depends on the Mexican government's position and the international rules on NAMA crediting.

CONAVI plans to play a central role in the investment board and supervise the investments directed to each financing institution. As the government agency responsible for housing policies, CONAVI would also receive part of the funds to develop housing policies and other activities such as enforcement of buildings codes and capacity-building activities. In addition, CONAVI would be responsible for the coordination of MRV activities and reporting to the donors. The establishment of a single focal point within CONAVI is essential for successful coordination of international support for the NAMA and an effective management of MRV data received from auditors.

Under the proposed financial structure of the NAMA, the financing institutions would have a similar role as in the existing programmes, acting as intermediaries between CONAVI and the housing developers and ensuring that the minimum set of energy-efficiency requirements are met by the housing developers. Furthermore, the financing institutions would be responsible for hiring auditors and ensuring compliance with the NAMA MRV requirements. This can be done with support provided by industrialized countries.

In order to achieve energy-efficiency improvements and emission reductions through the NAMA, housing developers should design housing projects according to the technical specifications defined by CONAVI. This is the main eligibility requirement for receiving soft loans and support. Additionally, training and capacity-building activities are expected to raise awareness about energy savings and facilitate the integration of green technologies in new housing developments.

House owners would be reached by the NAMA through the marketing and awareness raising campaigns promoted through television, information brochures and the internet. Being the main beneficiaries of the programme, the house owners are expected to be attracted to the programme due to the energy and monetary savings they are expected to achieve.

The NAMA creates financial benefits to house owners and the Mexican government. The house owners will benefit from reduced energy bills, while the government from the avoided financial expenditure for subsidizing the baseline energy consumption of the house owners. The house owners could be entitled to all the financial benefits from the technology upscaling through energy savings and generation at his premises, which he could partly use for repayment of the mortgage. This will ensure repayment and potentially shorten the payback period. The financial benefits for the government could (partly) be used to refinance the investments over time. For example, the saved subsidies could be re-invested through the revolving NAMA fund or through the public utility, in which case the government would also be involved in the investment under the NAMA.

The supported NAMA and financial structure could help to pave the way for a low-carbon development strategy in the Mexican housing sector. The NAMA would be necessary to provide sufficient funds and support to initialize this development and to establish the basis for a sustainable market transformation.

4 Conclusions

NAMAs have become a prominent concept in the international negotiation. The key advantage of NAMAs lies in their potential to support the implementation of mitigation policies in developing countries. This offers the potential to move beyond project-based mechanisms such as the CDM. The three types of NAMAs (unilateral, supported and credited) are likely to target different niches of mitigation actions, mainly depending on their MAC and causality and timeframe of GHG impacts. However, the different types of NAMAs can be implemented jointly to provide a mix of public and private sources. The revolving NAMA fund proposed for the residential building programme in Mexico shows an interesting option for leveraging private finance by public money channelled through a supported NAMA, and possibly credited NAMA too. Given the limited availability of public finance, NAMAs need to seek a way to combine private and public finance to achieve substantial upscaling of mitigation effort by developing countries.

NAMAs will require a holistic approach to MRV of mitigation actions. This is because mitigation policies implemented under NAMAs will likely involve a much wider range of mitigation actions than CDM projects, which mainly focus on single, technology-specific mitigation actions. For example, the Mexican NAMA aims to implement a variety of energy-efficiency and renewable-energy technologies that directly result in GHG emission reductions. It will also implement a number of supportive actions that will likely result in indirect emission reductions in the long term (enforcement of building codes, capacity building, awareness raising, etc.). The whole-building energy performance benchmark approach proposed for the Mexican NAMA will capture GHG impacts of any mitigation actions implemented under the NAMA. Such a holistic approach can significantly streamline the MRV process because the GHG impacts of all mitigation actions are evaluated in an aggregate manner.

As we need to realize substantial upscaling of the mitigation effort by developing countries, it is important to design clear incentives for gradually transiting from the project-based CDM to the policy-based NAMAs. The Mexican NAMA suggests that one way to incentivize the transition is to use the NAMA-financed level of emissions as baselines of future CDM projects. This gives full recognition of GHG emission reductions achieved by mitigation policies implemented under NAMAs while adjusting baselines of the future CDM projects for the impact of mitigation policies. This approach requires a change in the E+/E– rule of the CDM. Therefore, the NAMA architecture needs to be developed in tandem with a reform of the CDM, so that the two mechanisms effectively create an incentive for mobilizing support for mitigation policies in developing countries.

References

Broekhoff, D. (2007) 'Expanding global emissions trading: prospects for standardised carbon offset crediting', IETA.

Cheng, C. and Zhu, X. (2009) 'NAMAs for dispersed energy end-use sectors: using the building sector as an example', in K. Holm, J. Fenhann and M. Hinostroza (eds) *NAMAs and the Carbon Market: Nationally Appropriate Mitigation Actions of Developing Countries*, Roskilde: United Nations Environment Programme Risø Centre, pp. 79–95.

CONAVI (2010) 'Estimation of housing demand in Mexico', Comisión Nacional de Vivienda. Personal communication (29 October 2010).

CONAVI (2011) 'Cierre Preliminar del sector 2010: Avances del sector diciembre 2010', Comisión Nacional de Vivienda.

Helme, N. (2010) 'NAMAs, crediting and the CDM: the path forward', paper presented at EPRI GHG Offset Dialog, Washington, DC, February 2010.

Hepburn, C. (2009) 'International carbon finance and the Clean Development Mechanism', in D. Helm and C. Hepburn (eds) *The Economics and Politics of Climate Change*, Oxford: Oxford University Press, pp. 409–29.

Hepburn, C. and Stern, N. (2009) 'The global deal on climate change', in D. Helm and C. Hepburn (eds) *The Economics and Politics of Climate Change*, Oxford: Oxford University Press, pp. 36–57.

Hirata, E. (2009) 'Strategic programmes to promote energy efficiency in the sustainability development framework', in AEAEE (ed.) *Zero Energy Housing in Mexico Workshop*, Mexico City, Vienna: AEAEE, p. 15.

Jung, M., Vieweg, M., Eisbrenner, K., Höhne, N., Ellermann, C., Schimschar, S. and Beyer, C. (2010) 'Nationally appropriate mitigation actions: insights from example development', Ecofys Germany. Online. Available: http://climate-action.kz/uploads/Nationally_Appropriate_Mitigation_Actions,_Insights_from_example_development.pdf (accessed 14 June 2011).

Kim, J., Ellis, J. and Moarif, S. (2009) 'Matching mitigation actions with support: key issues for channeling international public finance', OECD, IEA. Online. Available: www.oecd.org/dataoecd/53/31/44204193.pdf (accessed 14 June 2011).

Levina, E. and Helme, N. (2009) 'Nationally appropriate mitigation actions by developing countries: architecture and key issues', Center for Clean Air Policy. Online. Available: www.ccap.org/docs/resources/823/NAMAs%20by%20Developing%20Countries%20-%20Architecture%20and%20Key%20Issues.pdf (accessed 14 June 2011).

NAPEE (2007) 'Model energy efficiency programme impact evaluation guide', United States Environmental Protection Agency. Online. Available: www.cee1.org/eval/evaluation_guide.pdf (accessed 14 June 2011).

Odón de Buen, R. (2009) 'Greenhouse gas emission baselines and reduction potentials from buildings in Mexico', United Nations Environment Programme Sustainable Buildings and Climate Initiative. Online. Available: www.unep.org/sbci/pdfs/SBCI-Mexicoreport.pdf (accessed 14 June 2011).

Okubo, Y., Hayashi, D. and Michaelowa, A. (2011) 'NAMA crediting: how to assess offsets from and additionality of policy-based mitigation actions in developing countries', *Greenhouse Gas Measurement & Management*, 1: 37–46.

UNFCCC (2007) 'FCCC/CP/2007/6/Add.1 Bali Action Plan'. Online. Available: http://unfccc.int/resource/docs/2007/cop13/eng/06a01.pdf#page=3 (accessed 14 June 2011).

UNFCCC (2009) 'Energy efficiency and renewable energy measures in new residential buildings, AMS-III.AE version 1.0'. Online. Available: http://cdm.unfccc.int/filestorage/C/D/M/CDM_AMS02DI2P0YCXF0W6W3D6HV1KX6NWQ8O0/EB48_repan14_AMS_III.AE_ver01.pdf?t=aWF8MTMwODE1Njg3NS4zNA==|Mfk1vq_Eh-qQxapXN4IqCMoSMNc= (accessed 14 June 2011).

UNFCCC (2010a) 'FCCC/AWGLCA/2010/14 Negotiating text: Note by the secretariat'. Online. Available: http://unfccc.int/resource/docs/2010/awglca12/eng/14.pdf (accessed 14 June 2011).

UNFCCC (2010b) 'FCCC/CP/2010/7/Add.1 The Cancun Agreements: Outcome of the work of the Ad hoc Working Group on Long-term Cooperative Action under the Convention'. Online. Available: http://unfccc.int/files/na/application/pdf/07a01–1.pdf (accessed 14 June 2011).

UNFCCC (2011a) 'FCCC/AWGLCA/2011/MISC.7 Views on the items relating to a work programme for the development of modalities and guidelines listed in decision 1/CP.16, paragraph 66'. Online. Available: http://unfccc.int/resource/docs/2011/awglca14/eng/misc07.pdf (accessed 14 June 2011).

UNFCCC (2011b) 'Energy efficiency technologies and fuel switching in new buildings, AM0091 version 1.0.0'. Online. Available: http://cdm.unfccc.int/filestorage/Q/7/J/Q7JWKS0GR8ZH1F9MBL5T3E2NXA4OUC/eb61_repan03.pdf?t=eEp8MTMwODE1MjM1MC4xNQ==|87PK3_2vsC4DW3xJ1y2tgxpKYBA= (accessed 14 June 2011).

UNFCCC (2011c) 'Compilation of information on nationally appropriate mitigation actions to be implemented by Parties not included in Annex I to the Convention'. Online. Available: http://unfccc.int/resource/docs/2011/awglca14/eng/inf01.pdf (accessed 12 July 2011).

Wehner, S., Krey, M., Gusmao, F., Hayashi, D., Michaelowa, A. and Sam, N. (2010) 'Supported NAMA design concept for energy-efficiency measures in the Mexican residential building sector: final draft working paper', Point Carbon Global Advisory Services, Perspectives Climate Change.

8 Market mechanisms for adaptation

An aberration or a key source of finance?

Axel Michaelowa, Michel Köhler and Sonja Butzengeiger

1 Introduction: background to adaptation market mechanisms

While markets are as old as humanity, tradeable units were first proposed as instruments of environmental policy in the late 1960s. Initially, policy-makers did not take these proposals seriously and it took a decade until the first cautious attempts to test the instruments were made in the United States. However, since the 1990s, there has been a strong upswing of environmental markets, starting with air pollutants but eventually extending to include greenhouse gases (GHGs). The most famous and largest example of environmental markets are the carbon markets, mainly driven by the EU Emissions Trading Scheme (EU ETS) and the project-based mechanisms, the Clean Development Mechanism (CDM, see Chapter 1) and Joint Implementation (JI), but also by numerous other regional and national schemes throughout the world.

Environmental markets are based on the generation of demand for tradeable units through regulatory decisions. This demand then triggers the supply of units. There are different types of market mechanisms, such as 'cap-and-trade' schemes, in which the total amount of an environmental pollutant is limited and tradeable units can only be generated by reducing the pollution below that limit (see Chapter 6). Offset or 'baseline-and-credit' systems allow the generation of offset credits through projects that reduce the pollutant compared to a baseline (see Chapter 6). While voluntary markets have existed for some periods, in the long run they have always suffered from a collapse of prices due to the lack of sustained demand; the latest example is the demise of the Chicago Climate Exchange in 2010.

So far, markets have not been used to promote adaptation to climate change. Given the increasing recognition that significant climate change impacts cannot be prevented and the huge amounts of finance necessary to effectively prevent (some of) the resulting negative impacts, this is quite surprising. One reason might be that the adaptation discussion has been dominated by actors from the development assistance community, which is normally not focused on markets. But what are the financial sums currently discussed in the context of adaptation?

Poor countries already suffer from an 'adaptation deficit' to current climate variability. For 2030, the UNFCCC (2008) estimates annual global adaptation costs at US$49–171 billion, with US$27–66 billion accruing in developing countries. The World Bank (2010) estimates annual adaptation costs for developing countries at US$70–100 billion.

Given this background, adaptation has increasingly become relevant in the international climate negotiations, and industrialized countries have felt compelled to announce large volumes of finance for activities in developing countries. In the Copenhagen Accord, industrialized countries have pledged US$30 billion as 'fast-start finance' (FSF) for mitigation and adaptation in developing countries (see Chapter 5), with a view to increasing financing to US$100 billion annually by 2020. However, the modalities of financing remain vague and the risk of 're-labelling' funds that exist already appears substantial. By today, three multilateral funds under the UNFCCC earmarked for adaptation each contain around US$150–250 million of funding: the Adaptation Fund financed by a levy on the CDM (see Chapter 4), the Least Developed Countries Funds (LDCF) and the Special Climate Change Fund (SCCF) (HBS/ODI 2011). The Adaptation Fund has the potential to become the largest of the three due to the steady inflow of the CDM levy if there is an ambitious agreement on the international climate policy framework after 2012. However, it currently is much smaller than the Pilot Program for Climate Resilience (PPCR), part of the World Bank's Climate Investment Funds, whose commitments reach more than US$900 million, of which US$300 million have already been paid in (HBS/ODI 2011). At this level of resourcing, the figures show nicely that a significant upscaling is necessary to reach the required orders of magnitude as estimated by the UNFCCC Secretariat and the World Bank (see also the discussion on resources for adaptation in Chapter 4).

Against this background of significant financial needs for adaptation but insufficient resources, any adaptation finance mechanism should fulfil the following two key objectives:

- to mobilize additional funding for adaptation by involving the private sector;
- to use available funds as efficiently as possible.

Could these aims be achieved by an adaptation market mechanism?

2 General functioning of an adaptation market mechanism

The cornerstone of an adaptation market mechanism is the creation of tradeable units through a governmental regulation quantifying an adaptation target. In general, such units are defined in terms of a commodity that a government wants to be provided.

If the tradeable unit denominates a 'bad', its volume has to be lower than the volume that would normally be produced. If the tradeable unit denominates a 'good', its production must entail a cost while the benefit cannot fully be appropriated by the producer; and hence the volume has to be higher than the volume that would normally be produced. In both cases, the volume would be defined by the politically palatable maximum. Kuch and Gigli (2007: 16) passingly mention an adaptation trading system that limits 'risky activities', and thus would be similar to the trading systems for classical pollutants. Such a trading scheme might, for example, limit the number of building permits in a zone prone to storm surges or rock falls due to thawing permafrost in mountains, and hence would consider the fact that much of the loss that occurs to climate change-related damage is also a result of socioeconomic development and a tendency of mankind to select the most scenic spots for building houses regardless of their exposure to damage. Building permits would be made tradeable and the price required to pay for the permit would generate a disincentive to engage in the risky activity. The advantage of such a trading system would be that an efficient selection of risky activities would be triggered, i.e. those activities would be undertaken that generate the highest revenues or utility. Next to making regional or local risks more transparent – leading to more public awareness and better-informed decisions – the trading scheme may reflect secondary costs such as costs for required public infrastructure and then reflect a more comprehensive level of risk and responsibility.

Trading systems for 'adaptation goods' can be based on any type of adaptation whose benefits are measurable and verifiable. To generate a price and make a market for tradeable units that works, there needs to be a scarcity of them. A simple way of reaching this would be to define the target as 'additional adaptive benefit' or 'avoided damage through climate change'. Stadelmann *et al.* (2011) suggest combining two metrics to assess the adaptation benefits and effectiveness of activities: (1) wealth saved from destruction through climate change impacts (i.e. prevented economic damage) and (2) disability-adjusted life years saved (DALYs) as an indicator for avoided health impacts through climate change. They argue that both metrics are economically and socially relevant and widely used in public health policy and economic analysis: saved wealth could be expressed as the net present value (NPV) of property saved in a given region over time, expressed in current currency units, whereas DALYs calculate the number of years of life lost due to premature mortality and the number of years lived with disability on a standardized basis according to a methodology developed, inter alia, by the World Health Organization (WHO). In this approach, the basis for comparison is standard life expectancy, and different types of disability/illness get different weights (WHO 2010a, 2010b). Apart from those two metrics, Stadelmann *et al.* (2011) propose to use no-harm assessments in the environmental and cultural fields. Certainly, it would be possible to determine other metrics or to start with a single metric first before making an adaptation market mechanism more comprehensive. In any case, the unit should be applicable to as many types of adaptation activities as possible to enable maximization of the cost-reduction potential.

Those entities that want to deliver adaptation units would have to first identify adaptation opportunities, then define the adaptation action in detail and estimate the adaptation benefit. This should be done under consideration of the protected value, the development of this value over time and the risk of future impact through climate change. It is obvious that uncertainty about future development of value and climate risk exists and might be substantial. Hence, guidance by the regulator about how to deal with this uncertainty would be required. As safeguards of the integrity of the adaptation market mechanism, independent validators should check the correctness of assumptions, estimates and calculations. Here, one can draw on the experience made with the CDM (see Chapter 1), while bearing in mind that the system should be manageable. Figure 8.1 summarizes the basic functioning of an adaptation market mechanism.

It is obvious that the geographical scope of the market mechanism needs to be defined as well. Again, many different options are possible. One could imagine a sub-national, a national, a regional or an international scheme. The larger the geographical scope, the higher would be the liquidity of the market. If one assumes that adaptation actions are cheaper in less developed countries (LDCs), an international scheme would lower compliance costs for covered entities. At the same time, it is questionable whether politicians of industrialized countries would accept a scheme where adaptation money mainly flows to developing countries.

Finally, the adaptation market mechanism could make use of the concept of offsets. Offsets are tradeable units generated by projects that provide tradeable units in a region where there is no requirement to surrender such units. The units can be used by the entities that are required to surrender tradeable units, assuming that an offset can be converted to a compliance unit. A discounting of the value of offsets would also be possible. Offsets reduce the costs of attaining the target underlying the trading system, as their availability reduces the price for the tradeable units.

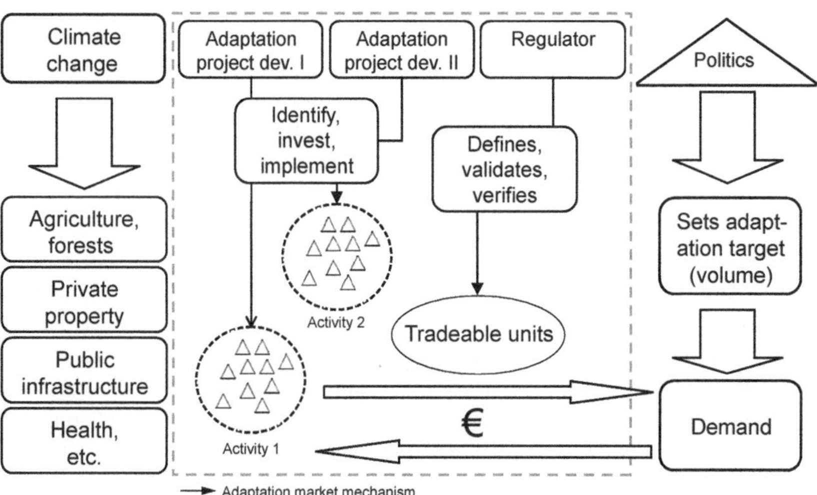

Figure 8.1 Overview: functioning of an adaptation market mechanism.

3 Major chances and advantages of an adaptation market mechanism

In the following sections we discuss the advantages of an adaptation market mechanism compared to the policy instruments used so far to mobilize adaptation.

3.1 Guaranteeing transparency

Usually, economic instruments are designed and adjusted in a negotiation between experts, lobbyists and politicians. Often, there is a lack of transparency of how and based on which principles and criteria decisions are made. In the fragmented context of international adaptation funding, a broad variety of financing institutions, including funds like those described above, have been established. Furthermore, multilateral banks like the Asian Development Bank, the World Bank or the Inter-American Development Bank, as well as implementing entities like the German 'Gesellschaft für Internationale Zusammenarbeit' (GIZ), the UK Department for International Development (DFID) or the Swiss Agency for Development and Cooperation (SDC) are engaged in adaptation financing (HBS/ODI 2011). All of them have set-up their individual governance structures, and thus use different approaches, evaluation criteria and indicators to assess the adaptive benefits of projects they are involved in. On the one hand, this situation could be interpreted as a competition of the best approaches, in which the most promising ones will prevail after time. On the other hand, these circumstances compromise transparency and prevent external control by civil society. Currently there is no evidence that the various approaches will be streamlined and standardized after a limited amount of time in order to enable independent control and comparability.

But even though there is no common institutional approach, the majority of these institutions provide at least partially transparent justifications for how they select projects for implementation and funding. However, if one analyses the monetary streams at the international level an astonishing fact becomes obvious: roughly one-third of the US$30 billion FSF is expected to be channelled into adaptation, while the rest goes into mitigation, with a significant element of avoided deforestation. Interestingly, only 40 per cent of these funds will be channelled through the institutions mentioned above, while 60 per cent are expected to be distributed bilaterally (WRI 2011; see also Chapter 5 for details).

Therefore, countries are almost unconstrained with regard to the general frameworks, indicators, assumptions, monitoring, reporting and verification (MRV) methods used for adaptation financing and need not provide any further justification for how the financial resources have been distributed. The resulting confusion becomes visible when one analyses the reporting of financial contributions in the national communications of developed countries to the UNFCCC. Here, double-counting of money for FSF pledges under the UNFCCC and ODA under the OECD is the rule rather than the exception (see also Klein *et al.* 2011). If an international agreement on such a key issue like 'additional financial contributions' is impossible to achieve, it can be expected that standardized MRV for adaptation activities will require even more time. Hence a lack of transparency and international control can be found at the bilateral level, which significantly increases the corruption risk as both the developed and the developing country state institutions and governments may have additional interests beside efficient and effective adaptation projects. Political sympathies and geostrategic interests, as well as trade and economic cooperation – especially regarding natural resources and sales prospects for national enterprises when deciding about the donations and recipients – are likely to play a key role. To avoid external criticism, active obfuscation will be helpful.

Summing up, a general lack of transparency seems to exist at all levels of international adaptation funding, usually due to inconsistent and unclear fund allocation procedures, but sometimes purposefully. Such a situation significantly increases the risk that funds will be spent for inefficient adaptation, maladaptation or even be fully lost through embezzlement and corruption. For national or international systems that should enable protection of wealth and health of large numbers of people worldwide, such risks are unacceptable, both from an ethical and economical perspective.

The methodological approaches applied to estimating adaptation benefits are determining the allocation of rare financial resources in an efficient system. But if the system lacks transparency an efficient allocation is rather improbable. Therefore, we propose a framework for the adaptation market mechanism that explicitly builds on a transparent process to enable a bottom-up methodological approach for a broad variety of participants. A possible adaptation market mechanism project cycle that involves several steps from a project idea until implementation could learn from the approaches applied within the carbon market. For example, under the CDM, private and public actors have already developed and applied hundreds of methodologies for GHG mitigation in several sectors from industry to agriculture. An adaptation project cycle could be built on the carbon project experiences. The following hypothetical example of a project developer seeking to build a dyke illustrates the process:

1 The project developer has to check if an applicable methodology/approach to determining the adaptive benefits for his adaptation activity is already available. If no 'dyke methodology' can be identified, the project developer needs to draft a new methodology.
2 The 'dyke methodology' is submitted to an independent auditor, either a private enterprise or a panel of experts selected by the regulator. During the audit, the methodology gets analysed according to applicability for adaptation projects, is published and comments from global stakeholders are solicited to be taken into account by the validator. Following validation, the regulator decides whether the methodology should be approved. This procedure guarantees international control and transparency of methodology development. In this example the 'dyke methodology' gets approved and is ready for the first project.

3 Based on the approved methodology, the project developer accounts for the adaptive benefits of his dyke project. Related data and climate change forecasts have to be gathered and implemented. Finally, project documentation has to be validated by the auditor. Again, all relevant documents have to be published and global as well as local stakeholders are asked for comments.

The example outlines an approach that is arranged as transparently as possible and allows international participation and criticism. This process enables participation from project developers, expert validators and actors from civil society, such as researchers or NGOs, which directly leads to increased transparency. Hence, this approach would effectively reduce inefficient adaptation, maladaptation or even embezzlement and corruption.

3.2 Mobilizing broad participation

One of the major advantages of an adaptation market mechanism is that it enables a broad participation. Participation in this context means both participation in funding adaptation activities, i.e. those entities that have an adaptation target and finally need to spend money for either creating or buying adaptation units, and participation in identifying, planning and implementing adaptation activities.

The first aspect is important to mobilize the funds that are necessary to adequately adapt to climate change. Certainly, both the ability to pay and exposure to negative impacts of climate change differ by region. But even looking at rich regions that are at relatively little risk – such as the European Union – it is clear that public money alone will be insufficient to quickly implement the desired measures (Yohe *et al.* 2007; Osberghaus and Reif 2010). In the case of an adaptation market mechanism that requires private entities to meet certain targets, the private entities will have to invest, so that overall the basis of available funds will increase.[1]

The second aspect is important as the definition of adaptation targets can boost a substantial search for adaptation opportunities. The experiences made with the CDM are impressive (see Chapter 1). In mid-2011, Point Carbon estimated the number of projects that have reached Project Identification Note (PIN) stage – including those submitted to the UNFCCC – at more than 9,000 projects, and the total number of CDM projects – including 'prospects' – to over 14,500 (Point Carbon 2011). Similar observations have been made in the context of the EU ETS. By today, the EU ETS covers over 11,000 power plants and industrial installations in 30 countries (EU Commission 2011). Although one cannot monitor the impact as easily as in the case of the CDM by just counting the number of project ideas, research has found that the EU ETS has clearly led to behavioural change. Rogge and Hoffmann (2009) analysed the impact of the EU ETS on the sectoral innovation system for power generation technologies in Germany, and found that the EU ETS, inter alia, affects the rate and direction of the technological change of power generation with the main impact within the large-scale coal power generation technological regime. They also argue that the EU ETS's impact on corporate CO_2 culture and routines may prepare the ground for the transition to a low-carbon sectoral innovation system for power generation technologies.

These two analogies strengthen our expectation that the simple existence of a (functioning) adaptation market mechanism can make a difference. First, it can mobilize a multitude of entrepreneurs to identify easy and effective adaptation action at all levels of an economy. Second, it can be a fundamental tool for raising awareness at the level of policy-makers, investors and the public – and finally make a difference in the day-to-day decisions of people.

3.3 Promoting efficiency

Economic theory shows that a market mechanism for environmental goods can achieve an efficient outcome as it will provide an incentive to embark on the cheapest options to procure the good. Markets for local pollutants and GHG emissions mitigation have confirmed that this theoretical result can be reached in practice, generating simple yet innovative solutions that nobody thought of before introduction of the market mechanisms. SO_2 trading under the US Clean Air Act generated the low-cost solution of transporting low-sulphur coal over long distances to replace higher-sulphur coal. In the CDM, projects that reduce the industrial gases HFC-23 and N_2O were developed rapidly, while earlier mitigation assessments and activities of public funds for GHG reductions had ignored these options (see Chapter 1 for a detailed discussion of industrial gas projects).

A key precondition for an efficient outcome of an adaptation market mechanism is the availability of a wide range of adaptation options with strongly differing costs. Evidence about costs of adaptation options is still scarce, but costs of adaptation projects seem to differ by several orders of magnitude. Economics of Climate Adaptation (2009) discusses measures to address adaptation to increasing drought risks in the Indian state of Maharashtra, and finds that 50 per cent of expected losses can be prevented by efficient irrigation systems at a cost of 1–10 per cent of expected losses. Likewise, in Florida 30 per cent of expected losses from hurricanes could be prevented by measures that cost less than 10 per cent of prevented losses, while another 10 per cent of expected losses could be prevented at costs ranging from 30–100 per cent of prevented losses (Economics of Climate Adaptation 2009). Given that adaptation projects differ substantially with regard to their technology, their lifetime and their size, it is very likely that the discovery process started by the market will lead to massive cost savings compared to an approach where policy-makers subsidize specific adaptation options preferred by powerful interest groups, or insurance that covers losses after they have occurred. Moreover, given the experience with mitigation markets, it is likely that many low-cost adaptation options would be discovered once an adaptation market mechanism has been introduced.

In order to maximize efficiency, the following principles should be applied:

1 Maximize the geographical reach of eligible projects.
2 Do not exclude any technological options.
3 Make sure that baseline and monitoring methodologies do not lead to advantages for certain technologies that are not justified given their adaptive performance.

Obviously, these principles may conflict with other policy targets such as preferring protection of people within one's own jurisdiction. Also, policy-makers may want to limit adaptation action covered by the market mechanism to the protection of public goods (see the discussion below).

4 Major challenges and disadvantages

Of course, the adaptation market mechanism also has relevant challenges and drawbacks that – if not prevented through a proper design of the mechanism – might outweigh its benefits.

4.1 Where does the demand option for adaptation units come from?

A key question that determines the success of the adaptation market mechanisms will be what policy will generate demand for the trading units. Without demand, the price will be zero and the market mechanism will remain an unused system. Therefore, three potential demand options will be outlined in the following: a governmental option focusing on domestic adaptation; a governmental option focusing on international adaptation; and a private-demand option based on the polluters-pays principle.

For all three cases, demand would be created through mandatory adaptation commitments specified by governments. The commitments would be defined in the trading units proposed by Stadelmann *et al.* (2011) for a specified period. For example, policy-makers could set an annual target of protection of €5 billion saved wealth (SW) and 10,000 DALYs saved health (SH).

The first option would be based on a national adaptation target that could be either pledged unilaterally or negotiated under the UNFCCC. In regular intervals, the government implements a tender round for adaptation projects. Project developers then submit project ideas that have been validated by accredited auditors, and the government does a cost–benefit ranking to identify the most efficient projects. As the result of the tender process the government will announce a number of selected projects that jointly fulfil the adaptation target, which will receive financing for the project period. Such a system could also be implemented in supranational entities like the EU. The broader the geographical area, the higher the efficiency.

Option two generally applies the same system as option one, but is specifically designed to promote international adaptation and transfers from industrialized countries to the developing world. It builds on the financial pledges made by developed countries in the Copenhagen and Cancun conferences. Instead of national governments, the UNFCCC Conference of the Parties (COP) defines a global, quantifiable adaptation target. An international organization like the Green Climate Fund or the Adaptation Fund would then receive industrialized-country financing in order to implement this target. The fund would then tender for projects as described above. In order to achieve an equitable regional distribution, as frequently called for in the context of the CDM, a one-sided allocation of adaptation activities could be avoided by country quotas or country caps. Obviously, this would reduce efficiency of the adaptation market mechanism.

The third demand option would make use of the polluter-pays principle. Internationally defined or nationally pledged adaptation targets are allocated to GHG emitters proportionally to their GHG emissions levels. The other possible allocation principles – ability to pay and inverse of vulnerability – are less compelling. To avoid overly high transaction costs due to the high fixed element of costs for MRV, the covered entities should have a minimum size. For instance, within the EU ETS, approximately 11,000 emitting entities are covered. Companies could comply with their adaptation target through different means:

- directly investing in adaptation projects that generate adaptation units;
- acquiring adaptation units from dedicated adaptation project developers;
- acquiring adaptation units from covered companies with a surplus of such units.

Contrary to the first two options, this system implements a broader market and stronger involvement of the private sector, including trading of adaptation units. The design and impacts are comparable to the existing instrument of emission trading schemes; related costs will be transferred to the final consumer at the end of the day.

Politicians would have to decide about the regional scope for adaptation project investment. From an efficiency point of view, a global scope would be preferable as well. A global scope would also enable accounting of flows to developing countries as part of the financial pledges for mitigation and adaptation, as under option two. If the adaptation benefit for the national/supranational level is to be maximized, the scope should be limited to the country or group of countries, e.g. the EU. Such a limitation would, however, increase the costs per adaptation unit due to the lower supply of projects. As a solution, the concept of supplementarity – as known in the mitigation concept – could be applied (see also Schulze *et al.* 2011). The challenging aspect of implementing the polluter-pays principle might be heavy resistance by emitters as they are already covered by emission mitigation policy instruments like taxes or an emissions trading scheme. Furthermore, the responsibility for adaptation is primarily not linked to current emissions; it is rather historical emissions that are responsible for negative impacts of climate change. In international negotiations this approach is under consideration as a criterion; emerging economies, in particular, are arguing for it. However, an allocation of adaptation commitments on the basis of historical emissions would probably not be enforceable both from an economic and from a legal point of view, as emitters could argue that they were unaware of the possibility of anthropogenic climate change before the 1990s. But the historical emissions principle might not be as far-fetched as it seems, as it has frequently been invoked in the context of mitigation (see e.g. the Brazilian proposal). Hence, the introduction of a polluter-pays principle for target allocation under the adaptation market mechanism would need further detailed consideration regarding legal issues, economic feasibility and ethical responsibility.

4.2 Public vs private goods

Market mechanisms are usually only applied in the context of public goods (or bads). Mitigation is clearly a global public good, whereas adaptation can range from a pure private to a pure public good. In some cases it is clear that the implementation of adaptation measures is a private good, i.e. the costs as well as the benefits accrue to a distinct individual or entity. This would, for example, be the case if a household living on coastal lowland builds an artificial hill to place his house above the reach of the highest storm surges, as has been done on the German North Sea coast for many centuries. Such measures will normally be undertaken if the benefits exceed the costs. Thus, theoretically, there is no necessity for public intervention except if the need to adapt is a consequence of a global public bad. If sea-level rise is caused by anthropogenic climate change due to GHG emissions, the polluter should pay for the damages. The challenge obviously is to make emitters liable for climate change impacts that will happen some time in the future.

Moreover, in many cases there is a high degree of uncertainty with respect to the benefits of adaptation measures. This is particularly the case when benefits only occur in the distant future. Then, even if today's adaptation costs are low, due to uncertainty and discounting, individuals might not take action. Thus, there would be a case for government intervention even in the case of pure private goods if lack of information prevents private action.

Many adaptation measures result in benefits for other people than those undertaking and financing them, and thus cannot be seen as generating a purely private good. Again using the example of coastal lowlands, several households may join in building a common hill, which has historically frequently been the case. Each participating household depends on the contribution of the others.

Finally, important adaptation measures or their consequences can be a public good, such as flood protection measures or the development of drought-resistant cultivars. In our coastal lowland example, building a dyke around a large area is likely to be more effective than having many individual hills for houses. But the dyke is costly and may be difficult to implement by private contribution, as households will try to minimize their own financial contribution. A famous German novel (Storm 1888) deals with the issue of how in the early modern period, private contributions to dyke building were insufficient due to free-riding behaviour and thus led to dyke failures. In other cases private adaptation measures lead to externalities. Under both circumstances a pure private provision of the adaptation measure leads to an underprovision of adaptation. Hence, there is a case for government intervention, and for the adaptation market mechanism.

Summing up, even for private goods, given that the adaptation need has arisen due to use of the atmosphere as a public good, there is no intrinsic argument against using market mechanisms, provided that there is no financing of private goods through other policy instruments. To avoid regressive impacts of private good financing – e.g. a billionaire gobbling up adaptation funding because his yachts need protection from storm surges – the trading unit can be defined in a way where large private fortunes are weighted less than the small savings of the poor. Given private myopia and the inability of insurance mechanisms to mobilize preventive action to prevent losses beyond the incentive provided by deductibles, an absence of public intervention to mobilize investments in adaptation of a private good character may lead to high losses. We would thus propose to include private goods in the adaptation market mechanism, as any limitation of adaptation market mechanisms to exclude private goods reduces the efficiency of adaptation.

4.3 No 'equitable distribution' of adaptation projects

The nature of the market mechanism will be to mobilize the cheapest options. It is likely that there will be some clusters of cheap options, whereas in other regions, no very cheap options will be available. Thus, the market mechanism will not lead to an equitable distribution of adaptation activities. In case such an equitable distribution is desired, maximum country or region quotas need to be defined, which will decrease the efficiency of the mechanism.

4.4 Applicability of the adaptation market mechanism in the context of 'soft- and hardware' adaptation activities

As discussed, the adaptation market mechanism should promote adaptation in as many sectors as possible. However, certain activities might not allow quantifiable calculation of adaptation benefits. As discussed by Stadelmann *et al.* (2011), the calculation of the trading units SW and SH requires a good understanding of the baseline economic development and expected impacts of climate change during the lifetime of the adaptation project. Ideally, project-type-specific methodologies will be developed that specify data sources and steps for calculation of the trading unit. Within this process, two technical criteria are critical to guaranteeing applicability, credibility and efficiency:

First, a forecast of adaptive benefits has to be possible to evaluate ex-ante how many trading units can be generated by a specific project. Either one needs detailed information on (local and regional) climate change, autonomous adaptation, change in socioeconomic conditions and effectiveness of measures, which often either does not exist or is highly uncertain (see Adger *et al.* 2007), or one needs to develop proxies.

Second, measurability of adaptation achievements has to be given in case of ex-post payments or issuance of certificates. Measurability/verifiability means that the amount of adaptation units (e.g. DALYs or SW) would need to be monitored and compared with a hypothetical baseline before trading units can be issued. The quality of data will be better than of those used for the forecast before project start: ex-post adjustments can be made and climate as well as economic models will improve over time (cf. Butzengeiger-Geyer *et al.* 2011).

Both predictability and measurability of adaptation units is easier for certain project types and very challenging for others. On the one hand one finds projects involving infrastructure development, improved health protection or agricultural activities ('hardware' projects), which seem to be appropriate for the calculation of adaptation units. On the other hand there are adaptation activities whose results are hard to quantify in terms of the proposed trading units, such as capacity building, raising awareness, building institutions or launching planning processes ('soft measures'). For those project categories, calculation of direct adaptive benefits might be tenuous.

Furthermore, policy instruments such as insurance mechanisms that lead to risk sharing will not generate benefits related to the reduction of climate change impacts, while providing the possibility to minimize indirect losses generated through economic disruption following the impact. It will be extremely challenging to calculate trading units for such indirect effects.

An alternative approach would be to try to take soft measures into account through the link of the adaptation market mechanism with the classical result chain of project evaluation that usually measures the effects of adaptation activities on the output, outcome or indirect/aggregated result level. Risk evaluation could be undertaken at the transmission point between project outcome and indirect/aggregated results, the so-called attribution gap. Process/outcome indicators could be translated into trading units, considering external risk influences and related causes. Particularly for 'building institutions' projects, the estimated value of SW or SH would be much more uncertain than for a concrete adaptation activity, such as reforestation or dyke construction. However, some of the adaptive capacity projects will not be able to give any indication of actual adaptive results. In these cases we generally recommend excluding them from the set of eligible project types for the adaptation market mechanism. These projects would then search for funding from other sources as is the case in the carbon markets.

4.5 Dealing with uncertainty

In contrast to mitigation, in which the benefit usually accrues once a specific technology has been installed, benefits of adaptation are not directly visible and depend on the vagaries of the weather. Compare a mitigation project that replaces coal with biomass as a fuel for an industrial boiler with a sea wall built as protection against storm surges. The fuel switch project generates mitigation units as long as biomass is fed into the boiler, whereas the actual benefits of the sea wall depend on the height of storm surges occurring. If chance leads to an absence of storm surges during the lifetime of the sea wall, the adaptation benefit is zero. If bad luck leads to the situation that only one storm surge happens during the lifetime of the sea wall but this surge is so high that it destroys the sea wall, the adaptation benefit is again zero. Only if storm surges occur that would have flooded the land in the absence of the sea wall but that are effectively held back by it do adaptation benefits accrue in full.

In the context of project-based market mechanisms in mitigation, the definition of the baseline situation is challenging. How would the economy have developed in the absence of the mitigation project? Would mitigation options have come up on their own because they are more profitable than high-emissions technologies?

For adaptation, one key uncertainty is the differentiation between natural climate variability and the extremes caused by climate change (Figure 8.2). Many countries and regions are not fully adapted to current natural variability. Differentiating between natural and anthropogenic climate variability is currently impossible.

In Figure 8.2 the black curve shows sea-level fluctuations due to natural climate variability, which is amplified by climate change; the black dashed line shows how sea level would have fluctuated in the absence of climate change. Damages are proportional to sea level. The parallel lines show three sea wall heights. Sea wall C would have failed under natural climate variability in the past, but not fail under it in the future; under climate change it would fail three times. Sea wall B would have never failed under natural climate variability, but will fail once under a changed climate. Sea wall A will not fail even under the climate change scenario.

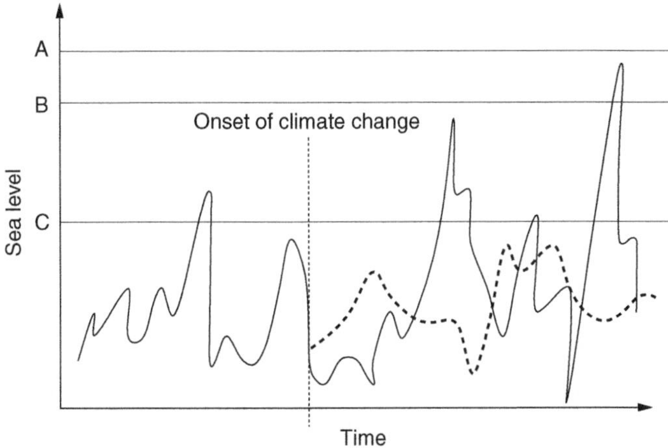

Figure 8.2 Natural variability and climate change.

Moreover, due to the high uncertainty of climate models and the difficulty of downscaling models to provide climate impacts on a small regional scale, estimating climate impacts may deteriorate into pure guesswork. Often we do not even know the sign of climate change, i.e. whether it will become wetter or drier. Therefore, allocating damage caused by extreme events to climate change and natural variability is extremely challenging. Literature on the evaluation of adaptation projects, such as Eriksen and Kelly (2007) and Hallegatte (2009), stresses the resulting difficulty of defining impact indicators for projects.

The easiest political solution to the uncertainty problem is to argue that we will not be able to detect climate change from natural variability and thus adaptation benefits should be calculated in absolute terms, i.e. no damage is assumed under the baseline. This will of course overestimate adaptation benefits.

A more complex solution would be to assume a natural climate variability baseline and value benefits against this baseline. This would be akin to mitigation baselines, where heuristics have been developed to specify emissions levels in the absence of the mitigation project. For example, for electricity sector projects under the CDM, the baseline emission factor is determined by the power plants built recently (build margin) as well as the power plants operating on the margin due to high operation costs (operating margin). Taking a similar approach, for example, the average damage incurred in the last three decades could be seen as the baseline damage level for adaptation market mechanism projects.

It is important to note that the uncertainty about future climate change does not only make it more difficult to apply market mechanisms to adaptation; it impacts on application of all adaptive activities. Only activities that have a benefit under all possible climate futures ('no-regret options') would make sense under a fully uncertain scenario. Of course, instruments such as insurance, which try to optimize societal reaction in order to minimize secondary economic effects of impacts of extreme weather events, do still make sense under full uncertainty of whether climate change impacts will ever materialize. But these instruments are very costly compared to activities that prevent damages.

Unless we define a clear, transparent procedure for baseline setting and calculation of project benefits, gaming by project developers could result, who would then get adaptation units for projects that actually do not provide such a level of adaptation benefits. If the loss estimates are consistently overestimated, inefficient spending would result. As there are incentives on both sides – the companies that have adaptation commitments and those that develop adaptation projects – the regulator needs to be impartial and uphold 'adaptation integrity'.

4.6 Transaction costs

Transaction costs related to the design, implementation and operation of an adaptation market mechanism can become significant, although their level strongly depends on the design of the scheme.

In principle, transaction costs occur for:

- designing the scheme and defining detailed rules;
- politically agreeing on the scheme;
- allocation of adaptation targets to the participants of the scheme;
- definition of rules and methodologies for offset projects;
- planning, approving and implementing adaptation activities/offset projects;
- MRV of adaptation activities/offset projects and compliance with adaptation targets;
- compliance and penalty schemes;
- in international schemes, reporting to and communication with an international supervisory body.

Experiences from the CDM show that transaction costs can reach a significant level. For a standard large-scale CDM project, costs for completing the approval cycle up to registration at the UNFCCC easily amount to €80,000–100,000 for external costs only (plus in-house costs for organizing the process, data delivery and communication with externals), plus another €75,000–100,000 in the event that no approved baseline and monitoring methodology is available. After registration, project developers need to conduct monitoring, which sometimes requires costly equipment. Costs for verification typically amount to €15,000–30,000. Besides this, the institutional capacity that has been established at UNFCCC level is quite impressive: in 2009 the expenditures for the 'Sustainable Development Mechanism' (SDM) (both CDM and JI) were US$21.2 million (CDM Executive Board 2010: 10). In the same year, 683 CDM projects were registered (IGES 2011) and 19 JI projects approved or determined (IGES 2011). Not considering that some of the UNFCCC CDM and JI budget was spent for longer-term investments (such as development of tools or new methodologies), this totals to about US$30,000 per project. On top of this come costs of national institutions such as Designated National Authorities (DNAs) in host and investor countries, and registry costs. Overall, the transaction costs for a standard large-scale CDM project with a ten-year crediting period and annual verification can be estimated as €300,000–600,000.

Looking at the EU ETS gives an impression about the transaction costs for implementing and operating a large-scale market mechanism. Many studies have analysed the transaction and opportunity costs accruing to firms – e.g. Schleich and Betz (2004) or Frasch (2007). However, an analysis of the total costs for setting up and running the EU ETS has not been conducted. It would go beyond the scope of this chapter to assess these costs quantitatively, but it is clear that costs have been very large. There has not only been two years of intensive lobbying: (1) against the introduction of the EU ETS; and (2) for or against certain allocation principles. There has also been extensive costs for collecting and verifying historical emissions data (as the basis for allocation) and proofs of so-called 'early action', elaboration and implementation of installation-specific monitoring plans, reporting of verified emissions data to national authorities via complex, specially built software schemes (varying between EU member states), and setting up compliance schemes at the national and EU level. The German

Emissions Trading Authority alone had, a peak times, employed more than 100 officers to supervise and administrate the allocation process.

The consequence is that one needs to be aware that the introduction of an adaptation market mechanism can cause substantial transaction costs at the national and international level. However, one can now draw on the experiences of both the existing offset schemes such as the CDM and JI and existing compliance markets such as the EU ETS. If there is a will to implement a simple scheme not trying to make everything perfect at the beginning, it should be possible to avoid prohibitively high transaction costs. Examples for reducing complexity are: using proxies/default factors for estimating future climate risk, and allocating adaptation targets on the basis of available data without (m)any special clauses. Given the different nature of adaptation projects compared to mitigation projects, one might also be a bit more relaxed about the economic additionality of projects.

4.7 Political acceptability

The political acceptability of an adaptation market mechanism will strongly depend on its design. A regionally limited scheme without offsets tendered by government might be acceptable to people because they know that the money will be used 'in the neighbourhood' (which could admittedly be as large as the EU) and will therefore benefit the regional welfare and possibly themselves. On the contrary, an allocation of adaptation targets to industry/private companies on the basis of a polluter-pays principle and the inclusion of offsets could cause severe resistance by industry – at least if they are already subject to GHG reduction policies – and might be perceived as less beneficial for local/regional welfare.

5 Conclusions

Given scarce public funds for adaptation, it is imperative to introduce efficient policy instruments for allocation of these funds instead of distributing them in a first-come, first-served fashion. Market mechanisms – either project-based baseline-and-credit, or target-based allowance systems – theoretically could achieve this policy target. Markets in GHG mitigation have been able to mobilize unexpected, cheap reduction options. Initial assessments of adaptation activities show substantial cost differentials that would lend themselves well to trading. The key challenge for adaptation market mechanisms is the definition of universally accepted trading units. Following Stadelmann *et al.* (2011), we propose the two distinct trading units 'saved wealth' and 'saved health' in order to prevent controversies about the valuation of human life.

One would also need to define, and eventually test in a pilot phase, which adaptation technologies would be appropriate for inclusion in a market mechanism. This is likely for technologies that directly protect against a specific meteorological extreme event such as a storm surge, river flood or drought. Moreover, baseline and monitoring methodologies should be developed for that set of technologies. The regulatory requirements necessary to prevent gaming by adaptation project developers should be assessed. 'Soft measures' like awareness raising and behavioural change projects are unlikely to be appropriate for the adaptation market mechanism. Moreover, adaptive activities that generate pure private goods might have to be excluded, especially if already supported by other policy instruments.

Generating demand for the adaptation units will be crucial, and several options are conceivable. The ideal form of an adaptation market mechanism would be driven by a policy target to achieve a certain amount of SW and SH. This target would be allocated to entities, preferably proportional to their GHG emissions level; this would be consistent with the polluter-pays principle. A second-best option would be a tender-based model where adaptation subsidies are tendered out and allocated to the projects offering trading units at the lowest costs. If emitter lobbies cannot be overcome, this would be a promising first step. The key challenge for an adaptation market mechanism is the specification of baseline and monitoring methodologies. Given uncertainties inherent in climate projections as well as economic development over long timeframes, baselines may be seen as arbitrary. The use of default climate models as well as default discount rates and input values for probability distribution curves for extreme events could reduce this arbitrariness. Given that most adaptation projects do not have recurring revenues other than the sale of trading units, some 'frontloading' of sales is necessary to provide sufficient incentives.

Politicians would have to decide about the regional scope for adaptation project investment. From an efficiency point of view, a global scope would be preferable, and it would also enable mobilization of flows to developing countries as part of the financial pledges for mitigation and adaptation. However, a global scope for eligible adaptation projects may encounter lack of data for baseline estimation. If this is the case, the scope could be limited to a region with good data availability with the possibility to import adaptation units from selected project types. If the objective of the mechanism is to maximize adaptation benefit for a certain region such as the EU, the scope should be limited to that region. Such a limitation would, however, increase the costs per adaptation unit due to the lower supply of projects.

Current financial distribution mechanisms implemented around and under the UNFCCC often lack transparency and broad participation from different stakeholders. Especially the bilateral distribution of scarce financial resources is devoid of external control. Multilateral financing institutions rely on different approaches for measuring and evaluation of adaptation benefits, which prevent comparability and transparency. The adaptation market mechanism would avoid these disadvantages by enabling a broad range of actors to participate in the mechanism. Furthermore, all relevant methodological backgrounds and project documentation will be published. This guarantees a high level of transparency which significantly increases the chances to avoid maladaptation, embezzlement or corruption. If the adaptation market mechanism is implemented at an international level comprising developing countries, MRV should be conducted by experts with considerable experience in development aid and related problems of effectiveness and sustainability.

The introduction of an adaptation market mechanism can cause substantial transaction costs at the national and international level. However, those costs can be reduced with wise design choices. There is now plenty of experience with market mechanisms on which one can draw. A crucial factor will be a willingness to use standard proxies for estimating the benefits of adaptation activities. Of course, these should be fair and not lead to advantages/disadvantages of competing projects, but it should be possible to establish a solid system without having 100 per cent certainty on everything.

Compared to the present ad hoc distribution of adaptation funding, an adaptation market mechanism would be a giant step forward. Before more money is wasted on a first-come, first-served approach, innovative policy-makers should test the different forms of adaptation markets. Learning from the lessons of mitigation, this will lead to an intense discovery process for adaptation technologies that will surprise all those who believe that incentive-based instruments cannot be used for adaptation. Instead of an aberration, adaptation market mechanisms might well be the instrument of the future.

Note

1 Certainly, an alternative is to increase taxes to generate more funds. However, such an approach would be less direct, transparent and reliable.

References

Adger, W.N., Agrawala, S., Mirza, M.Q.M., Conde, C., O'Brien, K., Pulhin, J., Pulwarty, R., Smit, B. and Takahashi, K. (2007) 'Assessment of adaptation practices, options, constraints and capacity', in M. Parry, O. Canziani, J. Palutikof, P. van der Linden and C. Hanson (eds) *Climate Change 2007: Impacts, Adaptation and Vulnerability – Contribution of Working Group II to the Fourth Assessment Report of the Intergovernmental Panel on Climate Change*, Cambridge and New York: Cambridge University Press, pp. 717–43.

Butzengeiger-Geyer, S., Michaelowa, A., Köhler, M. and Stadelmann, M. (2011) 'Policy instruments for climate change adaptation: lessons from mitigation and preconditions for introduction of market mechanisms for adaptation', paper presented at the Colorado Conference on Earth System Governance, 17–19 May, Colorado State University.

CDM Executive Board (2010) CDM Management Plan (CDM-MAP) 2010, EB 54 Report, Annex 37, Bonn.

Economics of Climate Adaptation (2009) 'Shaping climate-resilient development: a framework for decision-making', Economics of Climate Adaptation Working Group. Online. Available: http://ec.europa.eu/development/icenter/repository/ECA_Shaping_Climate_Resilent_Development.pdf.

Eriksen, S. and Kelly, M. (2007) 'Developing credible vulnerability indicators for climate adaptation policy assessment', *Mitigation and Adaptation Strategies for Global Change*, 12: 495–524.

EU Commission (2011) 'The emissions trading scheme (EU ETS)'. Online. Available: http://ec.europa.eu/clima/policies/ets/index_en.htm (accessed 13 June 2011).

Frasch, F. (2007) 'Transaction costs of the EU Emissions Trading Scheme in German companies', *Sustainable Development Law & Policy*, 7 (3): 48–51.

Hallegatte, S. (2009) 'Strategies to adapt to an uncertain climate change', *Global Environmental Change*, 19: 240–7.

HBS/ODI (2011) 'Climate funds update, pledged v deposited v approved v disbursed', Heinrich Böll Foundation, Overseas Development Institute. Online. Available: www.climatefundsupdate.org/graphs-statistics/pledged-deposited-disbursed (accessed 25 May 2011).

IGES (2011) '*IGES CDM Project Database*', Institute for Global Environmental Strategies. Online. Available: www.iges.or.jp/en/cdm/report_cdm.html (accessed 13 June 2011).

Klein, R. (2011) 'Show me the money: ensuring equity, transparency and accountability in adaptation finance', in Transparency International (ed.) *Global Corruption Report: Climate Change*, London: Earthscan, pp. 220–33.

Kuch, P. and Gigli, S. (2007) 'Economic approaches to climate change adaptation', Gesellschaft für Technische Zusammenarbeit (GTZ). Online. Available: www.gtz.de/de/dokumente/en-climate-adaptation-economic-approaches.pdf.

Osberghaus, D. and Reif, C. (2010) 'Total costs and budgetary effects of adaptation to climate change: an assessment for the European Union', *Discussion Paper*, 10(046), Zentrum für Europäische Wirtschaftsforschung GmbH.

Point Carbon (2011) 'Carbon project manager'. Online. Available: www.pointcarbon.com/trading/cpm/data/projects (accessed 13 June 2011).

Rogge, K. and Hoffmann, V. (2009) 'The impact of the EU ETS on the sectoral innovation system for power generation technologies: findings for Germany', *Working Paper Sustainability and Innovation*, S2/2009, München: Fraunhofer Institut.

Schleich, J. and Betz, R. (2004) 'EU emissions trading and transaction costs for small and medium sized companies', *Intereconomics*, 39 (3): 121–3.

Schulze, S., Butzengeiger-Geyer, S., Mechler, R., Michaelowa, A., Dlugolecki, A., Linnerooth-Bayer, J. and Köhler, M. (2011) 'Application of economic instruments for adaptation to climate change: interim report', Perspectives and Hamburgisches WeltWirtschaftsInstitut (HWWI).

Stadelmann, M., Butzengeiger-Geyer, S., Michaelowa, A. and Köhler, M. (2011) 'Universal metrics to compare the effectiveness of climate change adaptation projects', paper presented at the Colorado Conference on Earth System Governance, 17–19 May, Colorado State University.

Storm, T. (1888) *Der Schimmelreiter*, Berlin: Paetel.

UNFCCC (2008) 'Investment and financial flows to address climate change: an update'. Online. Available: http://unfccc.int/resource/docs/2008/tp/07.pdf (accessed 26 July 2011).

WHO (2010a) 'Disability weights, discounting and age weighting of DALYs'. Online. Available: www.who.int/healthinfo/global_burden_disease/daly_disability_weight/en/index.html (accessed 16 October 2010).

WHO (2010b) 'Global burden of disease'. Online. Available: www.who.int/healthinfo/global_burden_disease/en (accessed 16 October 2010).

World Bank (2010) 'Economics of adaptation to climate change study: a synthesis report – final consultation draft, August 2010'. Online. Available: http://siteresources.worldbank.org/EXTCC/Resources/EACC_FinalSynthesisReport0803_2010.pdf.

WRI (2011) 'Summary of developed country fast-start climate finance pledges'. Online. Available: www.wri.org/publication/summary-of-developed-country-fast-start-climate-finance-pledges (accessed 14 June 2011).

Yohe, G., Lasco, R., Ahmad, Q., Arnell, N., Cohen, S., Hope, C., Janetos, A. and Perez, R. (2007) 'Perspectives on climate change and sustainability', in M. Parry, O. Canziani, J. Palutikof, P. van der Linden and C. Hanson (eds) *Climate Change 2007: Impacts, Adaptation and Vulnerability – Contribution of Working Group II to the Fourth Assessment Report of the Intergovernmental Panel on Climate Change*, Cambridge and New York: Cambridge University Press, pp. 811–41.

9 Harnessing the financial markets to leverage low-carbon technology diffusion

Katie Sullivan

1 Introduction

The case for finding a means of making low-carbon development attractive to mainstream private sector investors is well known. The International Energy Agency (IEA 2010) estimates that more than US$1,000 billion per year of additional, non-economic investment in the energy sector alone is needed to achieve greenhouse gas (GHG) reduction targets. A very large proportion of this would have to be in the developing world. China and some other developing countries are focusing on the development of low-carbon technologies, hoping to sell those to the industrialized world and are prepared to create a home market as a platform. This is creating the impression that low-carbon technology will be economic across the world, driven by feed-in tariffs and regulation. Low-carbon investment funds and green bonds are being created on this basis.

However, most developing countries see no reason why they should pay for the incremental costs of making their development programmes low-carbon. There is a potential investment gap of hundreds of billions of dollars per year, for which countries in the South expect assistance from the industrialized world, preferably in the form of new dedicated grant aid for investment and capacity building. There is, however, no realistic prospect of direct aid from developed countries increasing to fill this gap. Therefore, developing countries will eventually accept private sector investment and loans at attractive rates if they do not want to be left aside. This investment needs to come from investors who have low appetites for risk and are able to think in terms of large-scale opportunities. Thus it needs to be leveraged by the support that the industrialized countries can afford. The scale and usability of the leverage instruments needs to be far, far greater than has been achieved by the Clean Development Mechanism (CDM) of the Kyoto Protocol, for all its success as a pioneer in global carbon pricing (see Chapter 1). No coherent plan is on the table for achieving this leverage; in the UNFCCC negotiations there are only vague references to upscaling the carbon market.

NAMA (nationally appropriate mitigation action) is a term being used in the UN climate change negotiations to mean GHG emissions policies or actions, usually large-scale, that will reduce a country's emissions profile below business-as-usual (BAU) (see the discussion in Chapter 7). The expectation is that developed countries will support them, or they will not be done, though in many cases proposals will have considerable ancillary benefits for the country concerned, such as public health or economic development. NAMAs are starting to be collected from developing countries by the UN. At least some of them are capable of being structured as large-scale calls for private sector investment. The definition of the term is still wide, and interpretations that are more consistent with a private investment opportunity are possible.

Below we develop a concept[1] intended to harness private finance for financing of NAMAs. Green NAMA Bonds (GNBs) are a proposed financial instrument aimed at combining conventional returns with guarantees and carbon returns. The type of instrument described attempts to blend a variety of ideas in order to stimulate this investment. It must be acceptable to borrowers, lenders and industrialized-country governments standing behind guarantees. Specific return-enhancement and risk-reduction mechanisms are to generate this attractiveness. Industrialized-world guarantees are enhanced by a link to emissions reduction performance. Both of these basic approaches have been well defined in the literature. Guarantees were comprehensively examined in the UNEP Sustainable Energy Finance Alliance (2010). There is an unavoidable need for some public sector, probably international, oversight body to certify the plausibility of lending propositions and to have the final word on whether emissions reductions have been achieved.

2 Green NAMA Bonds: the basic concept

There have been a number of proposals for more-or-less green bonds, aimed at getting the bond market interested in low-carbon investment. However, two big problems exist. First, the great majority of the investment necessary to make an impact on global carbon emissions reduction must occur in developing countries, many of which currently make the majority of bond investors nervous. Second, while some renewable-energy technologies are becoming mainstream and have the ability to make money without assistance, or with public tariffs and other support policies that are generally considered durable, most low-carbon investment simply do not work economically compared to high-carbon alternatives without a price on carbon to provide a subsidiary income stream.

Although a handful of green bonds have been issued in recent years, the nature and design of these instruments have, to date, failed to stimulate significant levels of private investment in developing countries' emission reduction activities. In addition, the more prevalent varieties of publicly backed guarantees have also been unable to mobilize material participation in abatement projects. If correctly structured and implemented, GNBs could help to unlock significant sums of private resources for emissions reduction activities in developing regions, while also helping to promote bottom-up solutions, realize co-benefits of reduction projects, secure developing country ownership of focused climate action, and introduce general efficiencies into project/programme implementation and evaluation. However, before any of this is realized, the concept requires a significant paradigm shift, particularly in the areas of international development, engagement with global guarantors and incentivization to maximize the interest for developing countries. Harnessing the true power of global financial markets to support climate solutions will, therefore, require new instruments and institutions designed to offer appropriate incentives, guarantees and risk–reward balances that appeal to the mainstream investment community.

3 Key design elements of Green NAMA Bonds

Green NAMA Bonds would limit industrialized country financing to the provision of guarantees provided to international finance institutions (IFIs), used to back green bond issues from host developing countries. These bonds would be invested in emission reduction policies that would eventually generate carbon credits. They could leverage lending by local banks for additional financing into abatement projects within a sector covered by a green bond issue, where a hybrid debt/equity bond structure is utilized. The amount borrowed by a country would be capped to prevent over-leveraging. Confidence and integrity in the system would be established through clearly established environmental standards and monitoring, reporting and verification (MRV) requirements.

Naturally, institutional investors would initially be cautious about the proportion of their return accepted in carbon reduction units; carbon largely remains unfamiliar to these stakeholders, and there is political risk involved. The carbon element could therefore be an additional benefit, a ‘carbon kicker’, diversifying the risk-and-return profile in an interesting way. In the event that emissions reductions fail to materialize on an ongoing basis, the GNB could switch to a loan facility along commercial loan lines; subsequently, if there is a default on resulting interest requirements, the IFI guarantees would enter the equation to lend support.

As familiarity grows and emissions reduction ambition by countries across the world increases, the appetite for a greater share of the return in the form of carbon will increase as well, and major steps will be taken towards the globalization of the idea of a carbon price, without which any effective climate change policy is doomed to failure.

3.1 Governance structure

The host developing country (or possibly a special purpose vehicle) would issue GNBs, with credit support provided by one or more IFIs. In the case of a potential default on repayment, investors would therefore take comfort in the existence of an OECD credit-support agreement. A GNB would not be issued without the formal approval of an international body in a position to certify NAMA objectives and GHG emissions reduction targets. This international entity, which would be entirely distinct from the CDM Executive Board (CDM EB), would be established to administer the proposed mechanism and declare whether the proposed investment is acceptable and appropriately follows a set of approved, agreed-upon standards and methodologies. Other non-national entities could participate in the development of projects within the NAMA. Rather than top-down target designations, municipalities, provinces/states, sector associations or coalitions could provide bottom-up nationally appropriate or sector-targeted proposals that would ultimately be endorsed by the national authority and promoted to the institutional entity for approval. Domestic banks could also potentially act as financial intermediaries, providing financing vehicles with additional support, if they became recipients of GNB financing. There would be no discrimination between public sector or private sector participants, provided they met predetermined eligibility criteria established by the national oversight body.

3.2 Standards and benchmarking

A benchmarking approach would be used, whereby standards are published in terms of the specifications that an abatement activity should attain and demonstrate in the design document in order to obtain approval. Standards should take into account national factors in terms of specific benchmarks and be administered by the international oversight body. Approved standards would remain untouched for a certain period of time (e.g. five years). After this fixed term, standards would be reviewed for future proposed GNB issuances, with a view to ensuring environmental integrity based on clearly defined criteria (e.g. baselines, additionality, etc.). By establishing rules at the outset, and maintaining those rules over a fixed period of time, the benchmarking approach would provide an acceptable level of certainty to investors and sponsors around what does, or does not, qualify.

The GNB would have MRV standards, overseen by the international oversight and administrative body. By establishing predetermined MRV benchmarks, in advance of the bond issuance, the design of this process would avoid the potential problems and delays that have plagued the CDM process since inception (see Chapter 1).

Under the proposed concept, the oversight body would be a necessarily depoliticized, full-time professional body. All decisions would be made in accordance with the principles of rule of law and sound administrative law process. An independent appeals tribunal would also be established, and a streamlined benchmark-based decision-making process would help to avert the problems of 'grey areas'. Written into its constitution, the established oversight body would not be able to make decisions on a retrospective basis, in order to provide a prescriptive certainty to investors and local sponsors regarding what is, or is not, acceptable. Of paramount concern is the need to ensure investor confidence through regulatory stability while, at the same time, ensuring environmental integrity and real reductions remain the basis for which carbon credits are generated.

3.3 Structuring of the bond

GNBs would be issued with a low-coupon rate and stream of carbon credits, the volume of which is tied to the host country's reduction target performance in the given sector or sub-sector. These bonds would be designed to be fully commoditizable and tradeable, and bondholders could be offered special tax advantages in jurisdictions to provide additional support. The bond issue would be fundamentally linked to predetermined baselines, standards and methodologies, as set forth in a Bond Issuance Design Document (BIDD) and approved by the international bond oversight and administrative body. The defined performance target, established by the BIDD and approved by the international body, acts as the cornerstone of this hybrid bond concept, as GNBs would pay holders a low coupon from the outset, plus a pre-agreed-upon volume of carbon credits, contingent on the national emission reductions having been achieved. With a view to providing indicative tenors, determining the term length of a GNB would likely be: (1) a function of the length of a compliance period(s) under future trading regime(s); or (2) determined on a case-by-case basis by the bond-issuing country, based on evolving policy landscapes and private investors' appetites (e.g. eight years or longer).

Funds raised for abatement projects via a GNB issue should be made available to both private sector and public sector entities in the host's relevant sector linked to the NAMA. Firms applying for GNB money would need to provide detailed cashflow and business plan modes in order to ensure that there are real projects with genuine project implementation intent. The projects that obtain the GNB financing will need to pledge that dividends to equity holders will not flow until interest payments have been paid. It is important to stress that all money from GNBs would only be disbursed by the host government against achievement of predetermined milestones, thereby creating an auditable trail. Investors would obtain a diversification element by investing across projects in a given NAMA sector; this approach would also reduce exposure from any one project becoming insolvent. Herein, capital equipment orders by Annex-I export credit banks would supply credit guarantees, which would help to alleviate and manage credit risk while reducing insolvency risk at the project entity level.

If pre-established and approved reduction targets are not met, the bond issuer (host country) would be obligated to pay a determined cash equivalent to holders, thereby increasing the coupon. In this case, the ultimate guarantors for the host country's payment would be one or more IFIs, providing the guarantee on behalf of (or via) a pool of guarantees from a subset of OECD government(s). Should the GNB's underlying sector fail to deliver a pre-agreed minimum level of emissions reductions, carbon credits would not be issued to bondholders; as a result, the interest rate payable by the host country would increase. In effect, the facility would become a commercial loan facility with investors receiving a higher interest payment as they would not receive carbon returns. The predetermined level of interest that would need to be paid in the event of the NAMA failing to deliver the intended objectives of emissions reduction (be that absolute or intensity in the given NAMA) will need to be set in advance of the investment funds flowing into the underlying activities. The default interest should not be set at a level that will trigger insolvency at the time that financial projections are evaluated. The project activities should demonstrate that, should the NAMA fail and a pre-agreed default rate of interest be applied, then the consequence will be diminished or delayed equity returns rather than insolvency. In particular, there is an argument to state that the presence of a strongly rated IFI guarantee should mean that in the event of a NAMA failure the investors have, in effect, invested into something that is giving them returns with a low-risk asset class and therefore, with the presence of returns from the underlying and low coupon, any additional interest component should be pre-agreed and set taking into account the present low-interest environment for low-risk assets. This is consistent with the default rate that should be set. A default rate is nonetheless required to let investors know that at a *de minimis* level they will earn a certain level of return in the event that carbon credits were not generated and also to incentivize the owners of the underlying assets within the NAMA as they will earn enhanced equity returns should the NAMA deliver upon its intended aims.

If reductions failed to materialize for a predefined number of subsequent years, and there was a failure to pay the resulting higher interest payments, the GNB would be declared in a state of default. In such a case of default, the guarantors would stand behind the issued GNB and repay investors accordingly, either on predetermined higher interest rates or principal payments.

The case might emerge where single abatement projects, funded under the umbrella of a GNB, successfully realize emission reductions even though their overarching sector fails to perform in delivering reductions (see also the discussion in Chapter 6). Under this scenario an international reserve might be required; therefore, it is recommended that performing abatement projects be allocated carbon credits (taken from the reserve), but that an equivalent amount of guaranteed carbon collateral units (see Section 3.4) be retained by the IFIs and not returned to the bond-issuing host country, thereby preventing the host from generating additional cheap green financing.

Given the possibility that some countries might prefer a zero coupon (no interest structure), a variation bond structure could also be offered. For instance, investors could have a guarantee on their capital invested with no interest paid, but all carbon credits generated would be returned in some agreed-upon proportion to both investors and project sponsors (e.g. 60/40 split). In addition, a hybrid debt/equity version of the bond could also be considered, whereby equity holders would obtain a greater share of issued carbon credits. These types of variations, and others, are ripe for further exploration and discussion.

3.4 Guaranteed Carbon Collateral Units

The limitation on the volume of GNBs available to borrower governments (developing host countries) could be expressed in guaranteed carbon collateral units (GCCUs). The global total of GCCUs could be linked to the total global GHG emissions reduction ambition by industrialized countries, which is the ultimate source of value for emissions reduction units, so that some balance between supply and demand is maintained. The formula should be based on two key factors: (1) the percentage of the host's measured emissions at a starting date for all countries; and (2) the amount of targeted overall reductions adopted by industrialized countries for 2020. Regarding the latter, although carbon credits generated from GNBs would be allowed for compliance purposes by countries (and eligible installations within those countries) under cap-and-trade schemes, a GCCU allocation must factor in total 2020 adopted reductions targets in order to lower the risk of oversupply while enhancing investor confidence in deploying capital; this factor would likely be revisited post-2020, once more ambitious emissions reduction targets are in place and greater volumes of GNB financing are required. The exact GCCU volume available to individual developing countries would be established by IFIs in the light of the emissions reduction potential and other characteristics of the country. Each time a host wants to issue a GNB, the host must transfer sufficient GCCUs to the IFIs supporting the bond against performance default. GCCUs would eventually be returned to the host by its IFI guarantors in a profiled amount, provided the bond reaches maturity. Failure to deliver emissions reductions not only depletes the facility, but results in an increase in the conventional interest rate of the GNB to compensate for the reduction in total return to investors because the expected carbon return has not materialized.

In the case of default, IFIs would be prompted to satisfy credit guarantees (i.e. repay principal and interest default), with guarantors retaining the GCCUs acquired through transfers that were originally relinquished by the host at the outset of the bond-issuance process. Under a default scenario, the specified amount of GCCUs would either be cancelled or retained by the guarantors.

Non-performing hosts should not be able to get the same volume of new GNBs they would get if they had performed. If a host falls below a certain percentage of GCCUs – against units issued at the starting date – that developing country would be excluded from any further GNB issues; that is, until the country has either: (1) replenished its GCCU inventory by acquiring GCCUs; or (2) reduced its domestic emissions below its initial GCCU inventory level, defined at the starting date. To reiterate, although carbon credits generated from GNBs could be used for compliance purposes, GCCUs could not be used towards meeting emissions reduction obligations by either countries or covered entities.

Even in the event of a breakdown of international negotiations, the GNB mechanism could still be used via bilateral or multilateral negotiations between industrialized countries committed to adopting future emissions caps and developing countries committed to engaging in emissions trading schemes with industrialized countries, while seeking to access cheap financing to enable green domestic growth opportunities. Under this bilateral/multilateral scenario, it is important to note that the amount of GCCUs issued must be aligned with factors taking into account developing country considerations and overall developed country demand.

With a view to reinforcing GCCU value and the integrity of the GNB system, at the end of the compliance trading period, it is checked whether the host issuing country has failed to perform and refused, or failed, to re-purchase its GCCUs. Such a host remains shut-out of the GNB mechanism, i.e. its new GCCU balance is frozen below the threshold required for new GNB issuance. The frozen GCCUs can be auctioned to other countries to allow them to increase their future capacity for additional issuance. If the 'value of carbon credit' points above hold, carbon credits should continue to increase in value and, as a result, GCCUs will be in demand.

3.5 Crediting a NAMA financed by Green NAMA Bonds

Carbon credits generated by the GNB could potentially be eligible for a range of compliance regimes, including the EU Emissions Trading Scheme (EU ETS). Over time, as Annex-I countries and the EU commit to more stringent reduction targets, at least to 2050 and likely beyond, the demand for such credits would likely increase substantially. Naturally, these regimes are not required to provide exact caps over the next 30–40 years, but they can commit towards long-term reductions by 2050 and beyond. Credit compliance eligibility, combined with the pursuit of more stringent targets, would ensure that carbon credits generated from GNBs would not only hold a 'hard value', but over time this inherent value would presumably increase. Further, with respect to credit fungibility, the long-term nature of these units would provide them with banking value channelled into future emissions trading periods. To note, prices for allowances in the EU ETS in the phase 2008–2012 have been bolstered due to their consistent banking value.

To ensure that supply does not exceed demand, the GCCU mechanism would effectively provide for a shortage in the system, ensuring that a positive demand would also exist for GNB-generated carbon credits. Ultimately, any concern over future oversupply in the system would be mitigated through GCCU management and re-adjustments, thereby limiting supply. Moreover, in light of the 'next commitment period' (to 2020), a greater proportion of the exposure would likely be tied to interest, with underlying earnings tied to carbon revenues expected to be ratcheted upwards over the post-2020 time horizon.

Compliance buyers would also be expected to play a significant role in terms of credits generated via GNBs, particularly as their own domestic targets become ratcheted-up over time. Compliance players would have the opportunity to invest directly into the bonds and/or enter off-take arrangements, similar to emission reduction purchase agreements, for carbon credits from local project sponsors. This investor option could also exist with a view to engaging in cooperative/co-development projects with local sponsors under the GNB mechanism. Investors would have the opportunity to participate in forward-selling credits (or through futures) in order to either: lock-out price risk exposure; or leave unhedged, depending on the existing risk profile. For investors seeking stable income streams, comfort would be provided via the weighted proportion of returns over the commitment period to 2020, derived from underlying revenues and/or interest payments.

In the case of GNBs linked to host-country energy or transportation sector reductions, the realization of underlying revenues would provide added revenue sources to investors while, at the same time, creating buffers that translate into credit protection for investors. For instance, power purchase agreements in the power sector – a sector accounting for the lion's share of growing emissions in emerging economies – could provide revenue streams beyond carbon credit revenue. This type of access to multi-type revenue streams supported by publicly backed guarantees would increase returns while driving mechanism buy-in throughout the investment community. In terms of a transport-related example, GNB financing might enable the construction of a host country's light-rail system. Under this scenario, a local municipality could take a percentage of the revenues forecast to be earned from the transportation project and discount by, for example, 50 per cent, while pledging those revenues to investors as: (1) an additional return; or (2) an enhanced collateral against insolvency, with perhaps this provision being a sum in addition to additional investor return (e.g. as a result, 40 per cent of forecast revenue for (1), and 10 per cent for (2)).

Once again, as demand-side countries (e.g. Annex-I countries) tighten their reduction targets (e.g. 80 per cent target by 2050 timeframe), the carbon price would increase, leading to the proportion of returns becoming more weighted to carbon relative to more traditional underlying revenue streams. Looking ahead, it is envisaged as carbon constraints in Annex-I countries tighten and the carbon credit value enhances from the projects financed via GNBs, it will even become possible for developing countries to start repaying the principal with proceeds derived from both carbon credits and underlying revenues.

Before 2020, it may well be that more traditional revenue sources would drive green bonds uptake at a large scale; however, it is expected that this return profile and investor incentive would change post-2020. Simply put, as new commitment periods are embedded into mechanism design and bond terms, investors would shift attention to heightened carbon exposure.

During the initial stages of instrument implementation, as an incentive to invest in GNBs, the option exists for there to be a subsequent additional issuance at a given price in the future, thereby providing existing investors with 'first rights' to a percentage of more heightened exposure to carbon, with the remaining issued to new investors. Here, the concept of a debt–equity hybrid in parallel with a 'rights subscription' element enters into the GNB design discussion.

It may well be that there should in fact be two tranches of returns, with one based upon a combination of just the interest rate coupon and a percentage of the underlying returns delivered in cash form to investors (with pension funds and insurance firms being the main target of this type of return) and a second class of investor that would receive returns encompassing the interest return, a percentage of the underlying and a proportion of the carbon credits (with the likes of utilities, major oil firms and industrials with compliance obligations in the EU and Japan being target investors, along with banks that have carbon finance/trading desks and pension and insurance firms that actually do wish for exposure to the carbon component). The ratio of split between returns would mean that in the absence of GCCUs in the pilot schemes and possibly out to 2020, the GNBs would be able to raise finance and deliver reductions without undue reliance on carbon credits in the run up to 2020, but thereafter carbon returns could increase in importance as targets ratchet-up and the demand side increases.

4 A pilot for Green Nama Bonds

In order to prove and demonstrate the viability of the mechanism, selected developing-world countries should work with industrialized countries to create pilots, perhaps initially via NAMAs for the power and transportation sectors, where it is relatively easy to measure emissions while testing the functionality of the GNB system prior to upscaling and roll-out to other sectors for NAMAs in the near future. To note, GNB pilots can also be devised for energy-efficiency and forestry sectors, then eventually rolled out across other countries once tested.

During the initial pilot schemes, the institutional framework (i.e. the International GNB Board) and GCCUs will not be in existence; however, the split in returns between different classes of investors can be established to take into account supply and demand balance along with an opportunity to examine how the scheme would have functioned with GCCUs present. Variations of the pilot should be tested, including working arrangements with municipalities and regional state governments, on key showcase initiatives that could be linked to GNB financing. There would need to be a pledge by the investor countries to accept the credits generated from the GNB pilots in order to enable the pilot schemes to function.

5 Conclusions

GNBs are a vehicle combining:

- conventional returns from sovereign or quasi-sovereign borrowers;
- the benefit of conditional and limited guarantees from IFIs that make developing country borrowers less risky and more acceptable to conventional investors;
- underlying project returns expressed in conventional financial terms; and
- returns in the form of carbon units that can be used for compliance by companies or governments with obligations under carbon trading systems (UN-linked or national) or can fulfil voluntary emissions reduction commitments.

Figure 9.1 shows the overall institutional structure of the GNB system.

Taking as an example a proposal by a developing country government or parastatal agency to modernize a part of the country's electricity supply industry, a borrowing proposition would be put to an IFI, which would use a new international assessment organization to estimate the emissions reduction impact as well as the conventional economics of the proposition. If satisfactory, the IFI

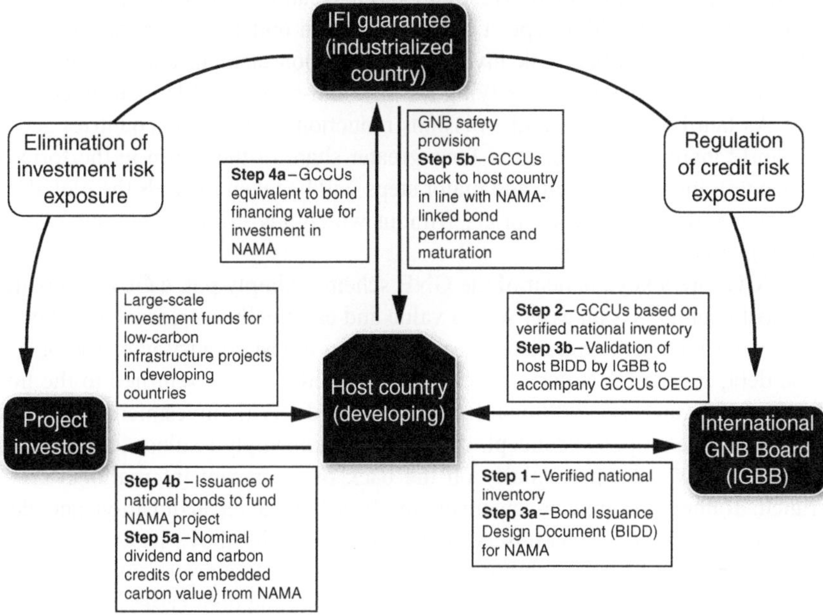

Figure 9.1 Overall institutional structure of the GNB system.

would authorize the use of part of a pre-agreed but limited guarantee and risk-reduction facility to allow the proposition to be constituted as a bond issued by the government or parastatal, attractive to the bond market at a low coupon reflecting the degree of IFI support. An alternative could be to create an implementation agent as a special purpose vehicle, receiving the bond proceeds from the government, managed by board members including the IFI and perhaps private sector representatives, and distributing the bond funding to the entities involved in the programme to use as part or all of their funding for the specific investments necessary to achieve the NAMA.

The return to bondholders would also include (the form, timing and balance depending on the judgement of the issuer) a share in the underlying returns from domestic electricity sales, perhaps de-risked, in the example – and some or all of the carbon return, meaning the emissions reduction units or proceeds from the sale of those units to wherever there is demand. The package could be enhanced by export credit support arranged between the borrower and developed country equipment suppliers for proposals involving major capital investment. Early real-world experiments could be possible, making use of some or all of the features outlined above. While the concept is unfamiliar, tricky balances would need to be struck to deal with existing policy or risk parameters of a host country, an IFI or investors, or elements might need to be left out. But this is the case with the birth of any new class of financial instrument. To begin with, it can be expected that institutional investors would be cautious about the proportion of their return they would accept in carbon reduction units: these are still unfamiliar, and there is political risk involved. The carbon element could be an additional benefit, a 'kicker' diversifying the risk-and-return profile in an interesting way. As familiarity grows and emissions reduction ambition by countries across the world increases, the appetite for a greater share of the return in the form of carbon will increase as well, and major steps will be taken towards the globalization of the idea of a carbon price, without which any effective climate change policy is doomed to failure.

GCCUs are a key element of the GNB scheme. Simply put, a GCCU – issued to a host country – is an asset with a value and essentially represents a 'ticket' to borrow. GCCUs will be transferred to IFIs from a host country in order for it to raise debt. As the GNB performs, relinquished GCCUs are returned to the host country so it can raise additional funds for clean domestic investment opportunities. Under the proposed concept, countries are not simply issuing, servicing and absorbing new debt, particularly on the back of the recent international credit crunch. Rather, the new mechanism involves both asset acquisition and debt management, and based on observations made under the above section exploring 'carbon credits and underlying earnings', there is a clear argument to be made against GNBs' propelling a new sovereign or subprime debt crises. Once again, value, stability and system integrity are realized through: GCCUs limiting how much finance and debt a host could take on via the new system; accrued debt would be backed by assets created in multi-revenue stream sectors (e.g. power, transportation); and IFI guarantees would ultimately back against defaults and political risk.

Industrialized countries committed to taking a leadership role in the support, design and roll-out of this proposed mechanism – which ultimately works to empower developing countries to realize low-carbon futures – would presumably reap significant economic and industrial development rewards. For example, export credit banks of participating developed countries could provide capital equipment to satisfy a host's GNB requirements and/or provide guarantees tied to credit issuance. At the same time, developing host countries would benefit through the acquisition of clean assets in the form of new technology and efficient modern production plants, enhancing domestic economies while enabling green growth and sustainable economic development. This scenario would inevitably lead to enhanced productivity which would eventually improve hosts' debt-to-GDP ratios. In addition, the construction and implementation of the clean infrastructure would lead to employment opportunities in the host country.

In conclusion, the GNB instrument is a new step for international climate policy and for the carbon market as it is currently known. But without it, or something like it, there is no chance of incentivizing substantial private investment at the necessary scale into technologies and activities that are simply uneconomic without a price on carbon and a reason to invest. The political consequences, as well as the climate change consequences, of failure to meet the expectations of the developing world in this uniquely difficult issue of climate change could be immense. Huge sums of money need to be raised; the private sector must be involved as never before; and there are tight constraints on expenditure, borrowing or disguised borrowing by governments. If there is an alternative to a GNB approach, it is very hard to see what it is.

Note

1 This concept has been described in some grey literature distributed at UNFCCC negotiations (IETA 2011), but is published here formally for the first time.

References

IEA (2010) *World Energy Outlook*, Paris: OECD, IEA.

IETA (2011) 'IETA response to the AWGLCA call for input regarding new market-based mechanisms', United Nations Framework Convention on Climate Change. Online. Available: http://unfccc.int/resource/docs/2011/smsn/ngo/236.pdf (accessed 29 July 2011).

UNEP Sustainable Energy Finance Alliance (2010) 'Publicly backed guarantees as policy instruments to promote clean energy'. Online. Available: www.unep.fr/energy/finance/pdf/guarantees_web.pdf (accessed 29 July 2011).

10 Climate finance and backstop technologies

Sonja Butzengeiger and Axel Michaelowa

1 Introduction

1.1 Background

In climate policy to date it has always been assumed that introducing low-emissions technology comes at a cost compared to fossil fuel technologies. However, what if a technology breakthrough enables large-scale utilization of low-cost power generation that comes with zero emissions of greenhouse gases (GHGs)?

One scenario for reaching this is the renewable-energy pathway. Imagine that the decreasing cost of renewable energy, particularly wind and solar but also tidal and ocean, and the increasing cost of fossil fuels leads to a situation in the not-too-distant future where an abundant amount of zero-carbon electricity is available at a cost that is lower than that of fossil fuel-generated electricity. This has been predicted by renewable-energy technology providers for the near-to-medium future (e.g. the aggressive and very optimistic forecast by Solarcentury (2009); Breyer *et al.* (2010) offer a more realistic timetable). Once capital costs have come down sufficiently, the negligible operating costs of most forms of renewable energy would lead to very low costs for electricity. New technical concepts such as wave and tidal energy could further improve public acceptability of renewable power plants, which has been a challenge in densely populated areas in highly developed countries.

Another scenario is a breakthrough in a technology that so far has not yet been used for commercial electricity generation. A candidate might be nuclear fusion – a process that is quite distinct from the 'conventional' nuclear fission reactors that are operated globally. Nuclear fusion is the process in which atomic nuclei fuse together to form a heavier nucleus. This leads to a significant energy release arising from the binding energy that formerly held the nuclei together. Fusion naturally occurs in stars and man has created artificial fusion in hydrogen bombs, but controlled fusion for electricity generation using deuterium from sea water so far has not been achieved due to the extremely high temperatures and pressures obviously required. For decades and with high financial resources, research groups worldwide have – so far in vain – struggled to overcome these obstacles. So the initial enthusiasm regarding an inexhaustible energy source has faded over the years. The International Thermonuclear Experimental Reactor (ITER) in France, which will be financed with a multi-billion euro budget, is the next step on the stony road towards a workable fusion reactor. However, there might be a much less difficult alternative. As early as 1956, a team of researchers at Berkeley University conducted experiments on a muon-catalysed fusion at low temperatures and observed the release of some energy (Alvarez *et al.* 1957). The main practical challenge encountered by subsequent research was that the muons required for catalysing the process decay very quickly and, in their lifetime, do not initiate a sufficient amount of fusion processes that would be required to achieve net energy gains. Despite numerous efforts over the past decades, a breakthrough has not yet been achieved. In September 2009, Japanese researchers showed optimism that in the not-too-distant future their work can lead to a commercial utilization of muon-catalysed fusion (Matsuzaki 2009). While, of course, it is uncertain when – if ever – a breakthrough can be achieved, it is obvious that if it happens, such a technology has the potential for a quick and large-scale utilization worldwide.

Hence, let us assume in the following that such a technology breakthrough becomes reality. What would be the consequences?

Actually, for generations, humanity has been dreaming of an abundant, cheap source of energy. Fifty years ago the technology assumed to achieve this utopia was nuclear fission (Brandt 1956). Anderson (2008) vividly describes the impacts of such a source of electricity on business and human behaviour:

> What if electricity had in fact become virtually free? The answer is that everything electricity touched – which is to say just about everything – would have been transformed. Rather than balance electricity against other energy sources, we'd use electricity for as many things as we could – we'd waste it, in fact, because it would be too cheap to worry about. All buildings would be electrically heated, never mind the thermal conversion rate. We'd all be driving electric cars (free electricity would be incentive enough to develop the efficient battery technology to store it). Massive desalination plants would turn seawater into all the freshwater anyone could want, irrigating vast inland swaths and turning deserts into fertile acres, many of them making biofuels as a cheaper store of energy than batteries. Relative to free electrons, fossil fuels would be seen as ludicrously expensive and dirty, and so carbon emissions would plummet. The phrase 'global warming' would have never entered the language.

It is obvious that such a technology characterized by low generation costs would bring tremendous economic, social and environmental benefits: electricity consumers and economies can benefit from lower electricity prices, the quality of life of people that today are suffering from restricted access to electricity or non-affordable electricity prices could massively improve; and eventually the climate change challenge could be mastered. At the same time, a sudden availability of such a technology would likely result in sizeable political and economic challenges. We discuss the implications of the availability of such a technology for today's climate policies and finance, and discuss how a 'power transformation levy' can be used as a cornerstone of an new era of climate and energy finance.

1.2 Past economic analysis of backstop technologies

Since the first oil shock of the early 1970s, economists have discussed the effects of a 'backstop technology', i.e. a technology providing a complete replacement of petroleum fuels at a constant level of marginal costs. The term was coined by Nordhaus, who defines it as 'a set of processes that (1) is capable of meeting the demand requirements and (2) has a virtually infinite resource base' (Nordhaus 1973: 547–8). Further research includes Heal (1976), Owen and Powell (1985) and Levy (2000). Since the advent of integrated assessment models for climate policy, backstop technologies have become fashionable in the climate community as well, especially when modelling a technology that provides an unlimited amount of zero-carbon energy, generally at a high level of marginal abatement cost (Bosetti and Tavoni 2009). Popp (2006) argues that a backstop technology improves welfare even without climate change risks and response policy. In a game-theoretic setting, Barrett (2010) analyses the impact of a backstop technology on international climate policy and finds that it increases cooperation. But all these analyses assume that the backstop has higher cost than the fossil fuel technologies.

In contrast to this, we assume that the technology will have lower costs – and this has not been analysed to any extent. We thus term it 'super transformational technology' (STT) to differentiate it from the 'classical', high-cost backstop. We also assume that the super transformational technology is characterized by short construction periods, and that manufacturers' capacities can be increased quickly so that the STT can be diffused rapidly. We also assume that it can be built close to the electricity consumers (as conventional thermal power plants) and therefore would not require significant grid infrastructure. On the contrary, it could even be established in very remote areas that today do not have grid access – as is the case for many regions in least developed countries (LDCs).

2 Benefits of a super transformational technology with regards to long-term climate policy

The STT's ability to provide low-cost, carbon-free electricity can have significant impacts on long-term climate policy if diffused broadly and quickly. First, the reference projection of GHG emissions (baseline emissions) would be lowered significantly, especially in the power sector, but also in other sectors where electricity consumption is large (e.g. the building and industry sectors). Second, the introduction of the STT would lead to a radical change in the set of mitigation measures. As the STT supplies carbon-free electricity at a low cost, other more expensive mitigation measures related to the production/consumption of electricity could be partially replaced or even be made obsolete. Consequently, the STT can lead to a reduction of overall mitigation costs.

This section aims to analyse the impact of the STT on mitigation and economic benefits. The result of the analysis is compared mainly with the *4th Assessment Report of the Intergovernmental Panel on Climate Change (IPCC AR4*, here cited as IPCC 2007). Where appropriate, other analyses published since the *IPCC AR4* are also considered. The analysis focuses on the time period through 2030 due to data constraints for the period beyond that date, and because this period matters most for the climate policy issues at hand.

2.1 Mitigation benefits of the STT

2.1.1 Greenhouse gas emission trends

The *IPCC AR4* emission scenarios project an increase of global GHG emissions from 40 billion tCO_2-e/yr in 2000 to 50–75 billion tCO_2-e/yr in 2030 (IPCC 2007). The projection is based on the IPCC Special Report on Emissions Scenarios (SRES), which describes a number of scenarios on how the future economy is structured.[1]

The lower end of the projected GHG emission range (50 billion tCO_2-e/yr) is based on the B2 scenario. The higher end of the range (75 billion tCO_2-e/yr) is based on the A1F1 scenario, which describes a future world of very rapid economic growth with emphasis on fossil-intensive technologies. The *IPCC AR4* projection of the baseline emissions and the mitigation potential beyond the baseline emission level are primarily based on the SRES B2 scenario and the IEA's *World Energy Outlook 2004* (IEA 2004). To be consistent with the *IPCC AR4* baseline emissions, we use the B2 scenario and IEA (2004) as the basis for our analysis, even if there are more recent IEA estimates available.

Table 10.1 shows the actual emissions in 2004 and the baseline emissions in 2030 by sector used in the *IPCC AR4*. First of all, it is important to explain the two different methods for allocating emissions from energy use: (1) point-of-emission allocation; and (2) end-of-use allocation. The first method allocates emissions to the sector where the emission takes place. For example, electricity-related emissions are allocated to the power sector. The second method allocates the emissions to the sectors that use the energy. Here, electricity emissions are allocated to the end-use sectors, mainly buildings and industry.

Based on the data available in the *IPCC AR4*, it is clear that the building and industry sectors are the major consumers of electricity. Providing carbon-free electricity to these sectors would have a positive spill-over effect of reducing the emissions from electricity consumption. There could potentially be positive spill-over effects in other sectors where electricity consumption contributes to a relevant share in the sectoral emissions. For example, further massive emission reductions could be achieved through the use of electric vehicles in the transport

Table 10.1 Overview of the global emissions in 2004 and the baseline emissions for all GHGs adopted for 2030 in the *IPCC AR4* (billion tCO_2-e/yr)

	Global emissions in 2004 (end use)		*Global emissions in 2004 (point of emissions)*		*Global emissions in 2030 (end use)*		*Global emissions in 2030 (point of emissions)*	
	Actual	*%*	*Actual*	*%*	*Actual*	*%*	*Actual*	*%*
Energy supply	–	–	12.7	27.4	–	–	15.8	27.7
Transport	6.4	15.5	6.4	13.8	10.6	19.0	10.6	18.6
Buildings	9.2	22.2	3.9	8.4	14.3	25.7	5.9	10.4
Industry	12.0	29.0	9.5	20.5	14.6	26.2	8.5	14.9
Agriculture	6.6	15.9	6.6	14.3	8.3	14.9	8.3	14.6
LULUCF/Forestry	5.8	14.0	5.8	12.5	5.8	10.4	5.8	10.2
Waste	1.4	3.4	1.4	3.0	2.1	3.8	2.1	3.7
Total	*41.4*	*100.0*	*46.3*	*100.0*	*55.7*	*100.0*	*57.0*	*100.0*

Source: Barker *et al.* (2007).

Note

There is a difference between the sums when allocating the emissions in different ways, which leads to a lower level for the end-use calculation. This is due to the fact that the electricity emissions from the agriculture and transport sectors are excluded due to lack of data. The total emissions in 2030 are only indicative as individual sectoral emissions are derived from studies that differ in terms of coverage and comparability.

sector, which would displace fossil fuel use. In other sectors, emissions from electricity consumption are considered a relatively minor emission source. Hence, we primarily focus on the emission reductions in the energy-supply (power), building and industry sectors, which represents about 55 per cent of the global emissions. This leads to a conservative estimate of the mitigation benefits of the STT.

In the following analysis, we adopt the point-of-emissions method because it makes more intuitive sense in analysing the impact of the STT, which mainly concerns the power sector.

2.1.2 Marginal abatement costs of the STT

We assume that the levelized electricity costs (LEC) of the STT amount to 2¢/kWh.[2] Based on this, the marginal abatement costs (MACs) of the STT are calculated as in Table 10.2. For simplification, the calculation assumes displacement of grid electricity in four regional categories: (1) OECD countries; (2) Annex-I economies in transition (EIT) countries; (3) non-OECD countries; and (4) global. The grid emission factors in these regions are derived from IEA (2008). The MACs are negative – consistent with the fact that the STT is the cheapest electricity generation option available.

2.1.3 Impact on the reference scenario

In its reference scenario, IEA (2004) projects that the world electricity demand will double between 2002 and 2030, and that most of the growth will be in developing countries. Coal- and gas-based power generation would take the lion's share in the growth of the world's electricity generation. The power sector could account for almost 45 per cent of the global energy-related CO_2 emissions by 2030. In order to quantify the impact of the STT implementation on the reference emissions in the power sector, the following steps are taken. First, the amount of CO_2 emissions from 2004 to 2030 are estimated. Second, a diffusion rate of the STT is assumed for the period through 2030 in order to calculate the amount of fossil fuel-based electricity that would be replaced by the STT, and consequently, the avoided emissions in the reference scenario. The diffusion rate

Table 10.2 Marginal abatement cost of the STT, including electricity sales revenues (US$/t$CO_2$)

	STT (US$/t CO_2)
OECD	–0.27
EIT	–0.04
Non-OECD/EIT	–0.13
Global	–0.20

Source: own calculation.

assumed for the calculations is a global average rate that results from the assumed regional diffusion rates as shown in Table 10.3 under consideration of the projected amount of electricity generated in each region.

Table 10.4 summarizes the average diffusion rates in the years 2015, 2020, 2025 and 2030, the projected global CO_2 emissions as per the *IPCC AR4* scenario, the projected global CO_2 emissions if the STT is rolled out only in the power sector ('STT scenario I') and the resulting gross CO_2 emission reductions. We assume that the STT is equally applied to replace fossil and non-fossil power generation.

2.1.4 Impact on the additional mitigation potential

The STT could also result in a change in the estimated mitigation potential beyond the reference scenario estimated in the *IPCC AR4*. This is because the STT offers a negative-cost mitigation opportunity, and hence will result in displacement of more expensive mitigation options. It is reasonable to assume that all power-related mitigation options will be displaced by the STT (i.e. nuclear, hydro, wind, bio-energy, geothermal, solar photovoltaic (PV) and concentrated solar power (CSP)) in the long term.[3] Given the low-cost characteristics of the STT, we also assume that carbon capture and storage (CCS) technologies will be completely displaced. Fuel switch and plant efficiency may still be implemented in conventional power plants in regions where the STT is yet to penetrate. Thus, we assume their mitigation potential will decrease in proportion to the diffusion rate of the STT.

Table 10.3 Assumed diffusion of the STT (% of electricity generation)

Country group	*2020*	*2025*	*2030*	*2050*
Industrialized + China + India	10	25	50	100
Other Asia + Latin America	10	20	50	100
OPEC	0	10	50	100
Africa	0	0	25	100

Source: own calculation.

Table 10.4 Assumed global diffusion rates of the STT in the power sector and impact on global gross CO_2 emissions

Year	*Diffusion rate of the STT (%)*	*IPCC AR4 reference scenario (Gt CO_2)*	*STT scenario I (Gt CO_2)*	*Gross emission reductions (Gt CO_2)*
2015	2	14.0	13.7	0.3
2020	9	14.6	13.2	1.3
2025	23	15.2	11.7	3.5
2030	49	15.8	8.0	7.7

Sources: own calculation, IPCC (2007).

Electricity savings in the building and industry sector[4] will also be affected by the STT. We assume that electricity-savings measures with zero or negative cost will be implemented anyway, but the ones with positive costs will be displaced by the STT. This is because the provision of carbon-free electricity would make it unnecessary to save electricity for a mitigation purpose and the low-cost electricity could also disincentivize electricity savings unless taxed (see the discussion on electricity taxation below).

However, the STT will make up only a fraction of the displaced mitigation potential. For instance, the global diffusion rate of the STT in 2030 is assumed as 49 per cent, leaving only the remaining 51 per cent as the opportunity for further mitigation. Therefore, we assume that in the year 2030 only 51 per cent of the total mitigation potential through substitution of power technologies (excluding electricity savings in the building and industry sectors) will be compensated by the STT, as the STT has already replaced 49 per cent of the conventional electricity generation.

In addition to the mitigation potential related to electricity production/consumption analysed above, direct fuel savings in the building and industry sectors will also be affected by the STT. We assume that all direct heating by fossil fuel (oil, gas or coal) will be substituted by electric heating.[5] This would obviously require a policy drive – for example, (partial) exemption from electricity taxes.

For the direct fuel use for heating in the building sector, we assume that 50 per cent of fuel used is substituted by carbon-free electricity by 2030. This would add further emission reductions of 3.0 billion tCO_2/yr in 2030.

In the industry sector, electricity could substitute fossil fuels used for generation of steam and heat. IEA (2007) roughly estimates that 20 per cent of total energy demand in industry is for process energy at temperatures above 400°C, 15 per cent for steam at 100–400°C and 15 per cent for low-temperature heat. Nineteen per cent is used in the form of electricity for motors and lighting. Moreover, 18 per cent of energy-related industrial emissions are due to processes that cannot be reduced by applying electricity, leaving 12 per cent for miscellaneous energy use. One can thus assume that close to 60 per cent of fossil fuel input can be replaced by electricity, which would account for 30 per cent of total industrial emissions (including non-fossil fuel-related emissions). Assuming that in 2030, 50 per cent of this potential would be tapped (i.e. 50 per cent of 30 per cent of 8.5 billion tCO_2 industrial emissions), fuel substitution for heat production would reduce 1.3 billion tCO_2/yr.

In the transport sector, a complete transition to electric vehicles fuelled by zero-carbon electricity could reduce emissions from the transport sector by 10.3 billion tCO_2/yr in 2030. However, it is unlikely that all transport systems worldwide can be transformed that quickly. We assume that a modification of 50 per cent of the transport sector would be more realistic. This would reduce global emissions by 5.2 billion tCO_2/yr in 2030.

2.2 Scenario analysis

To summarize the mitigation benefits of the STT, we categorize the STT scenario into three scenarios:

- STT Scenario I considers power technology substitution and electricity savings in the building and industry sectors;
- STT Scenario II further takes into account a partial (50 per cent) switch from direct fuel to electricity use in the building and industry sectors;
- STT Scenario III further assumes 50 per cent of all transportation vehicles will be fully run by electricity by 2030 in order to show the full potential of the mitigation benefits.

2.2.1 STT Scenario I: power substitution and electricity savings

This scenario concerns only the power sector. The change in the baseline emissions and the additional mitigation potential would in total lead to significant emission reductions (Figure 10.1). In the STT scenario, emissions from the power sector would be reduced to 8 billion tCO_2/yr in 2030. As compared to the

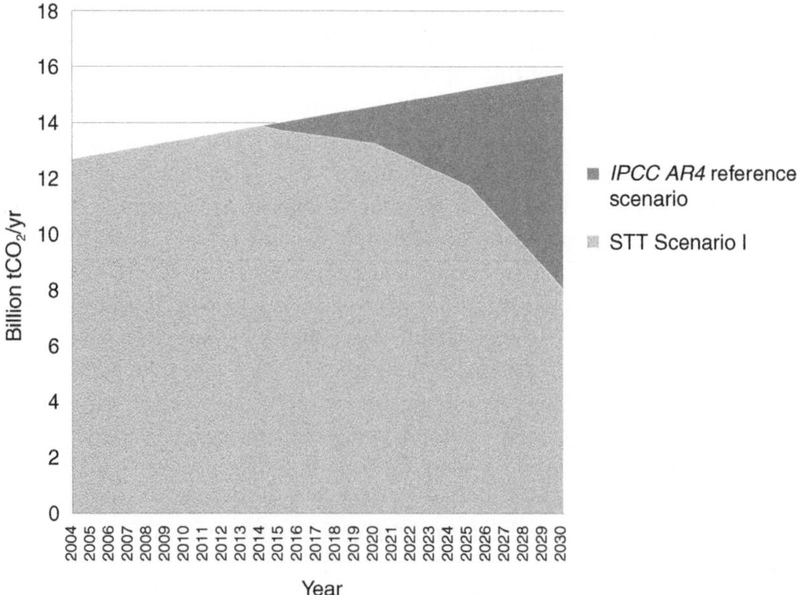

Figure 10.1 Annual emissions from the power sector from 2010 to 2030 under different scenarios (billion tCO_2/yr) (source: own calculation for the STT scenario I; adapted from IPCC (2007) for the *IPCC AR4* reference/mitigation scenario).

Note
Point-of-emissions allocation is applied.

reference projection of 15.8 billion tCO_2/yr, it represents a reduction of 49 per cent (see above).[6]

Consequently, the global emissions in 2030 are estimated at 49.2 billion tCO_2/yr, which represents emission reductions of 13.6 per cent from the *IPCC AR4* reference scenario.

2.2.2 STT Scenario II: additionally including switch in heat production in building and industry

This scenario achieves further emission reductions through the reduction of 50 per cent of the emissions related to direct fuel combustion in the building sector as well as the discussed fuel substitution for heat production in the industry sector. Thus, the global emissions in 2030 will be 44.6 billion tCO_2/yr, representing emission reductions of 22 per cent from the *IPCC AR4* reference scenario.

2.2.3 STT Scenario III: additionally including conversion of transportation to electric vehicles

In addition to the STT Scenario II, this scenario adds emission reductions by the partial use of carbon-free electricity in the transport sector (50 per cent). The

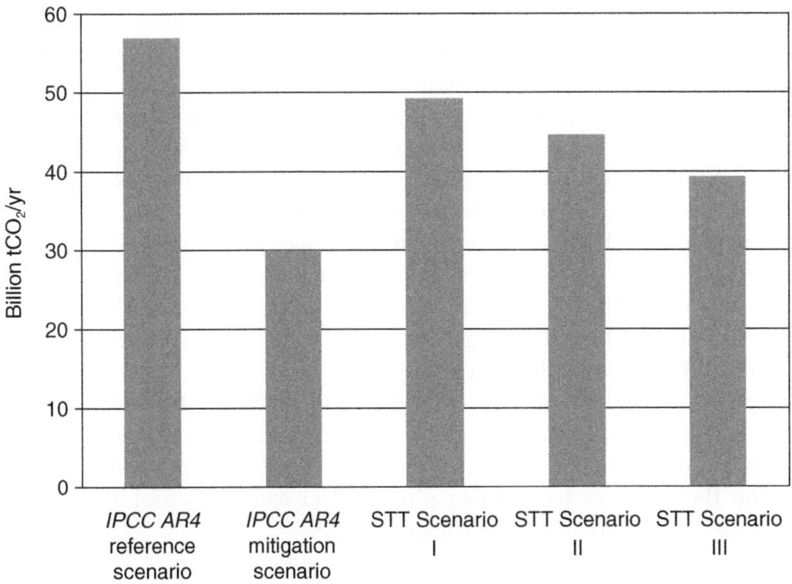

Figure 10.2 Comparison of annual global emission levels in 2030 under different scenarios (billion tCO_2/yr), regular scenario.

global emissions in 2030 are to be reduced down to 39.3 billion tCO_2/yr, i.e. emission reductions of 31 per cent from the *IPCC AR4* reference scenario.

Figure 10.2 summarizes the emission levels in 2030 in the STT scenarios as well as the reference and mitigation scenarios of the *IPCC AR4*. In 2030, the STT scenarios would reach the emissions level of 39–49 billion tCO_2/yr at the assumed degree of penetration of the STT and the utilization of other mitigation options, while the *IPCC AR4* mitigation scenario achieves 30 billion tCO_2/yr if all measures with costs of less than US\$100/tCO_2 are implemented (calculated using data from Barker *et al.* 2007).

2.2.4 Comparison with post-SRES analyses

As explained above, the *IPCC AR4*'s reference scenario mainly builds on the IPCC SRES published in 2000. Since the publication of SRES in 2000, a number of analyses have been published on the projection of the long-term GHG emission pathways. By the time the *IPCC AR4* was published in 2007, the emission levels of reference scenarios published since SRES were found to be comparable in range to those presented in SRES (Barker *et al.* 2007). Since 2007, however, there have been several studies projecting more pessimistic reference emissions levels than the SRES scenarios, largely due to the increasing economic growth of developing countries.

Garnaut *et al.* (2008) provide a synthesis of the post-SRES analyses and finds their own 'Platinum Age' scenario projection reaching the highest emission level in 2030, among other analyses. This is primarily due to the reflection of rapid economic development of developing countries in more recent years (e.g. China). The Platinum Age scenario projects an annual average growth in GHG emissions of 2.5 per cent over the period 2005–2030, slightly above the upper-end of existing scenario growth rates. By 2030, the annual emissions reach 83 billion tCO_2/yr, almost double their current level, 11 per cent higher than the 'extreme' A1F1 scenario of IPCC SRES, and a level of emissions reached only in 2050 in the reference scenario used by Stern (2006).

The emission levels achieved under the STT scenarios discussed above are clearly among the lowest of the existing major studies. Hence, the STT can play a central role in tackling the climate change challenge. Obviously, the quantitative impacts of the STT will strongly depend on the assumptions regarding the pace of the diffusion and utilization of the STT.

The global distribution rates assumed above might appear technically realistic, but the analysis of impacts on global GHG emissions has shown that these timelines are not sufficient to avoid dangerous climate change *alone* with the STT. The IPCC argues for limiting global GHG emissions to 11–30 billion tCO_2-e in 2030 to avoid dangerous climate change.

If, however, one assumes a quicker diffusion and utilization of the STT, this picture can change. For example, if one assumes a global utilization rate of 80 per cent for power generation and heating; and 60 per cent of transport in 2030, we estimate global GHG emissions at exactly 30 billion tCO_2-e (following the

IPCC reference scenario). This is shown in Figure 10.3. Obviously, the emissions in a single year are not decisive, but rather the cumulative emissions over time. However, looking at the year 2030 gives an impression of the order of magnitude that is required.

To sum up, if an STT is to become a cornerstone of international climate policies – which could become a blessing from God given the actual political situation in the UNFCCC context – then policy-makers need to find a way for a quick global roll-out and to make sure that the STT is utilized beyond the power sector. At the same time, national climate policies need to be continued, although in an adapted manner, to create a buffer against uncertainties related to the reaction of the global climate system to anthropogenic forcing.

3 Financial benefits of the STT linked to climate change mitigation

A major long-term benefit of a STT is its contribution to significantly reduce climate change and its negative economic and social impacts. As discussed above, a STT can play a central role in decarbonizing global electricity generation. As the share of power generation in global GHG emissions is around one-quarter and electricity could replace direct fossil fuel use responsible for another

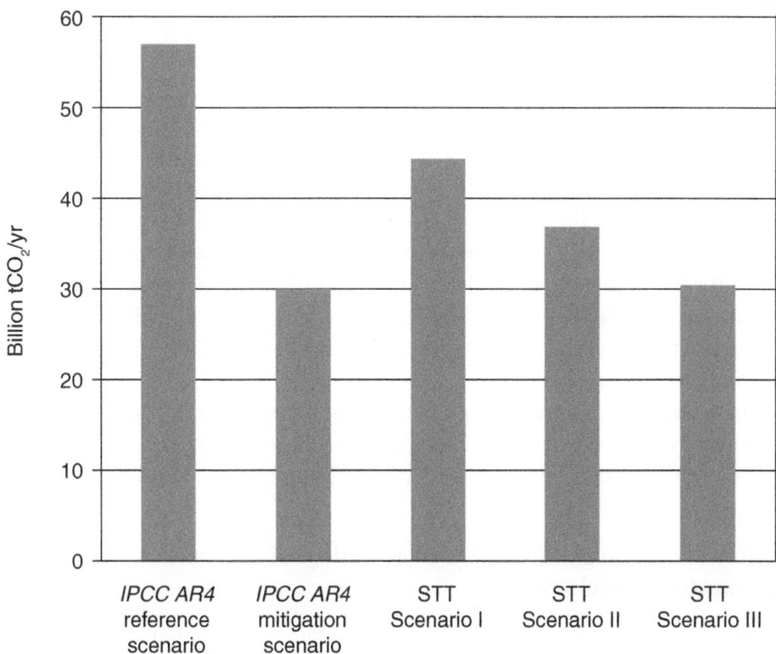

Figure 10.3 Comparison of annual global emissions level in 2030 under different scenarios (billion tCO_2/yr), aggressive scenario.

quarter of emissions, the STT can become a cornerstone in preventing or at least minimizing dangerous climate change.

The resulting question is: what are the economic benefits of avoided climate change? Over the last two decades, a multitude of studies has tried to assess the economic damage potential due to climate change (see an overview in Parry 2007). The most comprehensive analysis was done by Stern (2006) in the so-called 'Stern Review'. Their report analyses the economic impacts of climate change worldwide, and compares costs of climate policies with those threatened through climate change. The Stern Review estimates the total cost of climate change in the reference scenario to be an average reduction in global GDP per capita from 5 per cent to 20 per cent from the late twenty-first century onwards (Stern 2006). It also suggests that the appropriate estimate of damages caused by climate change may well lie in the upper part of the range of 5–20 per cent. On the other hand, much of the loss could be avoided through a strong mitigation policy (Stern 2006). Given that the negative effects of climate change will be felt with a certain time-lag, the total value of avoided economic loss will increase over time.

The IMF (2010) estimates the GDP for major economies[7] for the years 2020, 2025, 2030 and 2050. Total estimated GDP in 2050 is approximately US$240 trillion. Assuming the GDP loss is 1.5 per cent in 2050, costs of climate change could amount to US$3–4 trillion per year by 2050, just for these countries. The order of magnitude increases significantly for future time periods.

According to the *IPCC AR4*, the global GHG emissions in 2050 need to be reduced by –85 per cent to –50 per cent from the 2000 level in order to limit the global mean temperature increase above the pre-industrial level to 2.0–2.4°C (IPCC 2007). The 2°C threshold is currently the common reference for avoiding dangerous climate change. The required emission level would range from 11 to 30 billion tCO_2/yr in 2030 and from 6 to 21 billion tCO_2/yr in 2050.

In 2030, the STT scenario would reach the emissions level of 30–43 billion tCO_2/yr, depending on the degree of penetration of the STT assumed. As discussed above, the pace of global utilization in and beyond the power sector is the key factor for the climate benefit of an STT. Overall, the STT has a good potential to bring global GHG emissions down to what is required in 2030 for achieving the global mean temperature stabilization at 2.0–2.4°C, if it gets sufficient political support and dedication.

To sum up, although there is no guarantee that the STT can indeed avoid dangerous climate change, it can significantly lower its risk and hence the risk that the costs of climate change as discussed above do not become reality.

4 Economic challenges from the availability of a super transformational technology

If the cost parity between fossil fuel electricity and transformational technologies is broken, one can expect a revolution of energy markets. Since the super transformational technology could be spread rapidly, power markets would likely undergo a rapid transition.

A disorderly transition might mobilize negative forces. As economic history shows (Mokyr 1990, 2005), the replacement of an incumbent technology by a vastly better alternative can lead to disruption. This was the case when machine-based production replaced production by hand during the Industrial Revolution, or when wood energy was replaced by coal. The – often politically very powerful – lobbies of the incumbent technology will try to prevent introduction of the new technology (Mokyr 1998, 2000; Cooper and Smith 1992) unless they can directly profit from it.

Since a central feature of our STT is its low electricity generation costs, an uneven distribution of access to it can impact industrial production in two ways. First, electricity-consuming industry may benefit from a reduction of electricity prices if the lower generation costs are being passed to the consumer – which depends on the structure and price discovery mechanisms of the national power system. Second, heat-consuming industry may also benefit from lower energy costs if they shift energy input, e.g. from fuel oil to electricity. Required electricity can be sourced from the grid.

A reduction of industrial production costs will yield high benefits for the national economy. Particularly industries with high electricity and heat costs will benefit, and in the medium term entire new very energy-intensive industries are likely to emerge.

At the same time, an uncoordinated distribution of the transformational technology could lead to undesired impacts on industrial competitiveness, in particular in those sectors facing high international competition: in the case that an industrial sector in country A already benefits from lower electricity/heat costs while the same sector in country B does not, the latter will suffer economic damage. The damage occurs because country A would increase exports, and would displace products of industry from country B. Aligned to this would be the typical negative effects of a sudden economic breakdown of a sector, such as employment losses, reduction of tax revenues for the government, etc.

The effect will be the stronger,

- the higher the share of the sector's energy costs in total production cost;
- the higher the exposure of the sector to international competition and export/import options; and
- the higher the time gap of access to the STT – or better, to reduced power prices – between the countries.

Another issue is a reduced demand for fossil fuels that will result from a broad utilization of the STT. Fossil fuel exporting countries may suffer from reduced revenues from fuel exports. OPEC countries and countries exporting coal, such as Indonesia, Vietnam and Australia, would be affected most strongly (IEA 2009).

In the event that an STT becomes available, these issues require attention of policy-makers to make sure the transition to the new energy structure runs smoothly. In the following section, we therefore propose a power transformation levy (PTL) as a policy instrument avoiding potential negative side effects of the STT.

5 Cornerstone of transition policy: a power transformation levy to maximize global benefits of the STT

The discussion above has shown that despite its tremendous economic, social and environmental benefits, an STT can bring short- and mid-term challenges. A coordinated management of access to an STT would be a key element of a government-led transition policy to ensure that benefits are harnessed while negative effects are minimized. The overall scope and type of the policy would depend on the characteristics of the STT and its cost differential to incumbent fossil fuel energy technologies. Its overall objectives should be:

1 avoidance/minimization of negative impacts due to the introduction of the STT regarding industrial competitiveness and economies that depend highly on fossil fuel exports;
2 rapid global distribution of the STT to harness its economic, social and environmental benefits;
3 revenue creation that can be used for compensation of unavoidable negative effects of introducing the STT;
4 revenue creation for other measures beneficial to regional and/or global sustainable development and welfare.

To achieve these goals, the policy would have to include mechanisms to ensure a coordinated distribution of the technology, an appropriate and equitable flow of finance from all countries using the STT and an adequate governance structure to manage the funds.

5.1 Coordination of technology distribution

In this section we will analyse what impacts different distribution strategies of an STT can have. In a first step, we look at the options the technology developer has for distributing it in the national/global market, and then discuss how the potential impacts described above would develop under these options.

The STT could be developed through a publicly funded R&D project. In this case, the owners of the technology are either the researchers and/or the public agency/agencies that have been funding the research. One can assume that a contract will regulate ownership rights and intellectual property rights (IPRs). If a significant part of the money is from public resources, one can also expect that the country (or countries) that provided funds will claim ownership rights. Historical analogies, e.g. in the context of nuclear power and aeronautics, lead to the expectation that the respective country/countries would be tempted not to share the technological innovation in the beginning but to use it for promoting national wealth and gaining competitive advantages over other economies. A well-minded government would share the technology with other, allied countries. For example, an EU member state will likely share the technology at least with the other EU member states, and eventually with allies at the UN level or G20 level. However, in the context of renewable-energy technologies that develop incrementally through private sector activity, it is rather unlikely that this model applies.

The most likely situation is that a private energy technology developer achieves a breakthrough that leads to a decrease of levelized electricity costs below the level of competing fossil fuel technologies. From the developer's point of view, it would be economically rational to keep the IPRs and sole-user rights and follow an aggressive expansion strategy, first in the national/existing markets and then in new markets. Given that a single company would likely not be in a position to rapidly implement the STT on an international scale, it would rather be a 'slow-onset' event. Second, it has to be expected that the company would offer the electricity price at a level that is slightly lower than the price competitors offer (with the objective to gain market share), but at the same time maximize the margin on power sales. Hence, this can be considered as the worst-case scenario: cost benefits would not be passed to the power consumers; competitors would need to lay off personnel; and environmental benefits from reduced GHG emissions would not occur as rapidly as needed. The only one profiting would be the company that owns and operates the technology.

This leads to the question of how potentially negative impacts can be avoided or at least minimized. In the following we discuss whether different strategies for 'distributing' the STT at the national and international level can be a solution, where the technology developer collaborates with public institutions. This, of course, requires that governments watch the energy technology market and realize when an STT is likely to arise. We will analyse the following options:

1 partially coordinated distribution
2 fully coordinated distribution.

We assume that the technology developer cooperates strongly with the public authorities and/or an international supervisory body and makes the blueprints available to them. The motivation could be to maximize the global distribution of the STT or, besides receiving some financial remuneration, to contribute to tackling the world's challenges relating to economic development, living standards and environmental degradation. For the purpose of this analysis, we do not assess how a financial incentive for the technology developer would look.

A partially coordinated distribution can have many faces. One option would be that the access to the blueprints of the STT is coordinated in a way that all countries get access directly and then can make the best out of it. This would require a high-level political agreement of major economies and the establishment of an international body, eventually located at the UN, for coordination and supervision. However, even if it is possible to create the same starting point for every nation, this approach would likely favour rich countries as they have the financial resources to rapidly explore and utilize the new technology, whereas poor countries might not be able to harness the direct benefits of the STT at all. Hence, in a worst-case scenario, it might increase the gap between rich and poor countries. In addition, there would be significant inefficiencies as each country/company would need to learn how to transform blueprints to a reliably running power source.

Another option would be to regulate certain aspects of implementation, e.g. timelines and scope of implementation of the STT. One would need to develop a clear plan about which aspects of STT distribution are to be regulated and which ones are not. A fully coordinated distribution assumes that an international supervisory body manages the distribution and implementation of the STT worldwide. Hence, the international body would likely own the IPRs of the STT and would have authority to allocate STT plants at its sole discretion. The advantage of such an approach is that the body theoretically has the opportunity to maximize economic, social and environmental benefits of the new technology worldwide. However, one must expect that it will be subject to heavy lobbying and political pressure by major and minor economies. Hence, the overall question is whether such a body can have the political power to resist strong external forces. Below, we look in more depth at design options of such an international body.

5.2 The power transformation levy as the cornerstone of the transition policy

While a quick, global diffusion of any STT would be desirable due to its economic, social and environmental benefits, it is clear that it will take many years until a global utilization of the STT can be achieved. Having in mind the potential impacts of an uneven distribution of the STT on industrial competition as discussed above, we suggest implementing a power transformation levy (PTL).

The principle of the PTL is based on skimming off the power generation cost differential between the super transformational and traditional technologies, as shown in Figure 10.4.

The objective of the PTL is to keep power prices for consumers, including industry, at historical levels to ensure a level playing field in the years of transition. The PTL has to be paid by power consumers and equals the difference between current electricity market prices and the electricity price of the STT.[8] The tax levels can decline over time to allow for global convergence of power prices in the long run, once the policy aims of the PTL have been reached. The funds obtained from the tax can be used for activities that foster economic and social welfare and would be managed centrally by an International Supervisory Body (ISB). Both aspects will be described in more detail further below.

5.2.1 PTL collection system options

There are several options for how the PTL can be collected. In the following, we look at two options. In option 1, the PTL would be collected directly by an ISB;

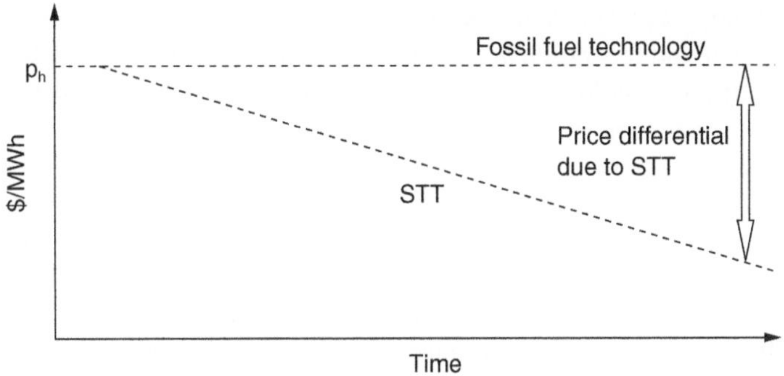

Figure 10.4 Electricity price differential.

Note
ph = historical/recent price levels for power generation.

in option 2 it would be indirectly paid through governments. A key challenge for a global programme is to ensure that all users of the STT pay the PTL. There is a clear incentive for consumers, utilities and/or countries to escape the tax and to benefit from the reduced electricity production cost. Given the highly scalable size of technologies likely to become STTs, 'energy havens' could mushroom in remote locations, in failed states or even in shadow economies within industrialized countries. The World Trade Organization (WTO) could be used to apply countermeasures such as border tax adjustments, if 'energy havens' abroad try to appropriate the benefits of the STT without paying the PTL. To avoid lengthy procedures before the dispute settlement panel, countries could engage themselves in a treaty applying border taxes against any 'energy haven'.

In option 1 the ISB would collect the PTL directly from the electricity consumers. Countries would inform the ISB which power plants use the STT. A practical barrier to this approach is the very high number of entities that the ISB would have to deal with. If manageable at all, this would result in huge transaction costs for the ISB. Even more problematic is the fact that the ISB would need to know (1) how much electricity is consumed by each end-consumer in a given period, and (2) from which utility/power plant the power was obtained in that period. The latter is particularly relevant if not all power plants in the country use the STT – in this case, the PTL only applies to some end-consumers or part of their electricity consumption.[9] This would pose severe monitoring challenges to the ISB. The above-mentioned challenge of national enforcement power applies as well. Overall, this option does not appear feasible.

In option 2, the countries would collect the PTL and pass it to the ISB. Either the energy consumers would be liable for paying the PTL, or the utilities. If energy consumers are directly liable to pay the PTL, the above discussed challenges of

- high number of actors involved; and
- detailed monitoring of power consumption patterns

are still going to be an issue. Again, this does not appear to be a feasible approach as long as the PTL cannot be applied uniformly to all end-users.

An option to avoid this problem is to make utilities liable for paying the PTL. In this case, utilities would pay the PTL based on the actual power generation using the STT. Payments would be made to the national government, which would pass the PTL to the ISB (see Figure 10.5).

The advantages of this option are that the existing monitoring and billing systems can be kept and that the number of actors involved is small: at the national level only the utilities would need to pay the PTL, while all end-users would not face any additional reporting/taxation duties; and at the international level, the ISB would only have to deal with the governments of the respective countries.

A general challenge of any solution that involves an international body is to ensure that it has sufficient enforcement power.

5.2.2 Principles for calculation of the PTL level

There are several ways in which the level of the PTL could be determined. The first option, described briefly above and in Figure 10.4, would be to make the PTL equal to the difference between current electricity market prices in each country and the generation costs – plus a profit margin – of the STT. This approach has the advantage of ensuring unchanged industrial electricity prices for the time being, and thus avoiding significant distortions of international competitiveness. A drawback of this approach is, however, its interference with national energy policies in the long run. Electricity prices would de facto be frozen at the level of the historical electricity price. Some resistance of countries

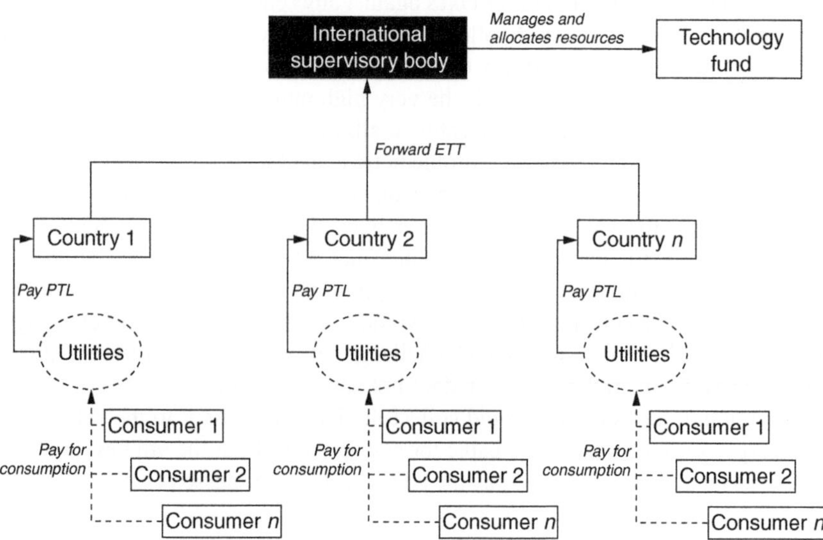

Figure 10.5 Indirect payment of PTL to ISB: payment by utilities.

must therefore be expected, especially those developing rapidly and thus changing their electricity pricing policies and market structures from a state-planned towards a more liberalized system, although overall benefits of the STT may justify the stringent intervention.

Another approach would be to calculate the PTL rate as the difference between current electricity generation costs and a uniform base price for electricity produced with the STT across the world. The actual electricity generation costs can, for example, be defined as the average weighted electricity generation costs of power generation worldwide. In this case, countries with a high share of expensive fuels in their actual energy mix would win in relative terms, profiting from cheaper power from the STT compared to their baseline generation costs (see Figure 10.6). These countries would therefore get a competitive advantage compared to countries with a historically 'cheaper' fuel mix. If countries aim to keep electricity prices constant, countries with higher than average electricity generation costs that currently subsidize electricity prices would profit because they could lower their subsidies.

Another option for tackling sovereignty concerns would be to use the weighted average electricity generation cost *per country* for calculating the PTL, instead of applying a global figure. In Figure 10.6, the columns for each country (group)

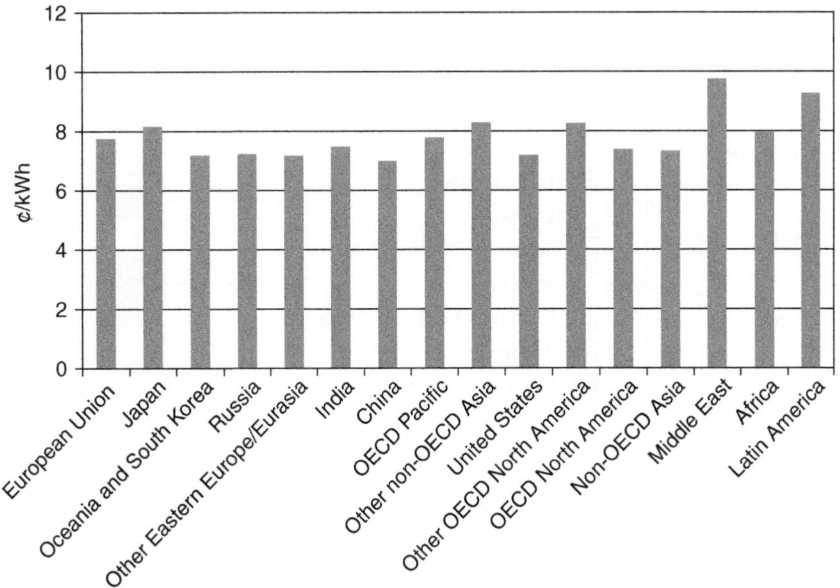

Figure 10.6 Electricity generation costs in selected regions/countries (¢/kWh) (sources: own calculation, EU Commission 2008; Fraser *et al.* 2005; Greenpeace and EREC 2007; Kaplan 2008).

Note
The average cost of electricity generation (horizontal line) has been calculated exclusively for the group of countries shown in the figure. It indicates the assumed base electricity price.

indicate this price. Compared to the approach to fixing the PTL rate to historical electricity price levels as described above, this approach has the advantage of maintaining national sovereignty with regards to electricity taxation policies. At the same time, it leads to a higher probability that national electricity price levels will change – simply due to the fact that all countries need to reconsider and adapt their electricity taxation system, which will 'invite' them to take measures affecting end-user prices. Hence, there is no guarantee that industrial electricity prices will remain constant. A change of relative electricity prices can severely affect competitiveness of those industries that compete on the world market (see discussion above). In the quantitative example below, we apply average electricity generation costs over all fossil fuel-based power generation per country.

6 Mobilizing development and economic diversification through the Power Transition Levy

Assuming that the STT will be diffused as shown in Table 10.3, with an electricity cost of ¢2/kWh, revenues from the PTL will develop as shown in Figure 10.7 if the option 'weighted average electricity generation cost *per country*' is chosen.

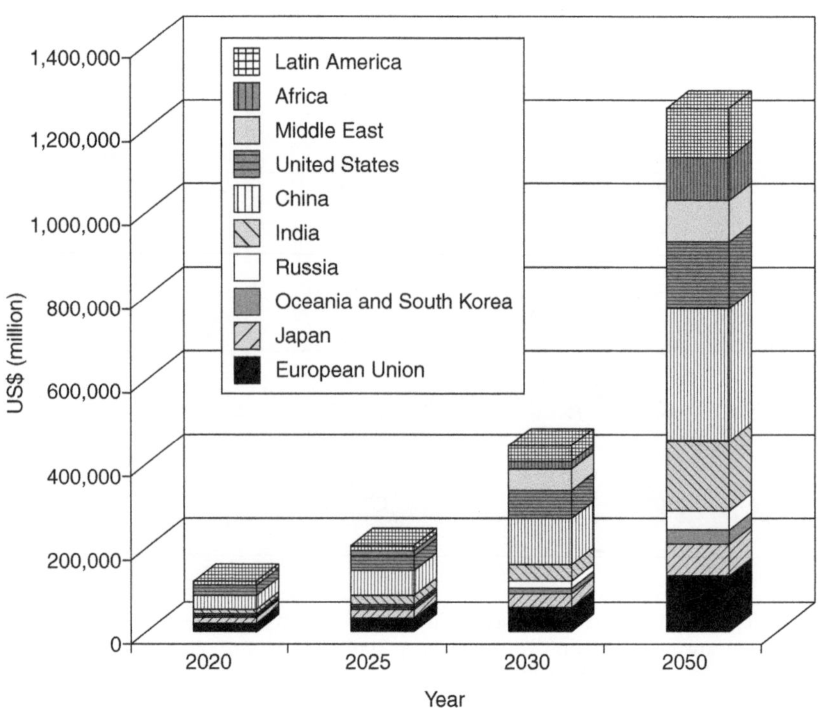

Figure 10.7 Annual revenues from PTL according to region (million US$).

While annual revenues rise from US$125 billion in 2020 to reach US$445 billion in 2030 and US$1.2 trillion in 2050, cumulated revenues from 2020 to 2050 would reach US$18.4 trillion.

We now discuss how the revenues from the PTL could be used. Obviously, there are many options for how to spend such large amounts of money. Given that such a tax would be a unique chance for raising sizeable amounts of money without putting a burden on tax payers, we feel this places a unique responsibility for using the funds in a way that benefits global social welfare. For this reason, in our view it would be beneficial if the following elements play a major role in the distribution plan:

- An Energy Development Programme (EDP) to reach a satisfactory level of basic energy needs in all countries by 2050. Developing countries should be integrated in the roll-out of the STT, particularly where electricity demand is highly suppressed.
- A Desert Greening Programme (DGP) focusing on countries that so far have benefited from fossil fuel exports. An economic diversification plan based on a DGP should be developed, communicated and implemented in a transparent manner.

6.1 The Energy Development Programme

Many developing countries are suffering from an electricity shortage whose alleviation would unleash a rapid increase in industrial production. In the medium and long term, availability of cheap electricity allows productivity increases.

The largest development benefits of electricity provision could be generated in circumstances where electricity supply is not keeping up with demand. For example, in India power shortages reached 9.3 per cent or 78 TWh in 2009/2010, while peak power shortages were 12.6 per cent or 15 GW. In such a situation, productivity is compromised through rolling or entirely unannounced blackouts. Costly back-up generation and voltage stabilization equipment is required. To improve the competitiveness of industries in developing countries, one short-term priority of roll-out of the STT should thus be on alleviation of suppressed electricity demand. Still, almost 1.5 billion people – one-quarter of the world population – have no access to electricity at all, and in BAU this would only slowly decline to 1 billion by 2050 (IEA 2009).

If an EDP is introduced, we suggest splitting it in two phases. Phase 1 is to achieve basic electricity supply throughout the world and should possibly be completed within five to ten years. According to IEA (2009), the basic electricity consumption of newly connected people is estimated to be 50 kWh/yr in rural areas and 100 kWh/yr in urban areas. Assuming an average of 75 kWh/yr and an average duration of consumption of six hours, we reach a capacity requirement of 50 GW, costing US$20–75 billion using current power plant technology (investment cost levels for gas and coal power plants as per Fraser *et al.* (2005)). The investment costs of an STT would probably lie at the low to middle end of this range. Main focus areas would be sub-Saharan Africa with 20.1 GW, India with 13.9 GW and the rest of Asia with 13.6 GW. The EDP should provide rapid STT deployment grants to all countries with populations with per capita electricity consumption below 75 kWh/yr. Electricity produced from the power plants financed through these grants should be exempt from the PTL due to the low ability of people in these regions to pay for electricity. Assuming US$20–40 billion are needed, phase 1 could be financed by just 15–30 per cent of PTL revenue of the year 2020.

Phase 2 can then support upscaling of electricity production in developing countries to the value typical of middle-income countries – 1,000 kWh per capita per year. This would require 615 GW at a price tag of approximately US$250–500 billion. The timeframe of phase 2 should be limited to up to two decades. The example of China in the 2000s shows that the roll-out of such a level of power plant capacity in a decade is possible if there is a firm political and economic development drive. To avoid moral hazard, phase 2 should require a certain amount of investment on behalf of the host-country government, especially in transmission and distribution infrastructures. At a 10 per cent participation level for the pure power plant component, PTL funding requirements would remain at US$225–450 billion, requiring about 10–15 per cent of PTL revenues during one decade. These plants should not be exempt from PTL payments.

6.2 The Desert Greening Programme

If electricity generation costs are sufficiently low, large new areas could be opened for agriculture through irrigation of desert areas by desalinated water. What volume of water is required to green the deserts? In 1995, irrigated rice production required 1.7–7 m^3/kg, whereas other cereals required 0.4–5 m^3/kg. The worst values were found in sub-Saharan Africa due to the low productivity per hectare. Water consumption per hectare reached 5,000–10,000 m^3 (Cai and Rosegrant 2003). How many hectares are available for such irrigation? Table 10.5 shows arid areas worldwide.

Table 10.5 Potential target areas for the Desert Greening Programme

Region	*Hyper-arid (million ha)*[a]	*Arid (million ha)*[b]	*Semi-arid (million ha)*[b]	*Dry sub-humid (million ha)*[b]
Asia (inc ding Russia)	277.3	616.4	764.9	458.8
Africa	672.0	505.2	507.3	280.8
Oceania	0.0	348.8	353.2	99.6
North America	3.1	37.9	343.6	208.1
South America	25.7	40.1	298.0	222.3
Central America	3.0	42.1	69.6	24.2
Europe	0.0	0.5	37.3	96.1
World total	978.0	1,591.0	2,373.9	1,390.9

Sources: a Noin and Clarke (1998); b Koohafkan and Stewart (2008).

We assume that one-quarter of the desert (hyper-arid and arid) area would be theoretically available for irrigation – the remainder would be stony or pure-sand deserts unsuitable for agriculture, at least in the medium term. For a more robust assumption, the soil characteristics of the world's desert regions would need to be analysed, which is beyond the scope of this chapter. This means about 0.5 billion hectares would be available in developing countries. Addressing semi-arid areas would add another 0.375 billion hectares. Assuming an average irrigation of 7,500 m^3/ha/yr in a desert climate and half of this for semi-arid areas, the pure water needed would reach 3.75 trillion cubic metres for the deserts and 1.1 trillion cubic metres for the semi-arid zones. For comparison, Rothwell (2006) discusses a DGP for 3.9 billion hectares, requiring a water volume of only 1.6 trillion cubic metres per year.

A key challenge for the DGP is the electricity requirement for desalination, as well as for pumping the water across long distances. The best desalination technology currently available – reverse osmosis – requires 5 kWh per cubic metre of desalinated water (*Encyclopedia of Desalination and Water Resources* 2010). Irrigating 1 ha with water from reverse osmosis desalination will thus require 25–50 MWh electricity.

Desalinating the 3.75 trillion cubic metres of water derived above would require 18.8 PWh per year, i.e. a power plant capacity of 2.1 TW – equal to half of the entire currently installed world electric capacity! Direct investment costs for the STT would reach US$820–1,640 billion. Water transport is also highly energy-intensive. The Government of West Australia, Department of the Premier and Cabinet (2006) estimates the energy use of a 1,900 km long, 1.8 m diameter pipeline delivering 200 million cubic metres of water per year over an altitude difference of 700 m at 5.8 kWh/m^3, with the value almost doubling to 9 kWh/m^3 if two 1.6 m diameter pipelines were used. Assuming that greening the deserts requires an average pipeline distance of 1,000 km and a head of 700 m, we derive a transport energy requirement of 3 kWh/m^3 for a 1.8 m diameter pipeline. Pumping energy for 3.75 trillion cubic metres thus would require 11.3 PWh per year and an installed capacity of 1.3 TW, with investment costs of US$520–1,040 billion.

These calculations show that the DGP could take-up the major portion of PTL revenues for at least one decade.

6.3 Considerations for a PTL allocation plan

As Figure 10.7 shows, PTL revenues increase significantly over time. Policy-makers or the ISB would have to decide how to spend the available funds wisely, and when to start reducing the PTL rate. With a view to maximizing economic, social and environmental benefits, they should consider the following priority fields:

- Preventing dangerous climate change: a quick global roll-out of the STT in the power, heating (industry and buildings) and transport sectors is needed to

maximize climate benefits. Note that (1) the installation of initial STT plants will require upfront finance; and (2) if the PTL fixes electricity prices at historical levels, there needs to be either a financial incentive for industry and consumers of heat to switch to electrical devices, or a respective regulation.
- Improving food production and availability through the DGP.
- Improving quality of life through the EDP.
- Quick reduction of energy prices to inspire economic growth.

It is obvious that not all of these targets can be reached at the same time. For example, the objective to reduce power prices interferes with the need for financial resources for the DGP, the EDP and also a quick roll-out of the STT, in developing countries in particular. Hence, the authority deciding on the allocation of PTL funds needs to make balanced and far-sighted decisions.

6.4 Structure and control of the International Supervisory Body

Given the huge amount of resources under its purview, the ISB would become a key institution in world politics. Countries would only be willing to set-up such an institution if it combined power, responsibility and accountability and did not become a bloated world-planning agency reminiscent of communist times. Thus it has to be as lean as possible. Ballesteros *et al.* (2009) define the following criteria for the three dimensions of ISB agency: power is the formal and informal capacity to determine outcomes; responsibility is the exercise of power for its intended purpose; accountability involves standards and systems that ensure power is exercised responsibly.

Issues relating to power in the ISB context are:

- distribution of vote and voice in the governance structure;
- authority and/or guidance of a multilateral governance body;
- imposition by contributors of conditionalities for the process of fund allocation;
- influence of bureaucratic discretion, technical expertise and civil society input.

Responsibility relates to:

- application of transparent criteria for allocation of funds;
- assurances that investments 'do no harm';
- enabling of 'ownership' of recipients.

Accountability requires:

- results-based management and reporting;
- fiduciary duties and financial management;
- environmental and social safeguards.

The ISB can only have the necessary power if governments are willing to accept decision-making by votes representing all relevant stakeholders. Obviously, interests and priority areas differ between countries. This would call for one ISB council representing all countries contributing to the ISB. Votes should be weighted according to the contribution – i.e. the PTL volume collected in a country – as is the case in the World Bank and IMF. This council would decide on the allocation of resources.

6.5 Limitation of the rent mentality of beneficiaries of fund disbursements

A key challenge in allocation of ISB disbursements is to prevent a 'rent mentality' that prevents economic restructuring in countries whose economies so far heavily relied on fossil fuel exports, which is required to create long-term sustainability. Therefore, payments have to be clearly linked to performance criteria, i.e. regular evaluation of benefits. Historically, successful large disbursements of funds have been provided under the Marshall Plan for reconstruction of war-damaged Europe. They were particularly successful when disbursed in a revolving fund system (see Baumgart 1961 and the discussion below). Moreover, large foundations have developed experience in using programme-related investments. The Ford Foundation, through loans, gave the now world-famous Grameen Bank in Bangladesh the necessary funding to demonstrate the viability of microcredit (Leibell 2009). These experiences have led to the rise of a concept called 'venture philanthropy'. According to Davis and Etchart (2001), its key elements are multi-year financing, an 'investment approach' (versus a 'grant-making approach'), capacity building as well as technical assistance to the recipient, an organizational focus, definition of quantitative benchmarks for success and clear exit strategies once agreed-upon benchmarks are achieved (or consistently failed to be achieved).[10] Recently, the Gates Foundation has decided to apply venture philanthropy to 10 per cent of its annual funding volume (Leibell 2009).

The ISB should thus define a clear maximum duration of payments. Even within this period, continuation of payments should be tied to indicators that show the productive use of the payments.

7 National challenges: strategy for transforming the energy sector

Broadly introducing an STT into a national energy system will pose interesting challenges to governments and utilities. If we assume that the technology has construction times comparable to those of coal-fired power plants, then national policy-makers would need to develop a totally new concept for the national energy system.

Any government would need to answer (at least) the following questions:

- How rapidly shall the STT be introduced?

- What share of electricity shall be produced with the new technology?
- Which other technologies and power plants should serve as reserves in case of technological problems with the STT?
- If national power installation capacities are already sufficient to meet demand, which installations should be replaced/shutdown first?
- What is the optimal energy mix of the future – under consideration of energy security needs, environmental impacts, price effects, other social effects?
- Shall the STT also be used for power consumption in industry and transport? When and to what extent?
- What infrastructure is needed to fully utilize the new technology? E.g. additional/other grid capacities, electricity fuel stations for transport?
- Once the new technology is implemented on a large scale, which old infrastructure such as unnecessary gas pipelines should be kept, which ones can be abolished?
- What can and should be the role of private power industry in the future? What role does the government need to play in the short, medium and long term?

It is obvious that the answers to these questions will strongly depend on national circumstances – such as structure and characteristics of the existing national energy system, perceived importance of domestic fuels and impacts on regional employment. In addition, the attitude of the population with regards to energy security, environmental aspects, social aspects and also acceptability of the new technology will play a decisive role.

In the following, we take a fictitious journey and explore what Germany could do if an STT was available by 2020. As of January 2010, 812 power plants at or above 50 MW were operated in Germany, or 544 plants at or above 100 MW (Platts 2010). Total installed capacity of these plants was 210 GW or 193 GW, respectively. A particular feature of Germany is that after the nuclear disaster in Fukushima in March 2011, the government decided to phase-out nuclear power generation by 2022; nuclear power generated 135 TWh in 2010, i.e. 22.6 per cent of total electricity production of 621 TWh (AG Energiebilanzen 2011a). The seven oldest nuclear power plants were shut down immediately after the Fukushima event and will not resume their operation. Hence, the availability of a super transformational technology would be the perfect match to fill the capacity gap created by the nuclear phase-out.

But apart from nuclear, which power plants would be shutdown first if the STT delivers cheaper electricity? Historically, both energy security and security of employment of coal workers in the Ruhr area and in eastern Germany have been high on the political agenda. Maintaining some coal in the national energy supply would support both targets. We therefore assume that Germany wants to keep a coal base of at least 15 per cent in its electricity production in 2020, to be reduced to 5 per cent in 2030 – compared to approximately 35 per cent in 2009 (BMWi 2010). This would amount to about 100 TWh in 2020 and 40 TWh in 2030, most likely from domestic lignite, which is the cheapest power generation technology at 2.9¢/kWh (Wissel *et al.* 2008). Hard coal plants are less competitive at 3.3¢/kWh and thus likely to be phased out earlier.

In addition, Germany may want to keep a 'cold reserve' of gas-fired power plants to deal with peak load, despite their high cost of 4.2¢/kWh (Wissel *et al.* 2008). We therefore assume that the actually installed capacity will be kept, but that electricity generation from gas is halved to approximately 6 per cent in 2025, i.e. 40 TWh, and will remain constant from then.

It is obvious that the first priority of the country would be to fill the gaps left by nuclear power plants. Then, the country may choose to shutdown the most CO_2-intensive installations while considering the defined minimum production of coal-based power.

We assume that the STT is available from 2020 at costs of 2¢/kWh and can be rolled out at a construction rate of initially 10 GW per year. These 10 GW would produce 60 TWh (at a load factor of 70 per cent). From 2025 the annual construction rate would grow to 15 GW. The replacement of power plants would be done as shown in Figure 10.8.

8 Summary

An STT which reduces electricity generation cost below the cost of the cheapest fossil power plants has the potential to change the world profoundly. If it can be

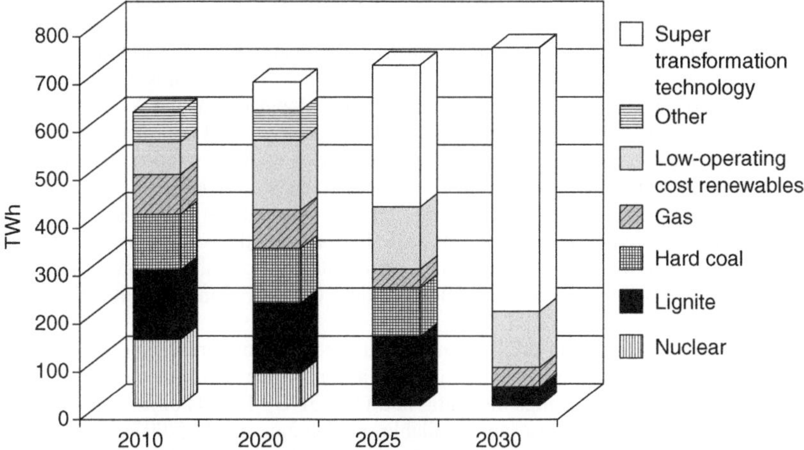

Figure 10.8 Penetration of the STT in the German power generation (TWh electricity generation) (sources: data for costs from Wissel *et al.* (2008); electricity production 2010 from AG Energiebilanzen (2011b)).

Notes

Assumptions: electricity production increases by 1 per cent per year; nuclear production in 2020 is derived from formal sequence on phase-out and 2010 production levels (Deutsches Atomforum 2011); 'classical' low-operation cost renewables are assumed to increase to reach the target of 30 per cent share of renewable power in 2020 and then decline by 1 per cent per year as plants reach the end of their technical lifetime).

installed in unlimited quantities and manages to reach a very low cost per kilowatt-hour, it can fulfil the age-old dream of limitless energy at low cost. Moreover, it can reduce global GHG emissions significantly and thus become a cornerstone of international climate policies. This is particularly true if it enables substitution of fossil fuels in the transport, building and industrial sectors.

Due to the STT's low costs, a sizeable share of the required outlays for GHG mitigation can be avoided. In addition to this, the availability of nearly cost-free energy both to industry and households can be expected to tremendously stimulate global economic growth.

In order to overcome some of the challenging side effects of such a revolutionary technology, we suggest implementing a power transformation levy as the differential between historical electricity generation costs and generation costs of the STT. Revenues from the levy can then be used for multiple purposes benefitting global society. Particularly the elimination of suppressed electricity demand in developing countries by a large Electricity Development Programme and the increase of agricultural production by a Desert Greening Programme would enable a diversification of economies that so far either have no relevant productive base or are uniquely built on the export of fossil fuels.

Notes

1 SRES considers four main scenarios: A1, A2, B1 and B2. The A1 scenario describes a future world of very rapid economic growth, global population that peaks in mid-century and declines thereafter, and the rapid introduction of new and more efficient technologies. The A2 scenario assumes a very heterogeneous, regionally oriented world that emphasizes self-reliance and preservation of local identities. The B1 scenario is based on a convergent world with the same projection of the global population as the A1 scenario, but with a rapid change in economic structures towards a service and information economy. The B2 scenario projects a world in which emphasis is on local solutions to economic, social and environmental sustainability (Nakicenovic and Swart 2000).

2 Note that throughout the paper cents are referring to the cents of US dollars.

3 Note that (some) countries may, for strategic reasons, decide to continue operation of alternative forms of power generation, in particular those with low operating costs and long lifetimes (hydro power). Such political considerations are not reflected in our calculations.

4 As mitigation measures in the building and industry sectors are very diverse, IPCC (2007) provides mitigation potential only at an aggregate level (electricity savings, fuel savings and other savings including non-CO_2 GHG). Details of mitigation measures in the building sector are available in Levine *et al.* (2007), particularly pp. 393–416 and Bernstein *et al.* (2007), particularly pp. 456–74 for the industry sector. The measures for the building sector include efficient appliances, thermal envelope, heating and cooling systems, heating, ventilation and air conditioning (HVAC) systems, building energy management systems, solar energy, etc. In the industry sector, key sector-wide energy-efficiency measures include efficient electric motors, high-pressure boilers and furnaces and process heaters. Fuel switching and heat and power recovery are also important sector-wide measures. There are numerous other mitigation measures available specific to each industry.

5 Electric heating has historically been introduced rapidly if economically attractive, as shown by the examples of Norway and France. This is due to the simple technology

that has very low investment costs. An obstacle to universal penetration could be lack of grid access in developing countries. However, those households able to afford fossil fuels are likely to have grid access by 2030.

6 Note that this is a simple estimate that does not consider secondary effects.

7 The United States, Japan, Germany, China, United Kingdom, France, Italy, Canada, Brazil, Russia, India, South Korea, Mexico, Turkey, Indonesia, Iran, Pakistan, Nigeria, Philippines, Egypt, Bangladesh and Vietnam.

8 For the purpose of the quantitative analysis below, we use a proxy – i.e. estimate the electricity price as generation costs of the STT plus 20 per cent to account for the profit margin of utilities, grid costs, etc.

9 At least in a transition period when a mix of power sources is still available, utilities would likely use cheap generation (the backstop technology) for base-load capacity, and the more expensive one (in this case, conventional energy) for peak-load demand. So, all consumers would partly use the backstop and partly other sources of energy.

10 Capers *et al.* (1998) discuss opposition to this concept among charitable institutions.

References

AG Energiebilanzen (2011a) 'Stromerzeugung nach Energieträgern von 1990 bis 2010 (in TWh) Deutschland insgesamt', Deutsches Institut für Wirtschaftsforschung, EEFA GmbH. Online. Available: www.ag-energiebilanzen.de/viewpage.php?idpage=65 (accessed 30 June 2011).

AG Energiebilanzen (2011b) 'Sondertabellen', Deutsches Institut für Wirtschaftsforschung, EEFA GmbH. Online. Available: www.ag-energiebilanzen.de/viewpage.php?idpage=139 (accessed 28 July 2011).

Alvarez, L., Bradner, H., Crawford, F.,Crawford, J., Falk-Vairant, P., Good, M., Gow, J., Rosenfeld, A., Solmitz, F., Stevenson, M., Ticho, H. and Tripp, R. (1957) 'Catalysis of nuclear reactions by μ mesons', *Physical Review*, 105: 1127–8.

Anderson, C. (2008) 'Free! Why $0.00 is the future of business', *Wired Magazine*. Online. Available: www.wired.com/print/techbiz/it/magazine/16–03/ff_free (accessed 26 July 2011).

Ballesteros, A., Nakhooda, S. and Werksman, J. (2009) 'Power, responsibility and accountability: re-thinking the legitimacy of institutions for climate finance', World Resources Institute (WRI). Online. Available: http://pdf.wri.org/power_responsibility_accountability.pdf.

Barker, T., Bashmakov, I., Alharthi, A., Amann, M., Cifuentes, L., Drexhage, L., Duan, M., Edenhofer, O., Flannery, B., Grubb, M., Hoogwijk, M., Ibitoye, F., Jepma, C., Pizer, W. and Yamaji, K. (2007) 'Mitigation from a cross-sectoral perspective', in B. Metz, O. Davidson, P. Bosch, R. Dave and L. Meyer (eds) *Climate Change 2007: Mitigation of Climate Change – Contribution of Working Group III to the Fourth Assessment Report of the Intergovernmental Panel on Climate Change*, Cambridge and New York: Cambridge University Press, pp. 619–90.

Barrett, S. (2010) 'Climate treaties and backstop technologies', *CESifo Working Paper Series*, 3003, presented at the CESifo Area Conference on Energy & Climate Economics, Munich, 16–17 October.

Baumgart, E. (1961) *Investitionen und ERP-Finanzierung*, Berlin: Duncker und Humblot.

Bernstein, L., Roy, J., Delhotal, K., Harnisch, J., Matsuhashi, R., Price, L., Tanaka, K., Worrell, E., Yamba, F. and Fengqi, Z. (2007) 'Industry', in B. Metz, O. Davidson, P. Bosch, R. Dave and L. Meyer (eds) *Climate Change 2007: Mitigation of Climate Change – Contribution of Working Group III to the Fourth Assessment Report of the*

Intergovernmental Panel on Climate Change, Cambridge and New York: Cambridge University Press, pp. 447–96.

BMWi (2010) 'Energiedaten: nationale und internationale Entwicklung', Bundesministerium für Wirtschaft. Online. Available: www.bmwi.de/BMWi/Navigation/Energie/energiestatistiken.html (accessed 26 July 2011).

Bosetti, V. and Tavoni, M. (2009) 'Uncertain R&D, backstop technology and GHGs stabilization', *Energy Economics*, 31: S18–26.

Brandt, L. (1956) 'Die zweite industrielle Revolution', in *Sozialdemokratische Partei Deutschlands: Protokoll der Verhandlungen des Parteitages der Sozialdemokratischen Partei Deutschlands vom 10. bis 14. Juli 1956 in München*, Bonn: Sozialdemokratische Partei Deutschlands, pp. 148–65.

Breyer, C., Gerlach, A., Schäfer, D. and Schmid, J. (2010) 'Fuel-parity: new very large and sustainable market segments for PV systems', paper presented at IEEE EnergyCon 2010, 18–22 December, Manama.

Cai, X. and Rosegrant, M. (2003) 'World water productivity: current situation and future options', in J. Kijne, R. Barker and D. Molden (eds) *Water Productivity in Agriculture: Limits and Opportunities for Improvement*, Cambridge: CABI Publishing, pp. 163–78.

Capers, C., Collins, M. and Gooneratne, S. (1998) 'Assessing venture philanthropy'. Online. Available: http://pages.prodigy.net/michael_collins/VP.htm (accessed 20 June 2011).

Cooper, A. and Smith, C. (1992) 'How established firms respond to threatening technologies', *Academy of Management Executive*, 6 (2): 55–70.

Davis, L. and Etchart, N. (2001) 'Venture philanthropy', Nonprofit Enterprise and Self-sustainability Team. Online. Available: http://forum.nesst.org/venture.asp (accessed 26 July 2011).

Deutsches Atomforum (2011) 'Kernkraftwerke in Deutschland'. Online. Available: www.kernenergie.de/kernenergie/Themen/Kernkraftwerke/Kernkraftwerke_in_Deutschland (accessed 26 July 2011).

Encyclopedia of Desalination and Water Resources (2010) 'Energy requirements of desalination processes', Desware. Online. Available: www.desware.net/desa4.aspx (accessed 26 July 2011).

EU Commission (2008) 'Energy sources, production costs and performance of technologies for power generation, heating and transport, Commission of the European Communities'. Online. Available: http://ec.europa.eu/energy/strategies/2008/doc/2008_11_ser2/strategic_energy_review_wd_cost_performance.pdf (accessed 26 July 2011).

Fraser, P., Stridbaek, U., Bertel, E., Condu, M., van Uitert, G. and Voss, A. (2005) *Projected Costs of Generating Electricity: 2005 Update*, Paris: Nuclear Energy Agency (NEA), International Energy Agency (IEA), Organisation for Economic Co-Operation and Development (OECD).

Garnaut, R., Howes, S., Jotzo, F. and Sheehan, P. (2008) 'Emissions in the Platinum Age: The implications of rapid development for climate-change mitigation', *Oxford Review of Economic Policy*, 24: 377–401.

Government of West Australia, Department of the Premier and Cabinet (2006) 'Options for bringing water to Perth from the Kimberley: an independent review'.

Greenpeace and EREC (2007) *Energy [R]evolution: A Sustainable World Energy Outlook*, Amsterdam: Greenpeace.

Heal, G. (1976) 'The relationship between price and extraction cost for a resource with a backstop technology', *Bell Journal of Economics*, 7: 371–8.

IEA (2004) *World Energy Outlook 2004*, Paris: International Energy Agency.

IEA (2007) *Tracking Industrial Energy Efficiency and CO_2 Emissions*, Paris: International Energy Agency.

IEA (2008) 'The electricity access database'. Online. Available: www.iea.org/weo/database_electricity/electricity_access_database.htm (accessed 28 July 2011).

IEA (2009) *World Energy Outlook 2009*, Paris: International Energy Agency.

IMF (2010) 'World economic outlook database, April 2010'. Online. Available: www.imf.org/external/pubs/ft/weo/2010/01/weodata/index.aspx.

IPCC (2007) 'Summary for policymakers', in B. Metz, O. Davidson, P. Bosch, R. Dave and L. Meyer (eds) *Climate Change 2007: Mitigation of Climate Change – Contribution of Working Group III to the Fourth Assessment Report of the Intergovernmental Panel on Climate Change*, Cambridge and New York: Cambridge University Press, pp. 2–23.

Kaplan, S. (2008) 'CRS report for Congress: power plants – characteristics and costs', Congressional Research Service. Online. Available: www.fas.org/sgp/crs/misc/RL34746.pdf.

Koohafkan, P. and Stewart, B. (2008) *Water and Cereals in Drylands*, London: Earthscan.

Leibell, D. (2009) 'Gates embraces philanthro-capitalism', *Trusts and Estates*. Online. Available: http://trustsandestates.com/wealth_watch/gates-foundation-venture-philanthropy1230 (accessed 27 July 2011).

Levine, M., Ürge-Vorsatz, D., Blok, K., Geng, L., Harvey, D., Lang, S., Levermore, G., Mongameli Mehlwana, A., Mirasgedis, S., Novikova, A., Rilling, J. and Yoshino, J. (2007) 'Residential and commercial buildings', in B. Metz, O. Davidson, P. Bosch, R. Dave and L. Meyer (eds) *Climate Change 2007: Mitigation of Climate Change – Contribution of Working Group III to the Fourth Assessment Report of the Intergovernmental Panel on Climate Change*, Cambridge and New York: Cambridge University Press, pp. 387–446.

Levy, A. (2000) 'From hotelling to backstop technology', *Working Paper*, 00–04, Department of Economics, University of Wollongong.

Matsuzaki, T. (2009) 'Muon catalyzed fusion for energy production', Riken Research. Online. Available: www.rikenresearch.riken.jp/eng/frontline/5976 (accessed 30 June 2011).

Mokyr, J. (1990) *The Lever of Riches: Technological Creativity and Economic Progress*, Oxford: Oxford University Press.

Mokyr, J. (1998) 'The political economy of technological change: resistance and innovation in economic history', in M. Berg and K. Bruland (eds) *Technological Revolutions in Europe*, Cheltenham: Edward Elgar, pp. 39–64.

Mokyr, J. (2000) 'Innovation and its enemies: the economic and political roots of technological inertia', in M. Olson and S. Kähkönen (eds) *A Not-so-dismal Science: A Broader View of Economies and Societies*, Oxford: Oxford University Press, pp. 61–92.

Mokyr, J. (2005) 'Long term economic growth and the history of technology', in P. Aghion and S. Durlauf (eds) *Handbook of Economic Growth, Volume 1B*, Amsterdam: North Holland, pp. 1117–79.

Nakicenovic, N. and Swart, R. (eds) (2000) *Emissions Scenarios*, Cambridge: Cambridge University Press.

Noin, D. and Clarke, J. (1998) 'Population and environment in arid regions of the world', in J. Clarke and D. Noin (eds) *Population and Environment in Arid Regions*, Paris: UNESCO, pp. 1–20.

Nordhaus, W. (1973) 'The allocation of energy reserves', *Brookings Papers*, 3: 529–70.

Parry, M., Canziani, O., Palutikof, J., van der Linden, P. and Hanson, C. (eds) (2007) *Climate Change 2007: Impacts, Adaptation and Vulnerability – Contribution of Working Group II to the Fourth Assessment Report of the Intergovernmental Panel on Climate Change*, Cambridge and New York: Cambridge University Press.

Owen, S. and Powell, S. (1985) 'Optimal supply of a depletable resource with a backstop technology: Heal's Theorem revisited', *Operations Research*, 33: 277–92.

Platts (2010) 'UDI world electric power plant data base'. Online. Available: www.platts.com/Products/worldelectricpowerplantsdatabase (accessed 28 July 2011).

Popp, D. (2006) 'The effects of backstop technology R&D on climate policy models', *Energy Economics*, 28: 188–202.

Rothwell, J. (2006) 'Cold fusion and the future', LENR-CANR.org. Online. Available: www.lenr-canr.org/acrobat/RothwellJcoldfusiona.pdf (accessed 27 July 2011).

Solarcentury (2009) 'Solar electricity as cheap as conventional electricity in UK by 2013'. Online. Available: www.solarcentury.co.uk/media/press-releases/solar-electricity-as-cheap-as-conventional-electricity-in-uk-by-2013 (accessed 27 July 2011).

Stern, N. (2006) 'The economics of climate change: The Stern Review'. Online. Available: http://webarchive.nationalarchives.gov.uk/+/www.hm-treasury.gov.uk/stern_review_report.htm (accessed 22 July 2011).

Wissel, S., Rath-Nagel, S., Blesl, M., Fahl, U. and Voß, A. (2008) 'Stromerzeugungskosten im Vergleich, Bericht Nr. 4', Institute of Energy Economics and the Rational Use of Energy, Universität Stuttgart.

11 Manoeuvring climate finance around the pitfalls

Finding the right policy mix

Axel Michaelowa

1 Climate finance: how can we prevent the current boom turning into a bust?

International climate policy has now been around for two decades and thus is still a young policy field. While the term 'climate finance' is recent, its different manifestations have been around for quite some time. Dedicated public climate finance emerged with the pilot phase of the Global Environment Facility (GEF) in 1990. But development assistance has supported renewable energy and energy-efficiency projects in developing countries already since the early 1950s. Market mechanisms took more time; the CDM was set-up in 1997, but registration of the first project took until December 2003. But only since the Copenhagen conference of 2009 and its fast-start finance (FSF) pledge of US$30 billion the all-encompassing term 'climate finance' has become fashionable. Glemarec (2011: 62) provides an excellent overview about all institutions currently involved, and all instruments included in the current understanding of climate finance, while a list of all relevant funds is provided by Ghosh (2010). Bredenkamp and Patillo (2010: 7) estimate a need for US$60 billion of subsidies to reach a flow of US$100 billion per year, whereas US$40 billion per year should flow as loans from a 'Green Fund' with a capital of US$120 billion. On the fringes of the debate, Friends of the Earth (2010: 19) propose a massive US$420 billion per year public climate finance programme financed through sources as diverse as 'cracking down on tax evasion by wealthy individuals and multinational companies' and a global 'Financial Transaction Tax'.

The current political willingness to spend billions for climate finance in developing countries is a double-edged sword. If used wisely, developing countries can be put on a low-carbon development path. If misused, climate finance will become political suicide in the not-too-distant future. How can we manoeuvre around the pitfalls and get an effective climate finance system? How can we learn from the frequent failures and less frequent successes of international transfer systems? What should be the relative role of market mechanisms and public funds? In answering these questions, I will draw on the preceding chapters, but also take a broader perspective.

2 Challenges to climate finance

The political salience of climate policy has been marked by twin peaks. In October 2007, Al Gore and the IPCC received the Nobel Peace Prize for their work on climate change. From then, multi-billion estimates of climate finance needs started to emerge – for example, see Project Catalyst (2009) for an annual estimate of US$65–100 billion. In December 2009, more than 100 heads of state met at the Copenhagen climate summit in the biggest such gathering ever held outside the UN headquarters in New York. But since then, there has been a marked decline in the relevance of climate policy due to several factors. The most important was surely the failure of the Copenhagen conference to agree on an international post-2012 climate policy regime. Moreover, the financial crisis of 2008 has weakened the public budgets of industrialized countries to such an extent that severe fiscal crises have followed. The EU, which used to be a leader in climate policy, is struggling to preserve its currency union. Policy-makers are thus preoccupied with restoring the fiscal health of their countries in the short term and have a tendency to ignore longer-term issues such as climate change. They are also more inclined to choose a narrow domestic policy perspective. Even if the health of public budgets was better than it is today, in a situation of increased industrial competition between advanced developing and industrialized countries, industry lobbies would object to climate finance streams that subsidize their competitors (see Ghosh 2010). So after the end of FSF, the mobilization of large volumes of public funds for climate finance seems out of the question (see also Chapter 9), unless innovative sources of public funds can be found that are directly linked to climate change. An air-traffic tax or the revenues from auctioning of emissions allowances could be such sources. In fact, the German climate finance programme has been built on auction revenues of EU allowances.

Van Melle *et al.* (2011) stress that the most difficult stage in financing mitigation measures is the upscaling of mitigation activities and that climate finance should focus on leveraging of private investments. However, Stadelmann *et al.* (2011) find that the leverage factor is not a convincing indicator for mitigation. For CDM projects, a high leverage factor might even be an indication that the project is not additional, and thus does not mobilize climate finance at all.

In a few years, the results of the FSF projects can be evaluated. Given the hasty procedures of finance allocation (see Chapter 5), and the lack of performance criteria in project selection (see Chapter 4), it is likely that performance will be mixed at best. A severely insufficient performance of climate finance would lead to a political backlash against future public climate finance. This has to be prevented by all means. The disillusionment with development finance in the 1980s and the ensuing impact on finance volumes and procedures give us a historical analogy.

The fiscal balance of advanced developing countries is much better than in most industrialized countries. As shown in Chapter 3, some of those countries have financed domestic programmes with massive climate benefits. If governments of these advanced developing countries want to promote export of the industries set-up in response to these programmes, they could become important sources of climate finance. However, this type of finance would certainly be tied to use of the technologies, which could lead to inefficiencies.

In the next decade we could thus find ourselves in a situation where public support for climate finance decreases even if climate finance needs to increase substantially. We discuss how the development assistance community dealt with a similar situation three decades ago.

3 How did development finance overcome its challenges?

The first large-scale effort in development finance was the Marshall Plan to rebuild European countries after the Second World War. The United States dedicated a much higher share of its GDP to this effort than to any later development programme. Especially in Germany, the Marshall Plan was a huge success as it provided the capital necessary to set up industries that were able to harness the idle human capital of the well-educated German labour force. So the first experiences with development finance were very positive and it was believed that these successes could be replicated in developing countries.

Parallel to the Marshall Plan, the first development finance flowed to developing countries, mainly to finance large industrial sites and power plants. In the 1960s, it pushed the 'green revolution', which led to a massive increase of agricultural yields in South and Southeast Asia. As the 1960s were an era of generalized economic growth in industrialized and developing countries alike, development finance was seen as contributing to this growth.

In the early 1970s, a wind of change in international institutions led to the promulgation of the target to allocate 0.7 per cent of industrialized country GDP to development finance. However, during this decade it became apparent that development finance achieved only a mixed performance. While some countries in East Asia managed to embark on an industrial take-off, the majority of recipients remained mired in poverty. Development success clearly was not linked to the volume of transfers received. Moreover, donors competed for the most attractive recipients, leading to duplication and inefficiency.

With the second oil shock at the end of the 1970s and the eruption of the debt crisis in Latin America, general donor fatigue set in. Electorates wondered whether development finance would ever reach its targets, and researchers struggled to develop new theories of how development finance could actually promote development. In this difficult situation, development practitioners started a serious engagement to develop criteria for the evaluation of development projects. Newell *et al.* (2009) argue that evaluation was absolutely crucial; it requires concrete metrics, and needs to address financial accounting, environmental integrity and social benefits.

Moreover, development finance bureaucracies identified new areas for development finance such as global environmental issues. With the emergence of new tasks for development finance, the downward trend in public budget allocation was reversed from the early 1990s. Moreover, doubtful performance in specific fields was increasingly masked by a proliferation of institutions, a tendency that is also currently emerging in international climate policy.

The lessons from development finance for climate finance are clear: an initial period of euphoria is followed by disillusionment, which leads institutions involved in financing to develop 'new' fields of finance and new institutions. Despite the disillusionment, development finance has never been completely abolished as a sufficient number of stakeholders had developed that lobbied policy-makers for a continuation of finance flows. A similar development can be expected in climate finance. So, after the first disillusionment, which we will probably get between 2015 and 2020 as the performance of the FSF push can be evaluated, a stabilization of climate finance flows can be expected. It might be linked with a drive to focus on cost-effective interventions, which might frequently try to maximize synergies between mitigation and adaptation (see Glemarec (2011: 16) for a call to maximize such synergies and minimize trade-offs). It is also likely that supporters of climate finance will try to intricately 'mainstream' it with development finance, as this will make it less likely that climate finance flows are reduced due to lacking performance. This, however, risks fragmentation of funding, coordination problems and lack of host-country ownership (as also stressed by Newell *et al.* 2009).

4 Preconditions for successful mitigation and adaptation in developing countries

As the history of development finance shows, only a relatively small subset of countries – mostly in East and Southeast Asia – has been able to successfully build development on grants received from abroad. Most of the countries that did so had been through a grave national crisis such as a war that had weakened the previously powerful interest groups. Therefore, governments were able to set conducive conditions for entrepreneurship without having to cater to the interest groups. They also provided basic infrastructures such as education systems.

More recently, large countries like China and Brazil were able to embark on a steady development path, mainly without foreign help. This was achieved mainly by liberalizing the economy, improving the education system and improving the physical infrastructure, mostly with domestic capital. As Chapter 3 shows, these large countries were able to embark on industrial policies that led to large-scale mitigation, and they essentially self-financed them. Ghosh's (2010: 32) proposal to 'separate and indigenize' focuses on multilateral banks providing guarantees for finance flows to the advanced countries. But it should not be forgotten that in other sectors, greenhouse gas (GHG) emissions of these countries increased rapidly. Here, the CDM has mobilized hundreds of projects, but did not achieve a decoupling of growth and GHG emissions.

As public mitigation finance is to flow not only to advanced countries that could emulate China's and Brazil's successes, but also to low-income countries, it is imperative to assess necessary conditions for successful mitigation. The key criterion is good governance. If the government is unable to credibly implement a policy, no NAMA will perform. This puts a lot of doubt on strategies to reduce deforestation, as there is generally a correlation between deforestation rates and bad governance. But even if government performance is generally promising, the availability of domestic producers of technology contributing to emission reduction is important to achieve persistent mitigation efforts. Building mitigation effort solely on imported technology will not work in the long term.

Bredenkamp and Patillo (2010) assume that mitigation financing would primarily be in the form of concessional and non-concessional loans, while adaptation would only be financed through grants. Proactive adaptation requires good planning capacity of government agencies and a full understanding of vulnerability. In countries with highly skewed income distribution and small political elites, adaptation finance will not flow to the most vulnerable.

Overall, mitigation and adaptation capacity is clearly linked to the level of development of a country. Expecting public mitigation and adaptation financing to succeed also in countries with bad governance and low levels of development would be expecting miracles. Even market mechanisms have rarely been able to perform in badly governed countries (see Chapter 1 for such an exception: the unexpected CDM success in Honduras).

5 Will market mechanisms or public funds prevail?

The question that pervades this book is whether market mechanisms or public funds are more appropriate means of climate finance. Both routes of climate finance have their role to play. Glemarec (2011: 43) rightly argues that a successful climate finance instrument has to be 'loud', i.e. it needs to substantially affect businesses' investment risk–reward profiles. On the other hand, the instrument also needs to be 'long', i.e. businesses have to be confident in instrument stability and clear with regard to the circumstances under which instruments are reviewed and possibly changed. Two minor criteria are credible means of enforcement, which applies mainly to instruments that provide a 'stick', and simplicity of the instrument. Van Melle *et al.* (2011) urge use of a mix of public and private financing to share the costs and risks of projects and programmes.

Market mechanisms can provide a powerful incentive for mitigation and – given political will – should also be applicable for adaptation. A key formal argument against them is that they contribute to reaching emissions and adaptation commitments of industrialized countries and should thus not be counted as climate finance, because climate finance should be 'additional' to any financial flows generated by compliance. Bredenkamp and Patillo (2010) implicitly accept this argument as their climate finance proposal does not count flows generated by the market mechanisms. However, in climate negotiations most countries see market mechanisms as a key part of climate finance.

The performance of market mechanisms is contested by some non-governmental organizations (see Friends of the Earth (2010) for a good summary of such arguments and their views on climate finance in general) as well as some academics. Neuhoff *et al.* (2010: 4) argue that market mechanisms do not provide sufficient incentives for innovation because of spill-overs or because regulatory frameworks limit upside profit opportunities. However, the same – or even more – applies to public finance that just covers mitigation costs and thus does not allow for any upside. According to Neuhoff *et al.*, time constraints limit the number of informed decisions by entrepreneurs and thus prevent implementation of otherwise profitable action. But market mechanisms provide direct awareness for such options. Where Neuhoff *et al.* (2010) are right is that regulatory uncertainty creates risks for investors and thus the market incentive is not generating changes in long-term investments. But again, this uncertainty also exists in the case of public finance programmes, whose long-term future depends on political decisions as well.

The force of market mechanisms is corroborated by the case of the CDM, which quickly harnessed mitigation projects in developing countries (see Chapter 1). However, they do not work in a vacuum – their incentives depend on the price per emission credit or allowance. This price depends on the demand for credits/allowances. While the initial price surge in the EU ETS was unexpected, since 2006 optimistic forecasts about persistent increases of allowance prices have not materialized and the early peaks have not been reached again. After Copenhagen, the willingness to set-up strong policy regimes that provide substantial demand for the market mechanisms has declined considerably. A pure 'pledge and review' system will be unable to provide sufficient demand to generate high prices. As Chapter 1 has shown, only the high price of the EU allowances in 2005 and 2006 mobilized the CDM market. Thus the ability of market mechanisms to contribute to climate finance is directly contingent on the political will to set stringent emission commitments.

A big advantage of market mechanisms is that they can only function properly if audited independently. This requires high transparency and strengthens accountability. The performance is thus likely to be higher than in the case of public funds spent in an opaque manner and without external evaluation. However, market mechanisms have not been successful in wholesale transformations of countries' energy systems. One reason may be that the CDM has focused on specific projects. But even the EU ETS – which applies to the bulk of CO_2 emissions from power production and industry – has not been able to change the structure of the European power production system. One key reason is that the carbon price is not high enough to justify a shift from fossil fuel to renewable-energy investment. But even if the price was high enough, companies might not believe that the system will survive in the long term, or think that carbon prices could fall again. Such thinking can only be dispelled if policy-makers credibly commit to a long-term future of the trading scheme. Therefore, in 2009, the EU Commission extended the EU ETS until 2020. This long-term perspective has been crucial to keep the price of EU allowances at a relatively high level despite a visible oversupply of allowances in the 2008–2012 period.

While upscaling of market mechanisms is currently being attempted in developing countries to cover sectors or entire nations, the crucial question of incentives for private sector players needs to be kept in mind (see Chapter 6). An upscaling needs to be thought through carefully. It will certainly not be a 'silver bullet' and requires a credible institutional structure.

Market mechanisms can also become the source of public funds, as the example of the Adaptation Fund – which is financed by a levy on the CDM (see Chapter 4) – shows. An expansion of the levy to all market mechanisms, including a domestic emissions trading system, and an increase of its rate could lead to considerable funding volumes. If the €160 billion turnover of the global carbon market had been taxed at 5 per cent, €8 billion would have been collected. Even larger volumes can be collected if emissions allowances are auctioned and the revenues allocated to climate finance.

Neuhoff *et al.* (2010: 8) provide a useful taxonomy of public climate finance instruments, ranging from upfront grants over funding during operation, provision of equity and loans to pure risk coverage. Usually, such instruments need to be administered by a public institution. Such institutions need governance procedures; they have been highly contested between donors and recipients of funding. Donors want to retain control, whereas recipients do not want to be constrained by donor interests. Due to these governance challenges, classical public funds are much slower than market mechanisms with regards to project implementation. Between 2002 and 2007, the GEF needed more than four years on average to approve projects, which was done on a first-come, first-served basis. The change to a formal resource allocation system, which occurred in 2007, did not improve this situation (GEF Evaluation Office 2010). Decision-making of institutions allocating public funds will be more political than that of market mechanisms (e.g. the country cap for projects under the Adaptation Fund, discussed in Chapter 4). Public funds generally suffer from the challenge to explain to the electorate why money should be spent abroad instead of domestically. Coordination is also a problem that is difficult to resolve. Thornton (2010) shows that in none of five Asian countries examined did the external climate finance funders coordinate their activities. Ghosh (2010) proposes that development banks should compete to become more efficient and better coordinated, as funding should be prioritized according to project revenues, whereas responsibility of monitoring should lie on the shoulders of market participants.

While it becomes more and more fashionable to discuss purely private finance flows in the context of climate finance (see, e.g. Mathews and Kidney (2010)), who believe that by some miracle institutional investors would be willing to issue climate bonds without any public subsidy), none of their supporters can provide an argument for how they can be mobilized without a subsidy element. But many analysts propose a mix of different finance sources. UNEP and Partners (2009) suggest several types of public finance mechanisms aiming to harness private finance – country risk guarantees, NAMA implementation risk insurance and currency risk hedges. This should be supplemented with low-carbon project development companies and public financiers taking 'first loss' equity stakes in carbon funds. Glemarec (2011: 98) recommends policy-makers 'to blend domestic and international, public and private, concessional, and grant resources to finance the design and implementation of the selected mix of public policies to catalyse climate finance'. While this sounds good on paper, it requires a highly informed decision-making process to avoid the country eventually becoming stuck with a complicated financing mix that is expensive and does not provide the correct incentive structure. Neuhoff *et al.* (2010: 32) propose an agreement on a social value of carbon that should drive all funding decisions, even if funding decisions are decentralized. Thornton (2010) stresses that the experiences of five Asian countries in climate finance show that specific institutional requirements of external funding sources can be inconsistent with the roles and responsibilities of host-country institutions. Furthermore, a lot of climate finance flows are supply-driven and not truly needs-based. One should also not forget that overly sophisticated blending of finance sources has contributed to the recent financial crisis.

6 Future climate crises and their impacts on climate finance

In a scenario of further reduced salience of climate policy and an unravelling of the international climate policy regime, mitigation efforts could falter for at least a decade. Thus, climate change would remain unchecked, and it would become likely that meteorological extreme events would increase in frequency and intensity. If such events hit major population centres in an industrialized or advanced developing country, this could lead to a reaction of the electorate clamouring for prevention of further events of this type. If the threat is seen as sufficiently strong, policy-makers might have a window of opportunity to mobilize a war-like effort. Given that classical mitigation through GHG emission reduction requires a substantial amount of time and will be costly, policy-makers will find alternatives attractive that take immediate effect and require a limited amount of resources. 'Solar radiation management' through putting SO_2 into the stratosphere or whitening clouds above the ocean through spraying of sea water could become such an alternative and provide 'climate remediation'. A crash programme could be financed by a single country, but indirect effects on other countries might be severe and therefore it is likely that solar radiation management would be controlled through an international treaty. Once the solar radiation management path is embarked upon, classical climate finance would lose its purpose. Emission reduction would become pointless and adaptation no longer required, as the 'world's thermostat' could be controlled by man. But the brave new world of climate management is likely to hold many nasty surprises, and thus it is by no means clear that this path will be taken.

7 A roadmap for climate finance

While the target to mobilize US$100 billion of climate finance per year might prove as elusive as the goal to provide 0.7 per cent of industrialized country GDP for development finance, there are several promising avenues for climate finance that would allow reaching annual flows of US$10–20 billion, i.e. one order of magnitude less. Despite the reduced magnitude, all of them require a political willingness to engage in serious mitigation measures, preferably coordinated globally. It would also need to be ensured that adaptation receives a sufficiently large share of climate finance.

From an incentive point of view, mitigation and adaptation projects in developing countries would be best promoted by a suite of market mechanisms based on stringent emissions commitments and adaptation targets of countries with a high level of development. Ideally, the project-based approach of the CDM should be continued when it comes to large-scale mitigation projects in the industrial and energy sectors. Dispersed mitigation potential in the household, commercial and transport sectors could be best mobilized by a policy crediting approach (see discussion of NAMA crediting in Chapter 7). Adaptation projects should be mobilized by a market mechanism as well (see the detailed concept in Chapter 8).

Mobilizing annual resource flows of US$10 billion each for mitigation and adaptation through these channels should be manageable (Project Catalyst (2009) also estimates the same order of magnitude). As that the current CDM has mobilized around 150 million CERs per year at a price of €10–15, it has generated annual flows of US$2–3 billion. Given stringent emission commitments driving demand, the price could easily double or even triple. A doubling of the annual CER volume should not be problematic, especially if the programmatic approach is taking off. And if policy crediting is added, the mitigation market mechanisms could generate finance flows of US$20–25 billion per year. For adaptation, the situation is a bit more challenging, as there is no experience with setting adaptation targets at national levels. Probably, over an initial phase of 5–10 years, a 5 per cent levy on all transactions of the market mechanisms could raise the required funds, which would then be allocated in a tender procedure. Alternatively, taxes on international transport could provide this amount, but the recent fight about the inclusion of air transport in the EU ETS shows that opposition would be fierce.

Public funding would also have its role in providing subsidies for non-quantifiable ‘soft’ activities, as well as capacity building and awareness raising. Especially in the context of adaptation, soft activities are likely to play an important role to change behaviour of populations exposed to extreme weather events. A coordinated soft-activity strategy will likely reduce the overall need for hard, technologically oriented adaptation projects. Assuming that reaching each citizen would cost as much as marketing a mobile phone (Turel and Serenko (2006) cite costs of US$180 per customer in industrialized countries, whereas Pyramid Research (2006) quotes costs in developing countries that are 10–20 times lower), covering the entire 5.5 billion people living in developing countries through an adaptation awareness campaign would cost US$50–100 billion. Of course, an in-depth awareness-raising strategy would probably be more expensive.

A crucial, hitherto neglected aspect of climate finance is the link with supportive policy action in recipient countries. For the market mechanisms this would mean that they work best in host countries with a supportive domestic framework, as shown by the case studies in Chapter 3. Likewise, public funding should be directly linked with governance. While recipients will not like such a linkage, it is indispensable to prevent low performance that would lead to a backlash against public climate finance in donor countries.

Summing up, climate finance needs to build on two pillars: one strong market mechanism pillar for quantifiable mitigation and adaptation activities; and a public finance pillar for non-quantifiable, but important ancillary measures. Each of these pillars carries the weight of a different part of the global mitigation and adaptation building. But believing that reaching a certain volume of funding flows to developing countries will be sufficient to address the climate change problem is a fallacy. We need to apply stringent performance criteria and evaluate the results of funding flows. Otherwise, our edifice will crumble when the first storm hits it.

References

Bredenkamp, H. and Patillo, C. (2010) 'Financing the response to climate change', IMF. Online. Available: www.imf.org/external/pubs/ft/spn/2010/spn1006.pdf (accessed 20 April 2011).

Buen, J. and Michaelowa, A. (2009) 'View from the inside: markets for carbon credits to fight climate change – addressing corruption risks proactively', in D. Zinnbauer, R. Dobson and K. Despota (eds) *Global Corruption Report 2009: Corruption and the Private Sector*, Cambridge: Cambridge University Press, pp. 41–5.

Friends of the Earth (2010) 'Clearing the air: moving on from carbon trading to real climate solutions'. Online. Available: www.foe.co.uk/resource/reports/clearing_air.pdf (accessed 20 April 2011).

GEF Evaluation Office (2010) 'OPS4: progress toward impact – fourth overall performance study of the GEF', Global Environment Facility Evaluation Office.

Ghosh, A. (2010) 'Harnessing the power shift: clean technologies, innovative finance and the challenge for climate governance'. Online. Available: www.princeton.edu/~pcglobal/conferences/GLF/ghosh_glf.pdf (accessed 20 July 2011).

Glemarec, Y. (2011) *Catalysing Climate Finance: A Guidebook on Policy and Financing Options to Support Green, Low-emission and Climate-resilient Development*, New York: UN Development Programme.

Mathews, J. and Kidney, S. (2010) 'Climate bonds: mobilizing private financing for carbon management', *Carbon Management*, 1 (1): 9–13.

Neuhoff, K., Fankhauser, S., Guerin, E., Hourcade J.-C., Jackson, H., Rajan, R. and Ward, J. (2010) 'Structuring international financial support for climate change mitigation in developing countries', *DIW Discussion Paper*, 976. Online. Available: www.diw.de/documents/publikationen/73/diw_01.c.347626.de/dp976.pdf (accessed 20 July 2011).

Newell, P., Timmons Roberts, J., Boyd, E. and Huq, S. (2009) 'Billions at stake in climate finance: four key lessons'. International Institute for Environment and Development. Online. Available: http://ccaps.strausscenter.org/system/research_items/pdfs/21/original.pdf?1282152999.

Project Catalyst (2009) 'Scaling up climate finance', ClimateWorks Foundation. Online. Available: www.project-catalyst.info/images/publications/climate_finance.pdf (accessed 1 August 2011).

Pyramid Research (2006) 'Subscriber acquisition costs are ten to twenty times lower in developed markets, says Pyramid Research', *Business Wire*. Online. Available: www.businesswire.com/news/home/20060928005729/en/Subscriber-Acquisition-Costs-Ten-Twenty-Times-Developed (accessed 31 July 2011).

Stadelmann, M., Castro, P. and Michaelowa, A. (2011) 'Is there a leverage paradox in climate finance?' Climate Strategies. Online. Available: www.climatestrategies.org/component/reports/category/71/324.html (accessed 31 July 2011).

Thornton, N. (2010) 'Realising development effectiveness: making the most of climate change finance in Asia and the Pacific', Capacity Development for Development Effectiveness Facility. Online. Available: www.oecd.org/dataoecd/23/51/46518692.pdf.

Turel, O. and Serenko, A. (2006) 'Satisfaction with mobile services in Canada: an empirical investigation', *Telecommunications Policy*, 30: 314–31.

UNEP and Partners (2009) 'Catalysing low-carbon growth in developing economies: Public Finance Mechanisms to scale up private sector investment in climate solutions'. Online. Available: www.unep.org/PDF/PressReleases/Public_financing_mechanisms_report.pdf.

Van Melle, T., Höhne, N. and Ward, M. (2011) 'International climate financing: from Cancún to a 2°C stabilisation pathway', Ecofys. Online. Available: www.ecofys.com/files/files/climate_financing_after_cancun_20110204.pdf.

Glossary

Absolute emissions Greenhouse gas emissions measured in tonnes of **CO_2 equivalent**.

Adaptation Adjustment in natural or human systems in response to actual or expected climatic stimuli or their effects, which moderates harm or exploits beneficial opportunities (text from www.ipcc.ch/pdf/assessment-report/ar4/wg2/ar4-wg2-app.pdf).

Adaptation Fund The Adaptation Fund is a Fund established under the **Kyoto Protocol** in 2001 and officially launched in 2007. The fund finances adaptation projects and programmes in developing countries that are parties to the Kyoto Protocol. It is mainly financed with 2 per cent of the **CERs** issued for **CDM** projects (text mainly from www.adaptation-fund.org/about). Chapter 4 discusses the activities of the Adaptation Fund.

Adaptation market mechanism An adaption market mechanism is based on the creation of tradeable units in form of '**saved wealth**' or '**saved health**' through a governmental regulation in order to increase adaptive activities. The government would quantify an **adaptation target** and allocate it to entities. These entities can then invest in adaptation projects themselves, or buy offsets from specific adaptation service providers. Chapter 8 describes a possible design of an adaptation market mechanism.

Adaptation target In order to provide demand for tradeable units under an **adaptation market mechanism** a government can define the target in the form of the number of adaptation units to be provided by entities covered by the target.

Additionality Additionality is given if a **CDM** project is not business-as-usual, which it has to prove through an investment test or a barrier test. Non-additional projects lead to an increase in global greenhouse gas emissions. For additionality relating to climate finance, see **new and additional**.

Aid – bilateral, multilateral See **official development assistance (ODA)**.

Alliance of Small Island States (AOSIS) The Alliance of Small Island States (AOSIS) is an intergovernmental organization of 42 low-lying coastal and small island countries. Established in 1990, AOSIS has been active in the international climate negotiations from their start and, through clever negotiations, managed to get seats on all relevant bodies of the **UNFCCC** and the **Kyoto Protocol**.

Annex-I countries The Annex I of the **UNFCCC** consists of a list of 41 countries (pre-1992 OECD members plus selected countries in transition) that agreed to take the lead in stabilizing the greenhouse gas concentrations in the atmosphere at a level that would prevent dangerous anthropogenic interference with the climate system.

Annex-B countries The Annex B of the **Kyoto Protocol** consists of a list of 39 countries which is almost identical with **Annex I** of the **UNFCCC** (Turkey and Belarus are members of Annex I but not of Annex B). Annex-B countries have taken legally binding greenhouse gas emissions commitments for the five-year period 2008–2012.

Backstop technology A backstop technology is a technology providing a complete replacement of fossil fuels at a constant level of marginal costs. For details, see Chapter 10.

Bali Plan of Action The Bali Plan of Action agreed at **COP 13 in Bali** in 2007 identified **COP 15 in Copenhagen** as the deadline for the post-2012 climate negotiations and defined the concept of nationally appropriate mitigation actions (**NAMAs**) for developing countries. It also defined the four 'building blocks' for these negotiations: **adaptation**, **mitigation**, **technology transfer** and **climate finance**.

Bali Road Map Besides the **Bali Plan of Action**, the Bali Roadmap included an agreement on a deadline for the negotiations on the extension/replacement of the Kyoto Protocol at **COP 15**, the launch of the **Adaptation Fund**, as well as decisions on technology transfer and on reducing emissions from deforestation (**REDD**).

Baseline A baseline is the reference from which an alternative outcome can be measured, e.g. a scenario without a **CDM** project is used as a reference in the analysis of a CDM project. Generally, a baseline is identical with the business-as-usual development.

Baseline and credit Under a baseline-and-credit mechanism, an **emissions target** based on **absolute emissions** or **emission intensity** is set against a **baseline** (which can be business-as-usual or some fraction thereof) and credits are created for activities that reduce emissions below the baseline. Activities with emissions above the baseline have to buy such credits. Baseline and credit is the main **carbon market mechanism** design besides **cap-and-trade**.

Baseline and monitoring methodologies Baseline and monitoring methodologies for **CDM** projects need to be formally approved by the **CDM Executive Board**. They calculate the emissions that would have been created in the most plausible alternative scenario to the implementation of the project activity, called the baseline scenario, and define how relevant data necessary for calculating the actual emission reductions from the project are measured.

Benchmark Benchmarks are default values for **baseline** emissions that are usually defined from a group of comparable installations.

Cancún Agreements The Cancún Agreements are a set of decisions adopted at the **16th Conference of the Parties** to the UNFCCC (**COP 16**). The Agreements import the essential elements of the **Copenhagen Accord** into the **UNFCCC**, including a collective commitment by industrialized countries for US$30 billion in '**new and additional**' resources (**fast-start finance**) in 2010–2012 to help developing countries reduce emissions, preserve forests and adapt to climate change; a goal of mobilizing US$100 billion per year in public and private finance by 2020 to address developing country needs (**long-term finance**); **mitigation** pledges and operational elements such as a new **Green Climate Fund** for developing countries; a system of '**international consultation and analysis**' to help verify developing countries' **NAMAs** and an aspirational goal of limiting global temperature increase to 2°C. Agreement was not reached on the more difficult questions of if, when and in what form countries will take binding emissions commitments. Also, the final outcome sets no clear path toward a binding agreement (text mainly from www.pewclimate.org/docUploads/cancun-climate-conference-cop16-summary.pdf).

Cap-and-trade An absolute overall emissions cap is set by the government and distributed to emitters. The covered emitters must reduce their emissions below their cap level or acquire **emission allowances** to cover emissions in excess of their cap. Emitters with a surplus of allowances can sell them on the market. The allowances can be auctioned or allocated free of charge according to certain parameters. If the quantity of allowances is below the emissions level of the covered entities, scarcity is created, which will create a price for carbon. The **EU ETS** is the most famous cap-and-trade scheme.

Carbon credit A carbon credit is a tradeable permit generated by a project that reduces greenhouse gas emissions. Carbon credits can be created by the project-based mechanisms the **CDM** and **JI** under the **Kyoto Protocol**. See also **emission credit**.

Carbon dioxide (CO_2) CO_2 is a naturally occurring gas, and a by-product of burning fossil fuels or biomass, of land-use changes and of industrial processes. It is the principal anthropogenic greenhouse gas that affects Earth's radiative balance. It is the reference gas against which other greenhouse gases are measured and therefore it has a global warming potential of 1 (Text from www.ipcc.ch/publications_and_data/ar4/wg3/en/annex1sglossary-a-d.html).

Carbon intensity The amount of emissions of CO_2 per unit of GDP. See also **emissions intensity**.

Carbon market mechanism Any policy instrument that allows trading of greenhouse gas units, be it under a **baseline-and-credit,** a **cap-and-trade** or a project-based **offset** system.

CDM Executive Board The highest rule-making body of the **CDM**, consisting of ten members and ten alternates elected by the Meeting of Parties to the **Kyoto Protocol**. It is supported by over 150 staff of the UNFCCC Secretariat in Bonn.

CER (Certified Emission Reduction) A tradeable unit created by a **CDM** project and issued by the **CDM Executive Board**, equal to one metric tonne of CO_2-equivalent emissions reduced or sequestered.

Clean Development Mechanism (CDM) The CDM is one of the three flexible mechanisms of the **Kyoto Protocol** and defined in its Art. 12. It pursues the two objectives of promoting sustainable development in developing countries and of helping industrialized countries to reach their emissions commitments. Projects that reduce greenhouse gas emissions in developing countries generate **CERs** that can be credited towards the emission targets of industrialized countries. The CDM is supervised by the **CDM Executive Board**. See Chapter 1.

Climate finance The term climate finance is used to describe all financial mechanisms under the **UNFCCC** and the **Kyoto Protocol**, including the **CDM** and **official development assistance (ODA)**. Besides these channels, **climate funds** are currently proliferating: funds under the UNFCCC include the **Special Climate Change Fund** for financing capacity building and adaptation, the Least Developed Countries Fund and the **Adaptation Fund**. Additional funds exist in other institutional settings, including the World Bank's **Climate Investment Funds** (text mainly from http://belfercenter.ksg.harvard.edu/files/HPICA_Issue_Brief_2_FINAL.pdf).

Climate funds See **climate finance**.

Climate Investment Funds (CIFs) The Climate Investment Funds (CIFs) consist of the Clean Technology Fund and the Strategic Climate Fund. They are administered by the World Bank Group and were established in January 2008 to operate until 2012. The bulk of the total amount of US$6.5 billion provided by 14 industrialized countries is dedicated to supporting the deployment of clean-energy technologies and making transformative reductions in greenhouse gas emission trajectories in developing countries (text mainly from www.wri.org/stories/2010/11/learning-climate-investment-funds).

CO_2 See **Carbon dioxide**.

CO_2 equivalent The emission of a non-CO_2 greenhouse gas, converted into CO_2 using the **Global Warming Potential** agreed in the **Kyoto Protocol** for such conversions. For example, 1 tonne of HFC-23 is equivalent to 11,700 tonnes of CO_2.

Coding In social sciences, coding is an analytical process in which quantitative or qualitative data are categorized in order to facilitate analysis.

Commitment period See **Kyoto Protocol**.

Common practice Under the **CDM**, proposed projects have to show that they are not common practice in the host country, i.e. that projects of this type have not been implemented in large numbers without applying for the CDM.

Conference of the Parties (COP) The Conference of the Parties to the UNFCCC is the highest body in international climate policy. It has met at least once per year since 1995 (see **COP 13**, **COP 15** and **COP 16**).

COP 13 in Bali **13th Conference of the Parties** to the UNFCCC in December 2007 in Bali. For outcomes see **Bali Plan of Action**.

COP 15 in Copenhagen **15th Conference of the Parties** to the UNFCCC in December 2009 in Copenhagen. For outcomes see **Copenhagen Accords**.

COP 16 in Cancún **16th Conference of the Parties** to the UNFCCC in December 2010 in Cancún. For outcomes see **Cancún Agreements**.

Copenhagen Accord The Copenhagen Accord is a political agreement struck by Brazil, China, India, South Africa and the United States at **COP 15 in Copenhagen**. It was hastily pieced together when utter failure of COP 15 became likely and provides for explicit emission pledges by all the major economies – including, for the first time, China and other major developing countries. Due to the formal opposition of a number of countries, instead of adopting the accord, the COP just 'took note' of it and opened the way for governments to individually sign on. Key elements of the Copenhagen Accord were later formalized in the **Cancún Agreements** (text mainly from www.pewclimate.org/docUploads/copenhagen-cop15-summary.pdf).

Crediting period The time during which a project under a project-based mechanism can generate emission credits. Under the **CDM**, the crediting period is either ten years without renewal or seven years, with the possibility of being renewed twice.

Desert Greening Programme (DGP) In case of the emergence of a **super transformational technology** that reduces electricity generation costs below the cost of fossil fuel-based electricity, revenues from a **power transformation levy (PTL)** could be used for a Desert Greening Programme, which would finance sea water desalination and irrigation of large desert areas. Such a programme should focus on countries that so far have benefited from fossil fuel exports.

Designated national authority (DNA) A designated national authority is a national institution that authorizes and approves CDM projects in that country. In CDM host countries, it assesses whether proposed projects assist the host country in achieving its sustainable development goals. If it finds this to be the case, it provides a letter of approval, which is a prerequisite for registration of the project by the **CDM Executive Board**. Countries that acquire **CERs** need to provide an approval letter by their DNA.

Designated operational entity (DOE) A designated operational entity is an independent auditor accredited by the **CDM Executive Board** to validate whether project proposals are consistent with CDM rules or verify emissions reductions achieved by implemented projects.

Direct access approach Direct access is a funding modality used in the **Adaptation Fund**, in which domestic entities with legal personality in developing countries have the status of **implementing entities** within the project or programme cycle and ensure fiduciary standards. A direct access approach stands in contrast with the traditional, indirect funding approach, in the sense that it does not require intermediary **implementing entities** such as multilateral institutions to apply for and access financial resources.

E+/E– rule The **CDM Executive Board** has clarified that, in general, a baseline scenario takes into account relevant mandatory national and/or sectoral policies and circumstances, such as sectoral reform initiatives, local fuel availability, power sector expansion plans and the economic situation in the project sector. However, there are two exceptions:

- E+ policies: national and/or sectoral policies or regulations that give comparative advantages to more emissions-intensive technologies or fuels over less emissions-intensive technologies or fuels. For these types of policies, only policies implemented before 11 December 1997 can be taken into account when developing the baseline scenario.
- E– policies: national and/or sectoral policies or regulations that give comparative advantages to less emissions-intensive technologies over more emissions-intensive technologies (e.g. public subsidies to promote the diffusion of renewable energy or to finance energy-efficiency programmes). For these types of policies, only policies implemented before 11 November 2001 need to be taken into account when developing the baseline scenario.

Emission allowances Tradeable units under a **cap-and-trade** scheme.

Emission credits Tradeable units issued from **baseline-and-credit** schemes.

Emission intensity The volume of greenhouse gas emissions per unit of income (GDP or GNI). See also **Carbon intensity**.

Emission target An emission target can be voluntary or mandatory. Mandatory targets exist for **Annex-B countries** under the **Kyoto Protocol**.

Emission trading Another term for a **carbon market mechanism.**

Energy Development Programme (EDP) In case of the emergence of a **super transformational technology** that reduces electricity generation costs below the cost of fossil fuel-based electricity, revenues from a **power transformation levy (PTL)** could be used for an Energy Development Programme to build power plants in countries with **suppressed electricity demand.**

Equity The value of an ownership interest in property, including shareholders' equity in a business (text from http://en.wikipedia.org/wiki/Equity).

European Emissions Trading Scheme (EU ETS) The EU ETS is a **cap-and-trade** system that covers all EU member states, including those that are not **Annex-B countries**. It was introduced in 2005 and covers over 12,000 installations. Legislation to extend it to 2020 was agreed in 2009. The EU ETS has the highest liquidity and turnover of all **carbon market mechanisms** and is a key driver for the **CDM**, as it allows import of **CERs** up to certain thresholds.

Extreme weather event An event that is rare within its statistical reference distribution at a particular place, e.g. floods and droughts. Definitions of 'rare' vary, but an extreme weather event would normally be as rare or rarer than the tenth or ninetieth percentile. Therefore, what is called 'extreme weather' varies from place to place (text from www.ipcc.ch/publications_and_data/ar4/wg2/en/annexessglossary-e-o.html).

Fast-start finance Fast-start finance describes the collective pledge by industrialized countries at **COP 15** to provide '**new and additional** resources, including forestry and investments through international institutions, approaching US$30 billion for the period 2010–2012 with balanced allocation between adaptation and mitigation'. Fast-start finance is seen as a testing ground for longer-term arrangements for climate finance. See Chapter 5.

Feed-in tariffs A guaranteed price per unit of electricity for a specific type of (mostly renewable) electricity fed into the grid by non-utility generators that includes a subsidy compared to the wholesale electricity price.

Free riding Benefitting from a public good without contributing resources for its creation or preservation.

Global Environment Facility (GEF) The GEF was established in 1991 and is a multilateral financial institution to fund projects and programmes related to biodiversity, climate change, international waters, land degradation, the ozone layer and persistent organic pollutants in developing countries. In the GEF council, its main governing body, developing countries have half of the votes, while industrialized countries and countries in transition countries have the other (text mainly from www.ipcc.ch/publications_and_data/ar4/wg3/en/annex1sglossary-e-i.html).

Global warming potential (GWP) The 'exchange rate' between CO_2 and the other greenhouse gases. Its value depends on the time horizon chosen. The Kyoto Protocol uses GWPs as specified in the IPCC Second Assessment Report for a 100-year time horizon.

Green Climate Fund (GCF) At **COP 16 in Cancún**, the international community adopted a decision in which it decided to establish a Green Climate Fund, to be designated as an operating entity of the financial mechanism of the Convention. A significant share of the longer-term pledge of US$100 billion annually by 2020 should flow through this Green Climate Fund (text from http://unfccc.int/cooperation_and_support/financial_mechanism/green_climate_fund/items/5869.php).

Greenhouse gas (GHG) Greenhouse gases absorb and emit radiation at specific wavelengths within the spectrum of infrared radiation emitted by the Earth's surface, the atmosphere and clouds. This property causes the greenhouse effect. Water vapour (H_2O), carbon dioxide (CO_2), nitrous oxide (N_2O), methane (CH_4) and ozone (O_3) are the primary greenhouse gases in the Earth's atmosphere. Moreover, there are a number of entirely human-made greenhouse gases in the atmosphere, such as the halocarbons and other chlorine- and bromine-containing substances, dealt with under the Montreal Protocol. Besides carbon dioxide, nitrous oxide and methane, the **Kyoto Protocol** deals with the greenhouse gases sulphur hexafluoride, hydrofluorocarbons and perfluorocarbons (text from www.ipcc.ch/publications_and_data/ar4/wg3/en/annex1sglossary-e-i.html).

Green NAMA Bond A bond to be issued by developing countries to finance **NAMAs**. Attractiveness for investors is increased by a carbon credit component. In case the NAMA does not perform, the interest rate will be increased. In the case of default of host countries, guarantees from **multilateral development banks** kick in. See Chapter 9 for a detailed description.

Gross national income (GNI) The gross national income is the market value of all products and services produced in one year by labour and property supplied by the residents of a country. Unlike gross domestic product (GDP), which defines production based on the geographical location of production, GNI allocates production based on ownership (text from http://en.wikipedia.org/wiki/Gross_national_product).

Halocarbons A collective term for the group of partially halogenated organic species, including the chlorofluorocarbons (CFCs), hydrochlorofluorocarbons (HCFCs), hydrofluorocarbons (HFCs), halons, methyl chloride, methyl bromide, etc. Many of the halocarbons have large **global warming potentials**. The chlorine- and bromine-containing halocarbons also deplete the ozone layer (text from www.ipcc.ch/publications_and_data/ar4/wg3/en/annex1sglossary-e-i.html).

Hardware project **Adaptation** projects involving infrastructure development, improved health protection or agricultural activities, in contrast to 'soft measures' whose results are difficult to quantify in terms of the proposed adaptation trading units, such as capacity building, raising awareness, building institutions or launching planning processes.

HCFC-22 Chlorodifluoromethane or difluoromonochloromethane is better known as HCFC-22 or R-22. The gas was commonly used as a propellant and in air conditioning applications, but is being phased out in these applications due to its ozone depletion potential and status as a potent greenhouse gas. See also **halocarbons** (text from http://en.wikipedia.org/wiki/Chlorodifluoromethane).

HFC-23 Greenhouse gas that is a by-product during the manufacture of **HCFC-22**. See also **halocarbons** (text from http://en.wikipedia.org/wiki/Fluoroform).

Higher-hanging fruits Emissions reduction activities in developing countries that are more expensive to realize than the so-called **low-hanging fruits** and that address reductions beyond the **no-lose target**.

High-level Advisory Group on Climate Change Financing An expert group established by the UN Secretary-General. The Group studied potential sources of revenue that will enable achievement of the level of climate change financing that was promised during **COP 15**. They published their final report on 5 November 2010.

Host country In the **CDM** context, 'host country' denotes the country in which the CDM project is implemented.

Implementing entities Implementing entities are the national legal entities and multilateral organizations accredited by the **Adaptation Fund** Board. In order to access funding, developing countries must either use a national (see **Direct Access approach**) or a multilateral implementing entity. Both national and multilateral implementing agencies have to meet certain fiduciary standards adopted by the Adaptation Fund Board (text from http://adaptation-fund.org/page/implementing-entities).

Inflated baselines **Baselines** used in **carbon market mechanisms** that are above the business-as-usual emissions scenario.

Intellectual property rights (IPRs) Intellectual property rights usually give the creator of an idea an exclusive right over the use of his/her creation for a certain period of time. Intellectual property rights can be divided into two areas: copyrights that concern the rights of authors of literary and artistic works; and industrial property rights (text from www.wto.org/english/tratop_e/trips_e/intel1_e.htm).

Intergovernmental Panel on Climate Change (IPCC) The Intergovernmental Panel on Climate Change is the leading international body for the assessment of climate change science. It was established by the UN Environment Programme (UNEP) and the World Meteorological Organization (WMO) in 1988, and it has so far produced four Assessment Reports (1990, 1995, 2001 and 2007). The fifth assessment report is planned for release by 2014 (text from www.ipcc.ch/organization/organization.shtml).

International consultation and analysis (ICA) **ICA is a term that relates to measurement, reporting and verification (MRV)** and is used for the first time in the **Copenhagen Accord**; it was confirmed in the **Cancún Agreements**. The emission targets of **Annex-I countries**, and their delivery of finance for developing countries, will be measured, reported and verified 'in accordance with existing and any further guidelines' from the **Conference of the Parties**, while actions by developing countries 'will be subject to their domestic' MRV, with the results reported in biennial national communications. The information reported will be subject to 'international consultation and analysis under clearly defined guidelines that will ensure that national sovereignty is respected'. Developing country actions receiving international support will be subject to international MRV under guidelines adopted by the COP (text mainly from www.pewclimate.org/docUploads/copenhagen-cop15-summary.pdf).

International Supervisory Body (ISB) In the proposal for a power transformation levy (PTL) in Chapter 10, the funds obtained from the tax would be managed centrally by an International Supervisory Body.

Joint Implementation (JI) **Project-based** mechanism under the **Kyoto Protocol**. In contrast to the CDM, JI projects can only be implemented in **Annex-B countries**.

Kyoto Protocol (KP) The Kyoto Protocol is an international agreement under the **UNFCCC**. The major feature of the Kyoto Protocol is that it sets binding targets for **Annex-B countries** for reducing greenhouse gas (GHG) emissions. These amount to an average reduction of 5.2 per cent against 1990 levels over the five-year period 2008–2012. The major distinction between the Kyoto Protocol and the **UNFCCC** is that while the UNFCCC only encouraged industrialized countries to stabilize GHG emissions, the Protocol commits them to do so. Recognizing that industrialized countries are principally responsible for the current high levels of GHG emissions as a result of more than 150 years of industrial activity, the Protocol places a heavier burden on industrialized nations under the principle of 'common but differentiated responsibilities' (text mainly from http://unfccc.int/kyoto_protocol/items/2830.php).

Least developed country (LDC) Forty-nine countries are currently designated by the United Nations as 'least developed countries'. The list of LDCs is reviewed every three years by the UN Economic and Social Council (ECOSOC). The following three criteria are used: (1) a 'low-income' criterion, based on a three-year average estimate of the **gross national income** (GNI) per capita; (2) a 'human assets weakness' criterion; and (3) an 'economic vulnerability' criterion (text from www.unctad.org/en/docs/ldc2010_en.pdf).

Levelized electricity costs (LEC) The cost of electricity generation taking into account the need to amortize the investment.

Long-term finance Pledge by industrialized countries at **COP 15** and formalized under the **Cancún Agreements**. **Annex-I countries** promise to provide US$100 billion annually by 2020 to support concrete mitigation actions by developing countries that are implemented in a transparent way. These funds would be raised from a mix of public and private sources (text from http://cancun.unfccc.int/financial-technology-and-capacity-building-support/new-long-term-funding-arrangements).

Low-hanging fruits Abatement measures with the lowest abatement costs.

Maladaptation Short-term adaptation that increases vulnerability to longer-term climate change impacts. For example, an irrigation system could be an excellent adaptation as long as groundwater remains available, but will lead to high impacts once the water sources run dry.

Marginal abatement costs (MAC) The cost of one unit of additional mitigation.

Market mechanism Another term for a **carbon market mechanism**

Marrakech Accords Agreements reached at COP 7 in 2002 in Marrakech, establishing a 'rulebook' for implementing the **Kyoto Protocol** with details on **carbon market mechanisms** including the **CDM**, reporting and methodologies, sinks and a compliance regime.

Measurement, reporting, verification (MRV) In order to preserve the credibility of mitigation action, the **Bali Action Plan** provides for measurement, reporting and verification of **NAMAs**, as well as the finance provided by industrialized countries for NAMA implementation. At **COP 15** and **COP 16**, MRV proved to be very contentious. Eventually, the process of **international consultation and analysis** could be agreed on. In a broader sense, MRV is also crucial for the credibility of **carbon market mechanisms**.

Mitigation Technological change and substitution that reduces resource inputs and emissions per unit of output. Although several social, economic and technological policies would produce an emission reduction, with respect to climate change, mitigation means implementing policies to reduce GHG emissions and enhance sinks (text from www.ipcc.ch/publications_and_data/ar4/wg3/en/annex1sglossary-j-p.html).

Multilateral development bank (MDB) Multilateral development banks are institutions that provide financial support and professional advice for economic and social development activities in developing countries. 'Multilateral development bank' typically refers to the World Bank Group and four regional development banks: the African Development Bank, the Asian Development Bank, the European Bank for Reconstruction and Development and the Inter-American Development Bank Group. They have a broad membership, including developing borrower countries and developed donor countries, which is not limited to member countries from the region of a regional development bank (text from http://web.worldbank.org/WBSITE/EXTERNAL/EXTABOUTUS/0,,contentMDK:20040614~menuPK:41699~pagePK:43912~piPK:44037~theSitePK:29708,00.html).

Multilateral environmental agreement (MEA) A multilateral environmental agreement is a legally binding agreement between three or more states relating to the environment. MEAs have been predominantly agreed under the aegis of the UN and after the Stockholm Conference on the Human Environment in 1972.

NAMA registry **COP 16** in 2010 decided to establish a registry to record **NAMAs** seeking international support, and to facilitate matching of finance, technology and capacity-building support to these actions. The NAMA registry will regularly update information on NAMAs seeking support, along with their estimated costs, emission reductions and the anticipated timeframe for implementation. It will also update information on support available from industrialized countries and support provided for NAMAs in developing countries. See Chapter 7.

National climate strategy/low-carbon development or emission strategy (LCDS/LEDS) The name for an integrated national strategy covering different areas of policy related to climate change, energy and development, with the aim to support development in a low-carbon way. Much of the recent interest in such strategies has come as a result of their proposal as a distinct mechanism under the **UNFCCC** at **COP 15** in Copenhagen. Uncertainty persists, however, about their specific content and the manner of implementation; they are currently mostly subsumed under **NAMAs** (text mainly from www.lcds-project.info/pages/what-is-an-lcds.php).

Nationally appropriate mitigation action (NAMA) Nationally appropriate mitigation actions are a concept for delivering, financing and recognizing emission reductions by developing countries in a **post-2012 climate regime**. The concept was first introduced in the **Bali Action Plan** and has given rise to the **NAMA registry**. See Chapter 7.

New and additional The term 'new and additional' is used in the context of industrialized countries providing **fast-start finance** and **long-term finance**

to developing countries. Countries use different baselines for justifying that their funding is 'new and additional'. The most commonly used definitions for 'new and additional' refer to funds beyond '0.7 per cent of GNI spent for ODA' or 'beyond existing funds', while the later definition may refer to climate or development, and past or promised funds. See Chapter 5.

New market mechanisms New **carbon market mechanisms** are potential elements of an international **post-2012** climate policy regime. The concepts underlying the discussion on these new market-based mechanisms for developing countries are **cap-and-trade** and **baseline-and-credit**. Crediting does not impose mandatory targets on a sector or country but rather works with a '**no-lose**' target. Trading on the other hand is based on the concept of **cap-and-trade** and imposes a mandatory reduction target on a certain sector or scheme. Important reasons for new market mechanisms are, inter alia: upscaling global investments in GHG reduction activities; providing a bridge for the transition towards a global carbon market and for the transition from a non-Annex-I to an **Annex-I country**; and overcoming the flaws of project-based **offset** mechanisms.

No-lose target A mitigation target for which a developing country is not punished when not meeting it.

Official development assistance (ODA) Flows of official financing to support the economic development and welfare of developing countries as the main objective, and which are concessional with a grant element of at least 25 per cent (using a fixed 10 per cent rate of discount). ODA flows comprise contributions of donor government agencies to developing countries ('bilateral ODA') and to multilateral institutions (text from http://stats.oecd.org/glossary/detail.asp?ID=6043).

Other official flows (OOF) Transactions by the official sector to countries on the OECD list of aid recipients which are not eligible as **official development assistance**, either because they are not primarily aimed at development, or because they have a grant element of less than 25 per cent (text from http://stats.oecd.org/glossary/detail.asp?ID=1954).

Offset Offsets are tradeable units generated by projects that provide tradeable units in a region where there is no requirement to surrender such units. The **CDM** is the most famous offset mechanism.

Ownership The OECD defines ownership as the effective exercise of a government's authority over development policies and activities, including those that rely on external resources. This means that the government articulates the national development agenda and establishes policies and strategies (text from http://stats.oecd.org/glossary/detail.asp?ID=7238).

Paris Declaration on Aid Effectiveness The Paris Declaration is a document adopted by the international community in 2005 at the OECD-organized Paris High-Level Forum on Aid Effectiveness. It builds on the experiences gained in development aid (see **official development aid**) and is focused on five principles: aid recipients shall forge their own national development strategies with their parliaments and electorates (**ownership**); donors are to support these strategies (alignment) and work to streamline their efforts in-country (harmonization); development policies shall be directed to achieving clear goals and for progress towards these goals to be monitored (results); and donors and recipients will be jointly responsible for achieving these goals (mutual accountability) (text from www.oecd.org/document/18/0,3343,en_2649_3236398_35401554_1_1_1_1,00.html).

Polluter-pays principle This principle was agreed on by the OECD in 1972. Polluters should pay the costs of abating their own environmental pollution – for example, by installation of filters, sanitation plants and other add-on techniques. The extended definition of polluter-pays demands polluters to additionally pay for the damage caused by their residual pollution (eventually also historical pollution) (text from http://srren.ipcc-wg3.de/report/IPCC_SRREN_Annex_I).

Post-2012 agreement By the end of the first commitment period of the **Kyoto Protocol** in 2012, a new international climate policy framework needs to have been negotiated and ratified. Although this deadline can already hardly be met, the legal nature of such a framework is still open. While some industrialized countries are reluctant to commit to a second period of the **Kyoto Protocol** and prefer a framework without binding emission targets (see **Copenhagen Accord**), for many developing countries the continuation of the **Kyoto Protocol** is their most important negotiating goal.

Power transformation levy (PTL) A power transformation levy is a global tax on the deployment of a **super transformation technology (STT)**. Such a levy is suggested as the differential between historical electricity costs and generation costs of the STT. Revenues from the levy can then be used for multiple purposes benefitting the global society. See Chapter 10.

Private good In contrast to public goods, private goods are characterized by exclusivity and rivalry in consumption; i.e. others can be excluded from consumption and the goods deplete the more that is consumed.

Programme of Activities (PoA) A PoA allows bundling **CDM** projects for a period of up to 28 years. The number and sequence of projects developed under the PoA need not to be known ex-ante. Only the generic documentation for the PoA and one typical project need to be validated, all other projects can be added without a further check by the **CDM Executive Board**.

Project and Programme Review Committee (PPRC) The Project and Programme Review Committee (PPRC) is responsible for assisting the **Adaptation Fund** Board in tasks related to reviews in accordance with the guidelines for countries to access resources of the Adaptation Fund, and for providing recommendations and advice to the Board on this issue (text from http://adaptation-fund.org/system/files/PPRCTORs.pdf).

Project-based mechanisms **Carbon market mechanisms** based on **offsets**. To allow the countries that have binding emissions reduction targets under the **Kyoto Protocol** to meet their obligations in the most efficient manner, two project-based mechanisms were developed – the CDM and **Joint Implementation (JI)**.

Project cycle The process from drafting the project idea to the eventual issuance of **emission credits** under **project-based mechanisms**.

Public good Public goods are goods that are non-excludable and non-rival in consumption; i.e. once produced, no one can be excluded from consuming them and consumption does not lead to depletion. Since no one can be excluded from consumption, **free riding** is likely where users of the good are unwilling to pay the producers for the cost of production. Therefore the incentives to produce public goods are often weak.

Reduced emissions from deforestation and forest degradation (REDD) While avoided deforestation was not included in the **CDM**, the realization that forest loss continued unabated led to the integration of avoided deforestation in the **Bali Action Plan**. Since then, industrialized countries have provided substantial funds to support REDD and the principle has been integrated in the **Copenhagen Accord** and **Cancun Agreements**. It remains unclear whether REDD will be integrated into **carbon markets**.

Renewable energy Renewable energy is any form of energy from solar, geophysical or biological sources that is replenished by natural processes at a rate that equals or exceeds its rate of use. It includes, for example, biomass, solar, hydro power, ocean, geothermal and wind (text from http://srren.ipcc-wg3.de/report/IPCC_SRREN_Annex_I).

Results-based management Results-based management is a management strategy focusing on performance and achievement of outputs, outcomes and impacts (text from www.oecd.org/dataoecd/40/7/43184177.pdf).

Saved health Saved health is a way of assessing mortality and loss of health due to diseases, injuries and risk factors like climate change, without valuing human life in monetary terms – which is an ethically questionable issue. It is a concept to quantify the burden of disability and death, expressed as the number of years lost due to disability and early death. It is proposed as a **trading unit** for an **adaptation market mechanism**. See Chapter 8.

Saved wealth The indicator specifies wealth protected by an adaptation project against destruction by climate change impacts. It can be either measured in absolute or in relative terms. It is proposed as a **trading unit** for an **adaptation market mechanism**. See Chapter 8.

Sectoral mechanism A **carbon market mechanism** covering an entire sector. It can either be a **cap-and-trade** or a **baseline-and-credit** scheme and is discussed in the context of **new market mechanisms**. See Chapter 6.

Soft measure **Adaptation** projects whose results are hard to quantify in terms of the proposed adaptation **trading units**, such as capacity building, raising awareness, building institutions or launching planning processes. In contrast, adaptation projects involving infrastructure development, improved health protection or agricultural activities seem to be appropriate for the calculation of adaptation units. See Chapter 8.

Solar radiation management Reduction of the incoming solar radiation by, e.g. injection of dust into the stratosphere, whitening of low-lying clouds through spraying of saltwater over the seas or painting roofs white. This would reduce the global temperature. Commonly seen as part of 'geoengineering' and as an alternative to **mitigation**.

Standardized baseline A standardized baseline for a **CDM** project is not calculated on a project-by-project basis by applying the relevant baseline methodology, but involves **benchmarks** or default factors. The aim of standardizing baselines is to reduce the time and costs associated with designing **CDM** projects and achieving registration of projects by the **CDM Executive Board**.

Super transformational technology (STT) A super transformation technology is a backstop technology that produces energy at lower cost than fossil energy, is characterized by short construction periods, can be built close to the electricity consumers and therefore would not require significant grid infrastructure. See Chapter 10.

Suppressed demand Suppressed demand for energy occurs when energy services go unfulfilled due to poverty or a lack of energy infrastructure. Chapter 10 discusses an **Energy Development Programme** to satisfy suppressed demand.

Technology transfer Under the UNFCCC, the 'developed country Parties shall take all practicable steps to promote, facilitate and finance, as appropriate, the transfer of, or access to, environmentally sound technologies and know-how to other Parties, particularly to developing countries to enable them to implement the provisions of the Convention' (Article 4.5). This commitment is echoed in similar provisions under the Kyoto Protocol (Article 10 c). See Chapter 1 for a discussion on technology transfer under the **CDM** (text from http://unfccc.int/cooperation_and_support/technology/items/1126.php).

Tradeable unit/trading unit Unit traded under a **carbon market mechanism** or **adaptation market mechanism**.

Transaction costs Transaction costs are the costs that arise from initiating and completing transactions, like finding partners, holding negotiations, consulting with lawyers or other experts, monitoring agreements, etc., or opportunity costs, like lost time or resources. In the CDM context they are the costs needed to complete the **project cycle**.

Transitional Committee At **COP 16 in Cancún** it was decided that the **Green Climate Fund** shall be designed by a Transitional Committee. This Committee comprises 40 members, with 15 members from industrialized countries and 25 members from developing countries.

United Nations Framework Convention on Climate Change (UNFCCC) The UNFCCC was adopted in 1992 and signed at the Earth Summit in Rio de Janeiro by more than 150 countries and the European Economic Community. It has now been ratified by 201 countries. Its ultimate objective is the 'stabilization of greenhouse gas concentrations in the atmosphere at a level that would prevent dangerous anthropogenic interference with the climate system'. It contains commitments for all parties, although **Annex-I countries** commit to taking the lead in the fight against climate change. All countries commit to publishing inventories of greenhouse gases, as well as national measures taken in order to **mitigate** or **adapt** to climate change. They agree to cooperate in **technology** development and **transfer**, in the management and conservation of greenhouse gas sinks, in adaptation, and in research and education related to climate change (text mainly from www.ipcc.ch/publications_and_data/ar4/wg3/en/annex1s-glossary-r-z.html).

Vulnerability Vulnerability is the degree to which a system is susceptible to, and unable to cope with, adverse effects of climate change, including climate variability and extremes. Vulnerability is a function of the character, magnitude and rate of climate change, and variation to which a system is exposed, its sensitivity and its adaptive capacity (text from www.ipcc.ch/publications_and_data/ar4/wg2/en/annexessglossary-p-z.html).

World Bank The World Bank is the largest **multilateral development bank**. It provides loans to developing countries and strives for the reduction of poverty.

Index

Page numbers in *italics* denote tables, those in **bold** denote figures.

T - #0062 - 230425 - C0 - 234/156/17 - PB - 9780415743433 - Gloss Lamination